HOMEFRONT

Homefront

A Military City and the American Twentieth Century

CATHERINE LUTZ

With photographs by elin O'Hara slavick

Beacon Press
BOSTON

Beacon Press
25 Beacon Street
Boston, Massachusetts 02108-2892
www.beacon.org

Beacon Press books
are published under the auspices of
the Unitarian Universalist Association of Congregations.

06 05 04 03 02 01   8 7 6 5 4 3 2 1

This book is printed on acid-free paper that meets the uncoated paper
ANSI/NISO specifications for permanence as revised in 1992.

Text design by Elizabeth Elsas

Composition by Wilsted & Taylor Publishing Services

Library of Congress Cataloging-in-Publication Data
   Lutz, Catherine.
      Homefront : a military city and the American twentieth
   century / Catherine Lutz.
         p.   cm.
      Includes bibliographical references and index.
      ISBN 0-8070-5508-5
         1. Fayetteville (N.C.)—History, Military—20th century.
   2. Fayetteville (N.C.)—Social conditions—20th century.
   3. Military bases—Social aspects—North Carolina—Fayetteville
   Region—History—20th century   4. War and society—North
   Carolina—Fayetteville—History—20th century.   5. War and
   society—United States—History—20th century.   6. United
   States—History, Military—20th century.   I. Title.
   F264.F28 L88   2001
   975.6'373—dc21

                                    2001001820

FOR GEORGE AND CAROL, MY BELOVED PARENTS,
JONATHAN AND LIANNA, MY TREASURES,
AND MICHAEL, MY FUTURE

CONTENTS

Making War at Home

I could see its seams as the huge warplane slowly lumbered overhead toward its twilight landing at a military complex near Fayetteville, North Carolina. It was mere feet above the flapping laundry and unlandscaped grounds of a trailer park. A few miles further away, people living in the houses of another, greener area of Fayetteville straightened wall hangings set off-kilter by the quiet boom of the post's artillery guns. Despite the chain-link fence separating these neighborhoods from the installation, together they make up the single, deeply entwined but often invisible world of America and its military.[1] There are many places like this across the United States that the nation's massive state of war readiness not only coexists with, but has helped form. Through the lens of the experience of the people of Fayetteville, this book traces how war preparation has shaped America through the twentieth century and how it is related to the country's inequalities and cultural contradictions. As home to a giant army post, Fort Bragg, Fayetteville may seem a very unusual place, but it is America's twentieth-century history of militarization writ on a small but human scale.

Bitterly contemplating the American rush to join the slaughterhouse of World War I, the writer Randolph Bourne asserted that war is "the health of the state."[2] He meant that a government's power grows in the bloody medium of war: It accumulates legal powers and the people's treasure to pursue the fight and often keeps an expanded role long after it has ended. The twentieth century has proved Bourne right, its wars enlarging the state while shrinking the rule of law and enriching both weapons makers and businesses that captured post-conflict markets. But no irony attaches to the now widely entrenched idea that war is the health of the nation, or of a people. That military spending not only preserves sovereignty but waters the social landscape, growing factory jobs, preparing young people for life, shaping values for the culture at large, and providing technological benefits to the economy and to households. The historical and contemporary experience of a military town such as Fayetteville, however, belies this common view, dramatically illustrating war's costs, physical and symbolic.

Much of the history and contemporary reality of war and war preparation has been invisible, though, to people both inside and outside the military—because it has been shrouded behind simplified histories or propaganda, cordoned off by secrecy laws, or been difficult to assess because so many of the consequences of running our military institutions are not obviously war-related. And so we have not evaluated the costs of being a country ever ready for battle.[3] The international costs are even more invisible, as Americans have looked away from the face of empire and been taught to think of war with a distancing focus on its ostensible purpose—"freedom assured" or "aggressors deterred"—rather than the melted, exploded, raped, and lacerated bodies and destroyed social worlds at its center.[4] And we have been taught to imagine the costs of war as exacted only on the battlefield and the bodies of soldiers, even as veterans' injuries and experience get scant attention, and even as civilians are now the vast proportion of war's clotted red harvest.[5]

Fayetteville's history of war is not only a chronicle of short wars remembered and of long mobilizations erased, but highly contested terrain: It is a past recalled in often radically different ways. For some, the violence to remember has been domestic and racist; for others, it is overseas, triumphal, and ethical. The city shares this contention with America more generally, some of whose angriest cultural debates have been the "history wars" and, more specifically, over the history *of* war, as in the 1990s battle over the *Enola Gay* exhibit at the Smithsonian's Air and Space Museum.[6] That is because war is often seen as a natural fact, a feature of a human nature, not historical possibility (as one Special Operations soldier put it to me, "Defense is the first need of any organism"). But in telling histories of war as something other than biology or national destiny revealed, many other issues are at stake: the role of the nation-state and international law in the twenty-first century; the role of individual will versus social constraint in creating wealth and class distinctions; the fairness of a myriad of government policies, military and civilian; the reality of "tribal sentiments" in a social evolutionary tale about the globe and its supposedly "primitive" and "modern" parts; the proper interpretation of biblical or other religious verse on war, compassion, and justice; and, not least of all, questions of who can or should take or risk a life. An alternative and more hopeful history of America's militarization can nonetheless be called out from the shadow of the view of war as predestination, as well as from the standard entertainment and triumphal accounts.

There are many places like Fayetteville in America, from its nearly nine hundred other domestic military bases in such towns as Norfolk, Virginia, New London, Connecticut, and Killeen, Texas, to the thousands of places from Seattle, Washington, to Binghamton, New York, where weapons and equipment are made.[7] In an important sense, though, we all inhabit an army camp, mobilized to lend support to the permanent state of war readiness that has been with us since World War II. No matter where we live, we have raised war taxes at work, and future soldiers at home, lived with the cultural atmosphere of racism and belligerence that war mobilization often uses or creates, and nourished the public opinion that helps send soldiers off to war or prevents their going. All of us consume cultural products and political rhetoric influenced by what sociologist C. Wright Mills called "a military definition of the situation." All experience the problems bred by war's glorification of violent masculinity and the inequalities created by its redistribution of wealth to the already privileged. All live with the legacy and rhetoric of national security, an historically recent concept that has distorted the definition and possibilities for democratic citizenship, discrediting dissent and centralizing power even more in the hands of the federal and the corporate few. And we all have lived with the consequences of the reinvigorated idea that we prove and regenerate ourselves through violence.[8]

FAYETTEVILLE: ALMOST ANYTOWN, ALMOST SPECTACULAR

A city of 100,000 souls near the interstate that runs between Boston and Miami, Fayetteville is a place both familiar and strange. Most cities share its mix of boosters and detractors, of gracious, friendly people and misanthropes, of activists and watchers. Most have a version of its tale of postwar growth and suburbanization, mushrooming malls and declining downtowns. And like almost every other American urban area, it is really two cities, one of pedicured lawns and plush square footage, and the other, small weather-beaten cottages and policed public housing. And this city is like the rest of America in its relationship to militarization—its people pay military taxes and send sons and now daughters to war, and it includes nationalists and interventionists, Quakers and libertarians.

Fayetteville is both a city of cosmopolitan substance and humane striving and the dumping ground for the problems of the American century of war and empire, the corner of the American house where the wounds of war have pierced most deeply and are most visible. With the post as its neighbor since World War I, the city has come to have among North Carolina's smallest tax bases, voter registration rates, and number of sidewalk miles, and its county appears near the top or the bottom, whichever is worse, in many lists of North Carolina's 100 counties' features, including those for poverty, child abuse and other crime, female unemployment, and auto accidents per capita. It has a striking number of pawnshops and strip joints, and of prostitutes and prostitute murders. And while many of its veterans are successful small businesspeople or civic activists, some live with horrific physical and psychological injuries, and they make up a quarter of the city's substantial number of homeless people.

America's international military interventionism is everywhere visible in the city, whose Okinawan, Korean, and Vietnamese residents stage an annual International Folk Festival but remain outsiders to city hall. Those twentieth-century military missions are also written on its citizens' memories and their imagination of Fayetteville's future. The refugees and veterans who now make up a large segment of Fayetteville's population have seen Guatemalan terror and the secret war in Laos and authoritarian regimes in Asia, and their politics have been shaped there. And while areas near the post are among the nation's least racially segregated, the city remains a place of stark racial tension and inequality. More generally, there is a widespread sense that someone else (on post or in the Pentagon) controls Fayetteville's people's fate. The city's wealth is in real estate and retail sales, with a virtual riot of shopping malls and "big box" outlets on eight-lane highways near the post where civilians and soldiers buy fashions and movie tickets with their literally billions of salary dollars. Many chain stores find their Fayetteville outlets produce more dollars per square foot than any others around the country, but the people who work there make lower wages than in any city in the state.

The drive into Fort Bragg and Fayetteville, if you come in from the west or the north, is through rural countryside dotted with the golf courses of wealthy Southern Pines on one side and with the multiple prisons and chicken processing plants of nearby Hoke County on the other. Entering Fort Bragg's open gateways, you feel the transition to a more environmentally pristine roadside, often dotted with enlisted men and women on litter patrol. Environmental management practices are evident in the burned-off underbrush and pine trees tagged with signs warning of nesting sites of the endangered red-cockaded woodpecker. You can drive for miles across the bottom edge of the post's 160,000 acres, passing sandy tracks into the piney woods where soldiers gather under camouflage tents for war exercises, parachute into the Sicily Drop Zone, or target practice into various "impact areas." Near the eastern side of the installation, you drive past the ammunition dump and a sprawling area of administration buildings, huge barracks, and family housing in neighborhoods with battlefield names like Normandy Heights, Anzio Acres, and Corregidor Courts. There live about half of the installation's forty-three thousand soldiers, the rest in town. Soldiers and their families head in and out of the Post Exchange (PX) to shop, the white-steepled church to worship, and their cars to commute to work on and off post. You pass a day care center with dozens of matched Fisher-Price toddler cars parked near its playground, recreation centers, golf courses, and after a wooded buffer, suddenly feel your arrival in Fayetteville itself, as miles of strip malls and strip joints appear. Its highway face begins with business flotsam and jetsam: a used car lot flapping with red, white, and blue bunting, a two-story pawnshop painted completely in camouflage, a sign with silhouetted thin-ankled strippers.

But two very different routes can take you, a few miles later, to downtown Fayetteville. One winds past the malls through miles of wealthy neighborhoods, from Van Story Hills to Haymount, with comfortable housing of most every era since the 1920s, reflecting the absence of any sustained recession in military salaries. Here are the people who sell car insurance to soldiers, market houses at a steady clip sustained by station reassignments, and own the fast-food franchises that feed young soldiers' appetites. These neighborhoods house most of the medical professionals whose incomes rival any of their peers around the country given the special market conditions of lush military medical funding and thin medical personnel supply.

Just a few miles to the east and directly below the residential area of the post, Murchison Road takes you through a very different landscape—an urban wasteland of razed and weedy lots and deteriorated housing untouched by the billions of dollars that have come into Fort Bragg over the years. In this area live many of Fayetteville's African Americans, the racial integration that characterizes some, more military-populated neighborhoods, absent. Sources of community strength are certainly evident—churches and a mosque, NAACP headquarters, and the new Sickle Cell Association building. And just before arriving downtown by this route, one comes to Fayetteville State University, an historically black college with an illustrious past and a promising future. It helped form a surrounding community at College Heights through waves of refugees who came from the 1920s on to find public education for their children and freedom from rural racial oppression.

These two routes converge and clash symbolically at the central rotary that twists around the Market House. This building means starkly different things depending on the road taken there: It is a former slave market and a current developer boondoggle for most coming down Murchison Road, but it is a nostalgic sign of a more glorious past for many coming down from Haymount Hill. The Market House's uses over the last two centuries do tell stories about the city's tragedies and transitions. It was a market for produce and estates—including slaves—before the Civil War, a meat shop swarming with flies until health regulations were instituted in the early twentieth century, an information center for America's first conscripted soldiers in World War I, a first-aid station for the hundreds of soldiers injured on town liberty each month in the World War II era, and, in the 1990s, a booster organization's headquarters and icon in a struggle for tourist dollars and rejuvenated land values as well as in skirmishes over what version of city history will prevail. For this past can be deployed as prologue, defining the city's present dilemmas and future directions in specific ways.

The physical view of the city for any newcomer is almost always preceded by an imaginary one, and it is less pretty. The city has a bad reputation, to say the least. Many people think of Fayetteville, as I have been told again and again, as a place to get a dozen beers and a sexual disease. People have long called its main downtown thorough-fare "notorious Hay Street," and the epithets collect—"Fatalburg" and "Fayettenam" have been among the most popular. And one can trace the transmission routes of that diseased reputation through every one of the now millions of soldiers and family members who have seen the worst the city has to offer or who have simply seen its unregulated highway detritus. But it is also viewed through the class- and race-inflected fantasies of people around the state who have never seen the city or met a resident. For it suffers the fate of all victims of poverty and racism, which is to be seen as the complete master and ar-chitect of their own sad fate. Working-class enlisted soldiers suffer the class prejudice as well, sometimes erroneously assumed to be a main source of the city's crime, at worst, its "lack of class," at best. The city's notoriety and neglect also result when people conflate the city with the wounds of war themselves or turn away from them in revulsion or fear.

THE RESEARCH AND THE BOOK

In what follows, I relate the larger chronicle already written of the American twentieth-century history of war and peace, and I try to explain Fayetteville's experience in light of those national processes and events. That story, while sometimes told through the social and cultural histories of ordinary people, is most often centered in the his-tory of elites and their decisions. And while soldiers' memoirs of bat-tle are widely available, the question is rarely addressed of how people live with and make sense of what haplessly becomes battle's other—"the home front"—and war's shadow—"readiness." I began visiting Fayetteville to learn how America's military has affected daily life in this country, knowing I would learn much from people who have lived with an army for part or all of their lives. While there are many military facilities within a several-hour drive of my day job as an an-thropologist at the University of North Carolina at Chapel Hill, Fayetteville drew me because its experience with the installation covers most of this century. The city had a significant population and economy and a distinct identity both before and after the post arrived, allowing me to see the problems of the military in society in that scale and relationship to each other.

I traveled to the city many times over the course of six years, visiting local archives and meeting with hundreds of people from all walks of life.[9] We met at street festivals and political or city government meetings, in the mall, restaurants, and convenience stores, and on post. About eighty people graciously gave me the time for formal interviews about their lives and views in their homes, church halls, public library, or, occasionally, by phone. As oral historians and cultural anthropologists who do this as a centerpiece of their methods know, such interviews are conversational gifts—the careful reflections, mind-widening challenges, and individual spirit of another person are the prize.[10] All the people I spoke with have lived lives remarkable in some way, many crafted in devotion to their images of the good person and the good society.

In my first visits to Fayetteville, I went to see what I and others construed as a "military city." While some in town may think of it that way as well, most people with longer residence prefer to think of themselves as living in a town next to a military installation. And in that distinction they hope to preserve their autonomy and, perhaps, the respect they might be accorded by others for whom they otherwise become latter-day "camp followers." This is despite the fact that, from the beginning, the camp followed them.

I also came to Fayetteville thinking that I would primarily study "civilians" living alongside "soldiers." I came to see, though, that this distinction between things civil and things military—while a distinction that in some ways is getting sharper over time and abrading political culture—has been for decades an illusion, artificially maintained. The blurred boundaries of the civilian and military worlds, and of war and peace, might have become visible to me because I grew up, like millions of other Americans, with a father who was a war veteran and then a military reservist. For all of my childhood, he was both and simultaneously in the military and in a civilian job. And like all of us, I grew up with that form of peacetime that is in fact war—war "over there" in Korea, Vietnam, Central America, the Persian

Gulf, or war threatened or held at bay by the wisp of deterrence theory, or war denied or spectacularized by daily Hollywood and television fare.

I remember vividly when I first became aware of the problem of how human communities can sustain or question organized violence. It was in the early 1960s and my middle childhood when, walking past my living room TV, I was stopped dead by ghostly images of ash and jumbled bones in Nazi ovens and skeletal human forms in the liberated concentration camps. And later, too, from the comfort of my home and through the mediations of those with the power to name the significant and choose the images, I saw the ravages of the Vietnam War on bodies and relationships. Two methods presented themselves to me for understanding how cultures and political economies came to shape people's view of war and the choices they had to make: anthropology, which demands listening and suggests how good people could disagree about important matters, how evil could be justified, how power shapes the currency of ideas and the well-being of individuals and groups; and history, which shows how things have not always been as we see them now, how we might have shifted from a nation suspicious of standing armies to one whose military patrols the globe in all of its corners, twenty-four hours each day.

With the tools of ethnography, history, and cultural critique, I ask: How did it come to be that we live in a society made by war and preparations for war? How has our social world been shaped by the violence our nation has made and threatened and by the other, more elliptical ways we have learned to name that violence? Are we all military dependents, wearers of civilian camouflage? What would America be like today if, at the least, the elites who opt for war had made other choices? Is it possible now to imagine another way? These are the questions that this book, I hope, will not so much answer as encourage readers to ask in their own way, in their own towns, and in regard to the personal problems that might seem unrelated to them—problems that a sociological imagination might help us link together in coherent ways. Some new way will be found when it becomes clearer how few really profit from the old.

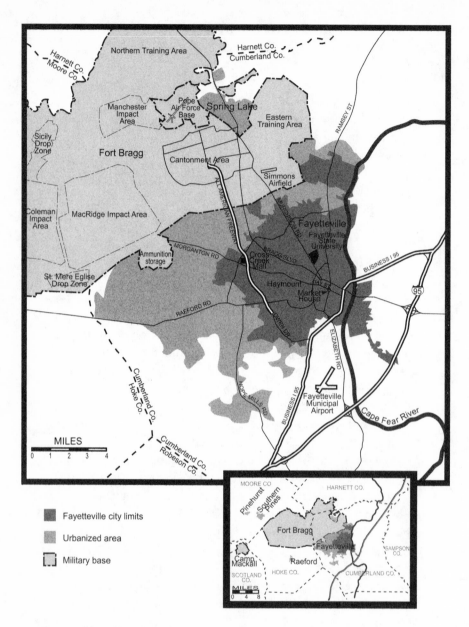

Fayetteville and Fort Bragg

CHAPTER I

Encampment

Boosters, Social Crisis, and a Military Solution (1918–1938)

It was the fall of 1916, and three men on a mission could be seen driving north on the road from Fayetteville, North Carolina, to Washington, D.C. A large poster mounted on the car's rear and flying streamers trumpeted their city's advantages as the location for a proposed federal armor plate factory.[1] Though this trio failed in their efforts, the chamber of commerce that sent them persevered and ultimately landed even bigger fish. Two years later, the government announced appropriations for a large military post near Fayetteville: Chamber emissaries then in the capital, the city's newspaper reported, were "overjoyed with the turn of events and there was much backslapping and hand-shaking when [local U.S.] Representative Godwin brought the glad tidings. Tonight they held a jollification dinner at the Congress Hall Hotel."[2]

Local boosters like these and decisionmakers in Washington were to turn many hundreds of American places into military landscapes over the next century. And like many local newspapers, the Fayetteville press was an ally, celebrating the men as "hustling, live wires," and their work as a bold contribution to the collective good. Then and in the future, they would be seen as community visionaries rather than salesmen, and the installation they brought as a wealth generator, essentially no different than a textile mill. And however important the boosters' role, their spotlighting would leave in shadow views of the military other than that of invited guest.

In stories about the events that brought Fort Bragg to the city, moreover, larger social forces have been lost to view. The push to join

World War I and to build a large peacetime army had come from a "preparedness movement" among wealthy elites. The battle they saw coming was not in Europe alone: They felt threatened by the militant claims of labor and the differences of race and immigrant cultures, newly bustling in American cities. Arguing for a military solution to problems of class conflict and declining American character, many were the same business elites whose enterprises required a more docile labor force at home and new markets overseas. A larger military would help create the former and open the latter. Also occluded was the role of emerging industrial warfare in reshaping American cities. It offered immense profits through manufacture of its new tools, and some, such as artillery that could toss shells over much longer distances, were sending the army on a determined search for larger tracts of land. And little noted were the antimilitarist activists whose sentiments—that war was "repulsive, uncivilized, immoral and futile"—were widely shared throughout the country.[3]

Banished from the Washington hotel celebration were local feelings as well, such as fears many had that the camp would dissolve life as they knew it. Those anxieties made brief appearance in the newspaper on a day in 1917 when hopes for a military facility—raised and felled several times—had been dashed yet again. The paper groused,

> Who wants to waste time and good money trying to grab an elusive military camp with a greased tail when there are so many fine business opportunities to be developed? . . . A large proportion of the people of Fayetteville are down in the mouth because a big machine gun school of training was not located here, but the pure in heart can rest contented and with a feeling of security: their sons and their daughters and their sisters and their cousins and their aunts will not be demoralized and corrupted by wicked, depraved young soldiers roaming the streets like roaring lions, seeking whom they may devour.[4]

Also absent throughout the public discussions were the voices of Fayetteville's white and black mill workers who would help pay for incentives the city offered the army. And the black sharecroppers and city residents who had already fled in the Great Migration north and for whom the changes came too late to matter in any case. Or the black, Native American, and Scots farmers about to be relieved of their land, their neighbors, and their churches. These perspectives were also absent from many histories later told, as the victors of domestic battles, like the foreign, have seized the right to pen the collective past.

So we must begin elsewhere than the boosters' hotel party to learn how homes in Fayetteville—and in every American town and city—have been transformed into home fronts. National myths lead us to imagine each war as overseas, all of them thrust upon the United States, and patriotism as the only motive for taking part. Regional stereotypes, in turn, might lead us to envision pre–army encampment Fayetteville as a quiet Southern place or a traditional turn-of-century American town of plowshares and tradespeople—a placid swimming hole into which a hefty military installation was tossed. But there was no simple peace for the soldiers of Camp Bragg to march into in 1918. For like America itself, Fayetteville had already made war and been made by it.

THE QUIET AND UNQUIET DEAD

The first was waged within Native American communities, the second—on a scale that dwarfed the first—by European colonists who claimed the New World as their own. The realities of violent conflict among the Native American groups who first lived in the Southeast about 12,000 years ago, as now understood by archaeologists, contradict the two most commonly imagined Native American pasts. One stereotype is of a gentle people, eating roots and berries and knowing nothing of conflict; the other, of ignoble savages at constant tribal war with other groups, a premodern Somalia or Yugoslavia. Both images are built on the common belief that human history is essentially the story of the replacement of the primitive by the modern, with civilization seen as either suppressing the violent brute within us or putting melancholy distance between us and a simpler, less grasping way of life.

In this region, however, the evidence is not helpfully slotted into either vision of antiquity. Living without apparent violent conflict by hunting, fishing, and gathering in small dispersed sites, the first people of North Carolina eventually turned to agriculture. By 1200, the surplus this produced had allowed the groups to be reorganized in many places into larger, ranked societies and permanent villages. It also seems to have precipitated war,[5] with evidence in the palisades

built around some villages by about 1400.[6] Violence exploded, however, with European contact in the seventeenth century, as Native
American slaves (sold to Europeans in the Caribbean and the rest of
the colonies) and pelts brought trade in guns and other goods.[7] Local
village life became more turbulent as people moved to serve the English deerskin trade coming out of Virginia and as smallpox and other
sickness spread along British trade routes through Native American
groups. The epidemic disease and warfare that broke out throughout
the New World, in fact, often occurred at some distance from actual
colonial settlements, as germs, weapons, and conflict over trade goods
sometimes migrated ahead of the colonists.[8]

In the early eighteenth century, disease was pushing an already
sparse population out of the Sandhills area that now houses Fort
Bragg when a set of three wars devastated native communities.[9]
Prompted by colonial conflicts over land, grazing, and trading rights,
the Tuscarora War led to the death, exile, or domination of all of the
colony's native peoples east of the Appalachians by 1715. This opened
the Fayetteville area to European settlement, which increased rapidly
in midcentury.[10] The wars, however, led some of the survivors to
align with the Catawba, to form the grouping now known as the
Lumbee, and to communicate more effectively among themselves,
the better to survive the challenges of the next century.[11] These people who had fled into the swampy area just thirty miles south of Fayetteville now constitute the largest, if legally unrecognized, Native
American community east of the Blue Ridge of the Appalachian
Mountains. Like many other areas of America today, it can be reimag-
ined as a landscape of war refugees.

So, too, does the local story of the American Revolution violate
the notion that a town's original families established a simple lineage
of patriots. Many of the Highland Scotch farmers who moved there
after the Tuscarora War were loyal to the British crown, and overall,
county residents were about evenly divided in their allegiances during the war.[12] Oddly, the Scots ability to claim premier citizenship for
themselves in the city through the ensuing decades was not harmed
by this untoward initial relationship to the nation. But their status
hinged not on revolutionary contributions but their hold on land and
local political power.

When the war ended, nation building centered on "Indian-fighting," which was one of the main ostensible purposes of militias established around the South. Despite the much earlier subjection of Native Americans in the area, the Fayetteville Independent Light Infantry (FILI) was formed in 1793 as the new federal government generated fear that Spain was "exciting the Southern Indians to war against the country," as well as in the immediate wake of the beginning of the revolution of Haitian slaves in 1791.[13] Historians commonly describe the early U.S. Army as a constabulary defined by its appointed job of "Indian hunting" rather than defense of national borders.[14] Consistent with this, the Army enforced presidential orders in the late 1830s to evict the Cherokee from their North Carolina land. Fully a quarter of the group died on its forced march to Oklahoma.[15]

Some historical accounts set this violence to the side and present the next one hundred years as the area's era of glory. Fayetteville was, in fact, one of the South's most prominent places through the 1830s. Running from the town down to Wilmington and the Atlantic, the Cape Fear River nourished Fayetteville's fortunes as a trade center for more than a century. At the end point of the river's navigable waters, the city commanded a middleman location between the state's only significant ocean port and farmland to the west and as far north as Virginia. As many people lamented to me, Fayetteville was almost the permanent capital of the state—perhaps echoing their sense of other, more recent opportunities lost: Interstate 95 sited a few miles too far east of town, legislative largesse passed to the city of Charlotte. Even with Raleigh made the capital, however, Fayetteville was second in size only to Wilmington and New Bern by 1860.[16] Its Market House and town hall, still standing today at the center of downtown, were a glory of Moorish arches, clock, and belfry. Fertile farmlands, growing first cotton and later tobacco, ran along the river, and the area was a prominent center for the naval stores industry in the several decades leading up to the Civil War. Fayetteville's early investment in public schooling for whites and blacks, begun in the nineteenth century, was said to be a model for other North Carolina communities.

But if "the Indian question" could be set out of mind because now out of sight, slavery and its aftermath were more insistent. Their brutality, too, demonstrated that the problem of violence in the United States throughout its history has been the problem of race, each made in the crucible of the other.[17] In Fayetteville's county, Cumberland, the eastern section was a relatively heavy slave-holding area, like other sections of coastal plain North and South Carolina.[18] One descendant of slave owners from this agriculturally rich area, William Fields, became one of the area's most ardent chroniclers. As I set out to meet him, I headed to the rural limits of town on the opposite side of the city from Fort Bragg, where the post's influence on growth has been slight. Riding down his furrowed, unmarked drive, I wound through Spanish moss- and vine-dripping woods to a large, ramshackle house, its boards askew and once-tended garden spilling over stone borders. Despite appearances of a place out of time, the man who greeted me at the door was a vibrant, chain-smoking eighty-year-old working artist who had lived in Rome and New York City. We sat down to talk at a table sprouting exuberant towers of genealogical and historical research papers, with sooty portraits of his two great-great-grandfathers overlooking us from the high-ceilinged walls. In those papers he could trace the deed that put his family on this same land in 1779 and the documents claiming his ancestor's ownership of 104 human beings.

Mr. Fields had been raised by a nanny who was a child to his great-grandmother's slaves, and she had told him many stories about their entangled ancestors, including his black cousins. Some of them, set against the silences and terms of his "official" family biography, led him to a somewhat unusual ability to identify where existing accounts of the local past had hidden the work that went into them to make violence look like order. "My grandmother was born in 1854," he told me, "so she was ten years old when the Civil War came along. When she was five they gave her this little girl as her personal slave. The first thing that my grandmother did to demonstrate her authority was to order the child to put her foot up on a chopping block and she took a hatchet and chopped off her big toe. . . . My grandmother told me that, yes. I think she regretted it somewhat later, but . . . she already was learning the ropes of how to subjugate people."

The violence slave owners meted out to control their labor force came back in haunted fear of retribution. So it was that the FILI, like other Southern militias, explicitly stood ready to repress potential slave revolts, alarms of which "punctuated the antebellum years."[19] Real and imagined, these insurrections and the response to them were in essence part of a long-standing race war throughout the Americas. And so it was, too, that several federal and state arsenals were built in Fayetteville in those years.[20]

Nonetheless, free people of color held a special status in Fayetteville over and above those elsewhere in the state. They continued to vote, by local statute, when the rest of the state's free blacks were disenfranchised in 1834, and they totaled between 5 and 10 percent of the town's population by 1840.[21] They remained second-class citizens, however, required to wear identification badges and forbidden, among other things, to smoke or carry a cane in public.[22] That their situation was far less than tolerable is indicated by the large number of people (including Langston Hughes's grandmother) who left for the North in this period and by the fact that a son of Fayetteville, Lewis Sheridan Leary, joined and was killed in the insurrectionary raid on the Harper's Ferry arsenal in 1859.

In those years, a white Carolinian could argue that "the nature of our institution of domestic slavery and its exposure of us to hostile machinations, both at home and abroad, render it doubly incumbent on us and our whole sisterhood of Southern States to cherish a military spirit and to diffuse military science among our people."[23] During the fiftieth-anniversary celebration of the FILI, a local dignitary orated on a militia's value and against "larger bodies of regular [or] hired soldiery" on grounds that the militias "have ranks filled with those who have all at stake in the welfare of the community."[24]

The FILI still exists, the second oldest continuously operating militia in the United States. While it sent men to the wars of two centuries, and while counting veterans of World War II and the Gulf War among its members, the contemporary FILI has been drained of its status as a fighting force and of these elements of its history. Today, it appears more as the colorful, vaguely heritage-authenticating frontispiece of city parades than as a legacy of the problems of land and labor that Native Americans, Africans, and poor whites had presented the city fathers. Its headquarters, shown to me by one generous member, is downtown in a crenellated building of deep red brick. As we entered through locked iron grilles and bolted doors, it was as if into a combination museum and men's social club. We passed through small exhibits of old militia uniforms, Civil War sabers, and group photographs of former members. Other photos showed the militiamen with their wives in elbow-length gloves and gowns in the 1950s and 1960s. And like the mounted antlers or petrified bass trophies that line some men's spaces of other eras, we passed displays of war loot members had brought home in their duffel bags from a variety of overseas campaigns. On one pedestal sat a large bust of Hitler, liberated from Berlin by an FILI member. And over the dark wood bar where members gather for drinks was a gigantic pinup-style pencil drawing of a lounging, sparsely dressed woman taken from a German POW in World War II Europe.

The defense of slavery was the FILI's moment, however. As the Civil War approached, the FILI and white residents of the city were more concerned with "the enemy within" than the Yankee without. The federal arsenal's presence in the city provoked more disquiet about its potential use by local slaves than by the North. Some began to ask themselves around Christmastime, "when the negroes were generally supposed to be taken with annual longings to 'rise,' [whether] the munitions of war should prove a temptation too strong for them to resist? . . . The scent of war was in the air. The negroes might take the infection."[25] Taken over by the Confederacy in 1861, the arsenal employed many local women, young boys, free blacks, and slaves in making cartridges and other equipment for the war.[26] Union soldiers destroyed it in 1865, when Fayetteville's great misfortune was to be one of the few North Carolina cities in the path of General William Sherman's march. Sherman also torched the offices of the local newspaper (which had the second largest circulation of any paper in the South) and the half dozen mills that had made the county the main site of the textile industry in the state.[27] He destroyed railroad property, shops, tanneries, and other factories as well, and dropped a social hurricane of twenty thousand to thirty thousand refugees and camp followers in Fayetteville.[28]

Over the next decades, Fayetteville's people struggled to recover from the war. Many farmed the land as tenants, as whites continued to own prewar plantation lands. New textile plants set up shop in the county, with mill owners paying low wages to a mainly white female and child labor force.[29] This economic activity helped Cumberland County grow at the same rate as the rest of the state. Democracy made some headway, with blacks voting and gaining office (if in disproportionately small numbers). But the Ku Klux Klan, a terrorist organization that operated through North Carolina soon after the war, led by the old Democratic political elite, tried to reverse these gains. By the mid-1870s, the white-dominated Democratic Party took over the reins of town government and held them for the next two decades.

As the century opened, Fayetteville, like the United States as a whole, was in the throes of many social and economic changes, sometimes of crisis proportions. Prices for cotton were cripplingly low. Depression had been followed by the devastating boll weevil. The area's once-strong turpentine and naval stores industry had been decimated along with its source, the longleaf pine, while the timber industry more generally was being rapidly depleted. Likely connected to the deforestation, silt clogged the city's link to the Atlantic, the Cape Fear River. City population growth lagged the state as a whole in the 1910s as such places as Raleigh, Charlotte, and Greensboro thrived on new rail connections that Fayetteville did not get and industrialized more rapidly. Despite an influx of new mills, the city, once third in size in the state, had fallen behind thirteen other North Carolina towns by 1910, a stinging fact if growth is equated with progress.[30]

As the new economy stumbled haltingly forward, racial violence lent it a guiding hand. Confronted by a political coalition of black Republicans and white Populists that had gained power statewide and in this county in the 1890s, the conservative elites of the Democratic Party organized a new white supremacy campaign intended to drive a permanent wedge between black and white voters and workers. Fayetteville played an important role in this movement that brought what amounted to a coup d'etat and racial massacre to the nearby city of Wilmington, the disenfranchisement of blacks throughout the state, and the one-party rule by the Democrats for the next seven decades.[31] State Democratic Chairman Furnifold Simmons's 1898 call for the restoration of North Carolina as "a white man's state" was vigorously answered in Fayetteville, where a White Supremacy Club was established.[32]

In 1898, the city hosted Ben Tillman, the South Carolina demagogue of the supremacy movement, with a major rally that turned out a crowd of as many as ten thousand citizens.[33] Tillman arrived at the railroad station with a cornet band and the Cape Fear militia and proceeded through downtown with the city's mayor, county chairman, and newspaper publisher. Banners flew around a four-horse-drawn decorated float ridden by young women in white dresses: twenty-two in all, one for each county precinct. Protecting the honor of these and like maidens was the pretext for the fearsome capstone to the parade, three hundred crimson-shirted men on horseback. These "Red Shirts" would later ride throughout eastern Carolina, as one contemporary account noted, "a yelling file of horsemen, galloping wildly. They were men who meant violence if fear was not enough."[34] Thousands of people attended, their "vehicles filling all the streets and thoroughfares . . . evidence that the white people of upper Cape Fear had left the plow, the machine shops, the kitchen, nay, the very neighborhood school-room."[35] Also attending were bankers, wealthy farmers, and the editor of the *Fayetteville Observer,* who heralded Tillman as the "liberator of South Carolina." In his speech, Tillman called for the murder of any African American who insulted the white women of North Carolina and thunderously called for the overturn of "negro rule."

This supremacy movement helped effectively evict blacks from the voting booth via a 1900 state constitutional amendment.[36] More horribly, the campaign lent further legitimacy to the idea that white women were everywhere in constant danger of rape at the hands of black men and that any means of "defense" were righteous. As historian Leon Litwack has chillingly described, it fueled the ongoing "climate of hysteria [that] would reap a grim harvest" of torture, castration, and lynching. This violence, as well as abuse via the police and court system, was to serve far into the new century. It provided the stick behind Jim Crow–era laws mandating segregation in transportation, mental institutions, prisons, tax records, and the militia. And it supported the idea of an inferior people whose wages could be brought low alongside their status and helped thwart their alliance with working-class white people.[37] Many came to see the South's military tradition—and the prevalence of other, less legitimated violence—as a feature of the region's timeless culture. But this violence was nourished first and foremost in attempts to create and preserve a strictly hierarchical racial order.[38] And it was understood at the time as a form of war, if overwhelming force was in the hands of one party.[39]

The events of 1900 were fresh in mind and soul when two years later the local United Daughters of the Confederacy erected a large Confederate soldier–topped monument in a Fayetteville square. Chiseled "They died in defense of their rights," it was the largest memorial ever made in the city, and the first in twenty-five years. While the monument could directly address a few still-living disabled Civil War veterans and grieving families, at another level, it clearly hailed the Red Shirts and the newly militant white identities they had spawned. Like all monuments to war, it was a "landmark of power" and a political statement.[40] Its stones did not so much cry out in accusation as sentimentalize the brutality of both slavery and war.[41] And it was certainly not the statement former slaves, populist farmers, textile workers, or the children of civilian victims of the Civil War might have made.[42]

Despite all of these attempts to right the state through white authority, civil control could be tenuous. In one famed incident, Sheriff James Benton was shot by a black man, Sam Murchison, who gunned through town in 1907, the context of his act of no interest to the report given in the white press. When he was caught, the crowds who gathered at the ringing of the Market House bell were so eager to lynch him on the spot that they obstructed the path of the wagon taking him to jail.[43] The editor of the local newspaper appeared satisfied with a trial and hanging a few months later.[44] Fayetteville's prison population around this time showed the system's racial bias: It had thirty-seven black inmates and six white ones.[45]

The forces of political corruption and bureaucratic modernization were periodically in full battle. In 1920, Mayor John Underwood and Chief of Police P. H. Merker resigned in the wake of an auditor's report showing incomplete and erased items in the records of the police chief and mayor's court, suggesting they had been taking bribes and pocketing fines.[46] While bootleggers could count the expense of jury-rigging as a regular cost of doing business, there were also physical risks for all concerned.[47] When Sheriff Pate was shot by a white bootlegger, David Marshall Williams, on the east side of the city in 1921, he was the fourth deputy killed in a year.[48]

Despite this climate, which included periodic downtown meetings of the Ku Klux Klan through the 1920s, rural black people moved steadily into Fayetteville. They came to escape even more intense racial terror and an unfair sharecropping system in the countryside. It

History wars: the Markethouse as city
icon and as slave market in street mural

was around this time, as one man remembered, that "one of my grandmothers was killed in a racially motivated incident and I don't have any direct evidence but I strongly suspect, based on hearing my mother and aunts talk, that was one of the things that motivated them to leave the [southern part of the county and come to the city]. . . . There was a greater sense of security to be around other families."[49] Many rural migrants also wanted their children to enter the locally prestigious city schools that had sprung up immediately after the Civil War. Once in Fayetteville, they joined the company of skilled laborers: From the black population came nearly all of the town's mechanics in the post–Civil War period, the leading undertaker, as well as tailors and shoemakers, carpenters and bricklayers. Many of these artisans gradually lost their livelihoods, however, as manufactured versions replaced their handcrafted goods. At the same time, they were excluded from employment in all but one of the textile mills that had come to town and absorbed the labor of white artisans.[50] Nonetheless, some blacks continued to own substantial property in land and housing, and there were more black professionals in town than anywhere else in the state.[51]

The economic troubles of Fayetteville's white entrepreneurs and land developers, however, are what sent the city's chamber of commerce looking for new sources of income.

WOOING CAMP BRAGG: BOOSTERS,
BUSINESS, AND AMERICAN MILITARY GEOGRAPHY
The chamber search for economic help intersected with the army's quest for a large tract of land for its new guns. New engineering and mass production techniques—pioneered by the army in the Harper's Ferry and Springfield arsenals rather than by Henry Ford—had increased the deadliness and scale of war.[52] This industrial and scientific mode of warfare had produced field artillery that could fire shells over a mile and a half. These new weapons would mean two things. Soldiers—and civilians, to their dismay—would find that the traditional close-combat "battle was to be greatly opened out in both space and time."[53] And civilians would confront an increasingly land-hungry military. The largest bases cropped up in the West as the century wore on—the size of these, too, was weapons driven, with faster jets and nuclear testing requiring more land. Technocentric accounts of war

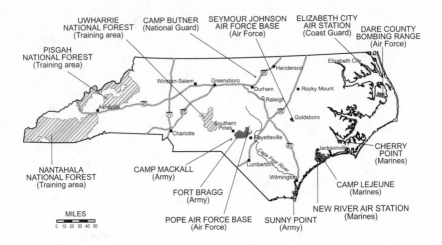

A geography of war preparation: North Carolina military bases

and social change often begin and end with the invention of such weapons, such as the machine gun or atomic bomb.[54] But the social relations surrounding war and the interests driving its pursuit provide more than sufficient incentive for the shaping of war's geography.

So it was, in June 1918, that the boosters' work helped bring representatives from the office of the chief of artillery and the U.S. Geological Survey through Fayetteville on their search for a site for these weapons. The visitors are said to have valued the Sandhills area for its adequate water supply, railroad lines, temperate climate allowing for year-round training, and remarkably sandy and well-drained soil.[55] This latter factor made it much easier to move the heavy new weaponry of industrial war. Its attractions might also have been clear to an Army whose soldiers had been felled by the diseases of moist environments—not by bullets—in relatively recent operations in Cuba, the Philippines, and Panama. The axiom that tacticians often fight the last war rather than the present one applied to the home front as well. But the land's choice seems not to have been hurt by a local boy's connections to the chief of staff, General William Snow. This lawyer and soldier, Captain Donald F. Ray, had family born on Fort Bragg land, and he had "pressed the case for his hometown" as the site.[56]

Local boosters and such insider allies have been key to patterns of military base and military-industrial geography in the United States. They helped bring the Navy's principal West Coast base to San Diego, for example, and the space command center to Colorado Springs.[57] Land developers, city officials, newspapers, and other business interests have often worked to lure military projects in attempts to generate higher land prices, a larger tax base, or more jobs. They have used the same incentives offered to corporations or sport teams, such as land, infrastructure, and tax breaks. Once established, they have promised an ethos of military support or acceptance to draw further bases or arms industries.

Nonetheless, Congress has been the institution most criticized for "skewing" location decisions for military facilities. While this has been overplayed—the Department of Defense and already-positioned military-industrial facilities initiate most decisions on where money will go—there has always been potential for more significant congressional lobbying for base locations than for other types of military spending. In the case of Camp Bragg, support came from the district's U.S. Representative Hannibal Lafayette Godwin and the white supremacist and now U.S. Senator Simmons. During negotiations for the post, the two raised questions of "fairness" in distributing war largesse. When Secretary of War Baker questioned labor availability in the Fayetteville area, Senator Simmons threatened to go to the president about regional discrimination in locating military bases.[58]

Later summing up the soundness of the army's decision to locate there, a chamber of commerce brochure noted, "Within a radius of forty miles of Camp Bragg there are a number of well known resorts, such as Pinehurst and Southern Pines. . . . So then Uncle Sam in selecting Camp Bragg had a kindly purpose in giving the soldiers who so loyally serve him the same climatic advantages that, as a rule, can be obtained only by the favored few" and gives them "a maximum of wholesome recreation" in the pure air and water of the area.[59]

On the other hand, official army sources today describe land taken for the post as "acres of desolate sandhills and pine trees."[60] While the land was not as agriculturally productive as that along the Cape Fear River, this description does no justice to the area's substantial agricultural community. On the more than 550 plots into which the land was then divided, farmers cultivated corn, cotton, fruits, and tobacco, attended the many churches they had built, and made the long trip into Fayetteville to buy and sell goods.[61] Their attachment to the land has been carried down to the present through their descendants, who hold an annual reunion each year at the Longstreet Church, still preserved on the installation.[62] But states not uncommonly have portrayed the resources they take as of little value to their original owners.

The displaced farmers were both owners and renters or sharecroppers, and they included Scotch, black, and a small number of Native American families, with substantial biological kinship between those categories.[63] While popular history-telling in many quarters tends to nearly erase the black and Native American residents, they made up in fact about half of those in the Camp Bragg area.[64] Black and white families were members of some of the same churches and were buried in some of the same graveyards.[65]

As the government began to buy land, its work was simplified by options the chamber of commerce had already acquired on several

Historic resource: nineteenth-century church graveyard on Fort Bragg land

thousand acres.[66] It could also buy tens of thousands of acres from a single extended family, the Blues, who had pulled timber and turpentine from the land through the late nineteenth century; they had also built a local railroad that might have benefited from a military facility.[67] Along with many Northern industrialist families, the Rockefellers had purchased North Carolina land around the turn of the century as a private resort. Although they gave one midsized parcel to the government for a nominal fee, to the resentment of some, they were not forced to sell their huge Overhills estate and game preserve; it was only in the late 1990s that a sale of those eleven thousand acres was negotiated with the family.[68] It also appears that some Scots families and larger landowners had moved into area towns in the years leading up to the army's coming: The black and Native American farmers, as well as smallholders and renters, who were then in the majority were more easily evicted.[69]

Also helping Washington acquire land—beyond its simple power to confiscate it—was the simultaneous disruption in some families whose sons were conscripted or volunteered for the army. Turk McFadyen was sixteen when the land purchases first became an issue, and his father John, a county commissioner, was the first to sell. In that year, two of John's older sons went off to war, and he was afflicted with influenza in an epidemic that killed nearly ten thousand in North Carolina alone.[70] This devastating plague in fact began its fatal acceleration that very September via the mass movements and clustering of young people in military camps which, unlike Bragg, were already in use.[71] But with these troubles of missing sons and poor health, the elder McFadyen soon took the government's appraised price. "Finding a place to move to was a job too," his son remembered, because area sellers knew the displaced had no choice but to move and could demand premium prices. The McFadyens bought an eighty-six-acre farm several miles to the south, with the help of a family friend. "They [the neighbors] were cussing my daddy for letting Fort Bragg come in," he remembered. But his father's advancing years, absent heirs, and the idea that they best "get on out of the woods" to put the next generation in school, all argued for the sale.[72] Many other farmers followed suit.

Others may swiftly forget the displacements of war, but even when the fighting is elsewhere and the dislocated are paid, some pain is uncompensatable. As one resident described it, the installation's coming "worked a real hardship on most of the people of the community. There were hallowed associations in the families, the community, and the church life that no appraiser could value and no purchaser could buy." But he went on quickly to assert his loyalty to the state even above home: "Let no one imagine that this fact is recorded in criticism of the Government. It is not. If the fort is a military necessity—a fact that no one in the community attempted to disprove—the needs of the whole country abundantly justif[y] the hardship imposed upon this small section. It is a pleasure to record that the relationship between the church and the government as represented in the authorities at Fort Bragg has been most cordial."[73]

The government dropped no windfall on the landowners, and some, much more reluctant to sell, fought the first offers. The Scotch landowners who did so had a strong ally in Henry Groves Connor, a federal judge who lobbied the government on their behalf and the lawyer who settled some of their cases in court. In letters to the secretary of the Navy, he warned, "I sometimes fear that the Government does not understand the temper of our people—they are loyal and law abiding but they do love their personal liberty and I sympathize strongly with them and they do feel that it is being unduly interfered with." Their "racial character" makes the injustice harsher, he argued, for these are "genuine Scotch, with attachment to their homes . . . which we find among these people." More sharply, he echoed a farmer's remark that this act of removal completed what Sherman started in 1865.[74] Other races, he implied, could more easily be parted from their homes.

Beyond the landowners' unhappiness, residents worried what the post might mean for local women. One person who worked as a cotton mill secretary and then started her own insurance business remembered, in vacillating shades, that her father "fought it like everything. Well he didn't fight it but I mean he said it would be such a change. He knew he had all these girls and he loved his girls a lot and he didn't know what might start up with all of it."[75] But the only notes of caution that followed in the newspaper as the appropriations were announced centered on the danger civilian greed might pose: "Let's keep our heads," it said, "and not get carried away by visions of wealth, 'lest we forget' and attempt to overreach because we are in a position to do so. And, above all, let's treat the soldiers with the greatest consideration. Instead of seeking to profiteer on them, let's charge them a little less for what they get than we charge other persons. That's patriotism and the proper way to treat the men who are offering their lives for ourselves and our homes."[76]

UNSEASONAL MIGRATIONS:
WAR AND A NEW LABOR GEOGRAPHY

In a choice that might seem ironic for a federal military facility, Camp Bragg was named after a Confederate general and native son, Braxton Bragg, when it officially came into existence on September 4, 1918.[77] Local businessmen did not fare as well as the rebel general. When building began immediately that fall, the main contractor was a firm from New York State; and most subcontracts also went to out-of-towners.[78] Although agricultural workers on seasonal lull poured in from the countryside to help with construction, a labor shortage soon arose.[79]

Late in September, then, the Army arranged for a shipload of fourteen hundred laborers to be brought to Fayetteville from Puerto Rico. Their availability had to do with imperial ambitions at the turn of the century that had netted the United States the territories of Hawaii, Cuba, and the Philippines, as well as Puerto Rico, taken in the Spanish-American War. The general who led the American military into that island spoke the contemporary language of racial evolutionism that had justified American imperialism, however different it was from the European version: "We have not come to make war upon the people of a country that for centuries has been oppressed," he said, "but on the contrary, to bring you protection, not only to yourselves but to your property, to promote your prosperity and bestow upon you . . . the advantages and blessings of enlightened civilization."[80] What Puerto Ricans experienced first with Spanish and then American civilization, however, were unfavorable new tax and fiscal regulations and the replacement of household-based farming of varied food crops with corporate-controlled sugar plantations. Pulverizing poverty and widespread malnutrition were the results. When the war in Europe exacerbated food shortages by limiting imports, and U.S. citizenship was extended to islanders in 1917 to help defuse an independence movement, the labor exodus was fueled.[81]

The islanders' treatment once they arrived bespoke their place in the racial scheme of things. The Puerto Ricans arrived "scantily clad," the post contractor noted. He ordered them clothes and deducted the cost from their first paychecks. Also debited to their accounts was their daily food at a rate that could equal half their pay. Problems quickly arose. In his final report, the contractor wrote:

> Not being accustomed to American food and manner of living, the Port Ricans were assigned separate bunk and mess houses [as were black and white workers] and some of their own members put in charge of these. The natives could not speak the English language, had had no previous experience in our methods of handling work, were disinclined to work and as a result, the project received very little value from their services. The Influenza epidemic attacked these men and due to their unwillingness to submit to proper treatment, a number [forty-two, in fact] succumbed to the disease. Late in December, when other labor became more abundant, these men were returned to Porto Rico.[82]

Their deaths joined those of five hundred thousand others felled by influenza—deaths never memorialized given the distortions of war and racial thinking.[83]

The Puerto Ricans made a vivid impression on the community while they were there. Though Fayetteville already had experience with people it construed as foreign or exotic—several Jewish peddlers had come to stay in previous years, and three Greek brothers had opened a café in 1907[84]—their numbers were tiny compared with immigrant populations in the North and West. While the war was to double their numbers in Fayetteville, the foreign-born population beforehand was less than 1 percent.[85] This demography had in fact been a selling point in some city fathers' eyes. Wrote a judge touting Fayetteville to Washington for the armaments factory, "No more faithful, loyal American citizenship exists, between the Atlantic and the Pacific. . . . A smaller number of hyphenated individuals can be found in that section than in any other equal extent of territory within the Union."[86] No sooner said, though, than these Caribbean men arrived, followed by soldiers who spoke Russian and Italian and Swedish and Polish and German.[87]

But, happily for some, the Puerto Rican men who came swelled the ranks of customers in local stores, as one woman whose father was in the hardware business remembered: "They filled the store with Puerto Ricans buying implements that they would use, tools for their job because if you used a hammer or shovels or whatever you had to bring your own and of course that was a very lucrative time with money for Father."[88]

The workers were also significant to Katherine Samons, a resident who had refused to sign over her land even as most of her neighbors had already left their homes. The Puerto Ricans, whom she called "Cubans," came to use her well. She complained to post engineers who told her she could shoot if they came near her house. For a while, she carried a gun with her as she farmed, firing into the air as needed. But what finally led her to sign her deed was seeing the men burying their dead at night, two to a grave, "singing Cuban songs" by flash-light. She nonetheless came back to harvest her vegetables, driving her horse and buggy past the protesting guards at the entrance to the new installation. Apparently, she resented the Puerto Rican interlop-ers more than the government, wondering why the migrants were necessary when "we had plenty of cheap labor of our own."[89]

Another person who refused to leave the site appears in a late Jim Crow–era history of Fayetteville. John Nichols, a former slave, had stayed on post land even as artillery shells began to fly. Twice the camp commander sent a detail of men out to remove him: Twice the sol-diers carried him with his pigs, chickens, and "scanty belongings" and dumped them beyond the border of the reservation, and twice he returned and relit his hearth. The commander himself then went out to remove him, but he too ran into problems. As he drove up, "The old darkey was sitting in the door of his humble shack with an open Bible in his lap. He laid his book down and took his hat, walked over to the car and said, 'Good evening, white folks.'" When the general told him he had to leave,

> He said almost tearfully, "General, Suh, I can't do it." He explained fur-ther that at the end of the Civil War he had promised a white family that he would stay and look after them. He kept his promise to stay on the farm of Mrs. Ray, cultivated the sand hill land and chipping the few pines that were left for turpentine and made tar from the lightwood knots. Nichols told them the angels told him when the firing was going to begin and he got out of the way. Finally the general said "Well, Negro, you stay right here."[90]

This story is structured around the time's stereotypes. The John Nichols of the tale is a loyal, God-fearing, simple Negro whose life under slavery was so suited to him that he could not bear to breach the code of loyalty to a master. And the story ends with the demonstration that he can be removed from the land with no more ease than the Scotch stereotype from the white historian's cultural repertoire.

In reality, there was a mass exodus of African Americans from across the South as the war began and work opportunities beckoned from the industrial north. Thirty-five thousand left North Carolina in eight short months despite exhortations to stay at home: The Fayetteville newspaper gave space that spring to the president of the Colored Citizens Patriotic League, who argued that black migrants "would better be cultivating Southern food crops."[91] While many blacks had come into town from rural areas in the preceding years, Fayetteville's black population dropped precipitously as a proportion of the city total, from 47 percent in 1910 to 38 percent in 1920. Even as the war whitened the city, some blacks who stayed found jobs on the new post that improved their position in the local labor market.

> I can remember my father telling me about how some of his father's bosses were upset when Fort Bragg came here and the price of labor went up, because of providing employment for a lot of the African Americans who before only had the farmers and share croppers to [hire them, as they were excluded from most mill jobs]. Then there was this alternative source of employment then meant that the people on the farms had to pay more to keep the workers there and some of them were upset.[92]

Much building at Bragg and other camps around the country was done by black men drafted into the army rather than by free labor, however.[93]

The available men installed water, sewer, and road systems, erected hundreds of buildings, and within a few months, built a post that could accommodate sixteen thousand soldiers. But before it was completed, the war ended and so just twelve hundred troops finally occupied the buildings and ranges in 1919 and 1920.[94] The demobilization that had followed all previous American wars seemed to come to Fayetteville in 1921 as Washington announced it was closing the post. Once again, vigorous lobbying kept the facility in Fayetteville, despite the War Department's plan. This time the camp commander, General A. J. Bowley, spearheaded the campaign with the help of local civic organizations. A key strategy was a promise of help to the new secretary of war, John Weeks. He aspired to the U.S. presidency and was assured support from Bowley's party in North Carolina.[95] To help seal the deal, Weeks was invited to the camp where local women staged a gracious picnic of barbecue, chicken, and iced tea.[96] And so the story would go throughout the rest of the century, as military bases and military industrial facilities sprouted up in places where local businessmen, military personnel, and politicians lobbied for them and then would not lightly let them go.

PREPARING THE NATIONAL CHARACTER FOR A NEW CENTURY OF WAR

The push to build Camp Bragg came partly from a "preparedness movement" that pressured Woodrow Wilson into his reluctant April 1917 declaration of war.[97] Led by Theodore Roosevelt, Elihu Root, Leonard Wood, and some of the nation's wealthiest men, the movement claimed the country was dangerously isolationist and materially unprepared for a new international military role.[98] They argued the military must grow to deal with the European war in which America would necessarily become involved. And their crusade envisioned much more: Conscription was "to revitalize and protect America through the inculcation of military values," values whose benefits were seen more in domestic than military terms. The claim was that "military training would help restore harmony, order, and vitality to a society that they believed was being fragmented and debilitated by individual selfishness, class and ethnic divisions, and local and regional parochialism."[99] Military conscription would also help solve the problem they saw of American manhood gone soft. While the army was less than completely enthused about the camps and universal military training—it wanted not to train everyone but to draft and select the mentally and physically most able—it encouraged the movement, particularly given public sentiment about the draft. "As a War Department memorandum put it, universal military training, 'is a happier phrase than compulsory military service.' "[100]

The elites who campaigned for conscription felt this training would "Americanize" the mass of new immigrants that civilian institutions had failed to enculturate. Recruits would receive sociology and history lessons embedded in their English exercises: The primers would tell them, among other things, that strikes lead to decline in workers' wages, and that American national character is intrinsically peaceful while the European preferred violent resolution of conflict. The Army's relationship to recruits defined as "different" included what historian Bruce White has described as "constant attempts to apply the time-honoured army rules and regulations, [and] to fit all comers into a common mould. It is essentially an Anglo-Saxon mould, which is not surprising in view of the upper-middle class, Anglo-Saxon, Protestant background of most army officers."[101] And yet the desire to assimilate groups through military training was limited. There continued a debate over the separation of Slavic and other all-white units. And in 1907, the General Staff had already ruled that blacks lacked the intelligence to be artillerymen (although they could join separate black infantry and cavalry units), and they were excluded from participation in the model civilian training camp in Plattsburg, New York.

Wilson's decision to move from volunteers to a drafted army was influenced by the contemporary rise of enthusiasm for the value of efficiency. He would organize military needs, civilian mobilization, and the general economy through scientific control of the labor processes championed by turn-of-the-century business leaders. Obedience and rationalism rather than enthusiasm were to be rewarded now in contrast to American wars of the past. Through the preparedness movement, the newly consolidating wealthy class could seek to "rationalize the social order. . . . Efficiency, predictability, and order superseded older values of localism, individualism, and voluntarism."[102]

Social tumult was generated by the rumors and machinations that rose with the war in Europe. A wide range of views and interests were in play—a variety little evident in pithy, popular accounts of World War I today. This was a first in American history: a drafted and completely federal army, with no bounties to buy oneself out of service. To pull along the reluctant public, Wilson renamed a missile a peacekeeper: The draft "is in no sense a conscription of the unwilling," he said, "it is, rather, selection from a nation that has volunteered in mass."[103] Some of Cumberland County's youth may have resisted this "total claim of the state over the individual," however.[104] The local paper, at least, felt it had to resort to strong words in exhorting local youth to volunteer or register: "Be manly. Be true. Be patriotic," it said and, evoking the war dead among their ancestors, editorialized, "Are the grandsons and sons of these brave men going to be slackers and wait until they are dragged into the army? Have they degenerated and become a race of timid weaklings?"[105] Nationwide, between 2.5 and 3.5 million men refused to register, 12 percent of those drafted refused induction, and another large number suddenly married in search of a deferment.[106] Many young men from Cumberland County went to war, however, as did eighty-six thousand young North Carolinians; 2,375 of them died, fully two-thirds felled by disease rather than bullets.[107]

The war injected nativism's poison into the body politic. As war approached, questions about America's involvement held more generally among the population were often attributed to noncitizens. Disloyalty among the city's foreign colony "should be made public," a "contributed" note to Fayetteville's paper said in the spring of 1917. Their supposed betrayal was especially galling to the writer given they were "enjoying business opportunities and a peace in our midst impossible on their native soil." More threateningly, the paper noted "reports of disloyal utterances among a certain element in this community. It should be borne in mind that disloyalty goes beyond a magistrate's court and quite often disloyal or traitorous citizens are placed with their backs to the wall and shot."[108] That same week, a prominent mill owner, J. R. Tolar, called for patriotic demonstrations near Old Liberty Point, and the Navy came recruiting at the post office. Less visibly and across the country, military surveillance had moved against labor organizers, religious groups, and others, as well as "enemy aliens": "It shifted from counterespionage to counterdissent, from a small force endorsed by the secretary of war to find German agents, to a force for keeping the population in support of the war policies of the administration."[109] So, too, the government conducted a massive propaganda campaign. It portrayed political difference as sedition and constructed a "War Issues Course" for universities that dispensed a simplified world history in which German evil struggled with Allied good.[110] And the antiradical hysteria that emerged from all of this government work went as far as the arrest and unseating of legitimately elected socialists in various parts of the country and vigilante violence against pacifists and labor organizers.[111]

When the war ended in November 1918, jubilation ran through Fayetteville. The commemoration that followed was a ritual, to be repeated throughout the century, that culturally divided the territories of war and peace, even as the boundary was increasingly to blur. The armistice announcement sent a woman with two sons in France screaming down the street,[112] and Frances McColl remembered "great celebration": "When the man next door to us went to war, we went to the railroad station to tell those boys goodbye. Of course I didn't know where Bud was going. I don't remember it being a serious thing with me, but my mother cried when Turkey surrendered, from joy."[113] And, in an attempt to shape such feelings into a broader glorification of war, the state's Governor Bickett speechified: "Lest we forget, I write it down in this last chapter and certify to all the generations that the one stupendous, immortal thing connected with this administration is the part North Carolina played in the World War. Everything done in the field of taxation, of education, of agriculture, of mercy to the fallen, of the physical and social regeneration of our people—all of it is but a 'snowflake on the river' in the gigantic and glorified presence of the eighty-thousand men who plunged into the blood-red tide of war."[114]

THE "INTER-WAR YEARS," OR THE AGE OF ANTIMILITARISM

The years of peace and relative demilitarization from 1919 to 1939 have haplessly come to be known as the "inter-war" years. The past is often labeled or storied in ways that make some outcomes appear inevitable, others impossible. And so this concept of peace as waiting-for-war suggests the inexorability of the coming of World War II, the necessity of America's destiny being made by its armies. However undesirable war is thought to be, some ways of telling national history suggest that peace can only be enjoyed as a temporary recess. However, a still strong desire to avoid foreign entanglement, the repudiation of what was defined as the true enemy—Prussian militarism—and the push for a frugal central government won the day after World War I.[115] With public backing, an "antistatist and anticorporate" Congress rejected the Army's proposed half-million-man peacetime Army.[116] It authorized a much smaller Regular Army, which shrank to 150,000 men in 1921 and 119,000 by 1927.[117] No longer convincing was the argument that a great nation needed large armies or the most modern equipment to express that greatness. The reality of war had been made clearer both to those who had seen battle and those who experienced its disruptions and took care of its maimed and wounded back home. For, as George Orwell was to write, "If the war didn't happen to kill you, it was bound to start you thinking."[118] Antiwar literature and films blossomed during this time: Hemingway's *A Farewell to Arms,* the film *All Quiet on the Western Front,* and Picasso's *Guernica* are of this era. The forces that combined to circumscribe the military and Fort Bragg were not just the pacifism and antimilitarist feminism portrayed in the popular arts; they included "populists and progressives suspicious of eastern capitalists, unilateralists opposed to alliances, [and] conservatives more worried about the domestic order."[119]

Universal military training was rejected as national policy, although the aftermath of the war did not completely kill the preparedness movement. Some of Fayetteville's youth (mainly the wealthy who could be spared from paid work) would become members of the Red, White, and Blue teams at the Citizens' Military Training Camps held at Fort Bragg through the 1920s. Although the young men underwent physical training, rifle practice, and drill, their camp annuals read like high school or college yearbooks of the time. Prizes went to the "most handsome," "biggest show hound," "ugliest country boy," and "most sheikish," and there were wry descriptions of camp rigors.[120] The young women of Fayetteville, organized by their churches, put on entertainments and danced with the young men. A striking photo that opens the yearbook is not of a man in war-making pose, but a discus-throwing camper whose body's beautiful Grecian lines suggest art or eros more than aggression.

The business interests that were crucial in bringing the post to Fayetteville also held an alternative view of America's military needs. Their 1919 chamber of commerce brochure saw the turn in city fortunes as part of a permanent change in American lifeways: "So long as the institution of war exists and so long as we shall require a large standing army, and we probably shall for some years to come, any scarcely settled section that possesses advantages for the attraction and maintenance of twenty or thirty thousand men employed in pursuits for their moral, mental and physical development cannot but derive its special share in the general benefit."[121] This represents a radical turn of thought—as much a hope as an observation—in its accep-

tance of a large standing army. It is one that businessmen in a struggling region might contemplate more quickly and positively than
others. But despite their hopes for large numbers of soldiers, Camp
Bragg remained small, as did the U.S. military as a whole, even
though it was double its pre–World War I size.[122]

Those who were children in Fayetteville during Bragg's first two
decades remember quite different posts. For some, it was a place of
elegant West Point officers and their cosmopolitan children. Polo was
an obsession, particularly in the late 1920s and 1930s, with the army
playing every Sunday on well-kept fields against teams from the
wealthy resorts just to the west and north, including Pinehurst,
Southern Pines, and the Rockefellers' Overhills estate.

Others recall a less genteel, though still impressive, place. Wade
Thomas Saunders, born to a prosperous merchant in 1907, had vivid
memories. The young boy was mightily impressed by the installation's cannons and thrilled with the technical parts he was able to pil-
fer to build a radio at home. His enthusiasm for these articles, as well
as his father's automobile, was a piece of America's twentieth-century
faith in the power of new technologies to remake the globe and ensure human happiness. In the case of war, the faith was that these in-
ventions would create and preserve America's dominance and safety,
even make war more humane. Despite the fact that the arsenal on
Haymount Hill drew Sherman's wrath on Fayetteville, the next century began and ended with the confidence that safety lay in better
machines.

The people of the army were another matter, however. Saunders
was fired from his newspaper delivery job in 1922 when he refused to
take papers out to the post via the streetcar. The soldiers, he said,
threw "what we'd called 'Alley Apples.' They'd hum a brick at you
anytime and I wanted no part of that. . . . They were peacetime soldiers then, you see. They were just people who wouldn't work, the
ones who were soldiers, a lot of them, see, they didn't care."[123] Disdain
for the peacetime regular soldier was a mainstay of the entire century
that led up to the 1920s. In the peace periods from 1820 to 1890, soldiers came predominantly from the ranks of immigrants and northern city folk and were less than one-twentieth of a percent of the labor force. The stigma emerged not just from their low social standing,
however. Wealthier families whose men enlisted "probably did not
mention them in polite conversation" either, because the soldier's

lifestyle violated the imperatives of the work ethic.[124] Civilians observed them drinking and heading to brothels on paydays, and this and the leisure of some obscured the hard physical labor many in the army did.

A ninety-year-old retired army veteran, Uldrich Conerly, was one of those peacetime soldiers at Bragg.[125] He enlisted at age seventeen out of admiration for the uniform his brother wore home from World War I as well as to escape intense poverty in his rural Mississippi home. Although the enlisted soldier, he said, was "regarded as little more than a bum," few left the service during the 1930s in particular, when other prospects were dim. The sharp social stratification within the army mirrored society's as a whole. Like numbers of enlisted men, he was given a variety of personal service jobs for officers. He replaced horse divots after each polo game; maintained an officer's uniforms, boots, and equipment; and cared for his child when the maid was out. It was also officers' prerogative to sit in a section of Fayetteville's movie theaters separate from enlisted men.

The 1920s saw the consolidation of artillery development and training at Fort Bragg. It housed cutting-edge equipment such as wireless radios and smokeless gunpowder, but Fort Bragg and the army had difficulty recruiting new troops in an era of prosperity and plentiful job choices. Unit officers and enlisted men fanned out around the state looking for men to sign to four-year enlistments. Public relations was already a weapon of peacetime mobilization, with the post recreation officer taking local schoolboys on installation tours and arranging for theater entertainment that drew both soldiers and locals.[126] Overseas assignments were relatively rare, as interventionism diminished. Soldiers mainly manned the occupation forces in America's relatively small colonial holdings.

The Depression began to show itself in Fayetteville's textile industry immediately in the fall of 1929. While army families were relatively protected and their salaries, though cut, continued to fund some business activity in town, the Depression was as dismal and deep in Fayetteville as it was elsewhere. When rumors circulated that the mills were about to restart, children missed school to stand by for work. Diseases of malnutrition such as pellagra, which attacks the skin and nerves, stalked the families of the unemployed, and death by starvation was not unheard of.[127] Black tenant farmers in the county had an especially hard time and left the area in large numbers.[128]

Ruins of the textile industry, replaced by retail sales to soldiers

On post, extensive building was funded in the 1930s, including exotic Spanish Colonial Revival–style homes for officers, as well as a hospital, theater, golf course, administration building, artillery stables, and chapel.[129] The post had approximately three thousand soldiers through the 1930s and employed 350 civilians in its laundry, kitchens, and offices. Still, it remained a modest part of local economic life, with over seventeen thousand people employed at farmhand, mill, and other jobs outside the installation.[130]

The Depression brought Betty Hanford to Fort Bragg in 1931.[131] I went to meet her in an apartment on the west side of Fayetteville, driving through pleasant neighborhoods and past sprawling shopping centers, one of them, the Bordeaux, advertising itself to passersby with a several-story-high replica of the Eiffel Tower. Letting me in through several locks, she told me about her recent harrowing mugging (as did several other people I spoke with). But she continued to enjoy Fayetteville: Her attractive apartment, decorated with Korean and Japanese artifacts from her soldier-relatives' Asian trips, was affordable. And she often played bridge with the many friends made over her sixty-five years in town.

Born in Utah, her ancestors were Mormon pioneers. Many worked as land surveyors, their move West to escape religious persecution simultaneous with the Army's eviction of Native Americans. As World War I began, she remembered, her father was given the choice to work in a California naval yard or be drafted. They soon set out across the Mojave desert toward the shipyard job, water bags hanging from the side of the car to ensure their survival through the empty, endless heat. When her father stopped to help some travelers who appeared broken down on the side of the road, they stole the water bags and drove off. A few years after the war-time stay in California, their world was turned around again. "My mother died in childbirth when I was 13. It was like night and day. Day turned to night."

They were living at the time in Chicago, where her father owned a tile installation business. When his company was decimated in 1929, one of her father's youngest brothers "was an officer in the [Army] Air Force and he decided to take care of my grandmother, . . . and the brothers and sisters decided one of the granddaughters should live with this bachelor uncle and his mother." When her uncle was transferred from the Chicago area to Pope Field at Fort Bragg, the three of them moved to Fayetteville.[132] His army job provided all three of them an alternative to privation, each in a way particular to the gender conventions of the time. "Bob wanted somebody to help handle Granny. I prepared the meals and acted as, well Grandmother acted as more of a hostess. I was more of the housekeeper although we did have a maid, a colored maid. . . . My uncle paid for her to come maybe three days a week to clean house. . . . I used to play tennis and played golf. You might have thought I was a child of means, but I wasn't."[133] She lived in a comfortable three-bedroom house, and, as a nineteen-year-old, found herself in great demand as a date among the 150 officers then at Bragg. And in the post chapel in 1936, she married the stepson of an officer, a veterinarian who cared for the horses and mules still drawing military equipment around the installation.

Army people like Betty impressed Fayetteville youth with the ease of their lives compared with the children's own Depression struggles and with their worldliness. Betty could speak of Morman Utah and describe Chicago's elegant Drake Hotel where her father's Italian employees had installed marble floors. Bill Fields described his encounter with army children in school:

> We're talking about the Depression when everybody was as poor as church mice and they were the only kids there [whose] daddies had regular incomes. One girl had access to an automobile and periodically she'd fill up the car with her classmates and when they had parties, the ones who were lucky enough to know some of those kids would be invited out there to social events and then, conversely—not that there were that many social events—we did the best we could. We didn't know then that we were deprived, but of course it was a period of terrific economic deprivation. . . . [The military children's material situation], of course, it was just parson wealth, but at least it was secure income. More than that, they were people who had lived in other parts of the world. We just found them attractive people and interesting and little bit broader horizons. [Though] the town wasn't all *that* provincial. The better sort had been off to get educations and travel some and had connections elsewhere.[134]

The association between class and travel—which the army could promise people of the "rougher" classes as a kind of double mobility—structured Bill Fields's early life as well. His army classmates' adventuresome tales may have helped send him off to study art in New York and Europe: On his walls were portraits he painted of Pope Pius XII and the Maltese nobility in post-Mussolini Rome. And once home, he organized artists and the arts in his home county and across the state. As he told me about his experience with army dependents, though, he had to pause several times. For an unusual number of military jets flew over his house that day, drowning out his voice as they roared in preparation for the Balkan war then looming.

It was in the unhappy climate of the Depression that disillusionment with World War I and military institutions was resuscitated. Many blamed their economic troubles in part on that war's debt and economic disturbance.[135] Ex-soldiers felt a special anger over what they saw as government neglect. They formed a so-called Bonus Army of unemployed war veterans who came to Washington in 1932 demanding their service bonuses. To add insult to injury, the army itself evicted the protesting veterans and destroyed their camp. Then, in 1934, Senator Gerald Nye held congressional hearings into ties between the Navy, War Department, and major arms manufacturers. Testimony given there suggested war profiteers had led the nation into the European conflagration. The hearings—occurring at the nation's center and generating great public interest—questioned the militarization of American society. They were part of a larger movement of antiwar activists in the Protestant churches, on college campuses, and among socialists, labor organizers, and conservatives fearful of state power garnered through war making. Fayetteville's newspaper editor reflected the views of many southerners, particularly agriculturalists and businesspeople who saw nothing in war to serve them, when he looked back at World War I at around this same time. He told the famous tale of German and English troops who climbed out of their muddy trenches on a Christmas Day and celebrated together in No Man's Land, their "natural brotherly love" replacing "artificial hatred" for a few hours. Then he imagined what might have followed for two hypothetical soldiers and two of the war's wealthy English and German home front planners who pushed the war onward long after that day.

> Thomas Atkins and Hans Schmidt are dead. They killed each other somewhere near Ypres in 1915, or at the Somme, or in front of Amiens. Some of their comrades managed to limp home and live feebly twenty years in poverty because the taxes to pay for the slaughter would not permit business to function. Sir Edward Grey and [Chancellor] Bethman-Holweg died in comfortable beds amid weeping relatives and expensive doctors from ailments not faintly associated with mustard gas or gangrene, proud to the end of the fact that their firmness prevented Thomas Atkins and Hans Schmidt from ending the war on Christmas 1914.[136]

Coming forward to contemporary talk about America's need to fight the Germans or the Japanese, he went on to argue against the profiteering and loss of freedom that would surely follow. "When that killing starts if a sane man should stand up in the streets of Fayetteville or the streets of Nagasaki and say that it was a very bad thing for boys from Bladen [a nearby county] and boys from Yokohama to be killing each other for the sake of little groups of millionaires, there would be a dozen demagogues near at hand to call him a Communist and a traitor and to hustle him to the nearest jail or the nearest lamp-post."

Despite the absence of public support for interventionism and the widespread understanding that collusion between weapons makers and an ever more powerful state was both likely and undesirable, militarization soon returned to the country and to Fayetteville. It came on the greased skids of the New Deal, whose propagators freely drew war analogies to their work. The metaphoric turn would justify their centralization of power and facilitate use of the army itself in New Deal programs. Soldiers' labor and army land, for example, helped the Civilian Conservation Corps set up an encampment on Fort Bragg. From there, CCC members went out to public service work, including such things as landscaping around the post's new buildings.[137] When some military men saw the use of soldiers in the CCC as a "diversion" from the army's real tasks or as diluting its warrior spirit, they prefigured later complaints about the army's "humanitarian missions."[138] From another perspective, these army deployments and the New Deal's strengthening of the state contributed to the process of militarizing public welfare functions. Not de novo, though: The New Deal drew on the past, using the "legal authority, programmatic example, bureaucratic shell, [and] key personnel" of World War I. And it faced forward, legitimating the massive federal deficit spending used to wage all future wars in the United States.[139]

As the decade ended, the people of Fayetteville could not imagine how much more complicated their hosting of an army would become. Their chamber's recruitment of the base twenty years earlier had inexorably embedded Fayetteville into the federal war planning to come. So had the earlier "preparedness campaign," regional rivalries, and new war technologies and professionalism structured the American military geography that World War II's mappers were to work with. The antimilitarist sentiments and movements that so animated those decades were not so much to die as to undergo reinterpretation in World War II and in its historical rewriting. And the war would only amplify the race battles that had already been the scourge of several centuries of Fayetteville's life, albeit battles largely erased from public memory.

CHAPTER 2

Hostess to the "Good War"

(1939–1947)

It is a radiant image: twenty young civilian telephone operators, proudly posing for the cameraman on the steps of the Signal Corps building at Fort Bragg during World War II. All are women, their smiles free, shoulders back, hands interlocked in an affectionate sense of sisterhood, team or club. Each woman's hair is loosely curled, each is crisply dressed, each is white-skinned. Although two male officers stand above them, the women seem not so much their subordinates, as colleagues at important work together.

There is also a heartbreaking absence. Beyond the generic losses of time, missing are these women's black counterparts, less photogenically bent over the post laundry's brutal steam presses. And the men's black fellow soldiers were shunted to segregated barracks, their sometimes violent mistreatment officially unrecorded. Neither does the photo tell of the losses of war itself. The women on the steps were a temporary sorority of an institution defined by deaths and separations and by their own marginality as females. Poignantly, one of the main functions of these signal women, before they became lost to each other, was to connect young men to their families and girlfriends by telephone before they left for war, some for the grave, and none to return unchanged or with the same simple worldview. Some of the women may have fallen in love with soldiers who would die in Europe or, perhaps worse, live but never return for them after the war. And they were not alone in this. The army creates separations and new loves on a mass scale. All of this losing and finding gets mixed together when people call the war to mind today. It is remembered by many as the "Good War," a label that can be used as an unambivalent

Signal women: civilians at work, Fort Bragg, World War II[1]

catchphrase, intentional oxymoron, or implicit comment on the evil in most all other wars—not a good war but *the* good war.[2]

Like all photos, this one is more than just a snapshot of the world as it was—and it was a world of sharply distinct genders, of skirts and khaki, permanent waves and buzz cuts. It also retells cultural myths. Despite their shared space and shared mission, the two male officers were positioned to loom above the women, reinforcing the cultural assumption that the women are protected and the men protectors. Of course, the matter was not so simple. The female civilians who worked on bases or in war industries can be seen as no less guardians or risk-takers than people in uniform. Industrial workers were more likely than soldiers to die or be injured during the war.[3] And while national social memory may dwell on the anomaly of Rosie riveting,

Fayetteville remembers the mostly very traditional feminine roles women played in and around the army. Wearing organza dresses to USO parties, nursing, typing, and ironing uniforms, women were a section of the "tail" in the military's "tooth to tail ratio": that proportion in combat versus support roles, such as preparing food, ammunition, and weaponry; maintaining trucks; and doing public relations work with civilians.

Older people's memories in Fayetteville dance between the stereotypic gender lines of the photo and more complex realities of males' and females' lives. Many women remember a swirl of romantic parties for soldiers and family generosity as men in uniform were invited home for Sunday dinners as surrogate sons. They also remember arranging child care and long, arduous days of commuting through a slow sea of cars and military vehicles to work on the post. They recall returning home to a domestic workload made more difficult than usual by absent husbands and by soldiers they were often boarding in their homes. And refugee war brides from Europe recall those years as a thousand days of hunger, pierced by aerial bombardment or the threat of rape.

Mostly teenagers or young adults during the war, the people I spoke with often described the war they lived through in a personal way—the people they knew who died, the work they did, the amazing sights they saw—rather than through abstract ideas such as "the fight against fascism." Younger Fayettevillians I spoke with who had *not* lived through the war were more likely to assign such general political meaning to it, a common contrast in how generations of people in the United States, at least, see the past.[4] And some memories also thin when it comes to the demeaning treatment of black soldiers who were mobilized for a war that was at least ostensibly antiracist.

But we should begin at the beginning of Fayetteville's World War II mobilization. This was not Pearl Harbor, but two years earlier, in 1939, when plans were announced to enlarge the U.S. Army. That year, Roosevelt had succeeded in convincing a reluctant Congress to mobilize in a major way, although military spending itself had increased sharply around 1935 and rose 50 percent between 1936 and 1940.[5] But more important, 1939 was also the beginning of a shift from debate centered around the limited activities of war and defense to the more expansive, expensive, and potentially imperial concept of "national security."[6] This concept was part of Roosevelt's and others' argument that the world and war had changed radically in the twenty years since World War I. New weapons and the shrinking of the globe, he emphasized, meant that "when peace has been broken anywhere, the peace of all countries everywhere is in danger," and that "no attack is so unlikely or impossible that it may be ignored."[7] Joined by many intellectuals, Roosevelt also began to treat ideas—totalitarian or American—as weapons that could leap the ocean in attack and counterattack.[8] This conception of what the military was now for—a permanently mobilized force to deal with an intrinsically threatening world—meant there were no promises this time of a war to end all wars.

This rhetoric and call to arms were resisted, however. And not only by pacifists and others who focused on the debacle of World War I. So did promilitary anti-interventionists and businessmen, the latter not yet embedded in the sure profit-making system of what was to become the military-industrial complex. They feared the loss of civilian markets and worried about being saddled with superfluous productive facilities should they take military orders. The terms of debate about the need for military intervention often remained technocentric, however, with both pro- and antiwar positions centered around the power of military technology. The rhetoric claimed those tools could either defend us well enough without involvement in Europe or hurt us here unless we engaged in the battle overseas. But in these arguments, the economics, social relations, and the morality of war took second seats.

Whatever the actual threat abroad, national media tended to magnify it. This effect came out of journalism's reliance on official government sources rather than independent news gathering and because orienting consumers to a dramatic external threat could successfully compete with hometown print journalism's local stories in generating commercial revenues. And its coverage, as Michael Sherry notes, was often "vivid enough to be alarming but not gory enough to be disillusioning."[9] Local media, on the other hand, while diverse in orientation to the war, drew energy away from mobilization simply by focusing on the more immediate problems American communities had. In many places, this local news remained economic recovery, the problems of labor, crime, and the weather. In cities that gained the limiting sobriquet "military city," the local news would become an interesting combination of regional concerns and war reports. News reporting focused on new buildings erected and soldiers arriving, concentrated at least implicitly on the prosperity they brought, and remained relatively quiet on the destruction a military base would make possible and the global issues at stake. Anti-Semitism was widespread enough throughout the country that stories of German violence against Jews played minor parts in the mobilizing stories.[10]

The army grew eightfold to 1.5 million men from 1939 through the summer of 1941. It did so via the nation's first peacetime draft, instituted in October 1940. Military base construction mushroomed to accommodate the new soldiers, with North Carolina alone to operate twenty-four military installations through the war.[11] Some bases were made from newly condemned lands, as in the eastern Carolinas, where numerous primarily black farmers were dispossessed, sometimes with just forty-eight hours notice. Throughout the South, over one million acres were taken and fifty thousand people displaced. The burden fell disproportionately on black rural people for at least four reasons. One was the Southern Democrats' congressional seniority, something their states' one-party political system had given them and which had put them at the head of several defense committees. Political leaders excluded blacks from the groups deciding or consulting on base siting and their voting disenfranchisement made decisionmakers unaccountable to them. Moreover, the military looked for areas relatively less crisscrossed with civilian infrastructure, something that white-controlled state and local government had been successfully denying to black communities over the years. Finally, slavery's heritage clustered blacks in the temperate coastal areas amenable first to plantation agriculture and then to year-round military training.[12]

Fort Bragg's farmers had already given up their land several decades before, and so buildup of that post took place earlier than elsewhere, beginning in September 1940. Over thirty-one thousand workers—the majority farmers from neighboring counties, both black and white—were organized to accomplish what one historian enumerates as follows:

> 2,800 buildings, 75 additional miles of roads, and new sewer lines, new water lines, and new power lines. These buildings consisted of 938 barracks, 320 mess halls, 320 day rooms (enlisted men's recreation), 320 company store rooms, officers barracks, officers mess halls, field houses, service clubs, regimental mess halls, quartermaster warehouses, a refrigeration plant, and a hospital. $100,000 was spent on new rail lines. Total

construction cost $46,500,000. The population of Fort Bragg went from [5,400 in 1940 to] 20,000 in January 1941 to 67,000 only six months later [and 159,000 at its wartime peak].[13]

After the new soldiers arrived, eleven post theaters served 70,000 patrons weekly. Each month, the post exchange sold 900,000 sodas, 900,000 bottles of beer, and 500,000 packs of cigarettes. Sixty-seven tanks and tractors and 7,951 pairs of shoes were repaired monthly. The ordnance office issued more than two million rounds of small arms ammunition, and the Signal Office, with 2,600 phone lines, deployed 65 projectors daily to show training films.[14] Such lists commonly pepper historical accounts of World War II mobilization around the country and demonstrate how breathtaking was the scale of human effort made.

The Fort Bragg of 1939 was described as a place that "seems a beautiful park, every blade tended with polo, golf, swimming, and barracks that resemble college dorms."[15] And while the radically expanded post of just two years later is pictured as more of a beehive of activity, it is also depicted as a place of natural beauty, architectural order, and human accomplishment. In a book celebrating Fort Bragg's contribution to World War II, published in 1945, we see photos of barracks, Euclidean in their parallel-lined windows, clipped foundation shrubbery, and sun-dappled sidewalks; the white spire of the post's main chapel; a light snow outlining branching greenery; canoeists on a pristine pond.

One army private describing the Fort Bragg of 1941 was less impressed with the aesthetics of the post than with the problems associated with its massive size. He told of a man assigned to the installation, along with his brother, who had to write to their mother for help finding his sibling. "Fort Bragg is menacing!" he said. "It is menacing in size. It is menacing in the consciousness of that size; and in the grim realization of what this great size and potential may mean in a world like today's." The sight of the thicket of army equipment running through the woods, he noted, "would have gladdened the heart of the most ardent militarist." And of Fayetteville itself, "you may not like what Bragg's boom has done to Fayetteville. Its prices are higher. Red and green neon has made lovely old Hay Street look tawdry. And the city's charming outskirts have dirtied with the mushroom appearances of cheap squatters' camps."[16]

This soldier notwithstanding, it was difficult to find, in 1940 or 1945, photos or text showing the scale of social change this all entailed: the mass migrations in and out of the county, the challenge to the Jim Crow racial system, to ideas about how women should properly behave, and to the sense of what the nation was in the international scheme of things. Also absent from most accounts of home-front mobilization is the scale of civilian need not met by concerted public action. In Cumberland County in 1940, 29 out of 30 farm homes used outhouses, and 8 out of 9 had no electricity.[17] In the city, 1,773 houses were without running water and needed major repairs.[18] There is little accounting of the human *de*construction the preparations and war itself involved: the costs in marriages hastily made or disrupted, work lives reshaped and unmade, the racial humiliation exacted by whites concerned that the war would precipitate black rebellion, and the bodily and emotional trauma to which all this activity was ultimately to lead.

ONE GIRL'S WORLD WAR II

A war glamorized by the government's mobilization offices and by some postwar histories can leave uncomfortable memories in juxtaposition: glamour and gore, romance and violence, doing what is expected when what is expected transgresses existing social codes. It is not these contradictions that people speak about, however, when they remember World War II. Seeming so long ago and difficult to name, these unresolved events are described with personal experiences and sometimes with numbers, just as the historians have done: small ones turning into huge ones, overnight. With those counts, they try to communicate the mushrooming, exploding, uncontained scale of change that suddenly engulfed their town.

So it was with Anne, a hospitable and vibrant, raspy-throated woman who has been involved in historic preservation in town, a once (but no longer) rare native Republican. She offered me a silk sofa pillow for my back as we sat down to talk in her elegant Haymount home. She described the scene that emerged into her ten-year-old world, something that is still today

> vivid in my mind. It's just amazing. It was absolutely amazing . . . it was
> just a very small post. Even counting wives and children. And we ended
> up being 100,000 troops, not counting their wives and children. Over a

period of just no time. The population of Fayetteville jumped from 13,000 to 17,000 overnight. I mean it was just boom. And then all these people pouring in, moving in with their husbands and children, wives plus all those 25,000 workmen, who were living, my daddy used to say, as far as 25, 30 miles away.[19] Some of them were living in tobacco barns, where they would sleep in palettes on the floor. I mean it was just no place to house them. And then all the troops coming home, I know they set up two tent cities at Fort Bragg where those first soldiers stayed . . . until they could get some barracks built. And as I say, they were building barracks every thirty minutes for nine months. It was just unreal.[20]

Some of these numbers may have come to her via the newspaper's later retellings of war history. More unmediated was her memory of interruptions in her childhood routines: "I had a friend that lived on that side of the Fort Bragg Road just several blocks away but on the other side, and I knew that if I wandered across that road, by four o'clock in the afternoon, I couldn't get across, because—and I remember as vividly as I'm looking at you—they were literally bumper to bumper. A line as far as you could see, that came for an eternity."

Her family was among the town's wealthiest, her father in the successful hardware business that his grandfather had started in the nineteenth century. This war-related growth was good for business. New product lines were brought in for sale to the post—immense cauldrons and giant spoons for stirring an army's worth of food, and titanic orders went out for building supplies.[21]

Her father had been a soldier in World War I, and the stories he told—of being gassed and of laying pierced with shrapnel in no-man's land—had prepared her, she felt, to understand what this new war could mean for soldiers. What it would mean for the poorly named "noncombatants" was less obvious. Unlike the First World War, this one would kill civilians at rates often exceeding soldiers. By the end of the century, 90 percent of all war deaths would be of unarmed women, children, and men. Just as high infant mortality rates in the United States and Europe once meant death was associated with childhood, and now as death is considered a problem of the elderly, so war's protectors and its protected have experienced a great reversal, one still dimly understood by Americans far from battle.[22]

The most immediate effect of the war, however, was to bring not carnage, but celebrity, into Anne's home. Along with others of the local white elite, her family would sometimes entertain the higher-ranking officers in their homes, including General and Mrs. Eisenhower, General James Gavin, and General Courtney and Mrs. Hodges. Her memory of this is bathed in the shimmering light that washes many childhood memories. "We had a swinging door between the pantry and the kitchen and the dining room. I remember peeking through that little crack, trying to see all of them, seeing them seated at the table, and of course they'd wear their dress blues to come into dinner. That was so romantic and glamorous, really."

Exotic experiences also came in the form of new secrecy and new people, at once dangerous and attractive. Anne learned she should "zip the lip."

> I [was] even real scared to speak to the stranger on the bus for fear of releasing a war secret. . . . And then we soon later on had air raid warnings. Daddy was air raid warden of the neighborhood and he'd have to go out . . . but you'd hear the sirens blowing and you'd have to cut off all the lights and close the curtains. That really scared me, because it was dark in the house and dark outside. I was scared of darkness. And then he'd have to go out because they say, even a cigarette outside, an enemy plane could see. Whether that's true or not, I don't know, but that's what we were told.

The war brought all sorts of new people to the city. Anne met one memorable stranger when the Red Cross sent a worker into school to teach students how to make bandages and knit socks, scarves, and arctic duty helmets. Her Red Cross tutor

> was a very nice lady named Mrs. Poncha and she had moved here from the north somewhere—New York, I think. And she was kind of mysterious. Her husband had this Town Pump [which became the most famous bar in the city] . . . and I guess she was strange to us because we never seen anybody with dyed hair a different color every week. It would be red one week, black one week, one week blonde, one week natural. We'd just never seen anybody like that. And these long, fine fingernails. When she knitted, we were all *fascinated* with it. So she said "I want all ya'll to go out to lunch with me, as your exam break," which was very nice of her. . . . [On] the way downtown, she told us we were going to the Town Pump for lunch, [and] I was terror-struck. I thought, my daddy knows I've been to the Town Pump, he will *kill* me. All our parents will kill us. . . . It had a bar that was this huge . . . oval . . . built on glass brick, and it was enormous. And within that was another circle that had [been] built up [for]

the piano, and the place for the band up high, with another circle. And then it had all these half-round booths around the walls that were white leather. . . . It was all very mysterious. Well, they lived not very far from Mom and Daddy, [but] they left under cover of darkness one night, just boom, they were gone. Moved out of the house, didn't say anything to anybody, just gone. Then it came out that Mr. Poncha had been Al Capone's driver. I've never heard anybody say that's not true. So I guess it is true.

The new people in town were civilian workers and people looking for business opportunities. Some natives, though, saw the migrants as "camp followers, prostitutes, gamblers, flim-flammers, racketeers, pawn [brokers], bootleggers, dope peddlers, and all who look for a quick take and a fast dollar in a military town." This description was given by the son of a businessman who came to town at the turn of the century. He also said his father "found it ugly and distasteful" that wartime fortunes, legitimate and illegitimate, were made because "it took no business acumen to do it."[23] And he recounted downtown crowds so thick that people could not fit on the sidewalks, traffic at a standstill, and stores jammed with shoppers and shoplifters, with a police force that could not cope. By contrast, another woman reflected common local sentiments when she said,

> We got an awful black eye from *Life* magazine and a lot of other media at that time. The GIs came to town, some of them and rented places and then sub-letted them. And then of course ran the prices up and we got a black eye from having high rents and restaurants and what have you went sky-high. A lot of people came from out of town, unbeknownst to us and rented coffee shops and small restaurants downtown and some of them were run by the local people, but a lot of them weren't. And a lot of it went sky high. And we got a black name because we were jewing [sic] the poor GI out of money and really it wasn't our fault.[24]

With the influx of soldiers, Fayetteville was again exposed to the exuberance, panic, and anger of men about to go to war, which could manifest as behaviors ranging from public rowdiness to petty criminal activity.

> The troops got "battle ready," Daddy used to call it. . . . The bus station was right there in town, near the hardware store. It was a great big old kind of barn-y, warehouse-y building, but very tall with lots of windows

and many panes. And every Monday morning he had a standing order to send his glass cutter to come and replace all the windows. All the window panes, they had got drunk and knocked out, and I heard Daddy say that they'd be so strong and battle ready, they'd twist—it was when a license plate was not like it is today within the fender but [was] stuck up on top— they'd just twist it off . . . and throw it aside.

Before and since this time, people have tried to explain what war training does to young men. Anne's father's explanation was more positive than many others, but, as she noted, he made money repairing the aftermath.

The kinship-centered life of this town was also to be challenged, as the government sponsored its massive migrations to Fayetteville, and without sufficient new housing to support them. As new soldiers and post workers poured from the train station or stepped from road-dusty cars, they discovered the inns full and their resourcefulness tested. They slept in rows in downtown hotel lobbies, in auto back-seats and backyard sheds, and tramped up to people's front doors, asking for shelter. The newspaper printed impressive, full-page ads pleading for help with the homeless, who were often the families of soldiers. Anne proudly remembered:

> So many people took in people to live in their homes who never would have rented a room or something like that. But they felt very much that it was their patriotic duty and I know the people across the street here [did] and there was a garage apartment in that house and they rented a room in this house and they were just everywhere. And they knew always, *always* that it was standard procedure that you would have a soldier for Sunday dinner after church. You know, we would invite one or two. Mother would invite one or two for dinner in the middle of the day after church. And everybody did that. It was just, the most open-armed place I could imagine. [Although] we were scolded not to be too friendly [she laughs], the three daughters, you know.

And Anne would also have her first experience of the role not only of hostess to strangers but of mourner for young men whose experiences of killing and dying, or peeling potatoes so that others could kill and die, neither she nor the soldiers in training could truly understand. Some young women clearly kept their eyes resolutely focused on the party, and the fresh young men, and the world of possi-

bilities. Others could already see the foreshortening and hear the lam-
entations of after-battle days. Anne's voice became more unsettled
and her syntax troubled as she described the troop trains arriving and
soldiers coming in on "big trucks with the wooden seats on each side
. . . when the war really started. All that [other] would have happened
before, but then during the war, when the soldiers were riding those
trucks and they come down that road, down this road, I mean, all over
the place, they were there. Miles of them, just miles. And they would
toss out notes, 'please write to me.' Oh, it was so sad. It was so sad."

SEXUALITY AND THE CLASS OF SOLDIERS

While many families opened their homes to soldiers and often developed an affection that kept them in touch years after the men left for
other parts of the country, they put sturdy barricades between their
daughters and the enlisted soldiers. This was notwithstanding the
barrage of images of soldiers in ads, news stories, and military promotional material that showed every soldier, enlisted or not, as clean,
tidy, ironed, sexually innocent and nonaggressive, and good-
humored. One woman, who described her childhood neighborhood
as "lower, lower middle class," remembered, after the war,

> You would never have dated a military guy. That was unheard of. That
> would have been trashy, because you didn't know him and you didn't
> know his family and things could happen. You know, unspoken horrible
> things could happen. And so, it was written in concrete: "Who is he?" If
> you came home and said I had a boyfriend, well, who is he? Where is he
> from? What's his family? . . . You knew that you were not going to get
> permission to go out with a guy if he were a G. I. [They didn't speak the
> things but, what did you understand them to mean?] Well, as I got older,
> of course, the unspoken became, you could get pregnant. And, of course,
> he was from someplace else, so he would take advantage of you because
> you were this backward Southern girl. And he would leave . . . [or] you
> might get caught and have to marry someone whose family you didn't
> know, that wasn't from around here. And, I think for my parents [it was
> also that the soldier] may come and take you away to this other place [and]
> that would be terrible.[25]

The officer class was another matter. Many young women were
bused to three-times-weekly chaperoned dances on post. Lilyan Ray
remembered going to the officer's club at Fort Bragg in the summer:

"They didn't have air conditioning [but] it was just cool. We had a good time out there. Usually you had plenty [of dance partners] to select from, [and] you always wore evening dresses." For some families, officers were more than acceptable dating and marriage partners for their daughters.

> My sister was old enough to date the young lieutenants. . . . I remember how careful Daddy was about that. She could not go out with anybody that had not been personally recommended to him—not necessarily somebody that knew the boy from his birth, but somebody that had met him and knew something about him. See they were drafting the *loveliest* people in the country. All the Ivy League schools were sending hoards of young lieutenants. Daddy had a lot of friends, particularly his World War I friends [who] would write and say my nephew is coming and my good friend, and you know, please look him up. . . . A lot of Fayetteville girls married the young lieutenants.

For the middle class, officers were preferred dates as well, but some nonofficers were acceptable. One woman, whose father ran a small sawmill, described the importance of the social distinction between enlisted men and draftees.

> We'd go to the dances during the war, dance with all those draftees. But you always had to find out if they were draftees or enlistees. It made a difference back then, I don't know why, but it did. There was a regular army. Back then [in] the regular army, the enlisted people were uneducated and some of them just went in the service because they couldn't find anything to do. They were starving to death and they had to have some means of support. But we were just brought up that we didn't associate with people like that. We didn't date 'em. That's not just Fayetteville. That was all small towns, all little southern towns that suddenly had a lot of military because it just wasn't in their social way of doing things you know. . . . The officers were different to date. We'd go to those West Point dances and we would date an officer, but [the problem was with] what we used to call the regular army enlisted men.

Because the draft could put well-heeled men in the enlisted ranks, the distinctions had become more complex. Class has always helped structure marriage choices in America, and so the signs of military rank—correlated but not identical with socioeconomic class—were important in decisions about how to deal with the new permeabilities war brought to town.

From soldiers' perspectives, the issue was also class prejudice and being unwelcome as outsiders as much as it was about sexual control. This problem involved soldiers of any race. A retired, black officer remembered that having a Fort Bragg post sticker on your car meant you were unwelcome on Fayetteville State's campus. There were "all these people coming in from the farms and what have you and Fayetteville had its little section of elite black you might say and they didn't want to be contaminated by these germs invading the community," he laughed. "They had their gate closed around Fayetteville and you couldn't get in and out. You just couldn't drive in there and start talking to girls or something like that. . . . When the soldiers would come into town the mothers would lock their daughters up."

Local women were, in fact, objects of consumption in some eyes. A cartoonist for a Fort Bragg newspaper early in the war drew a thick-eyelashed, hourglass-figured woman in mini-shorts, halter top, and kerchief and captioned it "Monday night in Fatal-ville! See What I Mean?"[26] Whether this is a venereal disease warning or an invitation to see the town as holding sexual promise is not clear. But hostility is above the surface in several other cartoons that show women disheveled after assaults during dates with soldiers: "I didn't know he meant real wrestling," one says, and another, "My dress was torn between conflicting emotions." While townspeople may have shared the widespread fear of "sex delinquency" in young women—so-called Victory Girls who were not prostitutes but average women who cavorted with soldiers—they defended some local women when required. In 1945, the newspaper reported the arrest of two soldiers for striking a pair of girls. After accosting them with obscene language, an intoxicated soldier asked one why she wouldn't speak to him. When she replied 'Because I don't know you,' he struck her. By the time the police and a posse of citizens caught up with him, he was bleeding from a knife wound to the chest given by an unidentified assailant, presumably an outraged onlooker to the assault.[27]

Campaigns against prostitution occurred sporadically through the war years. The May Act, making prostitution around army installations a federal offense, went into effect in mid-1942, but there were periodic raids in Fayetteville before this time. In 1941, the newspaper told of a prostitution raid that netted twenty-five women. Two days later, headlines announced "Police smash at Negro immorality. 32

Negro women arrested overnight by Mayor J. Scott McFadyen."[28] Civic leaders had other responses to the problem of sex and the soldier as well. With city funding, the Women's Club began to house country girls who came to town for work after the club women heard that waitresses in local "spaghetti houses," who boarded in rooms upstairs from the restaurant

> were supposed to entertain the men that they served. That of course threw us all into a tizzy . . . [so] we did house as many as 30 girls at one time. They had rooms for a small amount of money and then we arranged for them to have kitchen facilities and they could cook their own meals and what have you and we chaperoned them. We had Christmas parties for them and Thanksgiving parties. A lot of them were married from the house and we had an awfully nice Baptist minister . . . a wonderful man and he used to come down and counsel the girls when we needed him. And he would come to our dinners and everything. It was just a wonderful thing to do.

As venereal disease rates soared, in spite of such limited morality campaigns, North Carolina's Health Department criticized localities for condoning prostitution, evident in what they saw (despite some spectacular raids) as a failure to prosecute known places of prostitution. To garner public support, they warned that those who contracted venereal disease were rejected from military service, "perhaps mak[ing] your boy next in line to take his place."[29] The army set up four venereal disease treatment centers in the county during the war including one at the Market House, although the State Health Department had already been attacking the problem with three hundred new clinics around the state in the several years prior to the buildup.[30] Nonetheless, venereal disease rates remained high in Cumberland County during and after the war, reaching eight times the national average in 1950.[31]

WAR'S DIVISION OF LABOR

A popular war propaganda poster shows a strong but long-lashed Rosie the Riveter rolling up her sleeves and inviting women to join the workforce. This image of women industrial workers has transfixed popular imagination about World War II's impact on gender in America. It has suggested to the generations since feminism that the war laid down the seeds for the second wave of feminism and was the most important initial step in women's journey into the paid labor force.[32] But recent historical research shows the effect of the war on gender was more conservative, temporary, and complex than this simple image suggests.[33] Millions of men did leave for army work and military-industrial production expanded dramatically, both factors that opened new jobs for women. But many of the new home front war jobs went first to white men who had been unemployed and to rural migrants leaving sharecropping. Propaganda both drew women into the labor force and sent them back out at war's end with the message that their work was an emergency measure, their essential role still domestic and maternal. This meant that they were less likely to be broadly trained in the jobs they got and it convinced many not to enter the workforce in the first place. So it was that the percentage of all women working for wages went up relatively slightly during the war, from 28 to 36 percent, and dropped again afterward to near prewar levels.[34] While female employment in manufacturing mushroomed, it ended with the war. The proportion of women doing blue-collar work even declined slightly during the 1940s.[35] In other words, this was not the revolution that popular memory suggests had occurred.

Changes in the division of labor prompted by the war represented an "intensification of long-range trends related to the changing structure of the American economy and to the changing demographic characteristics of the female population."[36] For example, women expanded their job opportunities dramatically but relatively unnoticed in the lower-paying category of clerical work.[37] This field had already been increasingly feminized in the decades leading up to the war. Its low wages meant that women kept many of those jobs after the war, with men taking back the higher-paying, union-protected manufacturing jobs. Such processes contributed to the drop in women's pay relative to men's, from 62 cents on the dollar in 1939 to 53 cents in 1950, and black women made half what white women did by that point and had fallen further behind black men.[38]

The war also did not change the view that battle was men's work or that women's work need often not be paid. Some women— 350,000 in all—went into auxiliary units of the military services but many more put in monumental hours of volunteer work for the Red Cross, USO, and war bond sales. It was mostly men who died and men

who were "cast . . . in heroic roles." And men who received the nation's financial gratitude in the form of educational and mortgage
benefits.[39]

In North Carolina, women were hired at the massive Wilmington Shipyards and continued to work in the textile mills that provided
50 percent of the national production of cotton combed yarn.[40]
North Carolina workers, male and female, also produced ammunition, rockets, electronic components, parachutes, food, and airplanes.
Industrial work in Fayetteville continued to be mainly in textiles.
Often converted to war production, the mills in Fayetteville included
one where about two hundred people made nylon stockings. That
mill went into high-speed production during the war, moving to
three shifts. While other textile factories had converted to produce
uniforms, tents, and parachutes, hosiery was also apparently a wartime necessity. As a worker there remembered, it was "unspoken . . .
that the guys were taking them overseas to trade. My uncle was in the
Air Force, or, the Army Air Corps as it was back then, and I can remember that it was really important that [my parents] shipped him
lots and lots of stockings. . . . Cigarettes and nylon stockings."

Men make war and war makes men. That is the familiar dictum
about the military and gender. Responses to men who did not go to
war and women who did are the most telling cases for understanding
what gender and war norms were. There was sharp discrimination
against young men not in the army during the war years. Whether
they were exempted for conscientious objection, health problems,
or their war-related civilian work, such men could expect hostile
comments on the sidewalks of Fayetteville and elsewhere around the
country.

On the other hand, the draft law of 1940 was in truth hardly popular. While some men may have responded positively to their draft
notice, fully 40 percent of all twenty-one-year-old men got a sudden
urge to marry within six weeks of the new law, many presumably for
a draft exemption.[41] An extension on the draft bill passed by only one
vote in the House of Representatives and would have failed had it not
banned use of the drafted soldiers outside the Western Hemisphere.[42]
The attack on Pearl Harbor was to change some of this sentiment, but
men were under much pressure to be, as men, unafraid of death and
unexpressive about any reluctance they might feel to take up the gun.

One man recalled his induction, which occurred just before another new exemption went into effect: "The day I went out, they said everybody married over 28, step forward and you can go home. Like a damn fool, I just said, 'No, I'll go.'" We both laughed and I asked, "What were you thinking?" He rejoined, "What do you mean? I already said goodbye so I might as well just go ahead into the service. Besides, you had a guilty conscience if you didn't join. Everybody, every healthy male was in the Army."

Women were not permitted in combat, the very nature of war predicated on its masculinity. Women who joined the military did so with the trepidation that they would be assumed loose or lesbian. One woman remembers her sister-in-law, a college graduate and teacher, who first asked her family if they would be embarrassed if she joined the service. "It was her tendency to always want to help others," that woman told me fifty years later, aiming to paint her relative's behavior in feminine colors.

Women also did the work of hostessing and entertaining the soldiers, extensions of the typical domestic routine of women of a certain class. Pinkie Jackson and her husband produced radio plays to raise money for war bonds, gave dinners for soldiers, and chaperoned dances at the USO. "There were some real nice young boys, college boys and they were a long way from home, you know. And we'd have dinners and [plays], that kind of thing to cheer them up." Other war jobs women did evoked contemporary comment that celebrated women's war contribution in stereotypic terms: Women, they said, did office work with "the qualities that are peculiarly women's: their quickness, their capacity for detail, their deftness, their alertness." On the other hand, under the welding masks these pundits found "a new woman . . . different from her mother. She parcels out her emotions, she packs them away out of sight during her work hours with the inanimate tools of the factory and only takes the lid off in the after-hours life."[43]

While many poor and working women, and particularly black women, were already long-term workers, others found work for the first time. Fayetteville women worked as secretaries for the Red Cross, directed plays for production on post, worked as x-ray technicians at the dental clinic, and did administrative work at Womack army hospital. In late 1941, Lana Hill was a young woman already working at a downtown jewelry store, when her neighbor, whose husband was a Fort Bragg personnel officer, tried to recruit her for work on post. "She kept asking me didn't I want to go work at Fort Bragg and I said, no, I really didn't think I did. I was kind of afraid I guess and so one day she said I'm going to take you out there to make an application. And so she put me in the car and drove me out to Fort Bragg and they gave me an examination. . . . I passed the examination and they put me to work for three weeks on a temporary assignment and so I stayed for 29 years and 9 months," she said, laughing.[44]

Bernice Burris's work at Fort Bragg, begun during the war, also lasted for decades. Like many black women, she faced the more purgatorial challenge of the heat of the laundry and steam presses. When I visited her, long into her retirement, her wall displayed an official letter of thanks from President Kennedy for her years of ironing work, along with graduation and military service portraits of her children and grandchildren. Other black women did laundry and assorted domestic work for white families on Haymount Hill and child care for their own families and neighbors whose mothers worked. Finally, some women took new leadership of family enterprises. When Mildred Evans's husband was drafted late in the war and sent to Burma, she took over running their furniture business.

Working women dealt with an intensified version of the more usual female double day of paid and domestic work. Working overtime, having husbands away, and often having to feed extra boarders were just some of the conditions that made the double day seem triple. While the federal government administered thirty-one hundred day care programs in "defense-impacted" areas around the country, the need was far greater than the available help.[45] Just nine thousand children were in such programs in North Carolina, and in Fayetteville, only 150 families could use the child care area at the Honeycutt Housing Area, built off post for civilian and military workers in mid-1943. Others counted on informal child care arrangements in their neighborhoods, but there remained a strong stigma against group care. While wanting women's help in war work, the government warned that such care could damage children's development and it remained officially opposed to employment of the mothers of children under fourteen.[46]

Fort Bragg provided jobs for African-Americans that paid more in wages than did jobs in town (which would have occurred simply when the installation followed new federal minimum wage laws instituted in 1938). The jobs were also more likely to pay benefits such as retirement. As one older man said, Fort Bragg "helped blacks in general because, number one, there were more jobs opening up that everybody didn't have to be a maid or chauffeur or a yard boy." The new jobs on post continued to be racially limited, though. "[There was] caddying. We also used to go out there and shine shoes. In fact, you could go out there on payday and you could make as much shining shoes as your Daddy made in a week," he said, laughing. And the black employment patterns that the war started continued when it was over. Jobs were passed down in families or neighborhoods, with children knowing that if their parents worked out there, they would, too.

While some wealthier families continued to hire black women and men to work around their houses, many could walk away from these jobs when better-paying work became available on post or to do the preferable work of cooking and cleaning for black soldiers. They also walked away from oppressive forms of farmwork. Across the South, a government report noted, "[White] employers of farm labor complain that . . . the Negroes are becoming too independent [and] fear that out of the situation may come violence. They are accustomed to having the labor they want, and at the price they decide themselves."[47] While some of the women and men who left their farms during the 1940s for work went to the post, in the city of Fayetteville they were not being funneled into industrial jobs. That work was already mainly in the hands of white mill workers from neighborhoods that had experienced underemployment before the war.[48] Instead, the rural migrants went into trade and service work, fueled by the 1940s sixfold rise in retail sales, which was to become Fayetteville's postwar economic center.[49]

THE FIGHT AGAINST FASCISM AT HOME
The Allied victory in World War II destroyed German fascism abroad but in certain ways amplified prejudice within the United States, especially through racist imagery and annihilation in what historian John Dower vividly names the "War without Mercy" in the Pacific.[50] The war eroded the racial division of labor at home, as the demands

of war industry took precedence over racial sorting, but the war began and ended with a segregated army. Even African American blood plasma was kept separate from white, and black troops were assumed incompetent to fight, were much more likely to receive courts-martial, and were fully 74 percent of those receiving death sentences in military courts.[51] Many black soldiers were radicalized by seeing the contradiction of white supremacy twinned with the "fight for freedom." But despite the Double V campaign and their resistance, only pressure from war losses brought black soldiers into combat by March 1944.[52] Although they were never represented in the army or other civilian war work in proportionate numbers, many African American soldiers did the heavy labor and service work of the army (those units included the 41st Engineers). The handful of African American officers was mostly the medical staff who cared for African American bodies and the chaplains who specialized in African American souls. While some African American maids, laundresses, cooks, and truck drivers already worked at Fort Bragg, mobilization in 1941 required fuller use of African American labor, and so by that year, sixty-five hundred black soldiers had joined forty-six thousand white soldiers on post.

Jim Crow's choreography is everywhere in wartime photographs of Fort Bragg. Black and white inductees hold up their right hands swearing to defend the Constitution in separate rooms. Where they appear with groups of whites, individual blacks are pushed to the edge of the photos; where there is a unit of black soldiers, a white officer is often at the center. Aerial photos show the layout of the post with a small "colored troops" area, and the white area, unmarked as such, all the rest. Resistance to Jim Crow in the army included a campaign for the right to fight rather than simply to do the heavy lifting, for many agreed with NAACP leader Roy Wilkins about "the bargaining power of battlefield bravery in the struggle for advancement."[53] There was also a black antidraft movement based in resistance to the Jim Crow army, Muslim belief, and pacifist conscientious objection.[54] Discrimination in hiring for civilian war jobs helped draw support for A. Philip Randolph's 1941 call for a March on Washington to "demand the right to work and fight for our country."[55] To avoid that spectacle, Roosevelt issued Executive Order 8802 prohibiting employment discrimination in defense plants. But impression

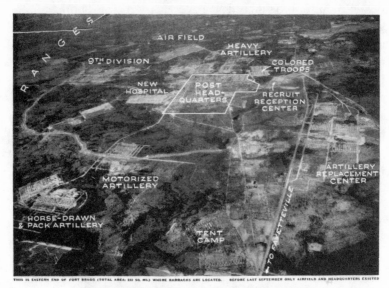

THIS IS EASTERN END OF FORT BRAGG (TOTAL AREA: 392 SQ. MI.) WHERE BARRACKS ARE LOCATED.   BEFORE LAST SEPTEMBER ONLY AIRFIELD AND HEADQUARTERS EXISTED

FORT BRAGG

WITH 67,000 MEN, IT IS ARMY'S BIGGEST CAMP

Segregation on Fort Bragg: *Life,* June 9, 1941

management, not reform, was the agenda. So it was that in 1943 the War Department could advertise for "competent, white female help in the Pentagon Cafeterias and Dining Rooms."[56]

Harassment and brutality were standard experiences for black soldiers. This was especially true where "a Negro in uniform symbolized a 'nigger not knowing his place.' "[57] Attacks on black soldiers and violent resistance occurred throughout the war, however, and across the country. In 1941, twelve black soldiers refused to take the rear on their bus ride to Camp Davis near Wilmington, North Carolina, and a riot ensued. A Private Spicely did the same on a Durham, North Carolina, city bus and was shot to death by the driver; a downtown block burned to the ground in the aftermath.[58] Lynchings continued apace. Private Felix Hall was hung on the reservation at Fort Benning, Georgia, that same year and his murderer(s) not brought to justice.[59] Major conflicts took place in Beaumont, Texas, Mobile, Al-

abama, Los Angeles, Detroit, New York, and Philadelphia, and Fisk
University's Social Science Institute reported that forty-seven American cities had witnessed 242 racial battles by 1943 alone.[60] One of the
earliest occurred in Fayetteville.

On an August night in 1941, Private Ned Turman of Ashton,
South Carolina, joined a group of African American soldiers boarding a segregated bus on the corner of Hay and Hillsboro Streets after
their off-duty night in town to return to the newly expanded post.
Like their colleagues around the country, the installation commanders had segregated their thousands of African American soldiers and
their tens of thousands of white soldiers into different buses, units,
barracks, and dining rooms. The civilians of Fayetteville provided a
clear set of lines separating the races as well. The section of town the
soldiers went to was a dusty set of streets behind the train station
where drink and women were available.[61] The area was patrolled by
military policemen operating out of the civilian police station who
had replaced their government issue equipment, as an internal memo
later revealed, "with long, hardwood night sticks, of unnecessary severity, that have been purchased commercially; many of them wear
holsters that have been cut away [for a quicker draw]; and many of
them carry personally purchased ammunition."[62]

As the bus was loading, a white MP approached a soldier, Mac
Poole, who happened to be walking by, and ordered him on. When
he protested that he had an overnight pass, the MP began to beat him
with a blackjack. Another MP joined in.[63] This kind of treatment was
considered normal enough by some that the white driver simply referred to it as an attempt "to quiet the colored soldiers." According to
soldiers themselves, however, the beating was so savage, Poole's head
"looked caved in." Some on the bus rushed to his aid, others tried to
escape, but the MPs stood in the front and rear exits, blocking their
way, and pounded on them with their nightsticks. Reports in the
black press said that when Ned Turman called for help for the first
bloodied soldier, he was cracked on the head by a Sergeant Hargraves
and several others. In the melee, Turman grabbed Hargraves's own
gun and shot him dead. Turman was himself shot and killed in turn by
another MP, Russell Owens.[64]

When word of the killings reached the installation, white MPs
were issued shotguns and proceeded to disarm, manhandle, and pen

Antifascism at home: *The Afro-American,* August 16, 1941

up all African American soldiers they could find, on post or off. Those who fell asleep during their confinement were kicked and beaten with sticks. They were released the next day, and shortly heard the news that the man who admitted killing Turman had been acquitted in a military court on the basis that he took "militarily necessary action."

The court of African American public opinion, however, was outraged.[65] An editorial accompanying the above cartoon bitterly announced "More and Better Riots Brewing" and critiqued War Department policy rather than universal racism within the ranks: "Between the majority of colored and white men in the ranks there is no ill feeling, and there never has been. It is easily created, however, by the War Department, which does everything by the jim-crow rule of the south and does not respect the absence of racial segregation that prevails in the Northern and Western States." A War Department investigation was prompted by such dramatic and persistent African American press coverage, a significant force, with as many as six million readers weekly during the war.[66] Also key was the NAACP's demand for an inquiry and the work of Judge William Hastie, a civil rights leader appointed the previous year as civilian assistant to the secretary of war to deal with equity and efficacy in the use of black manpower in the war. The press, NAACP, and Judge Hastie had already been trying to publicize and ameliorate the wider set of problems faced by African American soldiers. In historian Phillip McGuire's words, these included being "humiliated, despised, denied regular army privileges, insulted by post commanders, subjected to military and civilian police brutality, accused of crimes they did not commit, constrained by traditional mores, unfairly discharged from military service, denied adequate medical services, court-martialed excessively, and denied adequate entertainment."[67]

The War Department's Inspector General's Office examined the physical evidence and interviewed dozens of witnesses to the events of the evening of the murders.[68] Their final report began with detective potboiler tones: "a. Facts. (1) August 5, 1941, was pay day for a portion of the colored troops at Fort Bragg. The customary off-duty pilgrimage to Fayetteville, ten miles distant, for spending and recreational indulgences occurred. Late-hour returns to the post created a peak load demand for bus transportation and consequent large gatherings at a bus stop adjacent to a notorious colored section of the town known as 'little Harlem.' "

A stabbing earlier that evening of a soldier by a civilian, it says, "appears to have been a preliminary incident of sensation to start an infection of emotional excitement amongst colored soldiers collected in the district." The report writers did not portray the beating as a cause of the violence that followed or focus on the rationality of a righteously indignant response by onlookers. Rather, they home in on a kind of lower-order, physical sense-based response in the eye of the African American beholder: "The sight of his bleeding wound furnished a new influence upon the growing tenseness of the situation." Like any narrative, this was no simple report of events but an interpretation that framed the problem as one of African American indulgence and vice and of the soldiers' contagious, excited crowd psychology.

The report writers also framed the night as one where uncontrolled African American soldiers met courageous if overzealous and somewhat undertrained military police. The rounding up and terrorizing of African American soldiers back on post was a "logical necessity," and the incidents "were in no sense a 'race riot' or a clash between soldiers distinguished by color; and . . . as a result of these incidents no necessity developed for the adaption [sic] of special measures to allay racial feeling or conflict." In a separate letter to the NAACP, the inspector general transmitted these findings and warned the organization that the only problem was a belief that racism existed:

> The dissemination of such views, if accepted by all who read them, might possibly be provocative of such events of recalcitrance and public disfavor as this very one, imprudently chosen for their foundation. . . . [A] unified cooperative sentiment throughout all elements of the Nation . . . is earnestly hoped for in the furtherance of additional progress in the development of the morale and effectiveness of our defense forces.[69]

The report concluded that the murderer of both Sergeant Hargraves and Private Ned Turman was unknown, despite the many witnesses inside the bus who saw the man who shot at Hargraves, and despite Owen's own admission that he himself had killed Turman. Investigators failed to ask the black soldiers to identify the shooter by photograph, and the soldiers themselves knew not to offer truth to power when taken one by one for examination, as illustrated in one exchange:

> Q. When you first raised up from the position you had been in, what did you see?
> A. The man that was dead was on my leg.
> Q. Did you recognize this dead soldier who was lying on your leg?
> A. No sir.
> Q. Do you know Ned Turman?
> A. No sir.
> Q. Had you been drinking?
> A. No sir.
> Q. Do you have any further statement you wish to make?
> A. No sir.[70]

The report's deep desire not to know is visible in its composite sketch of the location of all people on and near the bus. Based on such interviews, it identifies almost all the dozens of men present, excepting the central figure to whom many eyes were drawn. He is labeled simply "soldier firing." The report drained the incident of any meaning at all, much less a racial one. With no explanation for the crimes, no action could follow, no responsibility be taken.

A few weeks before the report was released, however, Fort Bragg's commanding general was transferred to an all-white setting in the Deep South, on grounds he was not competent to deal with colored troops. The commander's error, in the eyes of his superiors, was failing to show forms of respect considered important even among those who accepted the necessity of Jim Crow laws. He had also brought unwanted publicity. A Northern journalist visiting the post gave a scathing report of the commander's free use of the word "nigger."[71] This newspaperman's account also communicated his distaste for the South in general, an attitude common in the Northern public.

Military investigators made much, as well, of the need for more attention to, or new forms of, "racial etiquette."[72] In line with this, they circulated, for the approval of higher authorities, the draft of a letter to be sent to Bragg.

> The permanent painted signs "For White" and "For Colored" on the wall above the two separate water taps [in a central post building] appear to be of exceptional size and prominence, unavoidably noticeable, whether one intended using the fountain or not. . . . It is desired that the signs referred to above be removed without delay. The installation and maintenance of paper drinking cup facilities in lieu of the separate fountain facilities for white and colored at your headquarters is approved.[73]

Also, behind the scenes, the investigators criticized the more "irregular" MP practices—their heavy arms and use of city jail and police facilities. Major blame was deflected, however, to the influence of "civilian police customs and [their] sense of inviolability in the exercise of authority."[74]

Within a month, a USO was established downtown for black soldiers, and within a year there were others at Seabrook Road and Spring Lake. A newspaper put together on post for black soldiers, however, claimed that its readers would usually rather remain on Fort Bragg because of problems in transport to town. They "only go when they have to," it said.[75] The hostility they could encounter was in dramatic evidence three years later when one of the USO clubs burned to the ground. One man remembered the scene: "When I was a little boy, my father and uncle took me out there and I saw the fireman standing there watching it burn with my own eyes without making any real effort to put it out."[76] A committee of black citizens went before city council to complain that fire trucks had failed to really attempt to extinguish the fire.[77]

Violence continued to be meted out to blacks, soldier or civilian, found in areas of town where they were not welcome. An off-duty soldier, Taft Rollins, was killed in a white area in October, and a civilian was killed, reportedly in a crash with a truck of uninjured white MPs while driving on the installation a few weeks after the Turman incident.[78] And this violence had a demonstration effect that went far beyond the grieving families of the dead. As Richard Wright observed, "the white brutality that I had not seen [but heard about] was a more effective control of my behavior than that which I knew," even as he observed, "I could not make subservience an automatic part of my behavior."[79]

Despite the changes military authorities made, black commentators felt nothing had been done to erode white supremacy in the army or in town: White officials had seen to the morale of white soldiers and obscured Ned Turman's resistance. Incremental changes in army practice were meant only to prevent further rebellion and loss of African American labor.[80] Of the case's outcome, the leading North Carolina black paper, *The Carolina Times,* headlined, "War Department Definitely Closes Fort Bragg Killing in the 'Usual' Manner."[81] The high-circulation *Pittsburgh Courier,* which had helped force the War Department investigation, made a more forward-looking claim: "One soldier has paid with his life that others might live like men. He is a hero to the colored troops stationed here and the colored population of this city. They are determined that Ned Turman shall not have died in vain."[82]

Almost sixty years later, as I went through the boxes of government papers on the incident at the National Archives, Ned Turman's face suddenly stared out at me from the morgue. Three small photographs, sharp as a knife, showed every detail of his smooth face, his eyes almost full open, his mouth as if about to form words, and his clothes in a small chaos, bunched up around him. A white hand reached in from the edge of one photo to point out the large bullet hole in his shoulder. The room kept busy around me as, sorely missing ritual, I disinterred him from his unmarked grave, this small coffin of a dusty, archived box.

Surviving black soldiers took their experience of the terrors and hypocrisies of white supremacy into their postwar sense of what should be. But while the war thus fortified the civil rights movement, the struggle for fair treatment was already long underway when it first began.[83] Glaring racial disparities in per-pupil spending on black and white students, for example, had been narrowed as the war approached through vigorous lobbying and fund-raising by the black community.[84] The local branch of the NAACP was reestablished in 1939, with one of the main prompts the beating and death of blacks in police custody, as well as the presence of the Ku Klux Klan, which older people remember enforcing a 9 P.M. curfew in black neighborhoods.[85] The charter members were local small businessmen, professionals, and working people: The first president, Frank McCay, was a barber, and other founders included a pharmacist, doctor, mechanic, day laborer, and the owners of a pool hall and of a local newsstand/ shoeshine stop that was a gathering place for soldiers, students, and others.

These were men whose livelihoods depended primarily on serving black customers and who would not have to fear firing or business reprisal in the way that school teachers or those working for white employers would. Fear of retaliation was such, one man remembered, that membership lists were kept as numbered code rather than names. When I asked him to characterize the extent of violence or fear at the time the branch was established, Robert Beatty—a charter member who was still a feisty and talkative member in the late 1990s—said, with an edge of humorous understatement, "Well it has been very warm around here. It has been no utopia, I can say that. But there [were] a few of us who were able to survive it and come along."

The war boosted these efforts, primarily by bringing a diverse mix of black soldiers and civilians to town. The current NAACP president, Raymond Shipman, a native and veteran, noted that

> Fort Bragg meant a lot to Fayetteville. It brought a lot of new people here who had new ideas and their ideas were different. . . . Fayetteville [was in]

a rural farming situation and we had not been exposed to certain things, but when people from all sections of the country came here then they brought their ideas here. And they were persons who were not used to being trampled upon necessarily but who usually would speak up. . . . And it's just like a melting pot because [the new people] did visit the churches, their children were into the schools and so it wasn't a typical southern situation. Because you had persons from the north, the south, from the east, from the west, all gathered together.

With his imagery of the melting pot, Mr. Shipman implicitly compared his city's experience with the Northeast's massive European immigration earlier in the century and with the American dream of strength and progress through pluralism. Paul Lewis, however, a retired African American Army helicopter pilot, remembered both Fort Bragg and the Marines' nearby Camp LeJeune as "hellish" places. Describing the Marines' resistance to African American recruitment, he credited the Japanese rather than an antiracist conversion among U.S. officers with allowing him to join, and the Japanese defeat with forcing him out of a job. The Marines, he said, "wanted to keep it mainly white and they displayed it every step of the way. It was the bastion in the breaking down of the services, and they tried to keep it lily white as long as they could." But, he added chuckling, "I guess the Japanese saw different. I can say that because I was there. The Japanese saw different: 'we're going to make you pay.' And so they opened the services, opened the Marine Corps to the African Americans."

City government had work to do if the wartime influx of black soldiers was not to disrupt the racial status quo. Those efforts to control the new racial mix of the city with the base's mobilization erupted into public view in the November 11, 1940, meeting of the Fayetteville city council. There, the council directed the city attorney "to draw up [an] ordnance providing that all restaurants, cafes, and eating places have two entrances, front and back, and prohibiting [them] from serving to both white and colored people."[86]

It was not this segregation that was the most onerous feature of life for black people in Fayetteville, but the abusive behavior of elements of the all-white police force. And this made a major milestone of the successful late 1940s campaign to employ black police officers. When the city hired them, though, it was neither first nor last among North

Carolina's larger urban centers to get a multiracial police force.[87]
Their authority, Mr. Shipman said, initially only "went as far as Hay
Street. . . . [They] couldn't arrest other people, [but] could only de-
tain them. . . . [They] could only arrest [people] of color. . . . They
were expected to not leave those neighborhoods." But as a young
man, he was deeply impressed that authority was finally in the hands
of someone with whom he could identify, and the names of the men
still roll off his tongue fifty years later: "Banks, Truitt, Taylor, and
Boone."[88]

A WAR BRIDE'S STORY

On the patio of her lush and nurtured backyard, Martha Duell told
me, still freshly grateful, about surviving her teenage years on the
World War II battleground of her French village. One of Fayetteville's many "war brides," she has lived in the city since her soldier
husband brought her there soon after the war. The coddled eggs she
served us in colorful china egg cups, rich in drizzled butter and herb,
spilled out of a pantry overstocked, she said, in proportion to her still
sore memories of wartime hunger. Plastic eggs sat on her kitchen
counter in a wire basket shaped like a chicken, and eggs came up often
in her stories. The Germans took her family's supply. As the hens went
hungry, they didn't lay as many. She loves an egg prepared in that way
or this.

The only regret she expressed was that she had not been born a
boy so she might have fought with the Resistance. While the Germans were their oppressors, occupying her home region of Alsace,
taking provisions, and rounding up Jews for extermination, the
Americans made things worse for her before they got better. U.S.
bombers destroyed her house as they aimed for nearby railroad tracks.
After ousting the Germans, the Army set up camp not far from where
she lived. While it provided Martha a job, she had to jump from a
moving military vehicle on two different occasions to escape being
raped by GIs ostensibly taking her to work.

She met and married her husband, who was the provost marshall,
and accompanied him to Dachau, where he judged at a war crimes
tribunal. She lived in the village during the trials and was dismayed to
hear the Polish townspeople deny being aware that they lived next to a
concentration camp. She challenged them, "How could you not have

TOP: Histories of foreign
intervention on parade: the city's
annual International Folk Festival
BOTTOM: Martha Duell, French
"war bride" and civic activist, on
Folk Festival review stand

known with all those trains going in and the smoke going up and no one coming out?" She and I did not talk about whether proximity to any war-making institution makes one more accountable for knowledge of what it does. Martha's courage, though, was to ask the uncomfortable question: Whose smoking bones are those? Who set the fire? Who bought the matches? Who could have prevented it?

Her first and most vivid impression on detraining at Fayetteville was of race and racism—she saw black people for the first time and the station's Jim Crow water fountains. The resonance of that vision with her experience of German fascism may be what led her, years later, to work with a local Jewish woman, Mildred Evans, to organize an International Folk Festival. The festival draws out a parade (and solidifies the categories) of the town's many self-identified ethnic groups. They include African Americans and Native Americans as well as a set that maps American military interventionism and occupations of the last century: Koreans, Vietnamese, Filipinos, Okinawans, Panamanians, Puerto Ricans, and Germans have the largest memberships. In a radical flattening of existing racial hierarchies, the festival made the Scots simply one group among the dozens who paraded on floats and set up booths of native food and artifacts. Where the 1939 celebration of the city's sesquicentennial was run as a virtually all-Scots affair, here all had equal space. It may not be surprising that Fayetteville, the most ethnically diverse city in North Carolina, hosted the first such fair in the state. It was not the diversity itself, however, but the experience of German fascism of an immigrant that made the festival happen.

Martha is also known for other civic contributions. She led in fund-raising to establish a botanical garden, hatched the plan to erect a statue of Lafayette (after whom the city is named) in a city park, set up a sister city program with a French town, and headed numerous clubs and service organizations in the areas of mental health and historic preservation. "I always wanted to do things in this community to show my appreciation . . . after being gifted [with a refuge and new home] . . . I love to go to bed at night knowing that I've done something for somebody else." She does not read the newspaper, however, when it focuses on negativity rather than on the real story, which is "the good that so many do."

Her first months in Fayetteville were lonely ones:

I was very sensitive with the fact that a lot of the officers' wives probably resented me being a foreign girl and said, "Why did he have to marry somebody when there are plenty of people here?" and plus my husband was twenty-five years older than I was and so maybe they didn't, but I felt a little bit strange. And I thought, "Well, I'm going to show them that he didn't make such a bad choice after all." So I really forced myself into learning English and doing things on a volunteer basis, and pretty soon I was heading organizations.

She also relived trauma as the boom of artillery practice on Fort Bragg reached her home. "Cliff [her husband] would hold me when the bombs went off and say, 'It's all right, it's all right.'" And she encountered misunderstanding of what war means for those truly in its midst. Speaking several years ago to the Kiwanis Club about the war and its privations, she was told by a man in the audience, "That's not so bad. We had rationing too." While rationing did in fact put certain uncomfortable limits on consumption, people in the United States ate better or at least more than they had before. Annual meat consumption per person rose from 134 to 162 pounds during the war and civilians bought 12 percent more goods and services in 1944 than they had at the war's beginning.[89] The Kiwanan's egocentrism might be extreme, but other war refugees encounter related myths. Among them: War is hell for soldiers but civilians are generally protected bystanders. American losses in the World Wars were equal to the other Allies'. And, most damaging for the war brides, women who meet U.S. soldiers overseas likely are prostitutes or in search of a free ride to America. And racial assumptions put barbed points on these negative perceptions when those women have come from Korea, Vietnam, the Philippines, or Latin America.

Martha's attitude toward soldiers is a very positive one, despite and because of her war experience and her love for her husband. After he retired, they worked for years publishing a newsletter with helpful consumer and other information for soldiers stationed at Fort Bragg. She had little sympathy for the anti–Vietnam War protestors of the 1960s and is currently the female auxiliary for the town militia, the Fayetteville Independent Light Infantry. She became convinced that soldiers, who she puts in the category of those who have suffered, are more magnanimous because of it, a belief also forged in her many years of fund-raising, when she found greater generosity in the city's poorer neighborhoods than in wealthier haunts. Nonetheless, she has limited compassion for some Vietnam War veterans who, in self-pity, she thinks, feel their war experience excuses them from work.

THE WAR ENDS,
THE WAR'S SURPLUS

Grief for the dead, relief for the weary, and anxiety about demobilization's effects descended on Fayetteville as the war came to an end in 1945. Over 7,000 North Carolina men had died, of the 360,000 who had gone into the wartime military.[90] Being host to Fort Bragg had exposed Cumberland County to more death, but it lost its children in the same way and same numbers as parents around the state.[91]

When the 82nd Airborne Division returned from its key role in the liberation of Europe to make Bragg its permanent station in 1946, it was the only large unit on the post. Most of the buildings the division did not need were mothballed and other buildings in town were turned over to civil authorities. Many buildings were cut from their moorings and were moved into the town of Spring Lake, and some continued in use into the 1990s.[92] The military population reached a low point of twelve thousand in 1947, as the Army shrank, and it was not until the Korean War in the early 1950s that it would return to something like its former size.[93]

The last hired, first fired policies for African Americans held in both civilian and military workforces, and so some black soldiers who wanted to remain in the military were pushed out. This was Paul Lewis's experience. Though he was later to enlist in the Army and come to Fort Bragg, he was a marine at Camp LeJeune, another North Carolina military facility, as the war ended.[94]

> Demobilization was in and anybody that wanted to go home they were sending them home. I wasn't ready, particularly say, to leave the Marine Corps, but they come around with a petition. It says in order to get the people to go home that want to go home, we're signing this petition. And if we can get enough people to sign it, we can let them go home that wanted to go. And I was thinking, this is a petition to assist those that wanted to go home, and that was what they were saying, those that wanted to go home, we get enough people to sign this petition, they would let them, they would let the others go home. And that's how they

caught me in that position. . . . [But] anything [such as this petition] that come from the orderly room in the Marine Corps, you didn't question. I mean anything. That was a hellhole.

Americans in general wanted massive demobilization, hoping that the country's economic strength would defend it from harm. To many, war itself seemed to be the enemy, not other nations. People focused especially on the horrors of the Holocaust and the atomic bomb–seeing these "as indicative of the evil of war in almost a generic sense, one transcending a particular nation's agency or a particular people's fate."[95] People immediately discerned the horrific implications of the A-bomb, seeing beyond the defeat of Japan. Among many such meditations on those repercussions, *Life* magazine published an imaginary "36-Hour War" scenario with dark drawings of ghoulish technicians taking radiation measurements in the rubble of a post–nuclear war Manhattan.[96] On the other hand, many news accounts and editorials were optimistic about the benefits that the science of war—including the split atom—would bring to civilian life. A cartoon in the Fayetteville paper showed Mars reading his last will and testament: "I do hereby bequeath to a world at peace all the marvels that have been achieved under my direction." His list included radar, jet propulsion, atomic energy, penicillin, DDT, and improved synthetics.

Intense anxiety about the postwar situation centered on whether the economy would collapse without war production, particularly given that the war seemed to have saved the country from the Depression. Some pundits predicted the imminent loss of two million high-paying war jobs. Responding to the fear, the owners of Erwin Cotton Mills, one of the largest in North Carolina, announced they would keep on all their workers even though their defense contracts were ending. The news also announced a cotton surplus and the return of hard times for many farmers, but nearly ten thousand people had jobs in the county's textile and lumber mills in 1946.[97]

There was in fact a civilian and military labor shortage at Fort Bragg in the fall of 1945, especially in jobs that had been filled by white women, such as typists, stenographers, and tailors. Calls for civilian workers gave preference to veterans and to men, while the army offered enlistment bonuses to veteran NCOs who returned to service. Full-page recruitment ads were needed. Smiling GIs with out-stretched hands beckoned, "Hey, Buddy," earn "travel, education, career." The ads stressed the army's new benefits and its democratization, none of which, they quickly added, are "to put a price on patriotism or make it profitable." Instead, it was to make the army representative of "the American way of life" rather than bottom heavy with the poor.[98] Here and throughout the century, recruitment has veered between the promise of a calling with character rewards or a job with financial incentives and has had to deal, above all, not with fluctuating levels of patriotism but with the health of the civilian labor market.

Another immediate postwar fear was that returning soldiers would create a havoc of crime and other unrest. In this, the city and the country experienced nothing new. Communities have treated soldiers throughout recorded history as requiring special treatment on their return from battle. Home communities often construe soldiers' sacrifice or the blood on their hands and minds as requiring a ritual bath or transformation to reintegrate them into everyday life.[99] Fear about the soldiers' antisocial tendencies was evident throughout World War II. The state's main black newspaper published a poem, for example, written in defense of the soldier:

> Everybody cheers a soldier,
> On his fighting way.
> And then they call him a "hero,"
> When in the grave he lay.
>
> Well, a soldier's greatest battle,
> Is in the time of peace.
> When every body scorn[s] him,
> And treat[s] him like a "Beast."
>
> And now with these few remarks, I must close
> And I hope you won[']t offend.
> But the next time you meet a soldier,
> Just treat him as a friend.[100]

At the same time, soldiers had been depicted in advertising and official rhetoric as "friendly, generous, easy-going, brave, the citizen-soldier[s] of America,"[101] and people knew that the ranks included people as loving, talented, young, good-humored, handsome, and healthy as their own sons, brothers, and husbands.

Newspaper readers could find fodder for either belief, though. In late 1945, soldiers featured in many stories of crime and auto mayhem, and newswriters sometimes provided an explanation centered on the disruptions of demobilization. So, a murder in the drug and prostitution zone on Lumberton Road in Fayetteville was committed, the paper said, by "a recently discharged soldier who had not gotten work." On the other hand, it also reported a North Carolina judge's prediction of an end-of-war crime wave prompted not by soldiers but by civilians because it was they who had "made the big money and had the easy times" during the conflict. Not tolerating the loss of their effortless riches, *they* would be the ones to turn to crime.[102]

The war's end affected civilian life in a variety of ways. The GI Bill, instituted in 1944 to boost morale as the war wore on, had perhaps the largest effect. With its support for veterans' mortgages, it helped fund the suburbanization of Fayetteville. It gave a great boost to the growth of several city colleges when its educational benefits plumped up enrollments. These schooling advantages went overwhelmingly to men, as did the mortgages, and both benefited only those with enough previous education and current income to afford to utilize them. It also instituted the idea of a two-tier social welfare system, one for the truly deserving—the veteran, and particularly the drafted veteran—and one for other citizens.[103] And citizenship became more firmly associated not with where one was born but with what one had done for the nation.[104]

Some things did not change. In Fayetteville, Jim Crow seemed undefeated by the crushing of Hitler. October 12, 1945, was "All Colored Day" at the Victory Fair, attended by eight thousand area citizens.

Some people returned to jobs they had before the war or simply continued in undisturbed civilian work. People who had owned or bought land did especially well. H. Lacy Godwin, for example, whose great-grandfather was one of the largest plantation owners in the area, and whose father was also a realtor and timberman, went into real estate in 1942 with great success. By the end of the war, with what he saw as little competition, he had become one of the five major realtors in the county. While he had suffered a reversal of fortune during the

Depression, he could build on his family history to profit during and after the war.[105]

Others, particularly older men who were drafted later in the war or people working in businesses that the war disrupted, had a more difficult time. Betty Hanford's husband had a tire and appliance business that was put out of operation by wartime rationing. Having been drafted early, he went off to war and Betty went to work on the base. When he was released from the army in the fall of 1945, he bought a run-down tire-vulcanizing business, but had a rough time making a go of it. As Betty said, "When he came back he had absolutely nothing, and had to start all over again, a man in his late thirties." I asked if he made use of some of the GI Bill benefits, and she replied, "No, none except that he died in a VA hospital."

In long retrospect, many people assume that the home front mobilizations of World War II gave a uniform boost to social progress and the economic health of American communities, with some recent popular accounts suggesting that the war created exemplary character in its generation. But the war's effect on social patterns in Fayetteville as in many other places can more aptly be described as an acceleration or temporary reprieve from social and economic processes already in motion. Los Angeles, for example, is often seen as a city made by the war. But it was already becoming a manufacturing powerhouse without wartime contracts, and the war did not alter the fact that its political culture favored the status quo.[106] Lowell, Massachusetts, experienced a boom in jobs during the war, a decrease in crime, and other social benefits, but there were fewer business owners in that town in 1948 than in 1939, and wages were among the lowest in the state by 1950. A meticulous study of that city's war and postwar experiences concludes that war "hinders fundamental social, political, and economic progress . . . hurt[ing] all but the few who control the American political economy."[107] And the study of California cities' experiences brings one leading scholar of the military and society to conclude, "The Second World War produced revolutionary consequences abroad, but largely conservative, rather than unprecedented, effects at home."[108] Finally, the call for racial justice that was so sharp and clear during the war slipped into a "liberal interracialism," at best, and continued Jim Crowism and violence, at worst.[109] This war had not ended that war or raised the hope of a permanent peace abroad.

One hundred thousand soldiers disembarked at Fayetteville's railroad station in 1940, and with them and the experience of World War II, the city's people struggled to deal with new social permeabilities, new anonymity, and new wealth. These phenomena challenged existing social relationships—between whites and blacks, men and women, and rich and poor. Black soldiers came to town with the promise of enhanced citizenship and manhood rights through soldiering, and black civilians had some new job opportunities. They also experienced a Jim Crow army and town made more obviously offensive by the prominent idea that this was a war against doctrines of race superiority, a fight against fascism. Despite the image of Rosie the Riveter that has dominated textbook understandings of how World War II affected gender roles, the years of war are remembered by older women today less as a time of gender revolution than as a crisis of logistics and work or an opportunity for finding romance and making money. Their stories exist alongside ones heard less often of profiteering tensions, prostitution, and anxieties about class boundaries that enlisted soldiers might cross.

As it had done after every war, the American government began to demobilize its massive army. By the end of 1947, there were eighteen thousand soldiers at Fort Bragg, well below wartime levels but far more than the three thousand who had inhabited it before the war. For the first time, the U.S. military fist was not fully unfurled. Popular historical memory takes it for granted (following the government's interpretive lead) that Soviet actions in Eastern Europe and the potential of Soviet A-bombs required the new militarized peacetime state. But historical research on how congressional factions came to sort out as they did in favor of remobilization shows that it was rather international investment banking interests represented in the Truman administration that looked favorably on an interventionist foreign policy and won out over those in the population at large and in businesses not served by orientation to overseas markets or commodity sources. It was their ability to redefine "the national interest" that prompted the growth of the military in the late 1940s.[110]

A revolutionary rupture in the American form of government was to open up between the past and the present, one that many observers date to the passage of the National Security Act and the variety of executive orders which together instituted what can be called a second, secret government or the "national security state."[111] It was made up of the new National Security Agency, the National Security Council, the Central Intelligence Agency, and a presidency that took on new, more imperial powers. The rupture did two important things. The first was to radically erode the rule of law in deciding whether to go to war. National security interests, while sometimes debated in Congress and funded with spending bills that were voted on there, were to be defined by the executive branch and take precedence over congressional "whim" or "politics." Policy documents NSC 4 and NSC 4-A, approved by the National Security Council on December 7, 1947, provided the central starting point for this process. Together, they claim to establish the government's right to conduct covert warfare. NSC 4 set up a coordinated and overt propaganda campaign and it was coded "confidential," which meant it could be discussed but not shown to the public. NSC 4-A, passed moments later, approved covert psychological warfare and was coded "top secret," meaning that its contents were "deniable."

Democratic process was foreshortened here and in other ways, such as black budgets in military agencies, assassinations of foreign leaders, and other layers of hidden work within the government. Truman set up a Federal Employee Loyalty Program in 1947 to probe into the associations, past and present, of every federal employee. Congress claimed the right to investigate any citizen's political beliefs, and people were purged from their jobs for their ideas.

The new regime came to Fayetteville as well. At Fort Bragg, Army officers were required to take loyalty oaths, and virtually any fort activity could be classified—even a photo of one of Fort Bragg's outdoor pools at the Officer's Mess.[112] Its legacy continues up to the present day, when local government planners trying to assess city needs are left wondering whether the true numbers of Special Forces or other Fort Bragg troops have also been hidden from public view.

The second effect of this new form of government was to install what the sociologist C. Wright Mills called a "military definition of the situation."[113] That is, everything the government did was to be justified in terms of its contribution to the military defense of the nation and its interests. A highway system would be fundable if it were able to move military equipment or evacuate communities under nuclear attack. Science education would become a budget item only if it could be argued to build a competitive edge over the Soviet satellite designers. Desegregation would be, not first an ethical or social issue, but either an impediment or a route to the social strength needed for the armed and moral standoff against Communism.

All of this was certainly not completely discontinuous with the preceding century and a half of U.S. history. The American state had already been dominated by ex-generals and by a commitment to military expansionism. There was first the drive across Native American and Mexican territory, and then the military interventions in Central and South America and in the Pacific. And some already thought of the world primarily in terms of its violent hazards. But this was to become the dominant mode of thought, one that crowded out all others. It would necessitate an exhaustive sorting of the world into friendly and unfriendly nations and the globe to be sliced comprehensively into military zones patrolled twenty-four hours of each day by American troops. Everything foreign was to be measured by its threat to "American interests," whether those be in trade or access to commodities or travel opportunities. This remains today a kind of cultural "common sense" that was once uncommon. The alternatives—the world as a wealth of knowledge or spiritual resources, a crisis of needs to be met, or a set of localities needing more freedom from the coercion of others—would be voiced in an unconquered wilderness.

With a vast demilitarization begun and then aborted, America missed an exit ramp where foreign and domestic peace might have been twinned with prosperity and justice. By the middle of 1948, the new political consensus in government led to revival of the draft. The Fort Bragg training center that had been in dusty repose since sending so many men to European battle was reopened, two hundred men arriving by the day. "Bragg's Ghost City Awakens" the local paper perhaps inaptly headlined. And so was to begin an unending and even more phantasmic new war.

CHAPTER 3

Simulating War at Home

Counterinsurgencies, Foreign and Domestic (1948–1963)

At first glance, the big wall map looked at once familiar and strange. It hung in the archives of the Special Operations Academic Facility on Fort Bragg, where a historian was helping me find documents on local war games. Looking more closely, I saw that it pictured the Fayetteville I recognized—its roads, creeks, and topography all clearly drawn in the fine detail of the U.S. Geological Survey. Until the eye reached the left bank of the Cape Fear River. Suddenly came not the city's cross-river section and its rural environs, but an empty bright blue ocean. This was Fayetteville as part of an imaginary country, "Pineland," described in great anthropological detail by the army for use in war games, but sounding like a parallel universe to the city. America's cities during the Cold War were often this kind of strange hybrid place, both tangible and fictional, where war was imagined and another American role-played the enemy. But the Pineland exercises were neither simple foreign-facing preparations nor fantasies at play. They reverberated in parallel with more local insurgencies against Jim Crow and laid the groundwork for very real violent campaigns in dozens of overseas places, some against people whose aspirations and methods were no different than those local ones.

Any military simulation attempts to draw an objective model of the world and its potential situations. But because it involves peering into the void of the future and the blurry shapes of the present, it must also be mythic: It has to draw on culturally tutored imagination, fears, and wishes. To look at Fayetteville's experience with war games, then, is to see certain American anxieties played out as if to tame them. War simulations are also experiments on how new forms of violence might work, and so they change as elites develop new technologies, strategies, and theories of the world. The main pair of war-making strategies in development from the late 1940s to the early 1960s was nuclear combat and counterinsurgency.

THE NUCLEAR MODE OF WARFARE

Imagine an April morning in 1954 in Fayetteville. Someone is just home from the graveyard shift at a textile mill and opens the paper over breakfast to find atomic war as front-page fare. Intimations of the new mortality were in a city map, overlaid with concentric circles radiating from an imagined downtown nuclear blast, and in news of Soviet atomic testing. But today, the newspaper told of a nuclear war simulation both more elaborate and concrete: Fort Bragg was conducting huge maneuvers to test ground and airborne forces under atomic warfare conditions. Dubbed Exercise Flash Burn, the games involved sixty-four thousand men, "frequent simulated use of atomic weapons," as well as practice in chemical and biological war tactics. Deploying six tons of maps, forty-six chaplains, and a maneuver historian, the exercises extended far beyond the post boundaries. In its struggle with the rapidly ascendant Air Force, proprietor of the weapon of the century, the Army meant with this exercise to demonstrate that the "foot soldier [is] still a vital cog in warfare."[1]

Some newspaper coverage of Flash Burn was in the style of *Reader's Digest*'s "Humor in Uniform": Soldiers participating in the games had mishaps as they bellied up to snakes in the woods or were bested by pickpockets on their bus trip in. And some featured a sporty rooting for the home boys against the "Aggressor Forces." That year's chamber of commerce brochure made Bragg's role in preparing for nuclear war a point of civic pride, reveling in Flash Burn's scale and the fact that the installation had "debuted" the new "atomic gun." Businessmen exploited the novelty of the games, calling local shoppers to the GI Surplus Store for "Flashburn Specials" of sleeping bags and khaki shirts or, in unblushing, bold letters, to buy a girdle with "An ATOMIC control" at the Capitol department store.

With World War II's ending, American political and military leaders began to install the nuclear "mode of warfare." This phrase points not just to the central weapon or strategy of a country or era's

TOP: Imaginary
nuclear war:
Exercise Flash Burn,
1954[2]
BOTTOM: Church
services, Exercise
Flash Burn[3]

military organization but to a wider array of social features to which this type of war making leads. In this reckoning, nuclear warfare is not simply war with atomic weapons, but warfare that allows smaller armies, puts a premium on scientific and engineering labor as the weapons become more complex and fewer in number, encourages secrecy to protect that technical knowledge, and diminishes the code of masculinity based on physical bravery and group camaraderie that characterized previous forms of war. The latter include the mass industrial warfare that came into its own with the nineteenth century and the emergence of the industrial might and democratic states of Europe and America. That mode of war required governments to extend civil rights and social benefits to gain the loyalty and labor of those larger segments of the population conscripted into the mass army. War in that style centered on manufacturing more than engineering labor, with many more workers required to produce the tens of thousands of relatively simple guns, tanks, ships, and, eventually, airplanes it was waged with.

With more emphasis than ever on technological development and less on quantities of weapons, the nuclear mode of warfare has been associated with increasing social inequalities in the societies restructured by it.[4] But most important, this mode of warfare drastically eroded the practical distinction between soldiers and civilians, as each was the target of the other side's weaponry. While military planners made fine distinctions between tactical and strategic nuclear weapons and proceeded to recode cities with military bases as military targets, millions of Soviet and American civilians were in the flash zone throughout the Cold War, and billions of people downwind. This has tremendously amplified the power of governments with nuclear weapons, both vis-à-vis other states and in relation to their own citizens. While some have argued that governments as political forms have always been a kind of protection racket, raising armies that safeguard the people from the threats of violence they themselves might simulate, provoke, fabricate, or wreak on their nation, many people since 1945 have had to strike a more lopsided bargain, trusting their nuclear government with the future of the human race.[5]

While the nuclear mode of warfare was already seven years old when he came into office in 1953, President Eisenhower made it more completely central to defense policy. "Massive retaliation," he

claimed, was the only path to safety, as it should deter any foreign attack, nuclear or conventional, and he immediately made it official
U.S. policy through a National Security Council directive. But he
also remained skeptical of nuclear war's survivability, saying of a government committee's call for a massive bomb shelter–building program: "You can't have this kind of war. . . . There just aren't enough
bulldozers to scrape the bodies off the streets."[6] He also officially proclaimed a healthy economy key to a good "defense posture," and,
consistent with his Republicanism, believed that this health lay in
controls on federal spending, including military allocations. Eisenhower feared high levels of defense expenditures "would leave the nation a militarized husk, hardly worth defending."[7] This drive toward
budgetary controls also suggested a nuclear bomb–centered policy to
the administration given the assumption that these weapons had a
lower dollar-per-death ratio than others. He also placed more stake in
the role of covert military action in pursuing what were defined as
U.S. interests, and this move was to fertilize the obsession with secrecy that nuclear technological superiority had already suggested
was required.[8]

This nuclear-centered policy was to have uneven effects across the
country because its consequences for each service differed. Despite
being a former Army general, Eisenhower's choices heavily favored
the Air Force and Navy, and shrank the Army, now seemingly made
combat-obsolete by air-delivered nuclear weapons. In his first month
in office, the Army budget was slightly more than that of the Air
Force. Two years later, it was cut nearly in half, and dwarfed by the Air
Force's. The Army's manpower shriveled as well, from 1.5 million at
the end of the Korean War to 860,000 at the end of his second term.
Eisenhower thought the Army's sole role should be to occupy postnu-
clear Eastern bloc countries and to police and maintain order in the
event that America was irradiated by Soviet weapons. This may be
one reason why no road or building on Fort Bragg bears Eisenhower's name.

The Army argued vociferously for the inadequacy, or even the irrationality and immorality, of the policy of massive retaliation. An
official Army critique in late 1953, for example, argued for the prohibition or minimal use of weapons of mass destruction.[9] (Such antinu-
clear talk from within the military was anything but unprecedented:

Six of the highest-ranking officers of World War II had criticized the atomic bombing of Japan.)[10] Officers in Army journals claimed the policy contributed to "the brutalization of war without purpose, to a preoccupation with mass destruction, [and] to the neglect of political realities."[11] A new Army manual implicitly questioned the policy with its opening statement that "indiscriminate destruction is unjustifiable in a military sense."[12]

At the same time, Army officials worried they were losing the public relations war with other services on the civilian front. In popular media, the likeable but hapless Beetle Bailey and scoundrel Sergeant Bilko with his do-nothing underlings were a sorry contrast to the handsome, techno-saavy, and competent airman Steve Canyon. The Army responded by trying to position itself as a high-technology service. It gained control of advanced rocketry, and recruiters' official cars had small mock-ups of the Ajax missile mounted on their roofs in the early 1950s. It also changed its uniform to a style more closely resembling a business suit, an adjustment one Army spokesman said would let the soldier "proudly meet and mingle with his civilian contemporaries."[13]

Alongside these moves, however, the Army continued trying, with exercises like Flash Burn, to compete in the nuclear combat field. When those exercises concluded, the Army broadly trumpeted their success. A few short months before, however, it had told the National Security Council that the new nuclear strategies overlooked " 'serious problems' of fallout that would enormously complicate the occupation of defeated countries."[14] But the political climate after World War II and Korea made deterrence an attractive concept for civilians, whose hatred of war seemed assuaged by the suggestion that the military's role now was to prevent war rather than fight it. This encouraged the Army to publicly use deterrence rhetoric while believing it to be either morally bankrupt or politically ineffective in comparison with conventional use of force.[15] Army leaders understood that nuclear friendly fire was a redundancy: Radiation's effects were known years earlier and certainly before the Yucca Flats tests, which sent U.S. Army soldiers walking under the still roiling umbrella of actual nuclear explosions. Nuclear war magnified the problem that some generals had already identified in earlier modes of conflict, namely, that "war ruins a perfectly good army." Each American war and war preparation period has done that in a different way, but this new form of ruination was self-inflicted. Said one military historian of the Army, "The irrationality of such a course did not escape thoughtful soldiers."[16]

Like everyone in the nuclear age, Fayetteville's people had to live with the nuclear choices elites made. They had fuel for fear of nuclear war, alongside occasional reassurance about the reality of deterrence, arguments for negotiated disarmament, and tips for surviving nuclear war. A single front page of the 1954 *Fayetteville Observer* pictured an aboveground nuclear weapons test in the Pacific, a story about a Soviet call for an atomic weapons ban, and a map showing Washington D.C. as a nuclear target. This could as well be Fayetteville in readers' minds, but it also permitted denial, showing Washington, not their city, in Soviet sights. Although military installations were prime targets for nuclear attack, Fayetteville, in fact, was not a first-strike target of Soviet nuclear weapons. Goldsboro, 60 miles away, was the only North Carolina site known to be so targeted, because its Seymour Johnson Air Force Base housed nuclear weapons.[17] But the nuclear risk to Fayetteville also included the unpublicized danger of accidents during the refueling of nuclear bombers in Fort Bragg airspace.

Schoolchildren across the country practiced "duck and cover" exercises in preparation for nuclear war. In some schools, children jumped under their desks, in others, they bent their small bodies into a huddle along hallway walls. And in a gesture that shows the importance of gender even in the face of annihilation, some teachers had their girls crouch down, eyes tight shut and ears covered against the blast, while the boys leaned forward on the wall, forming a protective arch over them. These exercises notwithstanding, there was local resistance to allocating money for civil defense. The North Carolina Association of County Commissioners argued "it will do no good for Nash County to have a full-scale civil defense program, if neighboring counties have none. And it is hard to engender enthusiasm for local civil defense appropriations, in the face of the substantial needs of schools and other county programs."[18] Nonetheless, Fayetteville by the early 1960s developed a plan for continuity of city government in the event of a nuclear or other disaster, and a sum was approved for a bomb shelter and equipment at the local radio station in the 1962–1963 budget.[19] The state's civil defense agency provided an "operational survival plan" that went into some detail on what to do after attack, such as "identify bodies and arrange for the transport of personal property to the mortuary area for safekeeping." Such fine points on body and personal effects management disappeared as new editions came out in the mid-1960s.[20] And it was to be taken for granted that these defense mechanisms, unlike missile silo hardening, would not be paid for by the Department of Defense.

Of all the many people I have asked about Fort Bragg's impact on their community, not one has mentioned a sense of increased risk of foreign attack for living near a major military facility. Whether this is nuclear denial or a realistic fatalism undefeated by government promises that civil defense measures were in place, Fayetteville's people have been no more plagued with a sense of conscious vulnerability than elsewhere, except, as we will see, when it comes to crime. The horror, challenge, and absurdity of trying to imagine nuclear war and to "be ready" for it have occupied Americans at some level in all the years since 1945, though, even as other kinds of war were to press forward and more obviously claim lives and treasure.

COUNTERINSURGENCY

It became apparent that the nuclear threat would not deter either peasant rebellions or anti-American propaganda. And so the rules and players in war games changed. On a melting August day in 1963, the same mill worker who read about Flash Burn would have been surprised as she stepped out of Fleischmann's Big Store in downtown Fayetteville. For she might have had to press back against the building as a band of irregular guerrillas rushed past, advancing on the Market House. She likely soon knew what theater of operations she was in, however, as a related previous exercise had used commercial radio and air-dropped leaflets to leave civilians throughout the Carolinas "saturated with propaganda" about the games.[21] The media told her that the men intended a coup d'etat and that Fayetteville's chief of police, L. F. Worrell, had defected to their cause. These "Red Forces" announced they were the city's liberators and offered the populace "independence from the capitalist war-mongers." Meanwhile, however, five hundred loyalists of the "Blue Forces," in regular army uniforms, were air-dropped into a tobacco field east of town and eventually succeeded in retaking the city.[22] They were but a fragment of the

100,000-man force conducting Swift Strike III, a month-long exercise that was the largest ever seen in peacetime.

The costs of such exercises could be substantial. Similar large 1951 maneuvers, Exercise Southern Pine, cost $3 million. Money went to rent land for use between the far-flung towns of Hamlet, Sanford, and Lillington to either side of the post, the adaptation of uniforms to give the helmets of the opposing force a high center ridge, and the printing of Aggressor Force propaganda. That material solicited membership in the "Trigon Federation," a military fraternity/political organization advertising itself as standing for "Constitutional Liberties, Free Speech, Share[d] Profits, Lasting Peace." It also cannily promised to "preserve the traditions of the South." Other propaganda addressed "Men of the 82nd" with a smiling, bikini-clad woman, Bebe Sloan, who "waits for you at our health camp." The propaganda of the U.S. troops focused on alerting soldiers to the presence of double agents all around them, in and outside the Army. "Can you be sure," one flyer asks, "that the man next to you is not an Aggressor agent?"[23]

While these games tested the theory of counterinsurgency warfare, Swift Strike III had a telling, perhaps unscripted part. It hinted there was more here than the international concerns that overtly organized the unfolding story line. While in its dress and rhetoric the exercise's rebel force evoked the communists of the Dominican Republic or Indo-China, a band of white soldiers suddenly appeared carrying the Stars and Bars of the Confederacy, offering the insurgents unexpected support. From the newspaper reports of the time, it is not clear who these men were exactly and what they imagined Civil War rebels might have in common with these Red guerrillas. Were they to be brothers in sedition or in a "Lost Cause," facing a technically more powerful foe, as strange bedfellow underdogs? Or were they demonstrating how quickly opponents can be domesticated once they are seen as weak or how doubled the enemy identity can be? The mystification thickens as spectator response to the "Blue Forces" advancing on the guerrillas included "one barefoot youth who excitedly screams, 'Look at those Bluecoats, the Damn-yankees are coming,'" an out-of-towner later reports. Whether this gesture pointed —in jest or not—to the resisted invasion of 1865, the invited incursion of 1918, or the federal armies enforcing integration elsewhere in

Can you be

SURE

That the man next to you is not an Aggressor agent?

What about the man who services the Coca-Cola machines—the men who collect the garbage-even the observers from higher headquarters?

The majority of the people in this area are loyal to Aggressor.

Can you be sure that any one of them is not an agent?

AGGRESSOR is looking DOWN YOUR THROAT

Simulating counterinsurgency: Exercise Southern Pine propaganda, 1951

the South that self-same year of 1963 is not clear from the journalist's report.[24]

But the episode demonstrates the confusions that anticommunism encouraged about whether the enemy was foreign or domestic, with the Confederate flag hinting at the internal social divisions and racial anxieties that the Cold War both papered over and used to its own ends. Fayetteville's history through this period, as will become clear, illustrates how the Cold War was connected to the idea of play and imagination on the one hand, and to the deadly serious business of preserving and contesting the racial caste system on the other.

War games like Swift Strike III came to Fayetteville as U.S. military planners proposed new forms of "special" or "unconventional warfare" to do those jobs. Special combat has gone under many designations, from the initial "limited war" to "counterinsurgency" to "low-intensity conflict" to the most recent "Operations Other than War."[25] Much is in a name, the changes more and more suggesting this is not "real" war, not something to activate the constitutional requirement for congressional decision making. And the list does not include "counterrevolutionary war," a name that will not do for most Americans who proudly trace their nation's roots to one. *Insurgency* was defined by the U.S. Joint Chiefs of Staff in 1962 as any opposition to an existing government that could be defined as illegal in the local context. It mattered not whether it was armed or foreign opposition, simply that it offended the governing (and often despotic) elite. This, then, explicitly included anything from urban political demonstrations to strikes, and from political parties to religious movements.[26]

The Army pursued modern unconventional warfare with the idea that conventional means could not rout the Soviets from Eastern Europe, although the center of activity quickly became the Third World. The theory was that small numbers of soldiers would be surreptitiously sent into those countries to engage in "harassment and guerrilla fighting." The new Special Forces soldiers, an official history says, "were all volunteers willing to work behind enemy lines, in civilian clothes if necessary. This last item was no small matter: if caught operating in civilian clothes, a soldier was no longer protected by the Geneva Convention and would more than likely be shot on sight."[27] The new soldiers were in one sense, *para*military—that is, neither legitimately civilian nor military, and organized as such in order that their superiors could avoid public responsibility for their actions.

Fort Bragg emerged as one of the central places where preparations for such operations were made. The distinctive ethos and personnel of the Special Operations Forces (SOF), established there in 1952, were to leave a lasting mark on Fayetteville's character as on America's. President Kennedy's intense interest in special warfare led him to visit Fort Bragg in 1961, and Special Forces soon mushroomed in size and funding. "Over army opposition based on a long-standing suspicion of elite forces within yet set apart from the army, he authorized the Special Forces to wear the green beret to symbolize that they were also special in status."[28] In the Army's vocabulary, *special warfare* by the 1960s meant psychological operations, counterinsurgency, and unconventional warfare, with the latter referring to subversion, escape and rescue, assassination, and guerrilla warfare. Special Operations today has three parts: combat Special Forces; psychological operations, whose goal is "to demoralize the enemy by causing dissension and unrest among his ranks, while at the same time convincing the local population to support American troops"; and civil affairs, described to me by one soldier as the unit that "fixes things up after an operation," remaking a country's social system after a war.[29]

Fort Bragg Special Forces soldiers were to be at the center of counterinsurgency in Vietnam, with Indo-Chinese officers attending the Psychological Warfare School at Fort Bragg at least as early as 1953.[30] Beginning as advisors in 1956 in their country and continuing as fighters through 1971, they suffered a reversal of fortunes after the war, as the Army turned to focus on more conventional fighting methods. Special Operations budgets and manpower would skyrocket in the 1980s, though most immediately in response to the Iranian revolution and hostage crisis.[31] Flush after the Reagan-Bush years, they had a sprawling new castle-like building on post by the 1990s.

Secrecy is at the center of Special Forces' power as a local icon and as a national institution. Some people in Fayetteville spoke of Special Forces soldiers in their families or neighborhoods as being "*at* but *not* at Fort Bragg," one mother-in-law of a soldier explained to me, "as far as the army is concerned." The secrecy that surrounds Special Forces extends from the public and combat spheres to the army itself, where even other soldiers can be handled as security risks. When the Military Police rushed one night to investigate unexplained explosions on Fort Bragg, they came up empty handed. The ruckus had been Delta Force soldiers (a subgroup of Special Operations operatives) engaged in a training exercise they had not informed post police about, although such notification was required. MPs had been kept in the dark "to keep *anyone* from observing their special tactics for taking down a bus."[32]

They have an in-between status, in a sense: both soldier and not-soldier, visible and invisible force. This would prove contagious to area residents, sometimes called on to be the sea within which they swam at home. Some area citizens assist directly in Special Forces training as weeks of field exercises can take soldiers into town, village, and public park, including the Uwharrie National Forest and the Sandhills Wildlife Refuge as well as Fayetteville and the surrounding countryside. There, soldiers practice land navigation, making their

way through the woods with heavy rucksacks to predetermined co-
ordinates where trainers will leave a cache of C rations for the next
day's maneuvering.[33] They also participate in unconventional war
games that use the services of civilians called "low-level source operatives." Soldiers might contact a woman, for example, with the assignment to count the trucks driving by her house during a certain period. She would do this while hanging her laundry or mowing the
lawn, trying not to draw the suspicions of opponent forces. In a "dead
drop," or contactless exchange, she would pass on her information,
perhaps in a black canister near the third tomato plant in her garden.
More often, soldiers practice making dead drops to each other, for example, via the back of the toilet in a local Hardees's men's room.

When exercise organizers imagine these local civilians, florid
stereotypes have sometimes emerged. A 1951 observers' handbook
mocks the "hillbilly types" supposedly to be found out on maneuvers. In one cartoon, nervous soldiers in a jeep are surrounded by
three gun-wielding, long-bearded, Confederate-uniformed locals;
They radio back to headquarters for help.[34] A late 1990s popular account of these exercises notes that the rural civilians who help the
guerrillas can also, by the exercises' script, betray them: "Any of the
corn-pipe smoking hillbillies and friendly farmer's daughters could
also be enemy informants."[35]

With these regional (and other, more vice-centered) stereotypes
dogging them, it is not surprising that many in Fayetteville have
hoped that the "elite" reputation of these troops would rub off on the
city, a theme repeated by many people introducing their town to outsiders. It comes up as well in both Special Operations and city self-
promotional material. In the eyes of one Special Operations fan,
"North Carolina's Fort Bragg [was to] become the Los Angeles of
U.S. Army bases, the place for soldiers seeking stardom through the
action and glamour of airborne and special operations."[36] One veteran who still worked on post told me, "It's just a pride thing. They
are highly trained, have special missions, they're higher ranking and
better educated. There are very few enlisteds in Special Forces." Even
a woman who found the military alien and frightening when she first
came to town was later to be impressed by Special Forces soldiers'
families. Invited to join a book club, she discovered "the women
in the book group who were the most interesting, dynamic, smart,

funny, you know, just the ones that I really felt like I would like to know better, all of them are married to Special Forces officers. One by one I found that out. I was like, oh, well that's interesting. 'Cause you know, somehow you would think that the women who were kind of left behind in the secret nature of that work, would be much less educated."[37]

The public image of Special Forces soldiers flashes differently not just by status but by gender. In the National Archives, I was struck as I moved from the World War II–era photos of soldiers in training at Fort Bragg—sometimes elegiac, often vulnerable and young, always ordered—to a 1965 photograph of "Special forces in training at Fort Bragg." These photos are meant to frighten, the men's faces smeared irregularly with camouflage paint, their weapons pointed in the direction of the camera. They pose as men being men, and they are older, wiser, and so more dangerous. They are enjoying their work, not just doing their duty proudly, unlike the men posed before them often have been. By reputation the most macho of all troops, some clearly play to the crowd's expectations. As I worked in the Special Forces archive, I met one such soldier who was born tall and with chiseled chin but had acquired an outsized motorcycle, wore a thick leather-skinned jacket, and a had German Shepherd briskly trotting alongside. His view of my occupational persona was somewhat skeptical as well, though: Like his own work, anthropology produced "interrogators," he said.

As the years have gone on, people in town began to complain about the unsavory types who were drawn either to Special Forces work or to be in touch with such soldiers. There is today much sentiment that blames the local drug problem on soldiers or veterans who bring narcotrafficking knowledge and contacts back with them from Asian and Latin American tours. "I don't know whether it was the base or not," said one woman, "[but] almost every day they are intercepting drugs from either like the bus station or drug money or something of that nature. They have an article everyday where at Spring Lake [next to Fort Bragg] we had this big roundup of people with drugs, and I can almost bet that the guys picked up were in the army at some point in time." Newspaper reports say recruiting for mercenary work and extremist groups has been especially focused on Fayetteville due to Special Forces veterans and their language and weapons training.[38] But the extent to which some of this is an attempt to place homegrown violence and social problems in others' laps might be indexed by the pawnbroker who told me that an infamous KKK leader and fugitive, Glenn Miller, was an ex-Bragg soldier who "joined the Klan and taught them how to use guns."

While soldiers have long had a reputation for sometimes being out of control in town, Special Forces soldiers are out of control, in another sense, even in their on-duty hours. What the town does not know about them could be imagined—both on account of the secrecy that surrounds them and because of the information about their activities that *is* known—to go far beyond the norms of acceptable behavior. The image of transgression and secret vices infiltrates not only the soldiers' but also the city's reputation.

But their work is also normalized. One woman was about to leave town when I spoke with her, following her daughter and retiring Special Forces son-in-law to his new job handling security for defense contractor Bechtel-Lockheed. Although his army job was very secret, she said, his retirement meant she could say something about it. He worked with the units that took care of things in other countries, such as "getting rid of leaders when that was needed" and other important matters. She knows and accepts the practice of assassination, although she and other Fayettevillians may not know how often it occurs or what laws it violates. Historians have documented involvement of U.S. military covert units from each of the services and the CIA in at least thirty-three assassinations or plans for assassination of well-known leaders around the world since 1945, including Chou En-Lai of China, Sukarno of Indonesia, Salvador Allende of Chile, Patrice Lumumba and Mobutu Sese Seko of what is now the Democratic Republic of the Congo, Charles de Gaulle of France, as well as the more familiar plots against Castro, Noriega, Khomeini, and Hussein.[39] This list includes the democratically elected and the autocrat; the communist, democratic socialist, and the inconvenient capitalist; the former friend and arms-trading partner and the implacably shunned. Many more common citizens armed and unarmed have been killed in over fifty-five unconventional operations historians estimate the United States has conducted or assisted in since the end of World War II.[40]

Not everyone on the home front accepts such covert warfare as ethical. Neither do all soldiers live happily with their knowledge of terror and torture committed by, for, or with the aid of the nation.[41] But either way, it can be asked of any society, "What do its people refuse to know?"[42] While official national security rhetoric suggests that citizens need not, or even should not, know what is done in the nation's name, there remains another strong tradition of belief. It holds that as a political system democracy is not built on trust of government employees, elected and not, but on their monitoring and accountability and that expertise does not entail a moral division of labor alongside the social. The belief that a free press provides "all the news" competes with the sense of being "famished with a few, poor facts" about the nation's military actions.[43] Such tensions between the impulses to innocence and to knowledge make up a key part of an American subconscious.

WHAT SIMULATION MYTHICALLY MAPS

An ally of the United States, the mythical Pineland territory of Fort Bragg war games has been described in great socioeconomic detail, along the lines of "country studies" that the CIA and Special Operations use around the world. While the study is not meant to exactly match Fayetteville's true social profile, it is often quite close, and both the deviations and the close matches show a cultural and cultural-military imagination at work. So Pineland is termed a democracy, but, in what would be a non sequitur unless an authoritarian paradigm were at work, the government is said to lack "tight control over its population."[44] It describes the area's social structure: an elite that can be "penetrated," a middle class that is "proud to be, . . . giving it various connotations of honor, patriotism, etc.," and a lower class that is small but "most dissatisfied with its lot and most susceptible to change," although many eligible for welfare do not apply because they are "too proud" and have been taught not to be a burden on others.[45]

At some length, it describes problems with the Lumbee Indians (who actually live south of Fayetteville). A "withdrawn and introverted people," they were not born but made so by the "passive racism and careless neglect by the rest of Pineland." Strategic data also includes the Lumbee's "legendary and magnificent fighting capability" and their "enormous amount of latent hostility against the remainder of the Pineland Populations. . . . Some fear that the hostility may someday manifest itself in a violent or revolutionary movement."[46] The report also gives important contact information for friendlies, such as a University of Pineland at Chapel Hill law professor who is "pro-U.S." Do's and don'ts for the soldier operative include being friendly, not offering bribes, and not photographing government or military installations in order to avoid being suspected of spying.[47]

In the Pineland exercise, Special Forces trainees get the roles of advisers, trainers, and assistants to a guerrilla force that is "liberating their country from oppression" and is pitted against a counterinsurgency force. The model here, oddly, resembles Special Forces work in situations such as Nicaragua or Afghanistan, not the more common situations of U.S. alliance with an existing government and its suppression of insurgents, as in Vietnam, Guatemala, El Salvador, the Philippines, Colombia, or Peru. Although special forces can either stabilize or destabilize a state, depending on who is in power and other U.S. military war games may model military assistance to counterinsurgents, the more-valued scenario in America is one in which the country helps those who most resemble the colonial American revolutionaries, Davids facing tyrannous Goliaths.[48] Reversals of reality within simulations are evident in nuclear games as well: The script for Nuclear Waltz II, a joint Fort Bragg and Pope Air Force Base 1970 exercise, had the 82nd Airborne preparing for a possible nuclear blast in a conflict with an "enemy [who] has used nuclear weapons in the past and therefore must be considered able to do so again," according to an official announcement.[49] As the cultural historian Tom Engelhardt has pointed out, Americans have been deeply committed to viewing themselves as having been defensively forced into each of their wars rather than pursuing them en route to their interests.[50]

The Pineland exercise replicates both the unreality in which war games swim, despite their attempt to do just the opposite, and Fayetteville's interesting relationship to actual geography. The Pineland map literally allows soldiers to navigate Fayetteville's real geographical terrain, but it also mirrors the invisibility and unreality that the city has for many of the soldiers who come, dislike or ignore it, and go. Pineland's map and the foreignness that the country study attributes to it also reflect Fayetteville's status as both a local and a global city, a place that is both in North Carolina and, in another sense, on and of the Korean Peninsula and the many other places that produced

Global city:
Fayetteville's Korean
Central Baptist Church

the immigrants of Fayetteville as well as the memories of many native residents, soldiers and civilians.

Fayetteville's use as stage for counterinsurgency games and as home to soldiers has posed special challenges to the separation between the foreign and domestic use of force and has potentially allowed cultural slippage between home and enemy. Whether under the rubric of training or straight-out assistance, Special Forces soldiers have demonstrated their nation building or psychological operations capacities at home. Psychological operations were deployed, for example, in a 1964 joint Cumberland County–Fort Bragg attempt to increase traffic safety. Special Forces soldiers did road building on Indian reservations around the country and, as an official history says, "provided free medical treatment to impoverished citizens of [North Carolina's] Hoke and Anson counties."[51] They have given survival training to some Boy Scouts and disadvantaged youth at a summer camp and developed civil disaster and economic development plans for several North Carolina counties.[52] In a 1970 counterinsurgency exercise, realism was provided by the 82nd Airborne's engineers battalion, which built school playgrounds, cleared roads, and did cemetery landscaping in a magically numbered eighty-two "civic action projects" in surrounding counties. These projects were meant to "win the people to the 'Pineland' government cause." This may have worked in both reality and fantasy, for, the newspaper said, stepping out of the gaming frame, "area civilians seem to share [the army's] high opinion of the projects."[53]

SIMULATION'S REALITY

If war games are a fantasy, they are also expensive. While not taking as much blood and sacrifice as the "real thing," exercises require a remarkable amount of labor, capital, and land. Moreover, war games and weapons practice conducted over the American landscape since World War II have taken the lives of thousands of civilians—most as nuclear test downwinders—and soldiers.[54]

America's bases expanded with the Cold War, covering 27 million acres by 1999. Vast acreage was taken, especially in the West and for the Air Force and nuclear weapons and missile testing. Nevada is a sensational example: The military holds dominion over 3.5 million acres of land and two-fifths of the state's total airspace.[55] Micronesia, an area in the western Pacific as large as the United States, is an offshore example. It has a U.S. Postal Service zip code rather than independence because the U.S. military has wanted to use its atolls for bases, target practice, and exclusion of other navies.[56] It includes Kwajalein atoll, whose people have been exiled to the festering, overcrowded adjacent islet of Ebeye so that its turquoise lagoon—the world's largest—can become the bull's-eye for missile tests sent up from Vandenburg Air Force Base in California.

While North Carolina already had significant land allocated to military purposes before 1945, the Cold War brought additional pressure, and, by 1983, over thirty-five hundred square miles, much of its public forest land, were available for military use (although many with the restriction that weapons not be fired there).[57] In 1953, the Army requested fifty thousand additional acres for Fort Bragg, most

of it in Hoke County, just west of Fayetteville, and much of it cultivated farmland. Local officials protested the decimation of their already weak tax footing, given that the post had taken more than half
the county's land area during World War I. There was also some fear
that the Army planned to fire atomic weapons on post.[58] While the
Fayetteville paper first editorialized against the expansion, pressure to
accept a military definition of the situation eventually won out. If the
Army was not able to acquire a more sparsely settled area, it said, "the
government could with some show of justice tell the Hoke County
people they would just have to grit their teeth and bear what is to
come, and accept a sacrifice, as soldiers accept sacrifices, in the interest
of their country." But, it said, land payments should be above fair market value: "Justice demands that the citizens removed from their an-
cestral homes should be compensated for the sentimental shock involved" and governments for tax revenue losses. While the paper's
rhetoric treated the citizens around the installation as soldierly, the
county did not defer to military authority when it went to the North
Carolina legislature for a resolution against the land taking. Even this
nonbinding resolution led one legislator to complain, however: "We
are engaged in a cold war. The time may be shorter than we think. I
don't think it's within our province to tell the Department of Defense
what they need or don't need for our national defense. And I say this
although I'm all for Hoke County. I hunt deer down there."[59] Among
the poorest people in a poor state, most Hoke County residents were
not in a position to pass up the chance to hunt in that wealthy legislator's home district.

Military target practice, atomic bombing, and toxic washing have
created a surreal landscape, particularly in the West, of bomb craters,
spent missile noses jutting out of the pierced earth, and giant pits of
animal carcasses poisoned by radiation.[60] Cold War games created environmental devastation no less extensive than some combat landscapes, both in the United States and in the Soviet Union's equivalent
Central Asian desert spaces (where fully 3 percent of the country's
area had military-induced damage of "irreparable, catastrophic proportions").[61] Nuclear war games have left deadly marks on the people of Micronesia as well, who never regained full sovereignty after
World War II. The United States has used the islands for A-bomb test
explosions and long-range missile shots.[62] When the damage done to

places home and abroad is acknowledged (and much remains classified), it is accounted by some as a "cost" of winning the Cold War,
with defense contractors jockeying for profitable contracts to clean up
their own messes and unreclaimable tracts called "national sacrifice
zones."[63]

The environmental impact of Fort Bragg on Fayetteville has been
considerably milder. It may even be possible (given data post officials
have made available) to argue that Fort Bragg has had some positive
effects on the land compared with the alternative in commercial
or residential development. Suburban lawns, for example, with their
monoculture of grass, gas-guzzling mowers, and weed killers, have
been excluded from most of the installation itself, and the Department of Defense has tremendous resources deployed to protect aspects of the local ecosystem, including, for example, the endangered
red-cockaded woodpecker. Installation foresters have also conducted
regular controlled burns, which replicate natural cycles of soil replen-
ishment and species change, something not permitted or feasible in
residential, developed areas.[64] On the other hand, the toxic chemical
use and greenhouse gases produced by the military airfields and heavy
vehicles of Bragg and Pope are far more substantial than civilian uses
and production.

While training exercises in and around Fayetteville are ludic moments for some participants some of the time, they are perilous work
as well. Parachuting airborne soldiers regularly snap leg bones, creating an otherwise inexplicable cluster on the nationwide map of or-
thopedic surgeons. At the least, many paratroopers told me, they are
one or two inches shorter after their stint as airborne soldiers. And
soldiers die in accidents with numbing regularity, the most calami-
tous including the drowning of twenty trainees at a lake on post and a
fiery crash at Pope Air Force Base that killed twenty-three soldiers
and injured about one hundred others. There are notorious cases of
equipment failures—for example, the M151 Army truck that consistently rolled over, crushing eighty soldiers over the ten years it took
the military to acknowledge and fix the problem.[65] Safety measures
are well enough developed, however, and enough soldiers are doing
office work that epidemiological studies show war making is safer
than some other types of work. A man has a better chance of dying
while working on a Fayetteville construction job, driving a taxi or

Jump training

truck, or logging than he does in military work, at least in peace-time.[66] During Exercise Flash Burn, there were seventeen men hospitalized, none for serious injuries, while in one weekend, rural highway accidents in North Carolina injured eighty-four.[67]

War games have many purposes—soldier training, "readiness assessment," tactical development, and public relations' warnings or reassurance to others, foreign and domestic—and so multiple audiences. The month after the 1963 exercises described earlier that brought rebels under the Market House, for example, counterinsurgency war was staged on Fort Bragg for visiting King Mohammad Zahir Shah and Queen Homaira of Afghanistan. Like many foreign military and civil leaders before and since, the Soviet Union–bordering royal couple were hosted at parties and watched military demonstrations. They saw a civic action team bring health care and education to a "liberty village," and observed a "Viet Cong village," complete with underground passages. Soldiers demonstrated a parachute assault, and a psychological operations team dropped leaflets picturing the king entering the village a mere hour earlier.

When one's work is preparation for a task more often deferred than taken up, like war fighting in the nuclear age, gaming becomes the dominant frame. And not just for the military, for the forms war gaming takes have proliferated in the civilian world as well during the Cold War and post–Cold War years. Battle reenactors pepper the landscape with pretend shot, paintballers splatter each other with bright faux fatal liquid, and children plan laughing assaults on each other with Super Soakers. For many civilians, the military itself has come to have the appearance of a sports team, especially in the post-draft years. For the people who watch the games—either indirectly through their neighbors' or media accounts or directly through staged demonstrations on post—war's reality, dangers, and ultimate killing objective can seem to recede. They recede behind the invitation to be an insider, to admire the tools and handsome young people of the trade, and to feel protected from unspecified dangers by preparedness. War game spectatorship redefines the role of citizen from one who questions and acts to one who observes and is entertained by the state and by power itself.

RACE WARS

The real war facing America throughout the 1950s was not about communism but, as for so long, race. It was fought with murders and bombing, threats of violence, and police brutality and the taking of prisoners.[68] And although the racially motivated violence was overwhelmingly white on black, black militancy sometimes included armed self-defense, as it had from the time of slavery.[69] Native American resistance was also not always simply political, from the Tuscarora War of the early eighteenth century to a famous armed routing of a Klan meeting in the county just south of Fayetteville in the 1950s. There were both fears that such violence was everywhere about to break out—some older Fayetteville whites remember "riots" or "near-riots" at many points in the past for which I can find no account—and suppression of stories of actual violence. The taboo on speaking of race violence was broken when it could be framed as a narrative of natural black depravity or presented as a humorous oddity. So it was when the Fayetteville newspaper told its readers in 1953 that a "Negro" woman was arrested after "making vulgar remarks to white soldiers on Donaldson Street." Brought to police headquarters, she "fell downstairs after resisting arrest" and was badly injured.[70] The

gender and race reversals this all suggested—especially the implication that white male soldiers had needed protection—may explain
the front-page position of the story and its "light" and turned-around
headline: "Cop Is Walloped by Irate Woman."

This war's front line was the color line, which in Fayetteville in
the 1950s and the 1960s remained as clear as high noon. As in many
other places in America, it ran between the black and white wards in
local hospitals, between balcony and mezzanine in movie theaters. It
created two waiting rooms at the train station and a back and front of
city buses. It cordoned off the voting booth for most blacks and excluded them from juries and from legal justice. And it ran between the
city's two high schools—the black E. E. Smith and the white Fayetteville High.[71] Public and private resources flowed down one side of the
line and trickled down the other.

> The [old] books that were coming from Fayetteville High were coming
> to E. E. Smith with a new back on them. The [old] desks were trans-
> ported from Fayetteville High to E. E. Smith [']cause they still had names
> carved in them. But they were [supposedly] separate but equal. The park-
> ing lots [at the black schools] were dirt and someone made a complaint
> and the man suggested they put pine straw in them, you see. These are the
> things that were separate and unequal that needs to be explained and
> taught to kids. Kids need to know that there were white fountains with
> white water in them and black fountains and black water in them, colored
> fountains. These are things that need to be included in our history be-
> cause they are part of it. You [a black person] work for ten cents an hour,
> you [a white person] work for 35 cents an hour. And at the end of the
> week you still didn't have but $13.50. Lunch counters you couldn't go to.
> You didn't even go under the Market House if I'm not mistaken. You did
> not. That was taboo, you didn't go near it. If you were going down on
> Person Street you went around. There are certain things that really need
> to be [in] a true history of Fayetteville. [They] should be told and then
> you can understand the problems we're having today because they've al-
> ways been underneath them.[72]

City contracts effectively drew a line excluding black businesses: The
first black man, for example, to get his wrecker registered in the city
towing rotation was an Army veteran who put himself forward in the
late 1960s. The color line in Fayetteville was drawn in part through
bank redlining practices common to most American communities of

the time, North, South, or West, which put black neighborhoods off-limits to mortgage money. It even ran through photographs: for the annual Employees' Month sale at a local furniture store, an advertisement lined up the pictures of several black workers under a grid of the many white men and women. In municipal reports, black men were assembled to the rear in portraits of city work crews (and women of any color were absent).[73]

Mental sirens went off when people came near the color line. One of Vivian Gregory's most vivid childhood memories is of her forbidden play, as a white child, with a black girlfriend. Crawling into the cool shade under her friend's foundationless, concrete-block–lifted house, where the dogs lay and the chickens would scratch out nests, she had her race revelation. "The floors were wooden, and when I was under the house, I was aware that you could see down through the floor. . . . I can remember the light shining down through the floorboards." The sunbeams coming through, the sounds and glimpses of the adults walking above, all illuminated their lives' differences. She knew later that their houses "were owned by these slumlords. They were terrible. Scarborough Realty and Haigh and Holland were two of the big ones. . . . I remember them putting notices on people's door and I didn't really know [then] what it was, but I know now that it was eviction notices."

North Carolina had a more race-progressive reputation through the twentieth century than such states as Mississippi and Alabama. This image grates, though, against the fact that the poverty rate among its black families has been nearly the worst in the United States and that some cities in the state were among the last to desegregate their schools. The historian William Chafe, in a study of nearby Greensboro, attributed this to the "civility" that many elites espouse. It prevents both change and overt racial conflict through the notion that "conflict is inherently bad, that disagreement means personal dislike, and that consensus offers the only way to preserve a genteel and civilized way of life."[74] As historian Timothy Tyson has said, the state's dominant politics were not progressivism but racial paternalism, whose goal was "to consolidate a social order carved out in murder and violence but preserved by civility and moderation. . . . Beneath the green ivy of civility stood a stone wall of coercion."[75] If blacks remember the violence and whites do not, that is the predictable politics of war and memory. And the Janus-faced technique—of glove and fist—was so similar to those of special warfare because they emerged from the same culture and social conditions of American racial supremacism.

By most standard reckoning, the long years of the Cold War were the outcome of the international struggle of the United States and the Soviet Union over their conflicting interests and ideologies. Alternative theories see the Cold War as an "imaginary war"—meaning a war fought through computer simulations of nuclear attack and counterattack and through the idea of deterrence rather than in actual combat.[76] It was imaginary not because no one died: Millions were killed when the Soviet Union and the United States trained, armed, or fought foreign armies in such places as Korea, Vietnam, Cambodia, Guatemala, and Afghanistan, and untold thousands died in military-industrial accidents or as uranium miners or nuclear downwinders around the globe.[77] It was imaginary in the sense that it fantasized the world as broken into two and only two parts—those free and for us, and those unfree and against us. It was a fantasy revealed by the question that, if this were a simple two-sided battle of democracy with totalitarianism, how could South Africa, Paraguay, and Indonesia have been coded *allied* and *free* throughout the Cold War, and how could China receive such differing levels of official U.S. hostility over its long communist history?

While the Cold War was ostensibly about the Soviet threat, looming peril to the local social order was more what must have made the world seem a dangerous place to some. The Cold War's ostensible rationale concealed and helped manage turbulent internal conflicts within the nation or the block of nations facing off against each other. In the United States, the Cold War allowed the interventionists and the business interests they served to counter the isolationists and theirs. A war mentality in the Soviet Union could help reproduce Stalinism and prevent the loss of Eastern Europe.[78] American labor and management were brought to an accommodation through a consensus that federal military spending would benefit everyone. And the movement for black liberation was prevented from succeeding earlier than it did when progressives were blacklisted for drawing attention to American apartheid and its connections with the control of labor. "That, however," as historian Michael Sherry has argued, "is the nature of militarization: it never arises solely out of military need, real or imagined. Its force [is] derived from the manner in which all sorts of conflicts become subsumed under or attached to dominant anxieties about national security."[79] Anxieties about changes in the racial order—particularly in those who profited from a docile and underpaid black workforce—were transformed into anxieties about communist infiltrators undermining American society. All goals had to take a back seat to the need to defend the United States against the Cold War enemy; those who called for racial justice were painted as unpatriotic and dangerous because, at the very least, any conflict was divisive and therefore weakened, they supposed, the American ability to present a strong front to the Communists.

The civil rights movement developed in close relationship to the Cold War. A death knell for the Jim Crow system rang with the independence of Ghana from English colonial rule in 1957, when it became clear to U.S. officials that a domestic antisegregation posture would be required to win hearts and minds in the emerging sovereign states of Africa. Communist states had been capitalizing on the American racial caste system: "State Department officials estimated that about half of Soviet propaganda against the United States focused on racial discrimination."[80] On the other hand, the Cold War climate coerced leading civil rights organizations into distancing themselves from the left to gain government civil rights concessions (as, for example, when the NAACP pushed out socialist W. E. B. Du Bois in 1948).[81] This helped strengthen the anti-Communist right and solidify high levels of military spending, with no one willing to be labeled soft on communism by questioning Pentagon budgets.

In Fayetteville, the Soviet threat was invoked in the fight to suppress the demands of the local civil rights movement. Regarding the new Negro city policemen of 1949, the newspaper editor said he could accommodate the change in what was politely termed "custom" because it might help alleviate black people's deficit in respect for the law. But, he warned, police leaders should direct the program wisely to avoid the "racial ill-will" which is "a number one aim of communism."[82] When, two weeks after the end of Exercise Flash Burn in 1954, the Supreme Court banned racial segregation in

schools, the next day's paper editorialized acceptance and concilia-
tion.[83] This is the end of segregation, it said, and the community must
face it calmly, for it is "within the realm of probability that the abolition of segregation will impose no tremendous problem on the public
schools."[84] Over the next week, however, the editorial staff came to
focus more on the problems of the ruling. Equal education, it said,
does not require similar education. The Court decision "pave[s] the
way with legal cement for Communists and fellow-travelers to insist
on an unrealistic educational amalgamation of the races, desired by
the majority of neither race, thereby creating racial bitterness and dis-
uniting America at a time when America needs the utmost unity in
order to present the strongest kind of resistance to Godless [Commu-
nist] aggression."[85]

The editorial saw race progressives as Communist inspired. Race
"liberals" were thought to be motivated by outsiders whose goal was
societal destruction—analogue to, if not the very person of, a Communist. Race change was painted Red because Cold War propaganda
had construed any dissent or controversy as seditious by definition.[86]
Disunity was not only dangerous, but the sign of subversion at work.
The editorial did not express concern about the dangers of interracial
dating or the notion of black intellectual inferiority—both ideas in
wide circulation—or the immorality of educational mixing. Editors
framed the problem as the necessity to be "realistic" about the conflicts desegregation would bring and about the higher claims of national security and anti-Communism, both of which it made spiritual
callings. In this way, Fort Bragg and segregated schools are symbolically drawn together as necessary to the safety of women and children
and the defeat of irreligion.

Anti-Communism could also be used to argue, however, for the
necessity of *de*segregation.[87] So the president of the Fayetteville State
Teacher's College at the time and prominent Fayetteville educator
J. W. Seabrook contended:

> The communists are nearly equal to the democracies in technological
> skills and nuclear weapons. If they succeed in gaining control of the tre-
> mendous pool of man power in Asia and Africa, America is doomed to
> suffer attacks with atom and hydrogen bombs, leaving millions of us ly-
> ing in unsegregated graves or interned in integrated prison camps. Our
> deeds must match our ideals and words concerning the rights of men and

their equality before the law, or the two-thirds of the world's population that is not white will turn to the communists for leadership. We need and must have unity at home and friends abroad if we are to continue to exist as a free, democratic nation.[88]

Several decades later there would be very different equations drawn among Fort Bragg, national greatness through military preparedness and integration. The army would come to promote itself as a racially progressive institution leading in an Americanism based in physical pluralism and racial tolerance. It would still, though, promote the view that disunity of thought about core values damages the country.

The fear of Communist subversion had been cultivated in the highest quarters of the American government. The McCarthy Senate hearings in the early 1950s were just the most visible circus of paranoia, but the suspicion had long tentacles: Government public opinion campaigns had promoted the notion that "the underground operating directorate of world communism" had the goal of weakening American society on its civilian front rather than planning direct military attack.[89] Officially generated fears centered on spies, double agents, and internal subversion. Voluntary organizations such as the PTA, labor unions, and national church organizations became suspect, as these were said to be the main points of attack for Communist subversion.[90] Even Fort Bragg officers were required to swear a new loyalty oath as Exercise Flash Burn took place.

THE GREEN AND THE BLACK

Black soldiers at Fort Bragg were to make Fayetteville's situation different from that of many other Southern cities in this period, however. Then and now, the African American soldier has been a powerful symbol, his uniform a claim to full citizenship, in a sense to "uniformity" with whites. This figurative power was amplified when the army was defined as the most important tool to fight other undemocratic and racist regimes. The power also radiates from the gun any soldier carries and from the fear generated by projected white hostility. The idea persisted, despite official acceptance of the equality of black and white soldiers, that true mature citizenship was mainly achieved by whites. If soldiering was even an advanced form of citizenship, or its sine qua non, the African American soldier would re-

main for many an oxymoron, at least, and an explosively dangerous error, at worst, and a challenge to the system in its own terms.

The effect of the military on Fayetteville's racial progress through
this period is complex. While many people in town claim the effect
has been beneficial, with the integration and tolerance on Fort Bragg
bleeding into town, the standard indicators of various kinds of black
advance show Fayetteville very much in the middle range of other
North Carolina cities. When the color line was crossed in city politics
for the first time since Reconstruction with Dr. W. P. DeVane's election to the city council in 1949, it was in the midst of a cluster of such
crossings in other North Carolina cities.[91] (Fayetteville's newsmen
demonstrated where they thought he should sit in the new order of
things, however, by ostentatiously publishing his photo below a line
of four photos of the white men elected.)[92] Black policemen came
to the post–World War II city, as already noted, no earlier than
elsewhere.

School desegregation, however, was begun on post very early,
started in 1951 by elementary principal Mildred Poole, a native North
Carolinian. With the approval of the fort school board and the installation commander, but without the intentional consent of the Pentagon's Office of Education, she brought black soldiers' children—2 to
3 percent of the total—into the schools (they had been sent into surrounding area black schools). She received several death threats for
her trouble.[93] This integration predated the Fayetteville city schools'
by eleven years, and North Carolina's other major military cities,
Goldsboro and Jacksonville, also began the process at about that time
(1962 and 1964, respectively). However, the state's five other major
cities started earlier—between 1957 and 1960.[94] Nonetheless, the
mayor's race relations committee at the time "praised Army leaders
for 'real help in the school desegregation.'"[95] The thirty-two black
applicants to Spring Lake schools in 1962 were, in fact, mostly or all
the children of military personnel stationed at Fort Bragg and Pope
AFB. An incentive to accept them came from the Department of
Health, Education and Welfare, which had recently threatened segregated school systems with cut off of "federal impact" funds, monies
paid to cities with large numbers of federal employees.[96]

It is mainly in the area of black economic status, as we will see
later, that Fayetteville stands out from its neighboring cities. Many
black soldiers were drawing salaries at this time that exceeded those of

their peers in other occupations, so that North Carolina's two main military counties had higher than average black median family income in 1959.[97] The influence of the black officer class on racial progress in Fayetteville has to be set in context of the progress and retrogression that had already happened in town. Black officers were in a sense simply replacing the black middle class that, we saw, was of a relatively substantial size until it was reduced by a variety of forces in the 1920s and 1930s.

Official narratives indicate little of this historical dynamism. Instead they suggest that the military marched ahead of society, doing in the 1940s what the Supreme Court only declared necessary in public schools in 1954 and pushed only by its own internal institutional values, such as explicit standards, discipline, and teamwork or soldierly brotherhood.[98] This view also ignores or downplays the role of dissenters—both inside and outside the military—in making Army desegregation happen. Refusals to observe Jim Crow laws, violent rebellions such as Ned Turman's on a Fayetteville bus, the vigilance of the African American press, and A. Philip Randolph's threatened mass march on Washington and civil disobedience, coming the year before Truman's 1948 reelection bid for African American votes, were all prime factors in producing Truman's executive order. They combined with near-crisis military manpower needs in a context of war weariness among recruitable youth, plentiful alternative postwar jobs, and the 1948 Army remobilization to push the army's civilian leader to sign an executive order desegregating the military.[99]

In 1951, the army conducted research on the effect of desegregation at several army bases around the country, including Fort Bragg. With 15 percent of its forty-four thousand men black, it was portrayed as an installation whose leaders had mixed views on race, with no "clear-cut, uniform policy . . . [which results in] a patchwork of contradictory opinions and practices."[100] An identifiable "colored part of camp" remained at that time, although its facilities were considered by the report writers to be approximately equal to the white. It was noted, however, that blacks were 30 percent of stockade residents. Soldiers and people in several of the surveyed Southern military communities said integration on the base had not affected the amount of "mixing" or social change in town. Soldiers saw locals as unconcerned or unknowledgeable about what was happening on base rather than anxiously fending off racially progressive influences from the base. It concluded approvingly, "The evidence supports the belief that a segregated community and an integrated post can exist side by side without special problems."[101]

"Special problems" were not presented to other military institutions, either. The National Guard remained all white in North Carolina until 1963, when it repealed its version of the widespread state laws preventing blacks from serving in militias. Even then, the Guard admitted only token numbers of blacks for many years.[102] But the military has made a difference in how the story of race and the civil rights movement in Fayetteville and America has to be told. To tell it in more detail, we can begin by passing on the stories of several black soldiers who lived in Fayetteville and some civilians who struggled to change the city during this time.

TWO MEN IN UNIFORM

When Paul Lewis joined the military at the age of eighteen in 1946, he was leaving the prospects in his hometown, Nashville, where, as a black man, "the only thing you could hope for basically in that city was to become a teacher, a bellhop, waiter, or a Pullman porter. Those were the limitations of the jobs. And of course you know all the domestic work was available. But other than that, when you're talking about professional, this is where we were going. We had one or two doctors and undertakers and things like this but that was about the extent of it." After his tour of duty, he went to college on the GI Bill. While this program took him and many African Americans to college, blacks, who made up 11 percent of the total population, were only 6 percent of the veterans eligible for such benefits. As a result, proportionately more of black than white taxpayers' dollars sent the eight million post–World War II army veterans to college and helped the eleven million veterans who got GI home loans, 97 percent of whom were white.[103]

He reenlisted in 1952 to get more GI Bill money to complete his education. He found a more integrated situation at Fort Bragg and other installations he was assigned to than he had in his first military stint, but he recalls having to make many requests for Korean War duty before being sent there.[104] And the city of Fayetteville was a less-welcoming place:

> [T]he community of Fayetteville did not want to embrace the soldiers. They did everything they possibly could to keep them out, and when I

say to keep them out, they set up speed traps, [and] they got as much money off the soldiers as they possibly could. It was just a regular old military town that you would read about in a storybook. They were designed to take what you had and you'd go on back to camp walking, if they could. The police was seemingly against the military man.

While soldiers both white and black were discriminated against, he remembers the speed traps as mostly on Murchison Road, the main route through black Fayetteville. The police would drag out the ticket-writing process as long as possible, knowing that harsh punishment would be meted out on post when the soldiers pulled in late for work.

In the 1950s, black soldiers and their families were still living in segregated housing in the Spring Lake area. Black soldiers did not hang out on the main thoroughfare of Hay Street, but on a black side of downtown, at Hillsboro Street. They were expected to use the Spring Lake NCO club rather than another, white NCO club at the center of the cantonment area. By 1960, integration on Fort Bragg was more extensive, but black troops continued to live mainly in certain areas of town and assiduously avoided others. Soldiers who traveled overseas were sometimes struck by the racial/ethnic integration there, but as one man said of his experience in Germany in the 1950s, the Americans brought discrimination with them. On patrol nights, he would go "to all the beer joints and you could hear rock and roll that black people like and two or three blocks down everything was different, with hillbilly and country music, and you could feel the tension."

Paul Lewis did not join the civil rights movement in town in the early 1960s, even though he belonged to a church that supported the demonstrations. He saw his contribution, instead, in enforcing federal school integration mandates: "I was in the military and if they called me to go to Washington to integrate school, I would go. They called me to go to Little Rock to help integrate schools, Alabama, or anywhere else . . . and you would have to go. That's me." Like many soldiers, he maintained residence in his home state because it did not tax military salaries. This also meant he did not cast a ballot in Fayetteville for thirty years. As soon as he retired in 1981, however, he switched his residency and started to vote in local elections. He also began to work with the local NAACP and has continued on there, alongside many other black veterans, fielding requests for help from

soldiers and civilians who call the busy office on Murchison Road
each day.

Describing corruptions and unfairness he had experienced in
Fayetteville, he said he thought he might someday leave the city.
Imagining his alternatives, he saw them through lenses his experiences had made both internationalist and nationalist. "I'm a world
citizen," he said, "I can go anywhere and live. But," he went on, "out
of all the places I've been and all the countries that I've visited, none
is greater than the USA. . . . So, I could live anywhere, but there's no
place greater than America." Navigating the contradictions between
the *is* and the *ought to be* of American life, his nationalism entails belief
in "God, honor, God and country, pledge allegiance to the flag.
That's my philosophy. Regardless to how rotten the system may be,
that's what I believe. I sincerely believe that but now, to come up [to]
the reason I'm here [at the NAACP] today is because I want to fight
against those injustices. And I suffered a lot of them when I was in the
services, a tremendous amount of it."

Another black veteran, ex-helicopter pilot Charles Easley, spoke
about race and the military in the 1950s surrounded by the artifacts of
his passion for the less politically freighted world of consumer technology. As I came up to his house for our interview, he was working
on a car engine in his tool-laden garage. We settled into his den surrounded by walls of computer, fax, and radio equipment, and I listened to his voice over the gurgle of a large fish aquarium. Native to
Chattanooga, Tennessee, where his grandfather was a lawyer and his
father a mail carrier, he came to Fayetteville in 1946 as an officer with
the Army.

> When I first got word that we were coming up here, it was like throwing a
> bucket of cold water on your head—all you heard about Fayetteville was
> negative. [What did you hear?] Well, small town, was rough on the sol-
> diers, not much here and I guess that was a pretty good characterization
> of the town at that time. Almost no recreation here. City fathers kept a
> pretty tight grip on the town at that time. But with time, they died out
> and the city expanded and got a lot of other people from other towns and
> other places in here and it began to grow.

Mr. Easley found little to attract him off post, with most restaurants and beer halls refusing to serve blacks. Some black soldiers found
entertainment at the 400 Club on Murchison Road, at special dances

Mr. Paye, a local funeral director, held at a hall down by the river, or at Mabel's restaurant. But a few years later, he had married a local teacher, noting, "Her parents were the progressive type, always trying to do uplifting things. Her mother started the first black library."

They moved into town and sent their children to the integrated Catholic school.[105] While Mrs. Easley became involved in the early 1960s segregation protests, he explained his own noninvolvement simply: "I was still on active duty then." On the post, he claims, "They paid no attention to it. . . . There was no problem [civil rights demonstrations]. If anything occurred there, I never heard of it." He lost a white army friend, however, when—resonating to the tenor of the times—he tried politely to encourage him to "deracialize" some of his talk.

Post commanders, he thought, did not try to intervene in "race customs" downtown, even though,

> [t]hey tried to take care of their soldiers. . . . but for the most part here, the soldiers used good judgment and for the most part, got along okay. Of course, some of them, when they would get their whisky or what have you, might get in trouble and downtown Hay Street used to be wide open, [though] it was mostly white. But there were a lot of joints there that people got in trouble with, you know, fights and what have you. I didn't see that personally. I just heard about it.

Commanders could and did place businesses off-limits if they price-gouged the soldiers but, as far as he knew, never for refusing to sell property or to serve lunch to a black man. Mr. Easley himself never tried to step over the color line, except when it was incompletely marked at the voter registration office in 1950. "I heard that a lot of [other black] people did have problems [registering]. But I guess the way you carried yourself might make a difference. I don't think I would sound like I was asking for something, if I went down to register, so I never had any problems." In 1958, Cumberland County had registered 24 percent of its potential black voters and 39 percent of its whites, with a literacy test still being applied by the registrar.[106]

The black soldiers who did not know or accept the codes of racial etiquette that some sons of the South knew and used were no doubt more likely to leave Fayetteville after their Army work, and so do not shape the current population and political culture of the town.

THE INSURGENTS

Given the relative political inactivity of soldiers at this early time, the day-to-day work of overturning white supremacy in the city was shouldered by the civilians who confronted it in hospitals, employment, and schools. They sometimes found allies and respite on the post, sometimes indifference, and sometimes special problems.

Three dozen students sat at the whites-only lunch counters at the Woolworths and McCrory's stores downtown in February 1960, soon after the famous Greensboro sit-ins. As was typical in other cities, the movement had already been operating out of the black churches, particularly Mt. Sinai across from the local black college, as well as through the NAACP and local barbershops.[107] A breezy tone of white assurance was struck in the next day's news accounts of the sit-ins. At Woolworth's, the reporter found a "nattily dressed insurance man was regaling two pretty store employes [*sic*] [with] the strategy he would have used if he had been coaching Carolina in last night['s basketball] game."[108] But others threatened violence, and gunshots came through the houses of at least a few activists. Sidewalk pickets of local movie theaters and eateries followed in 1961. College students were again the mainstay, though joined by older local people as well as some black and white soldiers from the post.

Massive demonstrations took place again in May 1963, and by the end of the month, a Mayor's Coordinating Committee had recommended the desegregation of restaurants and movies and a study of the feasibility of employment "based solely upon training, willingness to work, and"—in a gesture toward the heroics of joining this battle to the larger fight of the Cold War—"a sense of responsibility for the success and progress of our free enterprise which is so precious a part of our free democratic society."[109] The mayor also appealed for racial progress with an eye to the image politics of industrial recruitment, something ongoing throughout the South at that time but becoming especially pressing in Fayetteville.[110] If troubles continue, he said, "We will greatly harm our prospects for attracting new industries and business." The choice, he said, "is desegregation or bankruptcy—desegregation or bloodshed." But the city police continued to arrest blacks rather than the threatening whites who increasingly came to confront them.

Resistance by white businessmen and other citizens culminated, by June 1963, in a dangerous crowd of a thousand angry whites gathered to confront civil rights demonstrators. With "The Ugly American" advertised on the theater marquee behind them, the police threw tear gas and arrested 140 black demonstrators. The paper took particular interest in the role of a few soldiers: a white military policeman was charged with assaulting a black shoe shine boy, while a black soldier with the Engineers Battalion, said not to be a demonstrator, was charged with assault by a white man.

In telling the history of this period, many white leaders focus on how successful the city was in avoiding wider violence. While some attribute this to Fayetteville's more cosmopolitan culture or inherently sensible nature, a few make a more economic argument, pointing to the city's growth (much attributable to the growth of the post) as buffering it from problems others had. Said one man who had been involved in local politics: "I don't think we had the same battles that some of these other places had to go through. Especially when you're looking at job displacements and things like that. We were dealing just with prejudices, not job displacements and things. People weren't fighting for a shrinking job market."

Either way, there were notable successes in using negotiation to desegregate city facilities. Mayor A. Wilbur Clark appointed a Bi-Racial Committee, which issued a report of plans for desegregation of city facilities the next month, and the NAACP called off demonstrations. During the next year, changes were made in city employment practices, the police and fire departments, hospitals, cafeterias, drive-ins, bowling lanes, and professional organizations. In 1963, Fayetteville was ahead of other eastern Carolina cities in opening "public accommodations" and "tax supported facilities."[111] Allowing access and pushing for equity were two different things, however. For many whites no doubt agreed with the man who thought class would protect at least more affluent whites from the encounter with race. It was a black man who told him, he said, that "we can't pay—back in those days a hamburger was 55 cents—we can't pay 55 cents and we will not pay 55 cents for a hamburger, but we would like to know that we have the privilege if we chose. So it was just that simple."

Soldiers came out in numbers against segregation in July 1963. A very short news piece noted that ten MPs "stood by" while a sixty-person demonstration that included thirty-six soldiers took place downtown. Their signs read "First Korea, now Fayetteville, we will win our freedom" and "GI's and students unite for civil rights." The Department of Defense had recently announced that soldiers could demonstrate if they were off-duty and in civilian clothes.[112] Sippio Burton—then the head of the NAACP and a World War II veteran who had been sent to the back of the bus in uniform—pointed to the contributions of soldiers. But he noted they were short-lived: "Military personnel—both white and black—demonstrated with us until the higher-ups quelled that."[113] There was local concern about McNamara's additional command that towns that practice "relentless discrimination" be put off-limits. McNamara's 1963 directive, "Equal Opportunity in the Armed Forces," however, had given every military commander

> the responsibility to oppose discriminatory practices affecting his men and their dependents and to foster equal opportunity for them, not only in areas under his immediate control, but also in nearby communities where they may live or gather in off-duty hours. In discharging that responsibility a commander shall not, except with the prior approval of the secretary of his military department, use the off-limits sanction in discrimination cases arising within the United States.[114]

When Senator Fulbright of Arkansas complained about this Department of Defense order, McNamara explained that commanders were not to make the army an instrument of social change, but were to "work with and through local civilian community leaders with the object, not of desegregating the community, but of insuring that discriminatory practice bearing upon the effectiveness of men and women in uniform are eliminated in a reasonable, responsible manner."[115]

As desegregation of public facilities began to take place, the movement's focus turned more squarely to economic justice issues. The Fayetteville Area Poor People's Organization (FAPPO), active from 1964 to 1970, became a more militant nucleus of the local movements. One of its strategies was to have people load up their carts in the supermarket, ask for a black cashier at check-out, and when none came, leave the lettuce and melting frozen food in the aisle. Black cashiers were soon hired. In 1969, FAPPO complained to city council about its failure to improve black areas of Fayetteville, where streets remained unpaved, utilities unextended, and drainage problems foul and unremediated. In arguments to the council, Rev. J. B. Roseborough invoked white self-interest: "Deprived areas are a contamination to you," he averred. "These people work in your kitchens!" Levi Smalls appealed to a sense of fairness and delayed reciprocity: "We black people helped to build your places once. Now it is time for you to help us build ours."[116] FAPPO also helped organize a boycott and picket of a grocery store in a black neighborhood owned by white segregationists, actions later stopped by a court order enforced with an overwhelming police response complete with riot gear, shotguns, and rifles.

While the military commanders met regularly with city leaders through this period to solve mutual problems, they did not, as far as the mayor during that period from 1965 to 1969, Monroe Evans, recalls, place off-limits the institutions that continued to discriminate.[117] Control of city services was used as an integrating device, however. "One of the major problems was in the bars and the military," he remembered. "Most of the bar owners did not want the blacks to come in and have a beer. And we got together to try and figure out, what could we do to get rid of this prejudice. So we finally sent notices to all of the bars and said that if there were any fights inside the bars, and they were not integrated, we would not allow our police to go in and settle the arguments. They'd just tear the place up. . . . And one got torn up," he said, his laughter suggesting that this put an end to the problem of owner discrimination. But racial and interunit and other sorts of fights between soldiers continued to be a problem.

Attention also turned to a prominent sign erected by the Ku Klux Klan on the main road into the city from the interstate. It welcomed drivers: "Join and Support the United Klans of America, Inc. Help Fight Communism and Integration. Welcome to Fayetteville." With the vigorous support of Mayor Evans, city council passed a resolution in 1967 calling for the sign to come down.[118] The sign "does not express the sentiments of the vast majority of white people in Cumberland County," the Human Relations Commission head Ottie West declared. He noted, perhaps signaling more militancy among soldiers than civilians (or the town's dependence on the good-willed paychecks of soldiers), that the sign "engenders a lot of animosity at

Gertha Gibson, insurgent

Ft. Bragg."[119] A revival of the Klan, which had never disappeared since its 1868 founding by former slave owners, came as a foul wind alongside the growing civil rights movement. The seven thousand members in one hundred state "Klaverns" represented but a "tiny fraction" of Klan sympathizers, who showed up by the hundreds at nightly rallies between 1964 and 1967. They condoned or looked away from core members' acts of racial terror, from bombings to front-yard cross burnings.[120] These were among the local counterinsurgent forces.

THE RISK TAKERS

Cast among the ocean waves of change that titanic military institutions, powerful business interests, and organized racist violence created, an individual life is easily a fragile and inconsequential thing. But these visible parts of the civil rights revolution—activities that were public, downtown, and, however tersely, covered in the newspaper—grew out of daily choices people made to face down, obliquely ignore, and diminish white supremacism from violence to daily shaming gestures. Gertha Gibson was a gently gestured woman with a calm laugh who, when I met her, was trying to outlive her cancer.

She had first come to Fayetteville in 1957 as a young teacher, then a newlywed in her husband's hometown. The brick ranches of her current neighborhood were a short distance but decades of struggle away from where she first lived.

> It was very difficult, for us as Blacks, to get a place to live or to get a home. . . . Both of us were teachers at that time—but we really couldn't get a loan so we ended up in what existed by the projects, kind of, an apartment complex at Elliot Circle. And we stayed there for about a year or two. The rent was very high, and . . . so we had purchased a lot [nearby] and on Christmas Eve we got some blocks and got his friends and started building the house himself and that's how we started out.

While eventually this stranglehold on capital was to be broken with the establishment of a black credit union in 1947, its funds were limited and a handful of white landlords continued to control much of the available rental housing. Black soldiers lived alongside Gertha's family in their complex, paying the same high rents, and the pressure on housing produced by growth of Fort Bragg (and by the baby boom) continued to make life difficult for both soldiers and civilians. Those like Gertha who came from elsewhere—even if just a county or two away and even if they married a local man—could be drawn closer to soldiers both by this proximity in housing and by a shared sense of exclusion.

> It appeared to be two cultures for us. It was the army culture or the people who were moving in who were not what they called "ladies," and there were people who were reared here in Fayetteville, [who] made themselves a group in social activities. They sorta stick together, and those of us who had come to Fayetteville were forced to form other groups. . . . The base provided an awful lot of experiences for me and my children that we couldn't get elsewhere and I sort of meshed with army wives, particularly a lot of them that had children around my children's age and so I always got invited out there. . . . Like every Fourth of July, they had a family picnic and you'd go to the lake, and of course we didn't have a lake anyplace around here where blacks could go. Somebody would come and get us so that we could go out. We'd enjoy . . . going to the museums and we had the parades, and one I remember when President Kennedy [came], but any time any dignitary would come out they would invite us and we would go and see them. . . . And [we went to] the base library when they were little.

Like many, she tried to shield her children from racism. "I would put them in the company of people where they could not experience it . . . And not go anywhere we would be told to go to the back to eat or something like that." The owners of a local segregated department store, The Capitol, would not allow blacks to eat in their cafeteria, and, she remembered, laughing, "I don't think you could try on hats. And so I guess what I'd do a lot of time was go by myself and buy what I was gonna buy and bring it back for them to try on, like shoes or something like that."

In 1963, school district administrators pulled her from where she had been teaching and made her the only black teacher in a formerly all-white elementary school. A steady stream of racist incidents left memorial scars.

> Every time I walked out the door, the children, all of the black children were sitting in the hall. . . . [The other] teachers wouldn't teach them. [Teachers would send them out of the classroom?] Um-hm, with the desk and all outside. . . . There is no way they could learn, you know, and then sometimes when I'd go into the classroom, the black children's seats would be turned towards the wall [breathing out] instead of facing the teacher. I guess they couldn't deal with *looking* at them. . . . I just couldn't take it any longer and I resigned my job and with my church [Mt. Sinai Baptist] I started a daycare program. I said . . . if I can help black kids, I have to help them before they get to school.

Gertha went on to be pivotal in establishing model day care programs throughout the city and eventually the state. While she was struck with her military students' worldliness, she acquired her own when her day care achievements brought her into contact with the transnational women's movement. When I asked, she showed me the album of pictures she took in China and the Caribbean, where she had gone for international conferences.

I also spoke with Dr. Mason Quick and his wife, Beulah. While they saw Fort Bragg as a positive influence on the city's race situation, their stories emphasized the efforts of local people to make the city a place in which blacks could live. Born and raised in a black town near the resort of Pinehurst on the western edge of Fort Bragg in 1915, Mason Quick came from a middle-class family: His father ran a wood yard and his mother was a teacher and activist who got electricity run to their community. Sent to high school in Washington D.C., he went on to medical school. On his return to the area to practice, he bristled under the Jim Crow strictures on health care in Fayetteville. One of the city's hospitals, owned by Dr. Pittman, did not allow black doctors to practice, although it had a small segregated ward for black patients (where tubercular, cancer, and every other kind of patient were put in the same wards, categories that were separated for white patients). At the larger Highsmith Hospital, black doctors had to practice on the bottom floor.

When a new hospital was being built in the city with federal funds that required nondiscrimination, "I and a friend were young and decided to go and see if they would put us out." Sitting in on the first planning discussions, "We saw the blueprints and noticed a funny-looking entrance fifty feet to the left of the main entrance. Inside the entrance, there was a lobby with benches [for patient waiting]. The architects were describing everything but that door and so we said, 'we would like to see that closed up.'" He also worked to desegregate the local medical societies and, as an avid golfer, saw the segregation of local courses fall, one in part with help from officials on post. Several Fort Bragg soldiers, including a high-ranking black officer, came to play one of those courses and were told to leave. The installation commander came out and warned the owner that the course would be declared off-limits to military personnel if he continued to discriminate and Washington would investigate his operation given the federal funding he built it with. According to Dr. Quick, when the course then opened to all, it was financial trouble as much as this pressure that forced the owner's hand.

The early Cold War saw a language of national security replace that of war and peace. Whether one calls it propaganda or public relations, government campaigns shifted popular perception of the military from a temporarily mobilized group of citizen soldiers to a permanent force to deal with a world now construed as holding potential threat in every corner. In these years, political and military elites gave America's army massive new jobs—planning the potential nuclear annihilation of the world and surveiling and managing peasant societies around the globe. These missions brought war home to Fayetteville and other American cities in strange new ways. While nuclear war preparations gave Americans a sense of utter vulnerability, counterinsurgency suggested their omnipotence. Both enterprises put civilians on a quest for moral innocence that required denial of the violence's true scope and brought the urgent wish not to know what was happening on military bases and overseas. This quest made the idea of war as game compelling, as did the concepts of permanent war and nuclear deterrence and the increasing reliance on secrecy and domestic public relations to control information. War gaming in fact seemed to replace war itself and spilled over the boundaries of the post. Along with anticommunism, the simulations and dissimulations cast all citizens as soldiers of a certain sort and made the surreal a fact of daily life in Fayetteville and the nation. This was so not just for those many who participated in or heard about the games, but for those who lived with the idea of safety through mutual assured destruction or the idea of danger in the shape of impoverished but organized foreign peasants.

But by only seeming to identify where the battle lay, the military waging of the early Cold War at best had mixed consequences for and at worst set back the domestic struggle for civil rights, which pressed forward nonetheless in, through, and against the military. Fear of Soviet broadcasting of the facts of American apartheid to the decolonizing world put pressure on white supremacy. But when people subscribe to the idea that citizenship is something blacks earned through soldiering rather than acquired as birthright, the goal of demilitarization became more remote. And this case of mistaken identity—of confusing the problem of communism with the problem of race—paved the way for the much more visible dying and killing in Southeast Asia in the next chapter of our now seemingly permanent home front war.

CHAPTER 4

Carnival, Carnage, and Quakers

The Vietnam War on Hay Street (1964–1973)

Being new to Fayetteville in the early 1970s, criminal lawyer Kirk Osborne took a sheriff's nighttime "ride-along" to get his bearings. As the squad car he was in turned down one road just north of town, a great halo of light suddenly appeared ahead of them on the highway. The apparition drew closer, until they could see that this was in fact a salvo of sparks caroming off a car's underbody. The driver was a soldier just back from the war in Vietnam, so completely smashed he had not noticed his flat tire through the burning off of every iota of rubber and the cacophonous grinding down of the steel rim. For Kirk, this man's ride was a self-medicated delirium of both joy and horror. He had miraculously and dumbfoundedly emerged alive from a year of being shot at and he had seen and perhaps perpetrated horrors, murders, and mayhem. Kirk told the story with a great roaring of laughter at once aghast and sympathetic: The man who staggered from the car when it eventually stopped was barely twenty and had already been party to one of the century's most massive violations of the natural order of things—bodies turned inside out, lush forests reduced to moonscapes. Yet there he was, still, a human being, a mother's son, reenacting chaos but no doubt fervently wishing to recapture that order for himself.

Kirk's tale, offered as we spoke in his office, was one of many kinds of stories city people, like other Americans, have told about returning soldiers. Some center on the veterans of Vietnam as heroes, either on a noble or some other fool's errand, but in either case as men of valor. For others, they are simply men who suffered and sacrificed, their pain outside political time and moral space. Others either explicitly or secretly see the veteran as "damaged goods," his humanity or moral stature diminished by the grotesque task he performed, however set it was for him by his commanders, military and civilian. And this sometimes has meant he is assumed a danger to himself and others. Yet others see him as a victim of abuse only after the war, literally spat upon by the civilian world to which he returned.

What these views share, however, is an overwhelming focus on the returning veteran and his experience, healing, or betrayal. Hollywood fare and politicians from Richard Nixon forward have told Americans to focus on the U.S. soldier, rather than the political history of either Southeast Asia or America in that period. The soldier's huge cultural figure blocks discussion of the blundering and cruel choices leaders made, the devastation of Vietnam they wrought, or even their long denial of the ravages of Agent Orange on American soldiers themselves.[1] When the war itself is acknowledged, it is often simply called "unpopular," as if it were a television show or soft drink that failed on the market, or as if war is ever popular. Instead of discussion about the relevance of the past to the present comes unification around the ideas of mourning and remembrance alone, as Maya Lin's monument in Washington D.C. so famously allows. Silence is also a strategy of containment, for no one enters a conversation about the Vietnam War except as into a cultural no-man's-land of exposure and taboo. It may be for this reason that in Fayetteville there is no monument at all to the war.[2] And this is in a city, like any, where memorials to the dead soldiers of war pepper parks, roadsides, and post office plazas. The daughter of a local Vietnam War veteran did begin in 1998 to raise money for one. But while she received official thanks and the promise of a place for her memorial on the new army museum grounds, donations were tepid.[3]

Many of this city's residents, though, like Kirk Osborne, see much more than the cardboard soldier produced by the last thirty years of thin, officially and commercially mediated thinking about Vietnam. This is because they themselves were soldiers, close friends to soldiers, war refugees, or war resisters. It means that some know, even if there is little political space in which they can say so, that the great majority of Vietnam era soldiers—85 percent in fact—were not in combat, but buying office supplies, lubing trucks, or counting ammunition boxes.

Some know that the spitting on soldiers that occurred at that time was as likely to be found in fictional movies like 1978's *The Deer Hunter* or committed by older veterans against antiwar GIs.[4] That the powerful GI protest movement united soldiers in common cause with many civilians. That the movement tried to direct attention not to themselves as victims of trauma but to the Vietnamese people. That it said their officers and civilian leaders, not people assembling for redress of grievances on the street, were the root of the problem.

Official accounts of the city's history rarely make reference to such things and to those years, when Fayetteville made national news perhaps more often than at any other time. Yet to develop is a sociological imagination of the war as something that shaped the city and that the city shaped in return. It is difficult when the subject is experienced as a political minefield, when the psychological or autobiographical frame is preferred in a culture of individualism for explaining why anything happens, and when the most visible part of the war in the city was a flagrant and distracting carnival of vice and profits downtown.

The Vietnamese people, of course, call it the American War, because it came after the French War to retain their Indochinese colony and because it was not an indigenous war. The people of Fayetteville old enough to remember might think of it as the Vietnam War on Hay Street.

CARNIVAL BEFORE DEATH

By the mid-1960s, Fort Bragg had become one of the main sites from which the army deployed soldiers to Vietnam, with nearly two hundred thousand men training there during the war.[5] The downtown remained the vital shopping area it had been throughout the 1950s, with a JC Penney, Belk, and other big outlets, soda shops, and jewelry stores centered on several blocks around the central Market House. As night replaced day, however, hundreds of soldiers' cars pulled in where shoppers' had just backed out, and men headed for the many bars and clubs of the 400 and 500 block of Hay Street and its intersecting roads. There they found a free-for-all of alcohol, drugs, prostitution, and fisticuffs, as well as camaraderie and play. Other areas of license had existed in the city over the years, including Combat Alley, an area one block south of the Market House, which catered to sol-

diers and was much rougher than Hay Street, and the Old Wilmington Road area several blocks to the east in a poor black area of town.
It was here that police occasionally staged raids on houses of prostitution or illegal liquor. Hay Street was orders of magnitude more outra-
geous and generally allowed to blossom, many say, because the local
elite, including some city officials, owned most of the property there
and profited from the high rents their brisk business allowed.

Wallace Nelson had grown up in town and was in his teens as the
war intensified. Growing tall and shaving early, he would sneak off to
Hay Street at night, drink, and watch the scene go by. Its sidewalks
were literally filled to their edges with jostling people, ready to forget
what lay ahead or behind in Vietnam. Now a professional in town, he
did the work of remembering the past with enthusiasm, dressed in his
sharply pressed shirt and handsome if somewhat pear-shaped middle
age, with his small earring perhaps the remaining physical sign of a re-
bellious youth.

> It was a carnival atmosphere, truly. That's why I was asking you if you had
> ever been to Mardi Gras. Or to Bourbon Street. The only thing that I can
> equate Hay Street to at that particular time was Bourbon Street. If you
> ever have a chance to go, it's not criminal, it's care-free, people are drunk,
> they're engaging in all sorts of activities they normally wouldn't do sim-
> ply because it was okay to do it and nobody cared. Then they went home
> and were good citizens. [. . . You saw it as a child and as a teen, and your
> feeling was just that this was exciting and it wasn't scary?] Yeah. Every
> once in a while, there would be a fight and they would come and take care
> of things. At that time, the city police would have a military policeman
> sitting with them so if somebody misbehaved, in two or three minutes
> they clubbed him down, drug him away and they were gone. It was that
> easy, you know it's like, "you are not working or playing well with others,
> so you gotta go." And this is why Fayetteville got this horrible, terrible
> reputation because all this stuff went on and the city fathers did nothing
> about it. Because they were pumping millions of dollars into the com-
> munity.[6]

On payday weekends, the party took on even larger dimen-
sions. "Entrepreneurs" brought in extra groups of prostitutes who
they worked between Fayetteville and Jacksonville, Wilmington,
Charleston, and Savannah. Drug dealers, too, had more customers,
and, for a long time, he said, the police "didn't do that much about
it."

Even legitimate businesses sometimes joined in creating the car-
nivalesque climate. One jewelry store owner, said an employee of a
rival, "classier" store downtown, combined high interest rates with
discredited tactics to lure the soldiers in.

> This place was just swarming Thursdays and Friday nights when they
> were open to nine. It was literally shoulder to shoulder on the sidewalks
> with the crowds of people. And the atmosphere, because most of these
> guys were here for basic training and then they were leaving, and most of
> them were leaving for Vietnam and so these places were just sucking the
> money in and there's no other word for it. Many of them came from
> towns smaller than Fayetteville all across the U.S. And many of them were
> eighteen and nineteen years old and never had a real job and a real pay-
> check in their lives and they were getting all that for the first time and
> here we were going, "Hey, that girlfriend back home needs a little ring.
> She needs something to remember you by. Let me show you some stuff"
> and "You need a watch. That's not a watch you've got on—that's a
> Mickey Mouse. Let me show you a real watch." [The store manager] had
> a spider monkey and he had a little chain on him and had him clipped to
> the lapel of his jacket and the monkey would sit on his shoulder and he
> would go stand out on the sidewalk with these throbs of people and the
> monkey would jump on some guy and he'd go, "Oh oh, come in, the
> monkey wants you. And if the monkey jumps on you, you get ten dollars
> off the ring of your choice." I'm not lying, and he would bring him into
> the jewelry store and open him up a charge account and sell him a ring.[7]

While the jewelry store employees where she worked were outraged
at this low road to the soldier's wallet, "secretly," she said, laughing,
"we were going, damn, he's got a monkey. We need something. We
need a gorilla."[8]

But the carnival turned darker as time went on. By 1968 and 1969,
Wallace said,

> It got so bad that even during the day, I'm serious, I remember my mother
> sent me down to Sears and she had a Ford Pinto, and I remember coming
> out of Penney's and there were two prostitutes up on the hood of the car
> with their backs against the windshield and, you know, suggesting that I
> wanted to have sex and I was sixteen, and I said, "get off my mother's car!"
> It was that bad. At night, back up on these side streets the soldiers would
> urinate [and] the male and female prostitutes did their trades. . . . The
> Hotel Prince Charles, which is now a very upscale Radisson, had deteri-
> orated to the point where you could rent rooms in it by the hour for
> whatever service you wanted.

There are many points of view on what happened in those years. A downtown businessman who made money from the soldiers understands them sympathetically, as simply young and inexperienced boys who found themselves on the outskirts of civilization.

There's a big difference between a recruit and someone who's already been trained and gone into a unit. These people were just a lot less responsible. So you had a real young population and especially during Vietnam you have a young population that are going off to an unpopular war . . . and they know there're pretty good chances that they are going to get hurt over there and not come back. So it was not the same type of person, [the] professional soldier that you see at Fort Bragg today. [And how did you experience that downtown?] You had a lot of crime, you had a lot of drugs, a lot of fights. [Like during World War II or more severe do you think?] More severe because of the influence of the drugs. At the time it was like a wide-open wild west type of town probably more than anything else. [So on the street you'd be watching people come flying out of doors?] Oh yeah, yeah, absolutely. . . . It was booming for business, but it was horrible for the town. Fayetteville had an image, matter of fact, people from other areas used to call it "Fayettenam." I understand how that all happened but it surely didn't enhance the image of Fayetteville and probably because of that kept us from developing some of the finer, more sophisticated entertainment that some of the other cities were able to do at that time. [So the reputation of the city was not bad before that?] It was always what they used to call an army town, a town that was influenced a great deal by the military, but it wasn't a wide-open wild west type of free-for-all type town. It became that.

For many others, this very visible wildness was neither carnival nor anarchic, tamable frontier, but simply a moral embarrassment. Even thirty years later, a letter to the editor upbraided a politician who suggested otherwise. That person, a city councilman, had claimed that Rick's Lounge, a famous Hay Street strip joint razed in the mid-1990s, should have been preserved as a tourist destination for the veterans' reunions now pursued by the chamber of commerce. These differing definitions of the problem downtown matter because they suggest different solutions—if a carnival, more celebrants and advertising; if a frontier fracas, a new, high noon sheriff; if corruption of the spirit, a religious campaign. Whatever the explanation, the situation was made possible by the war and the problem of "morale" the "entertainment industries" theoretically served or symptomatized in a still overwhelmingly male army. The industry did not disappear with the end of the war or finally, in the 1990s, with the razing of the offending buildings. It continues today, just closer to the post and in Fayetteville's poorer neighborhoods.

For women, downtown in this period became an unsheltered place of catcalls, harassment, and relentless pursuit. They could avoid some of it as they began limiting their evening travel and eventually their days'. But no one could avoid the larger climate of objectification. It was in the proliferating strip joints, such as the Cellar Nightclub. Advertising on the side of its downtown building implicitly evaluated passing women with its larger-than-life nude and announcement: "30 Beautiful Girls and 3 Ugly Ones." While the sex workers made a living, other women literally became a type of war refugee, leaving town as soon as they became adults and never going back. People who were parents remember a job made more difficult by the attempts to protect their daughters and their sons from all of it, with the faintest family resemblance to the problems of parents in war zones far away. Said one woman, "I had my Scout troop up on this flat bed truck [for a parade] and there were these hookers yelling down at them [from the windows of a hotel, and I was thinking] I'm real sorry that we were in this. And the winos drinking out of the bottles on the corner. One guy was saluting our flag and drinking out of the brown paper bag at the same time and I thought, I'm not at all thrilled that we are watching this."

While the desperate bacchanal on Hay Street continued, it must have made the blood of war even harder to see, at least for those not in the army or hearing street tales of Vietnam from returnees. But distracting fog was generated by more than this wild street. Despite the prevailing sense that this was a very visible "TV war," its broken bodies were still disappeared. Throughout the reporting and writing of the history of this (and all modern warfare), writers have substituted unit names, equipment, and euphemisms for the people involved.[9] "The 4th Armored Division took out twelve enemy tanks this week, with minimal collateral damage," chroniclers might say. Or they use metaphors that make the army a natural process rather than individual men in uniform, their leaders making choices. The metaphors erase their dying and killing, as in this historian's description of the World

War I German army: "Advance units were trained to go across the trenches, to flow around strongpoints and to strike deep in the rear. Behind them other regiments would pour through the gaps they had made."[10] Wartime censorship and wars conducted in secret have also meant injured bodies are rarely visible to the civilian public. Given the division of labor within the military, they have often been hidden from most soldiers as well. When injured people are seen, it is the most "tasteful" examples that circulate—the naked but seemingly intact Vietnamese girl running from a napalm attack, or a soldier in one, if bloodied, piece being carried on a litter. These are substituted for those in which injuries are more horrific, where the hands and eyes can no longer be distinguished from mud or gristle, the very shape and substance of humanity destroyed.

The *Fayetteville Observer*'s regular feature, "News of Local and Area Men Serving with Armed Forces," listed the young men from area towns in basic training, reassigned to Europe, or stationed in Vietnam. War's hard realities were easily avoided in such mundane bureaucratic sorting and reporting. Not so by funeral announcements: Charles D. Bethea, 18, killed in action in Cambodia on May 8, 1970, to be buried after services at the Person Street Pentecostal Holiness Church.[11] His photo, the only one in the obituary list that day, radiates his luminous, youthful face. It could seem to readers either balm—this was a beautiful and good boy—or indictment—this is the insanity of war, that it kills one just springing from childhood. The passions ignited by his life and death are a sign not just that life is sacred and people have rushed to their own vision of its defense, but also of the danger of war's contagion within, even when it seems safely exported.

THE WAR AT HOME

The increasing disillusionment or disdain that many Americans felt about the war was reflected in the army. Many—draftees and volunteers alike—were not happy to be in the army, to be in Fayetteville, and to be headed to Vietnam, "where you were either [going to] get killed or have something blown off," as Wallace said. "The biggest thing written all over town was FTA—F#%@ the army. . . . There was [that] graffiti everywhere."[12] There were 1,907 court-martials at Fort Bragg in 1968 alone, and other thousands of dishonorable discharges, Article 15s (a punishment involving some combination of restrictions, extra duty, and reduction in rank), and AWOL soldiers.[13] Men escaped the draft through a variety of means, from self-starvation to gay posturing to flight to Canada. Incidents of soldiers sabotaging their equipment were legion. Some of the most costly occurred in the Navy, where seamen set fires onboard and dropped bolts and chains down the gear shafts of their ships headed for Southeast Asia. Soldiers regularly disobeyed orders and spoke out against the war to their commanders. Whole companies engaged in combat avoidance and refusal. All heard stories, before or during their experience in Vietnam, of colleagues who had killed their officers in the field.[14] And drug use was open and widespread.

The sources of discontent with the army were many: the lack of democratic process, including restricted rights of free speech and arbitrary military justice procedures, and the lack of a minimum wage or a forty-hour workweek. Most incendiary was some soldiers' moral criticism of the Vietnam War and of racism's role in it. Race hatred was ubiquitous in training, battle, and soldiers' relationships with each other. It was in the common coin of the epithet "gook" to describe the Vietnamese (a term U.S. soldiers used for the Filipinos, Haitians, and Koreans they encountered in earlier wars).[15] Other signs were the higher draft and combat risk rates for blacks and Latinos and how the war's costs contributed to the impoverished condition of black people in America.[16] Critics also saw an army still effectively segregated, unequal advancement opportunities, and unequal distribution of opportunities in its programs of transition to civilian life.

Racial incidents, as they were commonly called, became frequent in the army as the war ground on. They happened in Vietnam and at other overseas bases, especially in Germany, where there were armed revolts. And they broke out at home, from Travis Air Force Base in California to Alabama's Fort McClellan.[17] One hundred and sixty episodes occurred in 1969 at Camp LeJeune on the North Carolina coast, and two hundred white and black soldiers were involved in one such brawl at Fort Bragg.[18] Nearly every military prison experienced rebellions. Their populations had ballooned during the war, with many politically motivated "nonconformists" and a majority of black soldiers among the inmates. One of the largest uprisings was at the Fort Bragg stockade in 1968 after the beating of a black inmate.[19] Violence on military bases was sometimes labeled a race riot, as was a fracas outside the Fort Bragg enlisted men's club in August 1969. But the disturbances were instead often antiauthoritarian, pitting black and white soldiers from the lower ranks against white MPs and NCOs. The resistors were more often volunteers and from working-class backgrounds rather than from the drafted, college-bound, upper-middle-class ranks the stereotype pinpointed.[20] And the revolts involved much more than a fringe of the military. A 1970–1971 Pentagon survey found 47 percent of low-ranking soldiers had been either "disobedient" (insubordinate, refused orders, engaged in individual sabotage) or "dissident" (worked on a GI newspaper, demonstrated, went to a coffeehouse). Adding drug use raised the percentage to 55.[21]

In March 1969, Private Joseph Miles, a black soldier from Washington, D.C., began circulating two petitions on Fort Bragg. One was in support of the group, GI's United Against the War in Indochina, and the other protested the treatment of the Fort Jackson 8, soldiers arrested at that South Carolina installation for holding an antiwar meeting. Soldiers soon began assembling at a service club on post as a chapter of the group, which had begun with a core group of mainly black and Puerto Rican soldiers both at Fort Jackson and Fort Bragg.[22] Its call to membership said, "Many of us in the Fort Bragg GIs United are Vietnam returnees. As veterans we have fought and seen our fellow GIs killed for a cause the Army doesn't even want to allow us to discuss. . . . Many of us were drafted into the Army against our will—nearly all of us are kept in its grasp against our will—all in order to carry out this illegal, immoral and unjust war. . . . Many black GIs are becoming increasingly aware of the hypocrisy of fighting against other people of color who are struggling for the same rights of self-determination as they are." Like the broader black power movement, which had already been led by Muhammad Ali and others in conscientious objection to the war, they connected problems of race, class, and war here and overseas. The money used to support a dictatorship in Saigon, they said, "belong[s] to the American people. It should be used to improve America, to make our country the shining example all of us want it to be—a free society—free of poverty and hunger, free of racial oppression, free of slums and illiteracy, and the misery they produce." And in fact fully half of North Carolina's young men examined for the draft in 1970 and 1971 were rejected for health reasons or because their schooling had been too poor to let them pass the military's relatively simple entrance test.[23]

The army responded with surveillance and harassment of the group's meetings. New regulations required those passing out literature on post to submit a copy for authorization at least one week beforehand. GI's United questioned the regulations' constitutionality but complied at first, submitting for approval the Bill of Rights and the Army oath. The second, they said, was, "to explode the myth that the oath we took says anything about giving up our rights"; the first, to specify what those rights were.[24] Private Miles helped start an antiwar newspaper, *Bragg Briefs,* but was soon again transferred as punishment (as he had been from Fort Jackson), this time to an Alaskan post north of the Arctic Circle.

Published through that year and the next, *Bragg Briefs* printed alternative histories of the war in Vietnam. The war was already "lost," it asserted. The paper included accounts of army repression of soldiers' constitutional rights and said the army regulars referred to as "lifers" were more interested in preserving their prerogatives than their men's lives.[25] Commentary also claimed the authorities tolerated soldiers' drug abuse as a way of dampening dissent. And the paper counseled use of legal means to resist the war, from applying for conscientious objector status to going to Vietnam to take notes and potential witness names for future war crimes tribunals.

The publishers had to leave town to get the paper produced, traveling over an hour to use the layout tables at Duke University and employing another town's printer. Despite harassment and confiscation at distribution time, a Department of Defense investigation put on-post circulation at five thousand per issue.[26] Dozens of other GI newspapers continued to spring up around the country—from *Shakedown* at Fort Dix to *About Face* at Camp Pendleton to *Fun, Travel & Adventure* at Fort Knox.[27]

In 1969, a group of soldiers, half of them back from Vietnam, and Quakers from Chapel Hill, Durham, and Greensboro, established a peace witness center in a rented house downtown.[28] Called Quaker House, it held religious services on Sundays and provided an information center, to which hundreds of soldiers came each week, and meeting space for GI's United and Concerned Officers Against the War, organized by Pope Air Force Base personnel. And it offered sanctuary to a soldier whose CO application the army had refused. It was and remains based, as its director said, in "the Quaker style," or "witness done in a respectful way, in the sense [of] trying to distinguish the issue from the people."[29]

That same year, the U.S. Serviceman's Fund was organizing GI coffeehouses around the country. They sent one group to Fayetteville, which established the Haymarket Square Coffeehouse on Hay Street. Antiwar activity and literature were also found there. As these centers opened around the country's bases, military authorities moved in to surveil or in some cases try to place them off-limits to soldiers.[30] Other coffeehouses reported military police harassment of the soldiers who visited them, including punitive reassignments back on base.

Like the Fayetteville State students before them, soldiers and civilians in the late 1960s and early 1970s took to the public spaces of sidewalk and street. Seven hundred showed up for a Patriots for Peace Parade in preparation for the nationwide Moratorium in 1969, a march that included both local citizens and college students from around the state. While one hundred soldiers paraded at the head of the group, they were off duty and in civilian clothes, as regulations required. A late 1968 Army circular had reminded commanders troops were permitted to do so. The march ended up, as did many others, in downtown's Rowan Park where speakers included Dr. Howard Levy, a Green Beret sent to prison for refusing to train others "to do political medicine" in Vietnam, and Levi Smalls of the Fayetteville Area Poor People's Organization.[31]

During this same time, Fort Bragg soldiers were sent to Washington D. C. to police national antiwar demonstrations, as they had been the year before, while others went on riot duty in Detroit. Some Fort Bragg GIs were on an alternative watch. They joined the 1971 Vietnam veterans march on Arlington Cemetery (to honor the men whose bodies they had put in bags back in Southeast Asia), the Pentagon (to turn themselves in for war crimes), and the Capitol (to return their medals). Their peers back in North Carolina, it was rumored, were to be sent to break up their camp at Rock Creek Park. No such thing happened, however, for the authorities knew of the popular acceptance of the soldier/veteran protests.[32]

This all did not go down well in Fayetteville. Some disputed the protestors' right to use public parks, and a city council motion to re-

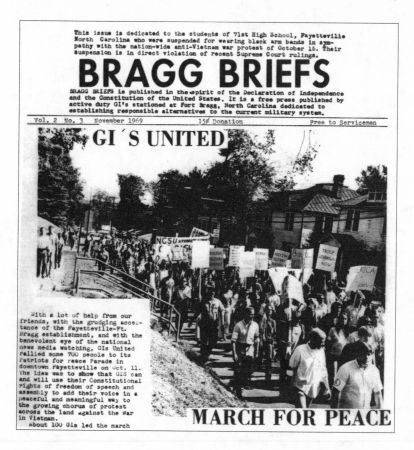

This issue is dedicated to the students of 71st High School, Fayetteville North Carolina who were suspended for wearing black arm bands in sympathy with the nation-wide anti-Vietnam war protest of October 15. Their suspension is in direct violation of recent Supreme Court rulings.

BRAGG BRIEFS

BRAGG BRIEFS is published in the spirit of the Declaration of Independence and the Constitution of the United States. It is a free press published by active duty GI's stationed at Fort Bragg, North Carolina dedicated to establishing responsible alternatives to the current military system.

Vol. 2 No. 3 November 1969   15¢ Donation   Free to Servicemen

GI´S UNITED

With a lot of help from our friends, with the grudging acceptance of the Fayetteville-Ft. Bragg establishment, and with the benevolent eye of the national news media watching, GIs United rallied some 700 people to its Patriots for Peace Parade in downtown Fayetteville on Oct. 11. The idea was to show that GIS can and will use their Constitutional rights of freedom of speech and assembly to add their voice in a peaceful and meaningful way to the growing chorus of protest across the land against the War in Vietnam.
About 100 GIs led the march

MARCH FOR PEACE

War protest downtown: *Bragg Briefs,* November 1969

strict their use was barely defeated. It drew the newspaper out, however, in defense of free speech.[33] Both protestors and soldiers, it implied, were Americans at their democratic best, defending the Bill of Rights—dissenters at home and soldiers abroad, via the domino theory. The true problem lay with two groups, according to the paper—people who "question the sincerity, the honesty, even the loyalty of all who disagree with the war," and law-breaking dissenters or those who "exhibit an appalling callousness toward the sacrifices many, many thousands of Americans have made in the pursuit of American policies in Southeast Asia. . . . It should surprise no one if this callousness is unforgivable in the eyes' of some who made the sacrifices." Despite the seeming evenhandedness, only one kind of error was inexcusable. This left the unpleasant question of what kind of community Fayetteville and the nation could go on to remake out of unforgiven neighbors and the unasked question of whether the war's planners were to be held accountable for their actions.

Nixon's invasion of Cambodia in early May 1970, with its clear expansion of the violence and its violation of that country's sovereignty, prompted massive demonstrations around the United States. Fresh outrage came with the killing of unarmed U.S. civilians—four whites at Kent State University on May 4th (none of them demonstrators and one an ROTC student) and two blacks at Jackson State College in Mississippi on May 15th (where the police had descended on the women's dormitory with an armored van and shotguns).[34] At 71st High School in Fayetteville, a school with many military dependents and within earshot of the guns of Fort Bragg, students wore armbands to protest the expanded war.

GI's United planned a march on Fort Bragg's Armed Forces Day Open House, inviting Jane Fonda and Rennie Davis (of the Chicago 8) to speak.[35] As a result, the military display was canceled, as were others at bases across the country.[36] Antiwar activists nonetheless marched on the post, were evicted, and reconvened at Rowan Park. Facing out over a sea of wooden crosses, *Bragg Briefs* editor, Private John Vail, called for a GI strike and Fonda urged soldiers to stay in the army and resist from within. By one estimate, 3,000 civilians and 750 soldiers rallied, the latter a remarkable number given that post authorities had restricted most soldiers to barracks during the march.[37] One rally participant remembered "they were so angry that they were confined on that Saturday—this was late in the afternoon—and about 7 o'clock that night they released the ban, and they all could go off post. And the Quaker House was just literally mobbed with people."[38] *Anti*-anti-war petitioners set up a table on Hay Street, and fifteen protestors against the protest sat in on the stage during the park speeches.

"Scene at Rally Site Relatively Peaceful," the evening headlines said. But the reporter had described no violence at all and few words even exchanged between war supporters and opponents there.[39] Despite occasional loose talk of violence at antiwar meetings, threats and attacks in Fayetteville were also more often directed at the antiwar movement than from it.[40] Elsewhere in North Carolina that month, President William Friday of UNC–Chapel Hill and the governor received death threats for not calling in armed force to prevent teach-ins and nonviolent protests on state campuses in the days following the Kent and Jackson State killings.[41] But the Army press release announcing cancellation of the Open House expressed concern for the "safety of visitors should planned anti-war activity in the open house area possibly develop into injurious action," a careful phrasing suggesting violence could erupt on either side of the ramparts, this both a projection and a warning.

Letters to the editor against the antiwar movement became increasingly enraged. One writer said she had attended a Rowan Park rally and urged "every American [to] make it their business to see and hear whats [*sic*] going on in their country. If they did[,] this would be halted and these doped up whining, dirty, non-working, non-tax-paying, dutiless, non-Americans would be behind bars where they belong. In spite of the (so-called) Supreme Court . . . their parents should beat the hell out of them and cut off their money and that failing they should be in prison or hospitals or insane asylums, depending on where they fit."[42] Much of the antipathy focused, like this, on differences described in cultural more than political terms. Another, after claiming that GI's United was made up mostly of civilians, said, "They are united all right! They all smell the same!"[43] Given the stronger public support for soldier than civilian protestors, Nixon, too, insinuated that the Vietnam Veterans Against the War was only 30 percent veterans. One VVAW member retorted, "Only 30 percent of us believe Richard Nixon is President."[44]

The readiness to question Fayetteville's new "cultural foreigners"—the long-haired men and bell-bottomed women who had come in numbers to live on Haymount Hill—was also clear in the infamous Jeffrey McDonald murder case. A volunteer Green Beret doctor, McDonald slaughtered his wife and two young children in their house on the post. Apparently high on amphetamines, he covered his crime with a few superficial self-inflicted cuts and the story that a group of demented hippies had overcome him and his family, Charles Manson–style, yelling "Acid is groovy. . . . Kill the pigs."[45] "Victims of Hippie Cult?" the paper bannered, and the local police followed suit, "leaning" on longhaired and bearded youth.[46] Widespread incredulity did not greet McDonald's story, despite its implausibilities: Belief in the violence of hippies and the peaceableness of at least this Princeton-educated officer was telling of the politics of social class and of the times. On the thirtieth anniversary of the murders, said one officer who worked on the case, people "couldn't bring into their minds that someone of his caliber did this. It's easier to believe crazed hippies did this. And still people believe this, to this day."[47]

Although McDonald was eventually charged with the murder later that year, it was in this hothouse environment that an anonymous caller phoned a member of GI's United to ask if the insurance on Quaker House had been paid up. Soon after, under cover of darkness in the early hours of May 20, 1970, the house was set ablaze. Several people sleeping inside leapt out of their windows and escaped, though those targeted elsewhere had not been so lucky. Two soldiers and two civilians were hurt when a Fort Dix GI coffeehouse was bombed several months earlier, and a Marine private was hit when someone sprayed a coffeehouse near Camp Pendleton in California with machine gun fire.[48] While an arson investigation was begun for the Quaker House, no one was ever charged in the crime. As one soldier who worked at Quaker House at the time said, the Fort Bragg military police had often sat in front "with their cameras taking pictures of the cars and the people going in. . . . If they'd been doing their job, there wouldn't have been the fire, is one way to put it, because if they knew who was there and what was going on, they'd have been able to stop it."[49]

The city, claiming zoning restrictions, would not allow the Quakers to move back into a rebuilt house at that location. And, according to a member of its board of overseers, "When we went to investigate about buying or renting a house, it would suddenly not be for sale or for rent, because of the feeling in the city towards Quaker House. And some people were afraid the house might be burned again if we opened up."[50] Although the *Fayetteville Observer* did not editorialize about the fire, it printed a critical letter from a woman and two soldiers. "The raw tactics of violence and destruction are the life style of those who oppose the peace movement," they said. "They flaunted this crass style by burning the Quaker House Wednesday. The violence of the burning is an extreme contrast to the non-violence of the weekend and demonstrates where the real controversy lies—between the supporters and the rejectors [*sic*] of violence. Non-violence shall prevail."[51] By October 1970, a recently separated soldier, William Carothers, using VA mortgage benefits, bought another house in the city and gave the remaining mortgage to the Quakers.[52] They chose a succession of students and other young people to run it—most from the "peace churches," the Quakers, Church of the Brethren, and Mennonites.

The pace of withdrawal from Vietnam quickened, diminishing dissent in the long run, but first bringing larger numbers of unhappy combat veterans to Fort Bragg and other bases. These are the soldiers whom a GAO study euphemistically described as "extremely difficult to motivate."[53] As 1972 began, the Army had announced an early-out program for anyone with overseas service or less than six months in uniform, both categories producing the most rebellion within the ranks.[54] The movement turned increasingly to issues of racism and quality of life, including a campaign to ameliorate the slum conditions that many GIs were forced to live in around the post. In early 1973, the Paris Accords ended the war, and by that summer, Congress ended Selective Service induction, and the shift to an all-volunteer army had begun. Notwithstanding the attention paid to civilian protests or the authorities' agenda setting, it was clear to some observers that the GI movement was the key factor in both.[55]

A CITIZEN'S JOURNEY
While war has often brought state repression of political dissent, in William Carothers's case it created a more active lifelong citizen. When he graduated from a Connecticut high school in 1966, his sister's husband helped him get a job in the small electronics assembly factory where he worked. Although the job afforded a military deferment, he grew tired of working with his brother-in-law, he said. "So I thought I'd go on ahead and join the army." Although his father encouraged him to join the Navy—"he thought I'd be more likely not to get killed"—since "he'd been in the Army, I figured I'd go in the Army." While the military option seemed reasonable to him, going to war was not his goal.

> I remember that spring [of 1968] I was riding across town, [and] the radio came on and said Johnson decided not to run again. And I just went "Woo-oo!" the war is going to be over 'cause he said the war was why he wasn't going to run again. So I thought well maybe I'll just get into the army and get right back out. . . . Anyway I got my draft notice and went to see a recruiter and this guy said if you'd sign up you wouldn't have any

reserve obligations once you get through your two years, so I figured okay but he lied to me. I had to do reserve duty anyway, but I didn't find that out until I got in the army for two years. So anyway I went to New Haven, Connecticut, and got on a bus to Fort Dix, New Jersey. Got there in the middle of the night [and the next morning] got up and started bayonets and all that kind of stuff. I never messed with guns or anything growing up in Connecticut cause there was no open land there or nothing. This was all wild to me. . . . They gave me a gun with real bullets.

He soon ended up at Fort Bragg, where his first monthly paycheck's $98 total was a bad surprise.

I said this is awful, . . . so this guy came to talk to us about Special Forces and paratroopers, and a guy with a beret on, he says, I want you guys to join up for jump school and jump out of airplanes. We'll give you another extra $50 a month. I thought what, that sounds pretty good, another $50, so I signed up for jump school [laughs]. . . . I finished basic training and then you go to advanced training and I got orders and I looked at them and they said guided missile repairman. I thought, wow, I'm gonna get over now! I went home and told all my friends I was going to be a guided missile repairman and I got orders to Fort Gordon, Georgia. I got there, [and] they put me in this camp, out in the middle of nowhere. I said this ain't right. I'm supposed to be a guided missile repairman, so I went back to the post. I was gonna argue with them. They showed me, says look here, you are infantry AIT [Advanced Infantry Training]. Ain't no guided missile repairman to it. They had given us all kinds of tests at basic and that was just a recommendation. That wasn't anything that was gonna actually happen. My orders were to be in infantry.

As Bill went to jump school, Richard Nixon was being nominated at the 1968 Republican convention. When he saw that protestors had "nominated a duck or a goose or something [it was, in fact, a pig]," he thought to himself,

"This is wild, I can't believe this". . . . Then at some point I saw the paper from the Democratic convention and it had a picture of two cops beating on this protester and he was just standing there and hitting him and all. I was thinking, is this what I'm going in to fight for? hitting people like this? . . . [And] I can remember this [TV news] show one night and it showed a big helicopter [with] a net under it, just full of bodies and they killed all these people that day and they said, "Well now it's just a disposal problem. We have to get rid of these bodies." And I don't know what they did, they buried them or burned or what they did. Just seeing something like that on TV, it's just like a click. You know this ain't right. No.

His army job was to pack parachutes. He and his fellow workers had a book to sign after taking care of each chute,

> so they know who packed it in case something happened and they could prove it was something not being done right. So we'd sign our name and put a little peace symbol next to it. . . . A bunch of us did it . . . I mean [we were] getting into Bragg and meeting up with other veterans, veterans who had been to Vietnam. There was one Green Beret who wrote a book about it. I read his book and then he came to Fayetteville to speak. And they had him back here at Rowan Park. . . . I went to hear him and I had this Hawaiian [friend and] me and him went. We were standing in the audience and I'd heard about GIs United. I don't know if it was in the Fayetteville paper or how I found out about it. . . . So I figured I'd go and check that out.

The next day, the newspaper published a large picture of him and his friend at the rally. "And I decided well I'd better hook up with these guys 'cause I'm sure the MPs and all have my number now." With this sense of already being an outlaw simply for attending a meeting, he joined the group and began to work on *Bragg Briefs*. He and other soldiers funded it with money they made painting properties for a local realtor, David Moose, a politically sympathetic veteran and former labor organizer. "There were GI groups at most of the major bases in the country at that point and some of them said they were real secret. We're not going to disclose who our members are and all this. So no, we said, we're proud of what we're doing. We're going to put our names on the paper and we did." The first article he wrote exposed the circumstances surrounding the deaths of three men on post: "We were living in the old World War II barracks [and] there'd been tile on the floor. They'd taken up the tile and they were going to clean the floor. And so this sergeant told these guys to get some gasoline and clean it up with a buffer. They turned on the buffer and the place exploded and killed three of them. I was hot about that. . . . They had a trial for the sergeant and they let him off."

People in the community he remembers as being "more supportive than not supportive, I'd say that. It's funny being in a military town at that point because you'd figure what the military was feeling [was pro-war]. Well I know what I [and others] was feeling, that this was a rotten war and we were murdering people. It's a lot different than people in the military now 'cause there's not a war, even though the stuff in Bosnia is going. It's not like they're out there killing people every week. There's really a different mind-set."[56]

After his release from the army in 1971, Bill continued working with Quaker House and helped buy their next building. He married, and he and his wife went on to work in a variety of progressive social movements. Together, they joined a work brigade to Cuba where he found, he said, "that socialism works." On his return, he moved to Charlotte, North Carolina, where he used veteran's benefits to get community college training in a trade. While he worked at a General Electric plant on machinery and welding for the next twenty years, he continued his activism, particularly with political prison cases. He also worked for many years in local efforts to end apartheid in South Africa through public education and political lobbying.

I talked with Bill Carothers about all of this at Quaker House, still an active, if less turbulent, place thirty years after the war. It was being run by Phil and Kaushaliya Esmonde, a couple who met in Sri Lanka, where Phil crossed front lines to do peace and humanitarian work through seven years of that country's brutal civil war. There he learned, he said, about "the ease with which the enemy profile is kept going, the ease with which people fall back into rationalizations of violence as the only way to deal with the situation, [and about] the day-to-day concrete result of violence in people's lives, of people disappearing, people being abused." In transferring those insights to Fayetteville, he focused on those enemy profiles and rationalizations, his preference being to see the enemy as "us," not the military. The day I met him in late 1998, the enemy image was the Iraqis: President Clinton had just ordered new bombing raids, even as devastating economic sanctions in place since 1990 continued.

Fort Bragg officials generally support the House's GI counseling, according to Phil, even though their rationale is not his.

> There are many, many young people who get into the military and they know it's the wrong place for them. They know they've made a mistake, and they have nowhere they can turn often to find out good information

Phil Esmonde, Quaker House director

about how to get out. Or they've gone into the delayed enlistment program and don't know where to turn. And this organization can be very
helpful to those kind of people who are questioning. Often even if they
believe that the military is the place they want to be, they suddenly find
out what the military is. . . . [They are told to] be all you can be or all you
want to be and they find out that it's sometimes all that they don't want to
be. But they don't know where to go with those first questions they have
about violence and the impact of violence and where it leads to.

Quaker House's work remains exotic for most people in Fayetteville.
Like other Americans, they are rarely exposed to the vibrant antimili-
tarist tradition it comes out of. This antimilitarism runs from the
American Revolution, fought in part over the issue of the standing
British army in the colonists' midst, to the large and sustained anti–
nuclear weapons movement of the last decades.[57]

THE BONDS OF WAR

Fayetteville's internationalists come both unarmed, as Mr. Carothers has been, and armed, like Gary Johnson, one of the many veterans now living in the city who see their Vietnam-era soldiering as a contribution to society. When I asked him "were you in Vietnam?" he sardonically answered, "Only four times." His brother went to Vietnam at the same time, something he thought, also somewhat wryly, was just as well so his mother "wouldn't have to worry about us but once."

In the Special Forces, his job was to train troops with the JFK Special Warfare Center and School. He traveled frequently in and out of Fayetteville to go to Vietnam, as well as to the Canal Zone, Honduras, Costa Rica, Bolivia, and Guatemala in the 1960s. We politely skirted around the issue of who was killing whom and how many were dying in these conflicts in favor of more general questions. I asked him what he thought was the most important thing he knew about war. His answer, with a blurt of laughter and the amplification of repetition, was "Stay out of it. Stay out of it. But if you are going to fight, fight to win. These containment wars are terrible. They're nothing but attrition."

This black officer also clearly admired the Vietnamese he fought. "Those were some ingenious people we were dealing with," he said. "They had been in those jungles for years. And they had their cities underground and they walked and they walked and they brought that stuff from Hanoi on bicycles walking those trails under the B-52 bombers down the Ho Chi Minh Trail. And they [the Americans] would rain those bombs down there and as soon the earth would stop shaking, they would come out and shake on down the road, going South." Hearing his poetic rendering of the kinds of shaking that were going on, I asked if he had some admiration for them. "Yeah," he said, "their determination for a sock full of rice versus that of being paid by the Americans. The South Vietnamese [were] being paid by Americans and the dedication that the North Vietnamese had was on their principles. Just two different people. Just two different people." The allies he admired were a local minority group, the Montagnards who, he said, "we had some real dedication from. . . . They were really into it. They didn't like the Vietnamese too well." Despite the race hatred many armies use to motivate soldiers to fight, some come to feel they have more in common with warriors on the other side than with civilians back home: They share, after all, a calling or at least a job, as well as temporary residence in the battle zone. While reducing the dehumanization that war making relies on, such bonds do not necessarily reduce the number of battle deaths or the social fragmentation at home.[58]

Although convinced his army work has been in service to the best principles, he spontaneously described the costs of being a warrior to one's conscience.

> We were fighters, and our mentality had been changed. We went to Sunday school and learned all about the Ten Commandments and things like this, [but as a military trainer] I've got to get you to the point that you would have a military mind and the military mind would be just like sitting here drinking coffee and [a signal would] go up and we grab our weapons and go out here and start shooting people. You see now that's the military mind. You see there's a method in killing and what that method is, is to justify killing people. If you go out here right now as a soldier, and we have some enemy out here and you could kill a great deal of them and I would tell you immediately that you provided a great service to your country. I would put a medal on you to justify it. And when I pin a medal on you to justify it, you have received a reward, so it's not as traumatic to your brain as it would be if you sit down and start thinking, Lord, what have I done? But when you start thinking like that, you look down on your chest and you see your ribbon, and you brace up and say by Lord [this is all right]! This is the way it's done and then once you have accepted that award, things like this, the country showed its appreciation, then the next thing you know you get a write up, and they have a appropriate ceremony and you sit out in front of the troops and they give you all the accolades and they tell you how brave and great you responded under fire, then you feel real good. Until you retire. [Is that hard?] No, it's not hard to retire, but until you retire you go up here and sit around out in the VA Hospital and you see these guys and they got some that got these headaches, and they can't stop them and they're wondering why they're having these nightmares. If you could have something [a gun], you'd blow his brains out. The luster is gone. He's no longer in uniform. Nobody knows what he's done. He's just a crazy bastard sitting out here in the hospital. [He's] just become a little bit less than a human. You know?

His laughter as he made this last observation was a bit manic. But he turned more serious: "Now we who embrace the military, you see,

Self-sacrifice:
Vietnam War memorial
on Fort Bragg

[we can say to ourselves,] 'I don't know how long it's going to be
before I'm up here doing this.'" In self-reassurance, he repeated the
common faith that army people take care of each other: "The military community sort of embraces [itself]." But despite this promise of
support, he seemed to tell me, the dead and disappeared are ever afterward the warriors' companions, too.

THE DEATH NEXT DOOR

Every death—whether the intentional ones of battle or the accidents
or inevitables at home—leaves a ragged hole in the social fabric and in
individual hearts. The dead remain always missing, and we hear them
leave messages. They are the 2,358,000 Vietnamese people and 58,184
Americans who died during the American war in that country, including 98 men from Cumberland County.[59] Most of these deaths are

uncounted on Washington D.C.'s wailing wall. And there are others—the after-battle deaths from Agent Orange or landmines left behind or grief or suicidal guilt and rage. Imagination labors over these
bare facts. The intrepid can try to glean the scale of human suffering
the war created, the large and ramifying web of death, like the web of
life, growing from each missing soldier and civilian into an ecology of
grief, of fathers, cousins, sisters, neighbors stunned, angry, mourning, resigned.

Because women do much of the work of weaving together family
ties, they do the work of filling the holes war leaves as well.[60] Said one
woman, of a gracious and outgoing personality, who had tended one
neighborhood family in particular:

> When I say that I lost a devoted friend that I knew, I'll cry right this min-
> ute. I remember him coming over here to tell me goodbye, and after he
> left, I just broke down and wept. He [had gone to] Korea and he fared
> well. He came and brought me this beautiful string of pearls, for looking
> after [his wife] and the children. Thanking me for looking after [her] and
> the children. And when he left my house after telling me goodbye to
> Vietnam, I just sat down and cried. I knew I was never going to see him
> again. I had never had that feeling in my life. I found out later after he had
> died, [his wife] had the same feeling. Isn't that strange?

Many attribute nothing but simplistic certainty to their political others and many assume a love of battle in military cities. But to my question, "How does that make you feel about war?" she replied, with intense but waffling feeling, "Oh, I feel terrible about war. I've always
hated it. But I think we have to do it, I guess. I mean I just hate it."

For younger women, the war shook their friendships and loves.
Like a muted version of the missing-in-action soldier, friends sometimes disappeared without necessarily dying.

> I remember some young people that I went to high school with immedi-
> ately went into the army because they were drafted. They went to Viet-
> nam and at least one of them was killed. [A friend?] Yeah, he had been a
> boy that had had a crush on me at some point. And, there was a lake . . .
> where lots and lots of youth went in the summertime and the military
> also went there because you paid by the day. . . . And some of them began
> going off to Vietnam. And, this was some of my earliest thoughts about
> the war and what was going on was having some guy come up to me and

say, "I'm not going to be in the club this summer because I'm going." No! You know, I can't believe. And then, most of them, you never knew what happened. You never knew whether they came back or not. A couple I kept in touch with, one of them sent me a picture of his wedding, but this was an awareness to me of the faces that we were *not* seeing any longer.

Men perhaps more than women, however, heard stories from other men, their neighbors and friends, who had been to Vietnam and returned. And what they heard, like every story, shaped the listener and revealed something of the cultures that produced the teller. Whether filled with contradictions or pure and simple, the stories made war sound nothing like the movies they had seen or the textbook celebrations of combat they had read. Said one once young man,

> I can't begin to tell you, you see, after I'd seen my best friend's father was blown to pieces, and I saw all my friends' parents and their brothers coming back dead, I was like, "and you want me to go and do this?!" If the United States had been attacked, just about anybody my age would have gone and fought. But we were not going to go to this strange place because you could talk to the soldiers. They would tell you what a horrible disgusting pit this was. And so, I was just not going to go. [So you heard a lot of stories about Vietnam first hand?] Oh yeah. You know, my friends' fathers . . . after a year's tour over there of seeing all this horror and all this kind of stuff, they were really bizarre when they came back. So, I had every possible negative reinforcement short of actually being dropped over there for me not to want to go to this place.

Many of these men—who included relatives as well as the fathers of his friends—could not understand his opposition to the war. While some were simply at a loss, others were threatening.

> A lot of the men that were here were serving their country and they were invested in this and then they thought that they were doing the right thing and you know how polarized the country was at that time. You said too much and somebody was likely to pop you. And I got called a long-hair commie pinko fag by a couple of my friends' fathers: go back, go live with the commies or whatever. . . . You better believe I took a lot of heat. I took it from my uncles who had been in service. I had one uncle who was in some part of the service and he still won't tell about it. He speaks fluent [foreign language]. He speaks like eight of those little bizarre languages fluently. We never knew, even his own wife never knew, where he

was. It was like, see ya, I'll be back, kind of thing. He was just short of executing me. Well, how could I have failed, how could I let the family down?"

But he could not understand, in return, how the same fathers who were so angry at him for his refusal were telling stories that did not make it sound like something any reasonable person would support. When I asked what soldier's story stood out in his mind, he answered tersely, "Executing people. Bam, you're dead." Were these soldiers describing their own actions, I asked. "Yeah, killing children." They told you? I asked. "Yeah," he said, clipped again. With what tone? I wanted to know. "Well, glee actually. You see they were gooks. That term *gook* [meant] they were subhuman. I don't know, on some level, maybe, who knows what they were feeling actually at the time, but when they relayed it back to me, it was a, it was like killing a batch of kittens. And, once again, [I said to myself] 'you think I'm going to go over there?! I don't think so. . . .'" I wondered whether their stories didn't also focus on their own suffering. "Well," he said, "they would come back, they would take off their boots and say 'check this out,' you know, the fungus growing out all over them. They were practically starved down because they'd been out doing this kind of stuff. And several [people I knew] came back with the most bizarre cases of malaria that you've ever seen. . . . And being separated from the family and all these kinds of things. There was *nothing* nice."

He recognized that if he had not grown up in Fayetteville, he might have been more oblivious. "I would have been much more likely to have gone," he said, "thinking, oh, okay, well, you know, it's a war but maybe I'll have a better chance. You see, I knew better, I just knew." How about other kids your age? I wondered. "Oh yeah, nobody wanted to go. Very few people were willing to stand up and be as vocal about it as I was, but not, definitely no . . . even the girls. By this point, the war had soured so badly and nobody was going to go, and people weren't supporting it. It was just terrible. . . . If I talk[ed] to my cousins [who did not live in a military city] or whatever, you know, they'd be like, I wouldn't go either. . . . [But] they *would* have [gone], and gotten their heads blown off." I knew the answer to my "why?" before he gave it: "Because it's the right thing to do: 'God and Country.'"

LOVING DAUGHTERS OF THE WAR

The military children of this time were bequeathed a painful dilemma. Some felt conflict between their love for their fathers—who would have usually been officers in those days—and their own or their friends' criticism of the war. Marcia Waters's toddler bounced between us and the Teletubbies as we talked in her living room about her teenaged experience during the war. Like many military dependents, she had attended nearly as many different schools—some of them overseas—as there are years of schooling. She spent her tenth grade in Fayetteville, schooled alongside civilians. But she made almost her entire social life with the children of military families and in the installation's teen club, movie houses, and playing fields. She had just one civilian friend and recalls more tension than older Fayettevillians do between the two worlds. The dependents were put down as "post toasties," and they returned the compliment, labeling the locals "townies."[61] Even though some post children had great success on the football team and in academics, she thinks the epithet said, "we didn't fit or we didn't belong. . . . Even now, there are people that I went to high school with here, they're all cliquey sort of, still." She also "imagine[d] civilians for many years thought that military brought bad things into the community." They were "probably right," she said, laughing. "I think the military brought drugs in, with Vietnam. [And] the prostitution was pretty bad in Fayetteville."[62]

The distance between the military and local children she thought of as an achievement gap as well as this social one. "In the tenth grade," she said of herself and other military children, "we were probably the smartest kids in that school. I don't know if it was pressure from home, or it was the one thing that carried you from school to school. . . . I think there was a lot of stress involved with succeeding if you were a military kid. Because you wanted to make your parents proud. And that's the one thing that carried you over from school to school, you would always go in as a good academic student, and then it would take time to deal with social life, and clubs, or whatever else."

But the intellectual and social spacing from civilians seemed based in class as much as in military status because it was repeated with enlisted families on post. Marcia's father lived on Colonel's Row, the housing around the parade grounds reserved for the highest-ranking officers. While there were many social events and friendly interactions between officers and enlisteds in the same unit, she remembers just one friend who was the child of an enlisted man. Nonetheless, the Vietnam War, she thinks, brought the two kinds of soldiers and soldiers' families closer together, if only temporarily. The father absence that war produced made the children of soldiers closer to each other and individual families tighter. By inference, then, they grew more distant from their civilian peers.

What made the separation from civilians especially sharp that year of high school and in her college years were the war's moral questions.

> We couldn't say anything against [the war] because our father was involved with the military. He was the leader of troops, and people died that we knew. So, when I went to college, one of my roommates was a civilian and then another one of my roommates turned out to be my girlfriend from the eighth grade that we had kept in touch with. Her father was a Marine Corps person and she transferred in after freshman year to my school. And we started rooming together. And she was anti-war. Again, her dad was in Vietnam. So, it was different. We didn't talk about very much back then. . . . It was hard. I guess I supported the war because I couldn't say anything otherwise because it was my dad and he was in Vietnam and he was shot down.

She focused on her sympathy for her father rather than anger at the military even as she described the horrible outcome of his exposure to dioxin sprayed over the Vietnamese countryside during the war. "My dad died last year of Non-Hodgkins lymphoma because of Agent Orange. So, it played a big part in our family life. He had cancer for seven years, but he was sick for twelve years off and on . . . Guillain-Barré is what started it, the legionnaire's disease. It deteriorated his muscles and then the cancer came. He kicked it for a while, [but it] came back with a vengeance the second time. It was pretty bad."

Her father had often been away in Vietnam, Korea, the Dominican Republic, Baltimore, and on his many maneuvers.

> I can remember every time Dad deployed. I can remember kissing him goodbye at airports when he went to Vietnam and Korea and [when] he went to Vietnam again, he missed my baccalaureate from high school. I can remember all of his departures and homecomings and I can't tell you

the names of my teachers except for one high school English teacher in
my junior year that was my favorite. Most kids remember who they had
and all about their school years and I remember when my dad left and
came back. Daddy's girl. . . . It was a different upbringing.

Perhaps unexpectedly, she went on to become a very active and
effective feminist reformer in a social movement whose development
ran parallel to the GI and civil rights movements. After marrying a
military man, she moved to bases, both overseas and at home, where
she organized chapters of the National Organization for Women
(NOW). When she moved back to Fayetteville, she helped found the
first domestic violence shelter in the city. She also did outreach to
abused prostitutes, some of them connected to the military. In this
work with NOW and the shelter, she found allies among both military wives and civilian women and in several male politicians in town.
And together they lobbied the county commissioners with balloon-
festooned, "friendly" protest when domestic violence funds were cut
during the Reagan years.

Whether military dependents like Marcia or others who had relatives in the war were prowar or antiwar, as a group they had distinctive
responses. A contemporary of Marcia's, who came to oppose the war
when she went away to college, noted, "I think because of being here
in Fort Bragg, I always understood that it wasn't [the soldiers'] fault.
They were being drafted. I didn't spit on any soldiers. That would
have been ridiculous. My cousin, who was over in Vietnam, I wrote
him regularly and sent him packages and I didn't even know him.
That was just the family thing to do. But it was a wrong war, and I
understood that politically and it was the old men who were sending
the young men off to die. I was very angry." She also saw the more
complex dilemmas of military people as well, and the drive to see
oneself, no matter what, as an ethical being: "Enormous numbers of
the population here are either active duty or retired and it's very important to believe in what you do. So, it's sort of ridiculous to think of
some retired military guy [saying], 'Yeah, my twenty-eight-year career in the military was [a part of] this militaristic war machine.'"

THE TRUE, THE TRUMPETED, AND THE SECRET
Walking for the first time into the massive, high-ceilinged National
Archives to find papers related to Fayetteville and Fort Bragg, I felt as

if passing through flying buttresses into an immense cathedral. There I was, in the orbit of the state's monumental power but also within the promise of democratic salvation from it: the covenant that the state be visible and accountable, that inquiry be free, and citizenship equal. Anyone, theoretically, can walk into this building just outside Washington, D.C., to read documents the government has produced. But virtually the first question I and other pilgrims to the archives were asked about our documentary quest was "military or civilian?" Like "paper or plastic?" this question only speaks to the obsessions of a particular point in time. When my answer was "military," I entered a labyrinth of badges and special military archivists and classified or missing documents. Archives personnel gave me a small tag to tape facedown on the Xerox machine as I made copies of the documents I received. "Declassified," the label said, and in another language: "Authority NND 824999 RMS." Women and men in uniform sometimes sat in one area of the huge research room, at a monitored distance from civilian researchers, working over documents they had clearance to see.

After decades of the power of suggestion, many take it for granted that some important common good—usually public safety—is served by this secrecy. One historian in uniform complained to me, though, about how rarely he had seen anything declassified in his twenty years in the military. During the recent occupation of Haiti, he said, even a requisition for lifeguards at an R and R beach was coded secret. While he implied sloth lies behind some of this—it is easier just to stamp things "safely"—he also resented military history's frequent transformation to mythic form and public relations purpose. Examples abound, as when the Central Intelligence Agency reversed and rewrote intelligence reports that suggested the Vietnam War would not go well for the United States and when military leaders silenced soldiers who testified about the devastation of civilians.[63] Military history's target should be truth, this soldier said, because its goal is to improve the science of war.

If truth was a refugee even in the laboratories of war, it is not surprising that it was often disappeared among the public as well. In Fayetteville, the courts upheld both the military's prohibition on *Bragg Briefs,* and the 71st High School principal's ban on the silent speech of armbands.[64] The judge justified this last ruling by arguing that the bands would have created a polarized, tense situation given that one-third of the school's students were military dependents. The first day of protest had been, he warned, "explosive. . . . There was confusion, disorder and demonstrations in the hall," and "fear of fights and disorder." The assumption that disagreement was inherently dangerous—not simply the noisy beauty of the democratic process—had been heard before, from World War I through the early Cold War. The courts felt their ruling was made easier by the fact that the principal had fairly banned "all armbands," but those bands—and the several antiwar students expelled for refusing to remove their armbands—had no prowar counterpart.

Common complaint has it that negative media coverage—especially television—undermined support for the war. National studies of archival war news content and journalists' own accounts show, however, that the press was "deeply committed to the national security consensus" even while seeing itself as independent of the political powers that be.[65] Until 1968, it was very supportive of the war and, afterward, continued to use American officials and soldiers overwhelmingly as its information sources. That did mean, then, of course, that it reported disagreement within those groups. But completely absent was the perspective of the Vietnamese farmer theoretically being helped. It was missing because journalists often focused on technical aspects of the war in chimerical hopes of being or appearing "objective" or outside politics. Their stories asked, for example, how accurate the Pentagon's body counts were or how effective the "strategic hamlet" program. The press never wavered from portraying the United States as noble in its intentions and helped support Nixon's long stage of the war by shaping public perception of it as a "mistake" or "tragedy" rather than a crime or predictable and intentional project. The 1971 Winter Soldier Investigation hearings in Detroit—a set of testimonies by Vietnam Veterans Against the War about wartime atrocities—received little and hostile media coverage. By that point, moreover, a majority of Americans had already turned against the war.[66] Media coverage of antiwar demonstrations helped draw support for Nixon's policies, as many people, seeing mainly the images of street disruption rather than the message, came to view the protests—as much as the war—as a threat to the social order.

Though delivered to many military households, the Fayetteville paper did not cover Fort Bragg or antiwar activism extensively during this period. For end of century coverage, its staff had to travel some distance to a university archive to get relevant pictures of Vietnam-era soldiers.[67] Many American media, not just those in military cities, skirted this issue. They strove to maintain readership by avoiding alienating those with one point of view or another on the war. This was at a time when there was no neutral language—of text or photograph—with which to describe any of it.[68] But the local newspaper did come to a critique of the war. While calling for an end to the war in May 1970, it tagged perhaps the key issue for many Fayetteville readers by emphasizing that withdrawal "would not diminish in any way the personal courage and heroism exhibited by many thousands of Americans there."[69]

The view that the press was the enemy of the army, however, has had "legs." Newspaper reporters today are not allowed to do any unescorted news-gathering trips on the installation. This holds whether they want to cover a traffic accident involving civilians, ask about work conditions, or discuss coming battles. And the simple human desire to know who one is living with and to do one's job well led a local reporter to tell me, "It's frustrating. . . . There are interesting people out there." It is not that the military has no use for the press, however. Via free transportation and with strict supervision, they are welcomed to follow military operations. Fort Bragg also sends out a huge volume of press release material each day. Although much of this is filed or tossed, public affairs story lines are omnipresent in local media. It is hard to measure the chilling effect, moreover, when official displeasure with newspaper coverage is expressed, as it has been in some cases.[70]

Military attempts to control the media in the wake of Vietnam represent just one way that war preparation has eroded social trust. Another is through the hostility that greeted opponents of the war, who sometimes silenced themselves for fear of social punishment. They could also fear the power of the state, as did one conscientious objector in town. He worried "that someday that [CO application] would be used against me. That was a real fear that I had, that if I were in some position somewhere . . . that this could be pulled out and said, here, this kid was, said this or this years and years ago. I guess it was just a distrust of the government."

This was not paranoia, given the spies and lies that have abounded in times of war, imaginary war, and war preparation. The Fort Jackson 8, for example, were originally the Fort Jackson 9 until it was revealed that one was a planted Army informer. Army surveillance of Americans began long before and on a massive scale during World War I, focused mainly on workers and unions. It continued through more peaceful times and accelerated in war. During World War II, over two million citizens were investigated. By 1963, the Army had developed a Civil Disturbance Early Warning System, as if the American people were incoming missiles. This transfer of military thinking and practice into the civil order was exactly what critics feared would happen when the military intruded into domestic policing of crime, much less political activism. Such an invasion seemed complete during the Detroit riots a few years later, when Major General William P. Yarborough, a psychological warfare specialist, sent his men out with the admonition to "get out your counterinsurgency manuals. We have an insurgency on our hands."

During the Vietnam War, 1,000 plain-clothes army agents did in fact fan out from three hundred military posts to spy on the antiwar movement.[71] Quaker House was under close surveillance by Army Intelligence and the FBI. Agents watched from outside the house, with as many as four men at a time recording license plates and the comings and goings of soldiers and civilians. They also went inside undercover and reported the minutiae of meetings:

> O'Brien suggested that GIUAWV [GI's United Against the War in Vietnam] distribute *Bragg Briefs* on Friday and Saturday, 30 and 31 January 1970, in downtown Fayetteville, Fayetteville area shopping centers (nfi), and possibly in church parking lots in Fayetteville on Sunday, 1 February 1970. O'Brien stated Noyes and Seiler were drafting a petition concerning GIs rights, to include wages, hours spent on "KP," working conditions and living conditions of individuals in the U.S. Army. Noyes and Seiler are also to circulate a petition objecting to recent violations of the haircut policy at Fort Bragg.[72]

And they accessed mortgage, court, and motor vehicle records as they saw fit. So it was that the FBI knew that Carothers had made a $3,000 down payment for the new Quaker House and that monthly payments were $118.[73] The only instance of violence noted in this official

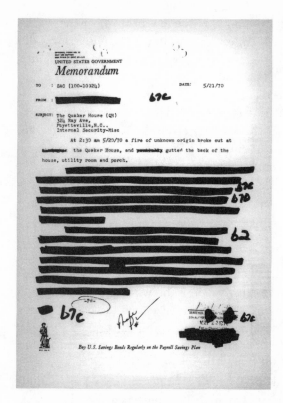

FBI report on Quaker
House arson

surveillance was the fire, but an FBI employee working on the Freedom of Information Act (FOIA) request twenty years later blacked
out nearly the entire "internal security" document that reported on
it.[74]

Secrecy may be the most important form of power that war and
war preparation cede to the state. Any hidden actor has a wider range
of possible action and narrowed accountability. The Vietnam War, of
course, did not create government secrecy: military, quasi-military,
and civilian government agencies had long before concealed their activities from the public. Officials hid the dire risks and their own cul-
pability in the sickness and death of uranium workers and nuclear test
downwinders during the Cold War. One high official with the testing
program, for example, gave public reassurance of the safety of the
Western desert tests but evacuated his pregnant daughter-in-law from
her Utah home.[75] As in that case, secrecy's more visible twins are propaganda and public relations. These have been pressed into service to

remake American public opinion at home, as in 1950, when the CIA fabricated a story for the American press in which an imaginary defector, Colonel Kyril Kalinov, "revealed" that Russia had plotted North Korea's attack on the South.[76]

In war and in life, secrecy seems to promise safety to all, but its protections are mainly for the powerful. Their crimes can go unpunished, and their posterity be but the good deeds they choose to record. But the corrosion of trust during the Vietnam War era was to come home to roost in some paradoxical ways.

LEGITIMACY, PARAMILITANCY,
AND THE ALL VOLUNTEER FORCE

The Vietnam War left the legitimacy of the American government in fundamental question in large segments of the nation. Oddly enough, this is true less on the left, where the war is viewed as a violation of international and moral law, than on the right, where government elites (military and civilian) are believed to have "tied the hands" of the American soldier, preventing him from winning the war. Sociologist James Gibson has identified this war-induced crisis of legitimacy as a source of rising paramilitarism, including both the growing militia movement and special forces and black budget military activities.[77] If government politicians and high-ranking officers betrayed the common soldier, leaving him out to hang as a mere target in the jungle, the new approach would be operating outside and around the law to achieve victory. But this new paramilitary hero is, as Gibson says, "only a short cultural distance from the classic American heroes who act outside the power structure in order to save society," like Western gunmen and noir detectives.[78]

There was a Mike Hammer feel to the estranged Special Forces soldier I met at a meeting of Fayetteville's Libertarian Party. Built like a fireplug with a short, almost sandpaper-like haircut, a vocal bark, and a combination of personableness and no-nonsense toughness, he had deeply resented criticism of the war by people who had not been there. And when he expressed a reserved admiration for the Montana Freemen, I was not surprised. A significant minority of Americans articulate sympathy for the militia movement or withhold judgment of it.[79] People in Fayetteville may have experienced a similar loss of faith as they watched their city crumble into "Fayettenam," their local government not victorious or even obviously at battle against the multifarious forces of disorder. The level of cynicism and displeasure with the city's appearance, culture, and crime rate is relatively high.[80] Such sentiments may seem to emerge simply from a reasoned look at the present state of the city, but some of its roots are in the Vietnam War on Hay Street.

As the war ended, the military had to change in the face of massive refusals to soldier, and the potential recruit's now pressing suspicion that an army job entailed more than career training. The government responded in 1973 with an All Volunteer Force. Stronger enticements would be needed to draw the required number of young people into this new military. Congress tripled the recruiting budget, doubled enlisted pay, offered bonuses to those who signed up for combat units, and opened nearly all military positions to women.[81] A new military culture would be needed as well. Changes were instituted— some of them begun in the late years of the draft: the end of shaved heads; the reining in of abusive drill instructors in basic training; a five-day workweek; less-arbitrary military justice; the end of reveille and bed checks; new, relaxed rules on hair length; and the installation of beer-vending machines in barracks, although to some degree these rules were changed to reflect practice rather than vice versa.[82] The rise of black nationalism and the problem of racism were addressed with many initiatives to attract black soldiers and defuse dissent.[83]

While the GI movement contributed toward making a more internally democratic and less authoritarian military, policymakers would continue to send trainers and troops to assist abusive and undemocratic regimes from Guatemala to Saudia Arabia. And they would continue to expose American soldiers to health risks as in the Gulf War syndrome, depleted uranium munitions, and experimental chemical warfare inoculations. The new volunteer force also paradoxically put upward pressure on the military budget to cover the steeply rising costs of recruiting and higher wages. And the massive new recruitment apparatus would have broad cultural effects.

Tens of thousands of people would now work each day at bringing in and retaining military employees. They would apply psychological and marketing science to this job, constantly assessing how "target demographic groups" feel about military jobs. So the Army slogan "Be all that you can be" was a research-based attempt to resonate with disadvantaged youth, telling them that opportunities to learn skills and express their talents would be unblocked for them in an Army that has their personal development in mind. While the military has long had recruiting offices, they now more aggressively target each and every American high school, cold-calling high school students to sell the military like Pepsi, or more aptly, a character-building after-school club. Over the years they have reached deeper into childhood, regularly visiting middle and elementary schools with a variety of programs to prepare students to see the military as an attractive choice.

The All Volunteer Force (AVF) has contended with a constantly changing set of conditions for its success. The first years of the AVF were, not coincidentally, a period of high unemployment as war spending dropped and massive capital movement sent many jobs overseas. And the baby boom was still providing a large pool of eighteen-year-olds from which to recruit. This all allowed the AVF to take off, albeit with declines in what the truly dismal science, military sociology, knows as "recruit quality"; that is, educational levels and test scores. Whether recruits have flowed to the AVF in the years since has depended on how entry-level military and civilian pay and benefits compare with each other. Other factors are the amount of money the military invests in marketing its jobs, the youth unemployment rate and cohort size, the recency and frequency of American war making (enlistment dropped during and just after the postdraft wars), and cultural attitudes toward war and soldiering.[84] The military can control many of these factors, at least with the help of congressional funding, and it has made a variety of calculations over the years about how to create the most favorable environment at the least cost. In the process of responding to changing social, economic and demographic conditions, the military's tremendous size has meant that its decisions in turn have affected those original conditions. Its TV wallpaper of ads during sports programming, its entrenchment in the schools, as well as air shows, and friendly Hollywood fare have shaped a culture of normalcy and celebration of, first, the military's people, and, quite secondarily, its purposes. A military staffed through drafted coercion rather than voluntary enticement would have trouble matching this cultural reach.

★

Vietnam veterans in front of Airborne and
Special Operations Museum diorama

The war in Vietnam brought massive new numbers of soldiers and, gradually, GI and civilian resistance, to Fayetteville. We can see this antiwar movement in the context of a wider and longer antimilitarist tradition in the United States, as well as see the returning soldiers' dilemmas. This war, like the others of this century, affected people's view of the morality of state violence in diverse ways, but those in closer proximity could view the soldier's complex humanity, meet war refugees, and make what they would of the relationship between war training and the violent social problems that beset Fayetteville and America. The crisis of legitimacy that the Vietnam War prompted, however, created the incentives for the turn to an All Volunteer Force. Post–World War II American access to global markets and resources made for affluence that gave recruitment problems to the still-huge standing army. The army found itself required to raise the standard of living its soldiers could expect on base in order to counter widening job opportunities and rising expectations in the civilian community.

The Vietnam War continues to send off cultural flack in Fayetteville and the rest of America. In the late 1990s, at a local conference on spouse abuse in the army, a civilian family services worker on Fort Bragg attacked *New York Times* and *Newsweek* articles that had identified higher rates of abuse in military families. They drew, he said, on the myth that the military attracts or produces more violent people. That fiction was created by the Vietnam syndrome, the common term that describes certain views of war and interventionism as an illness. "When individuals began to protest," he said, "the military was turned into a mean, evil force. Soldiers were spit on and called baby killers." Cultural myths like this "spitting image" have great power to shape what can be said and what cannot—that soldiers stopped the war.[85] This is true even in Fayetteville, where the war has most vividly walked the streets.

CHAPTER 5

Many Reserve Armies
The Faces of Military Dependency (1974–2000)

It is Fort Bragg payday and the people who own businesses at the megasized Cross Creek Mall and the owners of Lowes, Chili's, and McDonald's are feeling flush. This is one of the days that makes their Cumberland County stores wildly profitable. For on a dollar-per-square-foot basis, city commercial real estate exceeds the profits of virtually all others in the country.[1] Much of this is accounted for by the 35 to 40 percent of Cross Creek's customers who are soldiers and their families, most quite young and with both low rates of savings and the consumer needs associated with establishing a new household. And some profits come from sales to soldiers with a military-issued credit card, who might buy such things as office supplies or flowers or medallions for an awards banquet on the installation.

Not so favored is Bonnie Edmonson, a beautifully manicured and friendly clerk at a bath and beauty shop who serves the sudden spike of customers. As uniformed men and women, military wives pushing strollers, and teens on a rambunctious outing press into her store, she shared with me her resentments: her near-minimum wages, the military discounts she gives out but doesn't get herself, and her sense that her tax payments are disproportionately high because the military does not pay its way in local taxes. While she believes that holding on to her job depends on keeping soldiers at Fort Bragg, she feels that to do better, she has to leave town.

Many owners and workers join together, though, in talking about Fayetteville's economy in ways that obscure how spending for war preparation shapes their fortunes. First, many assume they are buffered from the slings and arrows of the business cycle that can afflict other American communities. That they live in a recession-proof city, a safe place to make a living because federal cash pours in ceaselessly. And people often use the image of open spigots or running streams to describe the money's abundance. Even those who live on very modest incomes and those who remember how recent deployments crippled some city businesses believe this. Many see these painful episodes as exceptions, not likely to be repeated. But throughout the city's past, it has been subject to the business cycle's even more unpredictable sibling, the war cycle. And some predict more volatility in the future.

Second, they assume, with the help of the nightly news, that there is a single economy. That when the stock market is up or consumer sales are growing or mortgage rates are down or, specifically in their city's case, when the military budget is increased, "the economy" is good. But at the same time, some people can see there are at least two economies in Fayetteville. One supports six thousand-square-foot homes with families who go to their beachfront property in the summer, and another, unpaved roads and the shells of abandoned businesses and four hundred-square-foot cabins perched on cinder-block corners. The vista in these places strongly suggests that the waters of military wealth are dammed somewhere upstream.

THE BOMBS AND BASES FOUNDATION
OF AMERICAN POLITICAL ECONOMY

Bombs and bases have been America's largest public works and public employment project over the last sixty years. Fifteen trillion dollars were spent from 1946 to 1991 on weapons, barracks, training, and warriors, with 1,250 military bases maintained in the United States and overseas by the end of the Cold War.[2] In 1992, fully 44 percent of all federal tax dollars collected went to military purposes.[3] Combining active duty and reserve soldiers and civilian employees alone, the military was the nation's second largest employer after the Post Office in the mid-1980s. Adding civilian employees of military contractors, it has been by far the largest.[4] By one estimate, 1 in 20 American jobs were directly or indirectly tied to military spending in the 1980s, and one-quarter of U.S. scientists and engineers were involved in military work.[5] While active-duty forces had been less than two-tenths of one

A tale of two houses

percent of the U.S. population in the 1920s, by the 1950s and 1960s they were ten times that proportion.[6] Adding military industry workers, there were almost seven million Americans in military-related jobs by 1987, two million of whom were added to this sector in the first five years of the Reagan administration.[7]

Setting the violent irony of a war economy aside, cultural common sense assumes that the military has contributed to America's wealth and development. It helps stabilize the business cycle, the logic says, and grows the economy. The military budget spreads paychecks and contracts for goods and services around the country. It creates work in jet engine and weapon construction and offers entry-level jobs, on-the-job training with transferable skills, and postservice educational opportunities to millions of young people. The army's massive R&D spending advances science and technological innovation. This progress spills over into the civilian economy and gives American industry a competitive edge over other nations. And, more indirectly, the money that soldiers spend and the profits military industry makes fire up other sectors of the economy.

Economic research, however, tells a very different tale. Military spending has produced *fewer* jobs per dollar than other kinds of government spending: A billion military procurement dollars create 26,000 jobs while the same amount in health care creates 37,000, and in education 48,000.[8] This happens because military industry hires scientific and engineering labor that it uses in relatively smaller numbers and pays more per capita; because many of those dollars go into the corporations' "gold-plating" of their weapons systems; and because these corporations reap a higher rate of profit than other businesses. Military spending has spurred innovation in the industries—such as aerospace, communications, and electronics—that provide the platforms for advanced weapons. But this focus has drained engineering talent, scientific research, and jobs from other fields, including auto and mass transit design, steel, machine tools, and consumer goods. Nations not investing heavily in militaries, such as Germany and Japan, put their research dollars and people into those other areas. Among other benefits, these countries reaped the American car market. While the pundits argued in the 1980s about whether Japanese *culture* made it more competitive, the U.S. government's military policy was driving industrial military specializations that grew the trade deficit and helped send jobs overseas.[9] While Americans driving

Nissans and Toyotas often provoked nationalist sentiment, the growth of the military-industrial complex helped put them there.

Military spending through the 1980s also contributed to the growing income gap between the comfortable and the poor in Fayetteville and across the United States. How did this happen? First, new high-tech weapons systems no longer used the mass production, assembly line manufacturing processes of the older war industries. The more highly skilled technical and engineering work they required employed fewer people. Moreover, inequality grows as unions weaken, and antiunion sentiment has been especially strong among military-industrial managers. And through the years, the Pentagon has actively encouraged companies to relocate to nonunion locations, sometimes billing taxpayers for the move.[10]

The formation of a powerful military has prevented the development of advanced social welfare policies, such as the universal heath care found in virtually all other modern industrial states. The sociologist Bristow Hardin has demonstrated in careful detail how this has happened. The military budget provided jobs and excellent benefits for many people during the post–World War II period.[11] The numbers of people whose social welfare needs have been cared for in this way are substantial: Tens of millions of veterans have gotten lifelong medical and educational benefits, and military production workers have had their company health plans and pensions funded through military contracts. This, Hardin argues, has led many of these groups to see no need for explicit expanded social welfare policies.

Moreover, the military budget's benefits are neither race, gender, or class neutral, with the white middle and upper classes and males being the system's disproportionate beneficiaries in intended and unintended ways. Despite relatively high levels of black employment as soldiers, military spending has funneled many more dollars into regions of the country where fewer African Americans live, such as the West Coast. The high-paying jobs designing and crafting advanced Cold War weaponry were in the engineering and technical fields whose workforces were overwhelmingly white and male. The women who did get jobs on military contracts found a gender pay gap even wider than in civilian work.[12] More well-known than this effect is the GI Bill's disproportionate assist to men, both in the late 1940s and now.

The result of this implicit labor policy of military spending is that

blacks of both sexes and women of all races have been left comparatively worse off and so more in need of welfare programs.[13] The idea
of unearned benefits is then associated with blacks and women in the
minds of many Americans. Hardin adds that "[n]ot only have the
benefits African-Americans received through this total system been
quite limited . . . but the direct and indirect effects of military spending have undercut the development of the political coalitions and
policies that are necessary to meaningfully improve African-Americans' life chances and socio-economic status."[14] Race and gender inequality is widened, then, in several ways: through the inequitable
distribution of the military budget's benefits, through the political
consequence of that distribution which has been to create racially divided sentiments on the necessity of a welfare state, and through the
solidification of the ideological association of full citizenship with
being male, white, and putatively economically independent.

While some military research benefits have trickled down to civilian uses, once identifiable civilian payoffs have been disappearing
over the postwar period. While R&D for early military aircraft was
used to develop civilian planes, this was no longer so with later military jet research. In *The Baroque Arsenal,* Mary Kaldor shows how
corporate designers began to favor embellishments, or "vertical development" on existing platforms. They built jets to endure blasts of
radiation or extremes of temperature and invented a $600 coffee-
maker that withstood gravitational pressure no commercial airline
would ever undergo. They made planes with so many elaborate features that, like the B-1 bomber, they cost a half billion dollars each, or
like the B-2, $2 billion.[15] Likewise, the adaptation of businesses
to military contracts—with their secrecy, guaranteed profits, and
indifference to cost containment—has often made them unable to
convert or adapt to the civilian arena where they emerge as noncom-
petitive and inefficient.[16] While corporate welfare has rarely needed
national security rationales, military industries have often been bailed
out of poor performance by government subsidy with the explanation that their production capacity had to be on line for a potential future need. An example is General Dynamics, whose insolvency in the
early 1960s earned it a contract for a jet, the F-111, that was inferior to
its competition.[17]

And there are the social costs not entered on standard balance sheets. The massive migrations funded by military spending have destabilized communities, moving thousands at a time as new military industry locations were chosen and contracts started or ended.[18] When weapons systems are completed, or large units moved around the country, cities can suddenly lose or gain whole classrooms of children. While American mobility is often celebrated and attributed to a continuing "restless, frontier" mentality, moves are often simply an uprooting to follow work rather than the heart. Environmentally, many military bases were to become solvent-soaked and ordinance-packed disaster sites that one administrator tried to cost-effectively rename "national sacrifice zones."[19] Finally, and most important, military spending has been an investment in deadly force. The damage done, often subsumed by the argument that it deters greater harm or even saves lives through war prevention, nonetheless can leave a burden of doubt and responsibility or a resignation to the notion of Armageddon.[20]

How have bombs and bases come to live in so many American communities and why are their burdens so little recognized?

It is, first, because much more is involved in military spending decisions than congressional pork barreling. Sociologist Sam Marullo has identified the "iron pentagon" of interests converging on ever larger budgets.[21] The five sides include military contractors (whose profits, as a percentage of return on equity, were double those of other corporations in the mid-1980s, and whose marketplace risks have been socialized),[22] the Department of Defense (which, like any bureaucracy with budgets and careers at stake, tends to push for expansion and also sends personnel in a revolving door into the military industries after discharge),[23] weapons laboratories (which have the same growth imperative), the Congress (whose members sometimes come from or work at the behest of corporate interests and are subsequently rewarded for bringing contracts to their home district's corporations and voters), and military industry labor. Each of these five interest groups put upward pressure on the military budget.

The sheer size of this public works program has restricted public input to and oversight of military spending policies. National security pretexts for secrecy have created the growing "black budgets" of various military agencies, estimated to have peaked at $39 billion in the late 1980s.[24] Even simple, local installation spending is difficult to uncover. Journalists at the Fayetteville paper, for example, had to submit an FOIA request to find out how the army spends tax money in the city on matters as nonstrategic as framing soldiers' photos for office walls.[25] And, finally, military boosters—with varied motives—have sold the notion of an army replete with social side benefits, in addition to its defense of the nation.

FAYETTEVILLE'S ECONOMIES IN THE LATE COLD WAR
Like every American place, Fayetteville's economies were remodeled by the changing military of the post–Vietnam War era. The reorganized All Volunteer Force became a more married army, as marriages were no longer officially discouraged and money and effort poured into recruiting and retaining not just the soldier but the whole family. Soldiers' wives came to Fayetteville looking for work, and their children headed out to city schools. It was an army more in search of off-post housing and shopping, an army commuting to work, and an army retiring into the city. It was an army with increasing numbers of dependents of all kinds, including the business community.

Fort Bragg's size dropped dramatically, along with the military's, at the end of the Vietnam War, but its doldrums were short-lived. Despite the many declarations that war making had undergone a revolution in form or doctrine with the "lessons learned," American war kept the same postmodern form it had had since 1945: nuclearism; low-intensity conflict and heavy reliance on providing weapons, training, and advisers to proxy foreign armies; a fervent if sometimes disavowed belief in technology; and military Keynesianism.[26] The standard historical narrative says that the Vietnam syndrome left the military budget a shadow of its former self in the 1970s and that only Reagan's new "morning in America" of national pride and conservatism in the 1980s revived it. While 1976 was, in fact, a low point for military spending, the budget was not much different than it had been in 1954 or 1960. It was still twice as high as in the late 1940s. Carter began the climb up the mountain of spending that was to accelerate with Reagan and peak in the late 1980s. For it was not ideology or a growing Soviet threat as much as the immense profits to be made by the military-industrial sector, interservice rivalries, and Pentagon and congressional officials' self-interest that drove the budget on. In any case, this leap in military spending flowed onto Fort Bragg and elsewhere as construction projects, weapons, and enhanced salaries.

The story of Fayetteville's economies through the 1970s and 1980s is often told as a boom town tale. The new army needed housing, and so huge tracks of farmland became subdivisions. Landowners and developers made small fortunes in residential and commercial building. But the noise and visibility of the city's boom hid other realities: that the rest of North Carolina's cities were growing faster and generating much higher average incomes and home values for their residents. Most had lower crime rates. And while many American downtowns atrophied with the suburbanization that road and car building prompted, the lure of land closer to the post accelerated the shriveling process in Fayetteville.

The new army would be sent on an increasing number of quick invasions and occupations abroad and a plethora of unacknowledged missions as well: There were fully sixty-six official engagements from 1975 to 1998.[27] Devoted to minimizing U.S. casualties and training other countries' soldiers, the military's used and new weaponry was on the international market in ever more voluminous quantities. It had become an army that Michael Sherry has compared with European armies before World War I. They, like the 1980s U.S. military, had "proclaimed the most dire danger, refrained from war except in peripheral areas, promoted sales of armaments abroad to shore up massive military industries at home, and conspicuously displayed weapons of dubious utility."[28]

Fayetteville and Fort Bragg were at the center of this action because Special Forces soldiers specialize in "undercover" work, and the Airborne is meant to be a first response, "Rapid Deployment Force." Sent to many small "trouble spots" (though that common label has suggested adolescent skin as much as a people in mortal danger), soldiers were coming and going from town even more frequently than before. Fayetteville's economies flew through even more turbulence, although with growing assurance that this post was here to stay or even grow.

As the city adapted to these changes in the army and its mission, it also dealt with the threat of economic capital's new hypermobility, something that rapidly accelerated in the mid-1970s.[29] In this so-called postmodern economy, where previous limits on the movement of factories and other productive resources overseas were lifted, Fayetteville and the rest of the American South were to lose their textile industry to the even lower wage, less unionized or regulated Third

World. Not coincidentally, but ironically, these factories moved to countries whose militaries—often supplied and trained by the United States—had successfully squashed the labor movement and other dissent and kept wages low.[30] Although several large factories —Purolater, Black & Decker, and DuPont among them—had been brought to the city in the late 1950s and early 1960s in an attempt to diversify its economic base, not all the fleeing textile jobs were replaced.[31] Fewer Fayettevillians got high-wage jobs in manufacturing compared with residents of other North Carolina cities. The new lush conditions of military spending, the sense of permanence about the post, and the growing antigravitational pull of Fayetteville's reputation as a place to live left the city in the backwaters of business recruitment.

THE COMPANY IN THE COMPANY TOWN

To understand Fayetteville's life with Fort Bragg in this period, begin by imagining a city dominated by one gigantic firm. While the majority of the county's population does *not* work for the firm, its influence is felt in many areas. The enterprise has distinctive hiring practices, employee pay, benefits, working conditions, and "product."[32] It is a (1) labor-intensive, (2) nonprofit, state monopoly industry that enjoys substantial tax exemptions. The firm also has a (3) very egalitarian pay structure, but is a (4) hierarchical, "total institution." And (5) its workers come and go at a rapid clip and remain (6) demographically distinct: Driving into the "plant" in the morning are a stream of young men of more colors than the average workplace has.

All of this matters to the company's town. And we can trace the effects of each of these six factors, beginning with its labor-intensive quality. The firm's huge labor force of about forty-five thousand employees makes the city highly dependent on its good will and vulnerable to its policy changes.[33] Most workers are brought in from outside by recruiters found in recruiting offices peppered around the country and by ubiquitous advertising. Unlike goods-producing military-industrial workers, the base workers provide services.

These many workers' salaries grow stores and retail jobs at the edge of the installation. In 1994, 31 percent of Cumberland County workers were in retail, compared with 13 to 22 percent in the state's five other large metropolitan counties.[34] Unfortunately, retail work

Mall retail worker

pays less than nearly any other of the nine major job categories economists use to type the workforce. The area's extra-large reserve labor
force includes military spouses, retirees (who can be as young as their
late thirties), and the local unemployed. Having these workers in the
wings means wages are depressed still further: Fayetteville's hourly retail wages are lower than North Carolina's other cities'.[35]

Store owners do well, on the other hand, especially with the All
Volunteer Force. It is more of a "shopping army" because its soldiers
are buying for whole families, and because—like all Americans—
they share the growing consumption ethos fed by ubiquitous advertising and more widely marketed credit.[36] (Even though the military
houses, clothes, and feeds them, many soldiers get into financial trouble with increasingly easy credit pushed on them by banks and retail-

ers and with the low rates of savings associated with youth in general.)[37] And because the army needs to recruit hundreds of thousands of young people, it has had to adjust its expectation of how spartan a soldier can be made to live. As one post official said, "You can't expect them to live out of a foot locker. They want stereo sets, barbells and a parking space."[38]

Jack Cox, a retired garrison commander at Fort Bragg, described this change in the lives of enlisted soldiers. Waving his hands in enthusiastic underlining, his heavy West Point ring now and again hit the glass table between us with dangerous gusto. Several interview hours later, his clearly very patient wife quietly checked on when she could serve dinner. But he had a whole life in the Army to tell, beginning with a movie he saw about West Point when he was seven in Illinois, through Korea, Germany, and Vietnam. After breaking his neck and back in a parachute jump in the mid-1970s, he went from combat unit command to running the installation support services as they adapted to the changing expectations of soldiers. In the "old days," he said, the soldier on payday bought

> two packs of razorblades, shaving cream, shaving lotion, shoe polish, and maybe a couple pairs of socks, for the month. What he had left, he either gambled away or drank away or some of them saved it. They didn't have any needs. There were no families to worry about. . . . Soldiers back in those days didn't wear civilian clothes. Soldiers had a wall locker and a foot locker, and their clothes were in it, and they had maybe one pair of blue jeans and one shirt, but that was exceptional. Nowadays, they have tons of [clothing].

Other aspects of his work as a kind of mayor of Fort Bragg began to differ from his predecessors' as well. The married army made its social life at home and in the community rather than in the many clubs and athletic facilities on the post where soldiers formerly went. In the past,

> A soldier would come to the service club for cookies, doughnuts, coffee, tea, fruit juice, everything was free. If he had no money, he could go to the service club at nighttime, he could watch TV or watch a movie inside. He could play pool, he could play ping-pong, and never spend a penny. . . . Now they go home to their families. They don't have to stay on Fort Bragg. They don't want to stay. They want to get off of Fort

Bragg. Downtown Fayetteville has three restaurants to every soldier, I do
believe. And soldiers get off post and go downtown. They have transportation. . . . They have two NCO clubs on Fort Bragg, and one officers'
club, and that's about all Fort Bragg can handle. Years ago, they had three
or four of each. Because everybody lived on Fort Bragg, everybody par-
tied on Fort Bragg.[39]

While restaurants grew in number and dependency on the post,
small businesspeople have been very unevenly reliant on or vulnerable to changes at Fort Bragg. While an estimated 30 percent of local
businesses make few sales to soldiers, the hotel/motel industry, residential real estate sales and rentals, furniture, and car sales suffer or
thrive with fluctuations in the post population, the wage level there,
and the number of deployments.[40] Also vulnerable are jewelers, people who sell movie tickets or menswear, and, if seldom mentioned,
sex industry entrepreneurs. Banks with many military mortgages are
hurt when deployments—even those as brief and limited as Gre-
nada—set the real estate market back for months at a time. Local government finances are also adversely affected.

The town's retail success was once more important to the local
economy than it became. While sales have gone up, hefty chunks of
the profits are now trucked out of town. When Cross Creek Mall first
opened in 1975, its stores were mostly locally owned. Today, 95 percent are regional or national chains.

Through these changes, however, the mall has continued to cater
to its military customers. Together with demographic and "psy-
chographic" information about the community, mall management
gives tenants advice on how they can be "military family oriented"
and keeps them aware of the latest deployments. It provides a military
discount (stores choose whether to participate) and lists those that do
at the mall information center. During the Gulf War, the mall owner
built a "military courtesy area" where family members could video-
tape messages for their soldiers.[41]

A second important aspect of the "company" that dominates this
town is that the military is a nonprofit firm whose activities have been
paid for almost entirely by tax dollars. Headquartered in Washington,
the firm is in theory accountable to those who hire it. In practice, national security laws and corporate influence have made congressional
and public oversight perfunctory or ineffectual. So has the militarized

Shopping soldier

cultural assumption that, as political scientist Cynthia Enloe points out, "no other public or private institution comes so close to being the sine qua non of a state."[42] For many this has come to mean that what military leaders want is by definition what the nation wants. While in this way its activities often go unquestioned, the army has more transparent and less exploitative hiring and promotions policies than many enterprises, although the soldier unions that have developed in the armies of many wealthier nations do not exist.[43]

A state monopoly with a heavy immovable investment in land, the Army offers the community the advantage that it is unlikely to flee overseas for economic advantage. It has, however, occasionally suggested it would have to go elsewhere in the country if the community tried to limit its flights, artillery practice, or growth. National politics and policy changes matter to the city, like coffee prices to a Central American monoculture. About twenty years ago, for example, a regulation was announced that starch could no longer be used on uniforms because new infrared scopes would pick up the soldier more easily. Those regulations were "like turning off a light switch" on the dry cleaning business, as one businessman said. Some traditionalists on post were unhappy about the new rules, however: "Everyone looked rumpled," he remembered. "They fought among themselves for a while and then the [traditional] military culture took over, they ignored the regulations, and let people go back to press in starch. The truth of the matter is the soldier's not usually in the scopes of the Russians." Dry cleaning businesses gradually recovered.[44]

Fayetteville, like all communities with military installations, loses revenue through the property tax exemption for federal land, through sales tax exemptions for goods sold at the Post Exchange (PX) and the commissary (equaling $12 million lost taxes in 1999), and through soldiers' ability to avoid state income tax by maintaining their home state residency. While the many soldiers who live off-post effectively pay property tax through their rent, the thousands of retirees who shop on post pay no sales tax. By one estimate, sixty-six major new factories would have to come to Fayetteville for the city to reach the tax base that similarly sized North Carolina cities have.[45]

Nonetheless and naturally, soldiers use public resources. While many military children go to Department of Defense schools on Fort Bragg, those who live off-post are educated in public schools, and all children go to the public high schools. Federal impact funds, available since 1950, are meant to offset this cost. But the amounts available have been irregular—sometimes adequate and sometimes grossly inadequate. In nearby Hoke County's case, they have been merely symbolic: $32,000 or about enough for one teacher's salary in a county that had almost 1,000 military children. With their poor tax base, military counties fall to the ranking depths on school spending. Of North Carolina's 119 school systems, Hoke County ranked 116th in local school spending, and Cumberland County ranked 113th in the mid-1990s.[46] The relatively poor schooling that results has ramifications further down the road: Fayetteville's students enroll at the flagship state university at nearly half the rate of Charlotte's and Raleigh's.[47]

The shopping siphoned off by the PX and other post businesses makes Cumberland County's per capita retail sales much lower than other urban counties'.[48] When Congress several years ago lifted restrictions on what items the PX could carry, allowing sales of higher-ticket items, local furniture and electronics stores complained loudly because sales tax exemption gave the PX an advantage in making sales to soldiers, dependents, and veterans. Local U.S. representatives, siding with business rather than the community as a whole, however, argued that soldiers should instead be exempted from sales tax at private businesses to level the playing field. Change is unlikely, however: PX profits totaling $2 billion nationwide have gone toward the military's "morale, welfare, and recreation programs" over the past ten years.[49]

The military's effects on the town come, thirdly, from its egalitarian pay. With an 8 to 1 ratio of the highest- to lowest-paid employee, the army pays more like progressive Ben & Jerry's than the many corporations in which the ratio of CEO to janitor salaries can be 1,000 to 1.[50] General Electric's head Jack Welch, for example, made over $93 million in 1999, while a minimum wage worker earned under $12,000.[51] The army's progressive pay scale makes the average income of military households (at $53,000 including benefits and allowances), 12 percent higher than the average of all U.S. households (at $47,000).[52] While soldiers' wages have not always been this high relatively speaking, they have made for a flatter class structure for Fayetteville, and a stronger middle class than the city would otherwise have. As one military retiree with a vivid sociological imagination said:

> The military population is the middle-class in this county. If you pull it out, we look like the surrounding counties. We've got a large, large poor population, heavily minority, a small middle-class, mostly white but starting to mix, and a very small upper class, one hundred families, and that's where the wealth is concentrated. But with the military mix in here, we look a lot more average in terms of what the rest of the United States looks like, but pull them out and its back to the old third world thing, you know, the big body of serfs, a few slave drivers, and then the boss.

Military policies have given the army comparatively high levels of racial employment, pay, and promotion equity. The military as a whole, at 33 percent "minority" (20 percent black) in 1998, was closely representative of young adult America, with the Army, at 40 percent minority (27 percent black), having more employees of color than the other services.[53] This is one reason the income gap between white and black county residents is much smaller than in other cities in North Carolina. Given the relatively strict class segregation in most U.S. neighborhoods, many black and white military families at near ranks can and do live in the same areas. As a result, Fayetteville is the country's fourth most integrated metropolitan area.[54] Although many in town say this shows the influence of the military's color-blind culture on people's willingness to live next to each other, the influence does not go much beyond the neighborhoods close to the installation where many soldiers in the same income brackets live. A clear dividing line remains between white and black neighborhoods elsewhere in the city, which developed very different housing stock given the past class backgrounds of Fayetteville's black and white civilians.

Fourth, despite its relative pay equality, the military is a hierarchical and authoritarian workplace. It is a *total institution,* the sociological term for an organization that makes claims on all aspects of a member's life rather than just, for example, the work or school hours or the time spent in a club activity. Living at their worksite, many soldiers are under more extensive surveillance by coworkers and supervisors. Soldiers, for example, once needed permission to leave post and had to wear their uniforms downtown. As these controls ended, others took their place, such as random and regular drug testing and nationally centralized personal record keeping. Even more important is the army's claim to "own" soldiers' bodies, no matter where they live, and to have a say about their sexuality and marital state. Soldiers, for example, once needed their first sergeant's permission to marry. Soldiers' rueful take on this was evident in the popular slogan, "If the army had wanted you to have a wife, it would have issued you one." Recruitment difficulties, especially in the wake of World War II and the Korean War, persuaded the military to relax this bachelor requirement and even to offer housing and dependent benefits as incentives for enlistment and reenlistment. The marriage rate among soldiers rose steeply.[55] The total control that the institution wields, combined with belief in male supremacy, has meant that female soldiers have far too commonly had to contend with sexual harassment and rape.

The military has long banned and punished homosexual behavior in its ranks.[56] When prohibition mutated to the "don't ask, don't tell" policy of the 1990s, the services were theoretically returning to their original focus on gay behavior rather than gay identity. The suggestion was that an area of privacy would be extended into sexual partner choices. But the soldier would have to collaborate and hide his sexual choices from others. And harassment and pursuit continued in any case. In Fayetteville, MPs would cruise the parking lots of gay bars, taking down license plate numbers (and they are now attuned to gay Web sites as well).[57] Soldiers, and especially women, have been routinely discharged for homosexuality.[58] The climate of hyperhostility has run from taunting to assault and murder. This is acknowledged in a Department of Defense inspector general's report prompted by the baseball bat bludgeoning death of a gay Fort Campbell soldier in 1999.[59] While this has not been exclusively a problem of the military, official policy makes gay men and women second-class citizens, and their treatment has been correspondingly shabby.

This has made gay life in Fayetteville especially difficult. According to one man, the "civilian homosexual" is also "deeper into the closet" because of the military. As a result, AIDS treatment and prevention services, which the gay population "drags" politicians into providing in most communities, are thin, he said. As one long-term resident woman who is a lesbian told me: "There is an enormous population out there [at Fort Bragg] that is very undercover, and when I have met them in social functions, their demeanor is very different. They are more oriented toward hoo-ha, the gung ho . . . more aggressive. I know this sounds weird, but probably in the past eight to ten years, they've been more covert than they used to be. . . . In [the past], there were more military people in the bars than there are now." She saw the change start in the mid-1980s, when "more bashings, more personal violence" began. While some gay people tried to collect data several years ago on the violence's frequency in town, they found it difficult given that much of it was not reported as such: "If you are gay and you are military and someone assaults you," she said, "you can't call it gay bashing, so you say that you were robbed, regardless of what they may have called you while they were beating you up. It will just be quietly taken."

Controlling the soldier, the army controls others. Because soldiers are employed twenty-four hours a day, their spouses are effectively on call to the military as well, and their work options narrow.

Volunteer labor was once an expected contribution of all wives, and a long struggle by ex-military wives was required to bring about the 1980s congressional action to apportion them some part of their husband's military benefits at divorce and to change the Defense Department's term for them from *military dependent* to *military family member*.[60] Company commanders can also require soldiers to exercise more control of their children with school discipline problems. An installation commander can also place any city business or location off-limits to soldiers. This sometimes protects soldiers from unscrupulous business practices. But it also protects the military from soldiers' behavior, as when head shops, gay bars, or neo-Nazi hangouts such as Adolph's Place were put off-limits. Very few businesses—and usually quite small ones—get added to the list each year. And the list was *not* used to push out of business the strip joints that so bedeviled downtown. A woman who had spent years working with development organizations to "clean up" Hay Street said, when I asked about the possibility of making the strip bars off-limits: "I'm embarrassed to say I have never thought about the question." With a burst of nervous laughter, she added "[If I had], I'd have *everyone* mad at me!"[61]

A fifth aspect of the "company" that communities with military bases must deal with is tremendous labor force turbulence. Despite the military's image as a place with strong labor control, turnover is high. Fifty percent of soldiers leave after one 4-year contract. Even more striking, one-third of recruits have left before their first term is over.[62] The official reasons given—misconduct, medical problems, drug use, pregnancy, or performance problems—no doubt disguise some problems, not of the soldier, but of mismatch between what recruitment ads and recruiters had often very aggressively sold the discharged soldiers and what they got. At least a few are mentally disturbed or addicted individuals, and some end up in Fayetteville's public and private safety net on discharge. One local homeless service agency estimated that veterans make up a quarter of the 2,000 clients it has served.

Fayetteville's chamber of commerce has tried to make this turnover an asset in appeals to relocating businesses. The city's Web site in the late 1990s featured a business-suited man with army boots parachuting in over the invitation: "Where else can you find an internationally trained labor force ready to jump into any situation? . . . 73%

of the approximately 8,000 people who annually move from the military to the civilian ranks have an associates degree or at least two years of college." Only a small proportion of this total stays in Fayetteville, however, and those who do remain sometimes simply compete for existing jobs when new business has not joined them in the city. Employers happily offer lower wages, knowing someone will always step forward to take them.[63]

Turnover became a more pressing issue for the Army when its work, while still often very straightforward and physical, got more complex. As Jack Cox described it, enlisted men at one time

> dug ditches. They piled rock on roads. They learned how to operate equipment and how to maintain equipment. They carried pipe. They were typical road guys. I mean, a lot of them, no education, got out of high school, didn't graduate, and joined the Army, and this was the existence that they had. . . . We used to call the soldier with a D-handle shovel a "light equipment operator." If he had a long-handled shovel, he was a "heavy equipment operator". . . . As we progressed more, the equipment got more exotic and sophisticated. [Back then] nobody knew what a computer was. Calculator? Slide rule? Soldiers had no idea what that was. A soldier knew one thing: he got paid once a month. . . . They didn't have all the exotic night vision equipment. We had an M-1 rifle and a compass. That was it.

With higher training costs for the new technologies, the army tried harder to create employee loyalty through the incentives of deferred benefits packages in education, health, and lifelong use of the PX and commissary. With some benefits location-based, the number of retirees in the city began to rise. But a cheaper route to prevent early separation has been "other than honorable" discharges. These can remain on a person's permanent record, like a bad credit report, and influence future employability.

Labor force turbulence also comes from mobility between bases (especially likely for Special Forces soldiers who have frequent short deployments overseas). This increased dramatically with the institution of the Rapid Deployment Force. On the other hand, the army does not move soldiers to new home bases as often as it used to. During the Vietnam War, soldiers and their families would often be at Fort Bragg for a year or less. The more typical three-year tour in the 1970s and 1980s became a four-year tour with the Gramm-Rudman-Hollings budget-balancing bill in 1985.[64]

This mobility has created a large transient reserve labor force of soldiers' spouses. Depressed wages and a high unemployment rate resulted (the female unemployment rate is near the highest in the state).[65] Employers perceive soldiers' spouses and teenaged children as ready to work for low wages given the soldiers' salary, transience, and their own lack of other options. Some, especially officers' wives, are overqualified for the jobs they do get in an economy centered on service and retail jobs. The woman who sells towels at one Fayetteville department store was formerly an assistant city planner in a major city, while the person behind the cosmetics counter there has an MBA. Soldiers' mobility also favors the efflorescence of pawnshops (there are 35 in town), used car dealerships (there are 102), rental housing and a highly transient school population (one-third are military dependents, and the other transients comes from poor families, who sometimes move to avoid rent or to take advantage of cheaper housing opportunities).

While many people think of the military as stabilizing local economic life, the numbers of soldiers and civilian workers at the installation over the postwar years has varied impressively, sometimes rising or falling by several thousands within a month.[66] So Fayetteville's county was the fastest-growing of all 100 in North Carolina in the 1960s, but then lost nearly 10,000 people between 1970 and 1973.[67] While the population at Bragg has been relatively stable since the end of the Vietnam War, even a small percentage change, with its large numbers, can shake the community. And while many people prefer an increase to a decrease, both directions create adjustment stress and pressures on public resources.

Finally, this is a company town with a still very male labor force. It results from hiring quotas, sexual harassment, and the continuing belief that war is a male job because men are stronger and more aggressive and women are life givers rather than takers. While women make up 14 percent of the Army, machismo norms mix with this man-heavy sex ratio to install a plethora of tattoo parlors, car lots, gun sales, and a flourishing sex industry.[68] Strip clubs and prostitution spill into the daily lives of people in the poorer neighborhoods in town. Sex workers are frequently the victims of crime, with prostitutes and exotic dancers murdered with regularity and seeming impunity (although a campaign was announced in 2000 to investigate seven unsolved killings of prostitutes).

War's gender business

And the army is young. Ninety percent of the active duty military today are under forty.[69] This relative youth places a special burden on public resources that go into support of children and young families, including schools, day care, divorce court, and policing. Family court days in the Cumberland County Courthouse are a bustling, crowded scene, with uniforms abounding in the waiting crowd.

TRAFFIC BETWEEN FORT AND FAYETTEVILLE AS FOREIGN TRADE

We can look at the post like this: as a special type of enterprise that has shaped and misshaped the city's economic life. Or, we can follow the advice of Carl Stolje, an ex–Special Forces soldier interested in the city's development, who imagines the situation as a problem of trade between two countries, Fort Bragg and Fayetteville. He and others in town worry about the amount of money that flows out of Fayetteville while, from the Army's perspective and that of some local elites, the flow seems clearly all the other way. Post officials have long worked at stressing their impact on the community. Said a former high-ranking officer:

> If you had $80 coming, you got four $20 bills. We wanted to make an impact on downtown, [show] how much Fort Bragg helped. Well, you got 14,000 soldiers going downtown in Fayetteville, armed with $20 bills on Friday night, the stores were wiped out on Saturday, because they had no change. Instead of making a favorable impact, we made a bad impact. Then we went to the $2 bills, which wasn't so bad, because the $2 bills permeated the system. [Then] we went to the silver dollar deal. A soldier with a whole pocket full of silver dollars, you know, it got a little bit cumbersome! So we tried these things to [show] the people downtown how much of an impact we had, but sometimes we went overboard.

As check and direct deposit replaced cash in pay envelopes, the Fort Bragg public affairs office began using a simpler method to advertise its importance to the city's well-being.[70] It calculated the base's economic impact each year and sent the figure to the newspaper, bottom-lining it at $4.1 billion dollars for 1999.[71]

An important question to ask, though, is, $4 billion compared to what? To the value to the city of high-tech corporations of the same total size as the post, paying taxes and employing local people at high wages? To the per capita impact of smaller businesses in the smaller city Fayetteville might have been if neither an installation nor substantial new industry had come to the area? To the city imagined as it is—that is, with all of the problems and strengths it has, some due to the post—and suddenly losing Fort Bragg paychecks and gaining Fort Bragg facilities and land? Or to a community without the population of retirees or dependents or war refugees brought by previous years of war mobilization?

The Army's multibillion-dollar figure, moreover, is all addition. It fails to subtract school costs; lost property tax; jobs lost when companies go elsewhere given the city's poor reputation; court, police, mental health, homeless shelter, and social service costs passed on to the community when individuals are discharged for behavior or health problems and they remain in town. Some of the $4 billion goes immediately to the outside companies who get construction or other contracts. Soldiers who pay no property tax because they live on post still use roads, parks, and police services and go downtown to bring suit or get a divorce. Fayetteville generates much of the state gas tax because of the amount of driving young soldiers do, but does not get its share returned to it to deal with the problems that it creates of pollution, road wear, and accidents.

Nowhere in sight are the less-quantifiable elements of the trade imbalance between Fayetteville and the fort: anxiety about violence and about living close to the war cycle, noise pollution, lowered local wage rates given the reserve army of unemployed the military brings with it, and the social and emotional costs of constantly losing or never getting to know one's neighbors. Also not counted, though, in a dollar-centric culture, are the cultural diversity brought by soldiers and soldiers' foreign wives and the vigorous participation and knowledge of bureaucracy that military retirees bring to the government and volunteer work they sometimes do in the city.

Fayetteville's physical environment is another item of "foreign" trade. The first Earth Day in 1970 drew initial attention to Fort Bragg's environmental effects. Focus was on smoke from its coal furnaces and the reservation's 56,000 privately owned cars; 11,600 jeeps, trucks, and other military vehicles; and 900 administrative cars.[72] And when the installation began massive burning of wooden World War II barracks in a modernization campaign, a newly formed Sierra

The unquiet dead: Civil servants Robert Judkins and Johnny Blount,
on the rounds of straightening gravestones disturbed by artillery

Club chapter took on the issue. "You could stand here on the main
street in Fayetteville and look that way to see the sky was black," said
Denny Shaffer, a dry cleaner and city councilman who was a member
of the original group, and who went on to become the national president of the Sierra Club. "We thought that wasn't a good idea. . . .
It became ridiculous because [Fort Bragg] decided they could do
this because they were training firemen . . . and then they ran out of
firemen [on post] to train so they sent the word out all around to the
volunteer fire departments and anyone who had firemen and they
were to subsidize them to come there and to train and so you can see
how this kind of thing would get publicity."[73]

The military also included those who peopled the environmental movement. Lt. Bingham, a medical officer from a politically active New England family, started the Fayetteville Sierra Club group, and soldiers made up about a third of the initial membership. The chapter disappeared by the late 1980s, however. According to one former member, this was due in part to the lack of interest in environmentalism or progressive political participation by the current active duty and retired soldiers. "It doesn't seem to me," she said, "that there's as much participation by military people in the community as there used to be . . . and the average retired military person is not an environmentalist. He's more interested in the right to bear arms and in low taxes." But she sees the problem of declining participation as a civilian problem as well: "I think people are struggling now to see whether they can't keep the library open, whether your kids are safe in school. . . . These are the kinds of issues that we're talking about here." Larger and seemingly less immediate issues take a back seat.

Despite the early environmental activism, no one in town talked—then or at any time in the next thirty long years—about the toxic chemicals, oil, and gas leaking from the post into the area's groundwater or draining into the city's Cape Fear River or the pollution created by the hundreds of thousands of yearly takeoffs and landings at the military airfields. Few even talked about the admitted problem of Fort Bragg sewage being inadequately treated before discharge into area waters. The reasons for this avoidance include lack of accessible and understandable information about pollution on the post, the illusion that toxics do not migrate outside the fort's boundaries, and the cultural taboo on questioning military procedures. As one person said, "It's not terribly socially acceptable [to say anything negative] about the military here. It's a major employer. You don't question what the military's doing quite like you might question what the guys at the gas station are doing."

Environmental problems generated in the city itself receive little focus either, however, beyond the emergency of E. coli in the backyards of the thousands of homes with overloaded septic systems. There is no curbside recycling, and public transportation is poor. Accounting for this is the city's weak tax base and atrophied public sphere—that is, the exceptionally low voting rates and the fatalistic sense that the public agenda is always already set by the military and the local elite.

If all this were not so, attention might be paid to the problems that plague military and other federal facilities across the country. The Pentagon itself has counted hazardous waste problems, some of catastrophic proportions, at twenty thousand sites now or once owned by the Defense Department. They are found at virtually every military base and in every state. In her comprehensive study of the military's environmental legacy, Seth Shulman describes the damage, from Jefferson Proving Ground in Indiana, whose one hundred square miles are an uninhabitable minefield of over a million unexploded bombs and artillery shells, to the Lakehurst Naval Air Station in New Jersey, where millions of gallons of aviation fuel and a toxic soup of other chemicals have been dumped into the soil and have entered the aquifer below that feeds a large portion of the southern part of that state. The Navy has accentuated the positive, however, giving awards for the base's cleanup efforts—an example, Shulman notes, of a pattern of "self-congratulation amidst unfolding environmental tragedy."[74] The problem runs across all federal agencies, even the EPA. The military is the prime offender, however, because of the immense scale of its use of fossil fuels and toxic and nuclear material, its intentional destruction of environments through bombing in training, and because national security rhetoric has often freed it from public oversight and accountability.[75]

The endangered red cockaded woodpecker is another story. The woodpecker has nested extensively on Fort Bragg, in part because its preferred long-leaf pine habitat has been lost almost everywhere but on federal land. The bird also prefers to nest in areas with clear understory, something the Army provides with its regular burn offs of underbrush to facilitate training maneuvers and prevent larger fires. Training activities were contributing to a decline in their numbers, however, leading the Fish and Wildlife Service to issue a judgment against the Army to bring it into compliance with the Endangered Species Act in 1980. The Army then began an elaborate program to prevent disruption of the birds' nests, protections that took many acres out of training use and revived the birds' declining population. Woodpecker politics heated up in 1995, however, when Senator Jesse Helms called for exemption of Fort Bragg from the Endangered Species Act, portraying the woodpecker as a threat to national security. While he was not entirely successful, many limits were removed and an eighteen-year outside monitoring effort was closed down.[76]

Some of Fort Bragg's environmental damage is exported overseas,

National security issue: Endangered species protection zone on Fort Bragg

and not just in wartime. One Fayetteville veteran who had been on Central American training exercises told of watching U.S. pilots drop a five-hundred-gallon "blivet," or giant fuel bladder, in a Honduran valley to test its durability. It immediately ruptured. They tried again the next day, adjusting the number of cargo parachutes used and the amount of fuel carried. Environmental laws, of course, might prevent such tests in the United States. In this soldier's eyes, it was just one of many examples of a dehumanizing attitude taken toward other people and a disregard of their homes. Evidence is found in dozens of countries, from South Korea, where raw sewage runs from U.S. bases into local water, to the Philippines, where residents on former Clark Air Force Base land drink water with high levels of mercury, gasoline, and bacteria resulting from the base's former operations.[77]

Everyone in Fayetteville has experienced the noise and concussion that emanates from the city's two installations—jets that thunder over neighborhoods and artillery shock waves that rattle wall hangings across the city. One young man who grew up under the flight path to Pope Air Force Base went on to join the military with great enthusiasm, but he told the story with a critical eye.

> We're in a primary danger zone now. . . . The neighborhood tried to raise hell about it, but I mean, what are you going to do? The flightline is that way, right? . . . We're looking at a distance of 300 meters [the width of the official danger zone]. I really don't think being 300 meters away from an Airborne crash is going [to make any difference in your safety]. . . . And so the airplanes, they fly anywhere in here. The fact of the matter is, when you have a C-5 costs, like, some $70 million, or $70 billion, some crazy amount of money, if the wind is blowing this way, they're going to fly their airplane wherever the heck they feel like they need to fly it to land it, you know?

At one point, F-16 pilots began making especially low landings over their house, their approaches, he said, "low enough that you could see the pilot's helmet up in the cockpit and stuff. They would come in *low.*" Although his parents' and neighbors' subsequent complaints and the contentious public meetings may have had some effect, he said, "I'm sure it was superficial. Because the Army or the Air Force is concerned about public affairs, but not to the extent in which it affects them, you know what I mean? If they can make people happy without hindering themselves, then they will, but they're not going to go out of their way." On the other hand, he noted, "Pope Air Force Base has been there for decades. And they knew when they bought the house that that base has been there forever."

Realtors, however, regularly call the post to find out when artillery practice will be in order to show nearby homes to their "best advantage." This young man and his neighbors also know that another option for the planned airfield extension is to build off the opposite end, which runs onto Fort Bragg property rather than into his neighborhood. That other end includes Army rifle ranges.

> Fort Bragg has, like, 350, I mean a *huge* amount of rifle ranges. And I've driven back there—this Manchester Road runs back there—a million times, and there's nobody ever using it. Ever. I've been there in the morn-

ing, in the afternoon, on the weekends, on weekdays. Nobody ever uses those things, you know? But the[re's] competition between the Army and the Air Force—the Army's not going to give up anything if they don't have to. They're not giving up anything. So it's a lot easier for the Air Force to simply pay off whoever owns this land and simply be done with it, because they can give a lot of money to whoever owns that, you know what I mean?

The military has hired consultants to interpret these problems for the public. A late 1980s impact study had the charge, according to one of its authors, of convincing local communities that unless they enforced "compatible land use" nearby, the bases would have to cut their activities at some cost to the local area.[78] Developers, of course, were dead set against any use restrictions on their properties. At the least, they wanted the military to pay for their losses should they leave land adjacent to the airfields undeveloped, something the military would not do.

Another hired consultant constructed a computer model of "Noise and Accident Potential Zones," which played down their size. In addition, as Carl Stolje argued,

> The Air Force and the Army have been playing games with their descriptions of where helicopters are flying. Sometime ago when they were talking about noise abatement, the newspaper printed large maps of the flight routes. Well, it turns out these are the flight routes out to the training area. There are no flight routes back. . . . The Air Force flat out lied. They suggested in the environmental impact statement that the noise levels would be fine with aircraft flying at 4,000 feet without their afterburners on. Well, they spent about three years flying right over the housing areas, afterburners on at 1,500 feet.

While plane crashes and misdirected artillery are always a possibility, most such accidents have occurred on the installation itself.[79] And although there have been uproars over the years about occasional grenades that children find in the woods, residents mostly push to the background the physical risks of living near a military base. Take the huge underground ammunition storage area that sits at the boundary of the post and city. In the mid-1990s, the army was contracting with a farmer to graze his cows on the grassy area above. When I asked about the possibility of a catastrophic accident there, one city planner reassured me the storage facility did not threaten nearby homes. If it ever explodes, he said, "It's designed to blow straight up."

What bargaining power the local community has vis-à-vis the military in these foreign exchanges is difficult to know. While city and county planners say they "keep the professional planners on the base informed" about their activities, information flow from the post to the city is more informal, or received, via Public Affairs, in the newspaper. As one planner told me, likening the army to a private rather than public enterprise: "Like any other company coming into the city, they [the military] like to make their own announcements" about such things as new construction plans. And I have found no civilian parallel to the Fort Bragg planning document that suggests the installation "continues to monitor planning board meetings in the civilian communities and explain more compatible development patterns adaptive to the mission of Fort Bragg."[80]

DUAL ECONOMIES

Rather than asking about the military in relation to Fayetteville or America as a whole, however, we can ask who has benefited from the military's federal tax dollars and who has not. For there are several Fayettevilles and several Americas. One reaps wealth from soldiers' salaries, and another only touches the money briefly as it works minimum wage retail jobs. Yet another is outside the whole system of exchange, treading water in a miserable pond of poverty, high infant mortality, and anesthetizing drug use. The gap between the first two Fayettevilles increased in the 1980s, as it did across the country.

One of Fayetteville's great fortunes was accumulated by J. P. Riddle in the home and commercial construction business. The minor league baseball stadium he donated to the city bears his name, and whole swathes of housing are his handiwork. Fort Bragg, he was reported to have said in the paper, is "your gold mine. When everything is good out there, the county is blooming. It's like a faucet wide open. Turn it off, and you couldn't sell nothing."[81] Many of the seven thousand houses he built were in the less-regulated part of the county and many were adjacent to Fort Bragg. But his control of the local military and civilian market depended in good measure on his campaign contributions: he claimed to have spent $100,000 in 1993 alone. Helpfully, his brother, Sheryl, was county commissioner from 1988 to 1992.[82] His political friends located highways and road-widening projects in his favor, rezoned areas for maximum resale profits, and awarded favorable property tax assessments.

This political power allowed him to turn some farmland between the post and the city into a cash machine of commercial property, beginning especially in the 1970s. It was then that people at Sears national headquarters made plans to move their downtown Fayetteville store into the suburbs, following a nationwide pattern. They had begun negotiations with another mall developer with property on the main road between the post and city. Along with suitable land a bit further west, however, J. P. Riddle had the ear of the state highway commission chair, Lauch Faircloth. In a three-way phone call with Mr. Riddle, Commissioner Faircloth assured the man from the Sears Tower that a new highway—to be called the All-American—would skim along the side of Mr. Riddle's proposed mall, with exit ramps to it from both Fort Bragg and the city.

Although knowing nothing of this phone call, the garrison commander around that time, Jack Cox, remembered resistance to the proposed highway on the installation. "They [the state highway commission] brought it to us . . . [but] nobody could conceive, initially, that we needed that road. 'What do you mean, put a four-lane highway onto Fort Bragg? You'll destroy Fort Bragg.' . . . People on Fort Bragg didn't want it. 'What do you want, to tear up our Fort Bragg? That's terrible! It'll look like over there, it'll look like Bragg Boulevard.' "[83] While it might appear from the outside, then, as if the military requested and got a highway, in fact, some entrepreneurs got the road in a bid to raise their land's value and give base salaries a quicker route to their stores (and Lauch Faircloth moved far up the political ladder with such largesse, becoming a U.S. senator a few years later). Most Fayettevillians tell the story of the mall's coming as inevitable, almost beyond human control. Economic geography, in these accountings, just naturally happens: The highway line is dictated by the need to connect population centers, its precise location simply following the lay of the land. The mall follows the highway, and Sears simply joined the crowd, jumping the downtown ship. J. P. Riddle presciently buys land in the best spots to draw customers.[84]

If the highway and mall had been located further to the east (and much base housing and offices are as close to the poor as the wealthy side of town), they might have helped diminish the sharp and racialized wealth and land-value gap between the eastern and western halves of town. But wealth followed wealth rather than population centers or human needs. On the other hand, those businesses that continued to operate in the eastern part of the city were more often locally owned firms, whose profits stayed in the city. Those dollars, nonetheless, often eventually migrate to the mall, in the absence of other shopping choices.

But there is a *third* Fayetteville. It is a community of relative wage equality, socialized health care, unsegregated public housing, excellent day care facilities, and cornucopic athletic and recreational facilities. It is Fort Bragg, whose community of mutual care any socialist nation might envy.[85] When these two stories are put together—the two cities the military economy helps produce and the socialized army—Fayetteville's overall numbers show relatively low income inequality compared to other North Carolina cities, especially between the races.[86]

But the third Fayetteville does not prevent the area from having the highest child poverty of any urban center of the state (in 1995), with the county near the top for infant mortality and black families in poverty[87] and far fewer doctors per person than other urban areas.[88] There is also nothing more visually striking about the Fayetteville area than its wealth of poor housing. The 1950s and 1960s established it as a state leader in trailer parks, substandard housing (including houses with seven-foot ceilings and unsecured block footings), urbanized neighborhoods without water and sewer hookups, and relatively poor road connections to other cities. Today, many of these homes with septic systems have reached saturation. Without street drains, pooling rainwater—swirling together with human waste—attends every storm, and septic system runoff reaches wells and other water supplies.[89] To explain the poor housing and public facilities, people often point to the slim salaries of the lowest-ranking soldiers, saying developers build to suit their income levels. But the poverty rate is much lower among soldiers than civilians.[90] What instead accounts for it is corruption and weak public regulation. Exacerbating the problem is the fact that many of the citizens affected by these problems are soldiers who bought property in the county in order to live close to the post, and whose transience and/or nonlocal voting make them easy to ignore when public priorities are set.

Also key was Fayetteville's 1959 exemption from a bill allowing cities to annex their suburbs.[91] Local legislators who pushed for the exception were responding to the desires of county developers who found it cheaper to put in septic systems and wells than pay for city hookups. And, more publicly, they acted at the behest of the county's volunteer fire departments who wanted to keep their autonomy and taxing authority. And they clearly reflected the sentiments of most county people, who anticipated higher taxes with city incorporation. Many agreed with the property rights rationale of a legislator who claimed involuntary annexation would make of the area "another Cuba." The state legislature went along with those rural legislators because, as one city official with a long history in town said, Fayetteville "had been a farmers' town. And just by past history and makeup, the legislature had been more powerful in the county. Fayetteville was generally disregarded as an urban community."[92]

So it was that city authority and services stopped far short of the boundary with Fort Bragg, leaving the large area of land that was to be built up over the next decades in the hands of a minimalist county government. And so it was, too, that much of the booming real estate development of the 1950s and 1960s occurred with the merest hint of infrastructure, and often on land that could not support it. A former Fayetteville mayor said people look at the housing and services problems of the city today and

> They blame it on the governments who allowed the real estate people to develop property without having to develop the utilities necessary to maintain them. And of course, the real estate, obviously strong, it's hard to insist that they put water, sewage and sidewalks in their developments. They said it raises the price of the house. Fayetteville has less sidewalks than any other city in the state of its size, which has always been a thorn in my side. . . . The city tried to do more but the county backed off quicker than the city did. Both of them are sissies.

Real estate developers had other methods of avoiding regulation. A pleasant-faced engineer with a decaffeinated style who worked for the city during this time described how the builders passed the required "percolation test," even in areas with poorly draining soil.

> Dig a little hole, about a six-inch diameter hole and pour water in it and if the water went away in a half a day then you got your septic tank permit. If it didn't go away, you couldn't get it. But you can solve that prob-

Freedom

lem by a quarter of a stick of dynamite and loosen up the soil, smooth the soil back over, dig the same hole and the water would go away. But then that doesn't mean it would be a successful septic tank operation for years, but that was the way things happened. . . . I haven't been involved in it first hand, but I'm told that there's whole subdivisions where the developers loosen up the soil with dynamite so they could [pass]. [So when they say Fayetteville had been booming in the sixties that's what they meant?] I suppose.

Only in the 1990s did the city pass regulations on the size and number of signs a building's owner could put up. What people see as a result is a town "visually littered," as one woman put it. But a veteran and member of the local Libertarian Party chapter brightened when I asked him about the tangle of signs and rough-and-tumble building styles of Fayetteville: "It looks," he said, "like freedom to me."

Fort Bragg itself, of course, has highly regulated land use, its ordered vistas often described by the military as a sign of its discipline and of the necessity that "soldiers give up some liberty so that civilians may have theirs." But for some in the city, the mess in town signals instead that off-duty soldiers are a blight, likely to create ugliness because that is what their freedom or irresponsibility looks like. Or they may assume that camp followers, not soldiers, are a less conscientious or clean lot. But the military is connected to these problems in less obvious ways than these.

Fayetteville's explosive growth during Fort Bragg's World War II expansion imported urban problems to an area with a rural and small town ethos. Because soldiers have extremely low local voting rates, politicians did not give due attention to the interests of the urbanized parts of the county, where many of them have lived. Voting rates have been low because many soldiers did not change their official residences when posted to Fort Bragg, particularly if their home states had no income tax, which North Carolina does. Just 25 percent of eligible voters were registered in 1970, with the percentage increasing over the next decades as the proportion of county residents who are active-duty soldiers in town declined. While it reached 49 percent in 1994, the other five large metro counties run between 70 and 74 percent.[93] At both the state and local levels, residents' concerns can be treated lightly and democracy becomes a slighter thing.

The lack of public investment and regulation and the city's poverty began to hurt the recruitment of higher-paying and revenue-generating manufacturing jobs. As the county's industrial recruiter tries to lure potential businesses to town, he rues how many places he has to avoid while giving them the area tour: "If I could bring every prospect to Cross Creek Mall in a helicopter," he said, "I would be fine."[94] One of the sights he would surely like to avoid is the Carolina Square shopping center near the base. On a shared theme of body parts for sale, there is Alpha Plasma, alongside strip joints such as Foxy Lady, Mickey's Lounge, or Boogies. While a razor wire–topped fence separates the square and the poor trailer neighborhood behind it, it is not clear who is being protected from whom.

While Fayetteville's crime rate has sometimes been among the highest in the state, it has been variable over the years, the city's reputation for criminality often more severe than the reality.[95] People debate how to account for the high rate, presumed or otherwise, with great intensity because there are many reputations at stake. While for some, it is obvious that the city's poor are its criminals, others blame Fort Bragg, saying it ejects into the community its recruits who are criminal or drug and alcohol addicted or that it attracts or produces violent men. Said one businessman, imagining his own offspring getting a military education: "If my son was out there everyday being trained how to decapitate the Vietnamese and other bad guys and then he came home to his wife and crying baby son, who knows what could happen." And residents can point to the many infamous cases of recent years: a soldier who killed four people in a local Italian restaurant (hurling invective against homosexuals as he rampaged), neo-Nazi soldiers who murdered two randomly chosen black people downtown, an officer who shot up his troops during morning exercises, the so-called Ninja murders in which two Fort Bragg soldiers dressed in black martial arts costumes stabbed a local couple to death, and a soldier who was on trial for the brutal battering of his partner's young child.

For some people, this military connection is still a question of wealth and poverty, of some "low-class" types who enlist for a job. Soldiers and ex-soldiers facilitate or conduct drug smuggling and dealing, they say, which then brings on the violence; there have been several high-profile cases through the years to corroborate this view. More widespread, though, are the drug dealers and prostitutes who invade certain neighborhoods every night, brought there by a wealth of military and other customers.[96]

One woman from a neighborhood that became a drug and prostitution center around the time downtown was being cleaned up in the late 1980s remembered this as only a child might. She and her playmates would sometimes shout out warnings to customers driving up to transvestites, assuming they were being fooled. And her bus driver would take kids home to the "better neighborhood" first, even though those homes were farther from school. She recalled days of too little food and of questioning why her mother had to work the long hours that she did. Calling home each day from the job, her mother insisted the children remain inside after school. "We spent ten years in the house," she said, summing up her childhood. "We never left. I was really proud of my brother for what he did, watching over me," and resisting the easy money to be made just outside their door in the drug trade. She eventually left the city and went to college.

But, in fact, active-duty soldiers relatively rarely commit crimes in Fayetteville in comparison with civilians. The military crime rate is low for several reasons. As a group, soldiers have a zero percent unemployment rate, and the good pay and benefits reduce the motive for property crime. Moreover, recruiters screen out many of the addicted and the mentally ill. Moreover, as one man told me, "The army does not want to recruit killers, it wants to train them." Closer surveillance of soldiers' lives also serves as a deterrent.[97] When soldiers wear their uniforms, they are very visible off-base, as one officer noted: "It's good for order and discipline . . . when you're in uniform, and you're in God's plain view, you're less apt to do something stupid than if you're in a pair of cut-off old blue jeans and a holey shirt and they don't know who you are. And, of course, with the Airborne, you've got no hair, it's quickly recognized who you are."

A few crimes, though, appear to occur more often in the military. Shaken baby syndrome occurs much more frequently in military than in civilian families.[98] Rape is committed more by soldiers than comparable civilians during wartime and at higher-than-expected rates (given the lower overall crime rate among soldiers) in peacetime.[99] And domestic violence rates are higher among soldiers and civilian men with military experience.[100] The domestic shelter movement developed early in Fayetteville in comparison with the rest of the state, and it currently has one of the busiest and most well supported programs in North Carolina. The military itself has instituted a variety of programs to curb domestic violence within its ranks, but public relations considerations and the patriarchal concern to maintain male privacy and privilege has meant that cases not reported to the civilian police often get no public oversight or punishment.

Though there is no getting around Fayetteville's high crime rate, residents must contend with an even more inflated reputation for criminality than their city merits. This stems from the very visible "deviance" of Hay Street during the Vietnam War, but also clearly from the class and race prejudice that Fayetteville—blacker and poorer than other areas of the state—would be victim to, no matter *what* its crime rate. And the crimes that it does throw out for examination, including military crimes, can become cannon fodder for television and print journalism's voracious and increasing appetite for sensational violence. While crime rates have been going down nationally—crime rates correlate closely with the decline in unemployment—media murder coverage went up 700 percent, according to one survey of local television's practices in the early 1990s.[101] While local boosters have worked hard to prevent these images from frightening away investors, fear still runs with fair freedom for those who already live in Fayetteville.

HOST, HOSTAGE, PARTNER:
INTERPRETING MILITARY DEPENDENCY
Fayetteville's people understand their economic dependence on the military in many different ways. Some feel savvy and fortunate to be able to profit from this well-populated niche of young customers. Some are angry about the unfair advantage the military has over their businesses, including both the military's ability to take customers at the PX, the corruption they see in the use of military credit cards, and the off-limits threat. Others feel some guilt about running away with the money of naïve young soldiers. And there are people who were in the army themselves and are either grateful for or resentful of what they did or did not get from their military years. Regardless of their feelings about the city, its soldiers, and its military economy, however, most are certain the town would collapse were the base to leave. Despite the fact that many American cities that lost military bases in Base Realignment and Closure (BRAC) closings have successfully remade their towns, the very thought inspires panic. "This would be a ghost town without the post." "We'd look like Sanford," they say, pointing dismissively to a smaller town up the road. But often they are imagining the installation packing its bags and abandoning the house it built: "There are just not enough natives in Fayetteville to support all those businesses and related activities," said one man.[102]

Living in Fayetteville requires people to carry the heavy cultural baggage that comes with being a dependent—literally or figuratively—of the military. By cultural definition, a *dependent* is someone not fully mature or capable. In a society that values independence and individualism, a dependent has an ambiguous status, perhaps even less than full cultural citizenship. Dependency has two faces, though. The dependent is both supported and disempowered. While abused military wives, for example, have a range of services offered to them, many have been afraid to report the violence they suffer. This is not only because of their husbands' likely retaliation, but because they could lose health care coverage and other benefits if their husbands are found guilty of assault and ejected from the army.

When people earn money in town, whether they are construction workers putting up a new fast-food restaurant or clerks selling Adidas running shoes to soldiers, their wages and profits can be interpreted in several ways. First, as "military dollars," belonging to that institution and coming into what should be grateful civilian hands. Or they can be parsed as taxpayer money, belonging to hardworking citizens around the country and coming, perhaps somewhat illegitimately, into the hands of people close to the trough. Or they can be seen as the money of hardworking Fayetteville entrepreneurs who make the cash on their own from their labor of repairing cars, preparing meals, and selling insurance to soldiers. The wages and profits are even viewed by some as a kind of glossy criminal money, because they come too easily to Fayetteville citizens from the hands of (relative) babes, eighteen-year-olds easily parted from their first paychecks.

For some who have profited from the base's economy, the attitude is simple: "What," as one man who made much money in the dry cleaning and real estate businesses said, "could possibly be wrong? There are nothing but advantages." But others within the elite have a more ambivalent take, some asking for their identities to be kept anonymous for fear of alienating their military customers. But they have already spent much time thinking about the larger economic picture and, depending on their business, feel more or less vulnerable to the military's decisions.

This was the view of Bob Ray, who had been in insurance for many years. A handsome, garrulous, and social man, he had a long list of local friends and characters he mentioned with appreciation or admiration. His family's deep roots in Fayetteville give him a sense of belonging that many do not have: "I am," he told me without meaning to say things quite this way, "a two-hundred-year resident of this town." But he steered me away from questions about his family history and was much more interested in the city's present and adroit in thinking about it sociologically. He saw evidence of the city's two economies in his own office. "My secretary," he felt bad to note, "makes as much per week as I take out of the cash machine for week-end out-of-pocket buys." Even with his membership in it, he was cynical about the city's elite and their exploitation of others. He saw himself as taking the cash he made from soldiers during the week and fleeing on the weekends, as do many wealthy people, to the North Carolina beach or the Blue Ridge Mountains. As we sat talking on the lushly pillowed furniture of their sunporch, his wife complained that the city is treated as a second-class citizen in the state. The legislature never sends it its fair share of resources, and even department and clothing store chains, she was certain, send the rejects from their Charlotte and Raleigh branches to be sold in Fayetteville's stores.

Bob Ray warned me not to believe all the business positives I would hear people rave about: The installation's impact, he believes, is massive and negative overall for the city's quality of life. The army, he said, is mainly a "blue collar type work force, not counting the upper level managers like the captains and generals." This produces plenty of Wendy's restaurants, Walmarts, and Chinese take-out joints, but not the demand for higher-priced goods and services. On the other hand, the volunteer army has greatly improved "the quality" of the soldiers, he said, and this has made even the lowest-grade enlisted person demand better housing and refuse to accept trailer living. As a businessman, he felt vulnerable on account of Fort Bragg: When deployed soldiers' families leave town to return to their mothers, their bills not always paid, he said, post officials stand behind the families, and he and others feel pressure to simply deal with it. He also felt hostage to decisions made in Washington and on post. And like many—from public officials to citizens looking for jobs that pay better than retail work—he argued that the city's economy should be more diversified, ideally into high-technology industries. He bemoaned the lax industrial recruiting that followed a misguided belief in the base's permanence. But he repeatedly described the business community as "raping" or taking economic advantage of the soldiers. With this language, he posed the fort as a helpless female, and the locals as criminal. While few spoke that strongly, many people sense the same degree of power some in the local economy have to make money without trying very hard and to take advantage of army consumers.

A related analysis of Fayetteville's economy came from the less-ambivalent perspective of a former soldier, a black veteran. Soldiers spend their paychecks at city businesses or deposit them with the local bank, and then the bankers "take it and turn 15, 18 percent on it and you come back and you get your 3 percent." The soldiers are both exploited, he was saying, and the ultimate source of all city buildings and assets. He suggested I go look at the local hospital: "Each room is named after some great person in Fayetteville, you see, they donated so much money. But all of this money, mind you, comes from Fort Bragg. They had no other source. They didn't get it raising tobacco. They didn't get it from cotton. It come from Fort Bragg."

Another soldier, also once an officer, might have been speaking of Fayetteville when he described what he has seen around American bases overseas. Wherever the Army set up a camp, he said, things start to grow around it, although much of that growth is "fueled by the exhaust from our big engine" of money and privilege and relies on the "subculture of selling your [women] and scrounging for leftovers [tossed out by the base]. We congratulate ourselves on contributing to the local economy, but," he caustically noted, "that is like living on a septic system and being proud of how green your grass is."

The people who have the strongest negative understandings of what Fayetteville's dependence on the military has wrought are not there. They come and eventually flee for what they hope will be greener pastures, and their views are missing when surveys are taken or anthropologists visit. There are more than a few women like Sara Waters, who grew up in Fayetteville and left once she reached adulthood in order to escape the sexually oppressive atmosphere created particularly by the prevolunteer army. While the impact of Fort Bragg on young local women was at its height during the Vietnam era, it was already a problem for her in the early 1960s. Her parents forbid her to go downtown on payday weekends. "I didn't think I had a normal childhood," she said. "There was just this horrible pressure from the soldiers." Her resentment shaped her description of the army as a kind of hostage taker of many women in her class: At her twentieth high school reunion, she said, many of the missing were the people who married soldiers and moved all over the United States and the world. "My own perspective on the city is that it was a lovely genteel Southern town that got ruined by Fort Bragg. There is a pawn-

shop and car lot on every corner, but economically who can argue?"
Still, she claimed, "most older people from Fayetteville are very ambivalent about the post."

Another woman who left, but who would add the economic costs
to the cultural ones, was Marcia Greenup. She grew up on the poor
side of town several decades later and married a soldier. She resents the
city's overwhelming attention to the military, rather than to "the
people who made the town," those who live and work there permanently. Marcia's view disregards the fact that the soldiers are also
workers, and sometimes were or become natives, and that many natives came to town to work in businesses that served soldiers, such
as her own grandfather. But it reflects common resentments of perceived privileges a military ID card garners. She would never move
back, she said, because everyone from her neighborhood is gone, and
"there's no real development. There's nothing for kids to get into but
trouble. You can go to the mall or you can go see someone take their
clothes off."

Some in Fayetteville would protest: If your wages allow it, they'd
say, you can see a play at the Little Theater or a Reba MacIntyre concert at the Crown Coliseum, meet people from all over the world at
the International Folk Festival, watch a basketball game at Fayetteville
State, or breathe in the gardenias at the Botanical Gardens. These advantages are connected, however, to the city's trials, to the need for
volunteers at the city's many homeless shelters and outreach centers or
busy domestic violence center. For, while Fayetteville's military dependency has made fortunes for some as the post continued to grow
through the 1970s and 1980s, its economy was increasingly based
on selling goods and services to soldiers, creating retail jobs that pay
less than any other category of work. Despite the egalitarian pay and
strong benefits packages military work brings to town, overall the installation established a low-wage economy, a vulnerable labor force of
dependent women and teens, the high crime rates that come with
poverty, and a weak democratic culture and public sphere. For many,
this has been reason enough to leave, for others reason enough to press
for change, and perhaps for most, reason only to endure.

CHAPTER 6

Military Restructuring, Civilian Camouflage, and Hot Peace

(1989–2000)

As the Cold War ended, doubt and uncertainty clouded military cities and towns across America. The stakes were especially high in California, Virginia, Texas, and Florida, where almost 40 percent of military dollars were spent, and in places like Connecticut and Massachusetts, where one in fifteen workers were in military-related jobs.[1] But people in every region were anxious. North Carolina—also heavily dependent on military transfers and contracts—nervously commissioned a study of the Department of Defense's socioeconomic impact on the state. Run by a retired military officer, the study identified the clear and present danger of the coming peace dividend: eighty of one hundred counties had procurement contracts, and each seventy-five retirees brought in a million dollars. "Any reduction (in military spending) is going to be felt all the way across," Colonel Woelfer said, and bluntly added: "When people start talking about the peace dividend, are [they] willing to give up that much economic impact in their county?"[2]

As I rode a bus across Fort Bragg eight years later to watch a military exercise and weapons display, the post had not shrunk, but instead looked as if it had been put on a course of steroids by those monumental events at the decade's beginning. It had sprouted gigantic new barracks, family life facilities, and shopping centers. This growth meant it was business as unusual at Fort Bragg and in Fayetteville. But all along, the city's people had felt relatively certain they would hold their own if the military shrunk, for their base offered an economy of scale most others could not match. And their units, the 82nd Airborne and Special Operations, specialized in the rapidly deployed and/or secret operations that had already been christened the wave of future war or semiwar.

Bases elsewhere across the country were closed or consolidated.[3] The number of active-duty soldiers shrank by a third, and the budget gradually dropped by 18 percent.[4] But a groundswell of aggressive lobbying by defense contractors, weapons labs, and the Pentagon repaired the damage: Budgets were projected to again reach the 1991 level by 2005.[5] Though the Cold War had ended, the victor was none other than war itself. Reconstruction happened, but it was of weapons systems, not Cold War–recuperating communities like Fayetteville.

Acceptance of unending war preparation could occur because, turning on their televisions during the 1990s, Americans had heard over and again that the world remained a perilous place. But danger was in the eye of an interested beholder, and so there was also an inflation, invention, and projection of threat. The public imagination was newly populated with rogue states and a China looking for military secrets and political influence, cyberterrorists and old-fashioned Islamic ones, tribal hatreds reemerging and destabilizing the once-steady areas of the world. Some of the sense of terror came from the notion that any change "out there" was bad. The fear emerged not from a world suddenly run amuck—"stability" was often purchased with unseen violent repression, and the new wars have had half the casualties of those of the 1970s and 1980s, worldwide. Rather it came from an elite political agreement that the American state must remain large and strong in the military face it showed the world, not its inward-facing, public welfare one.

This post–Cold War consensus found a supportive new *evolutionism* in the air. Warriors in suits such as Samuel Huntington, otherwise generously called "national security intellectuals," proclaimed a "clash of civilizations," the one Western and noble, the others barbaric and Eastern. Others predicted "the coming anarchy" of clashes between the haves and have-nots, but with an America triumphant because of its superior culture.[6] The punditry rehearsed, again and again, the idea that the Cold War's end lifted the lid from a bubbling cauldron of "ancient tribal emnities."[7] What remained unstated was the neocolonial assumption that this hatred of others was "primitive" peoples' natural state. An attitude, which anthropologist Hugh Gusterson has called "nuclear orientalism," suggested that some nations (such as India, Pakistan, and Iraq) were not "mature" enough to handle nuclear weapons; others (mostly the United States and European nations) were.[8] And a series of books, marketed and sold like hotcakes, promoted a domestic version of this evolutionism. These books gave a biological charter to the domination of one group by another: from fantasies of genetic white superiority in *The Bell Curve* to the understanding of sexual violence as evolutionarily compelled in *The Natural History of Rape.*[9]

The very idea of the lost "peace dividend" hinged on accepting that the nation had "invested" for almost forty-five years in a preparedness that kept it safe and brought peace. The half-hearted commitment to this theory, though, was evident in the continued aggressive budgets and the absence of celebration, even in Fayetteville. There were to be no streets renamed Hue or Jakarta or Santo Domingo, no Fort Bragg buildings honoring the "freedom fighters" of Nicaragua, the Shah of Iran, or the Guatemalan generals who were that war's Allies.

More importantly, examination of Soviet archives newly opened in the 1990s and attention to actual political events showed that the Cold War was not primarily ended by building U.S. military strength until it surpassed and exhausted the Soviets (it had always been more substantial). Instead, the transnational peace and human rights movements and changed political will in the Soviet Union brought at least some elements of the Cold War to an end; and severe economic problems by decade's end were brought on by poor decisions in the Soviets' centrally planned economy.[10] Beginning in the early 1980s, nuclear weapons were rapidly stigmatized by public education efforts of the transnational anti–nuclear weapons movement. Led especially by scientists, who successfully lobbied the Soviets, and by religious leaders such as the National Conference of Catholic Bishops, it produced the largest ever demonstration in New York City in 1982. While one-third of Americans favored abolition in 1981, a tipping point was reached two years later and the figure was suddenly 80 percent.[11] The human rights movement provided an ethical language beyond either anticommunism or anti-anti-communism to help bring down the police states of Eastern Europe and thwart the U.S.-supported war against civilians in Central America. And it contributed to the dramatic rise of international law regulating war. The 1980s and 1990s saw a near universal set of signatures on conventions against the use of landmines, child soldiers, chemical and biological weapons, nuclear weapons testing, and state-sponsored torture. Despite this international consensus on the need to control the more obscene forms of state violence, the U.S. government refused for years to sign or ratify most of these treaties, often finding itself alone or with a handful of "rogue states" in its rejection of them.[12]

HOT PEACE AND MILITARY RESTRUCTURING

The U.S. military restructured itself in important ways as the Soviet empire was collapsing. Externally, it applied itself more vigorously to the new forms of what can be called Hot Peace: training other people's armies and police, drug interdiction, hurricane relief, hostage rescue, the quelling of civil disorder, and what it called nation-building assistance. Internally, it reorganized itself in the manner of American business: It downsized, outsourced, and privatized.

Both of these kinds of restructuring, new modes of warfare and institutional renovation, heated and reshaped civil-military politics. On the one hand, there was intense renegotiation over the moral status of soldiers versus civilians, with the army generally emerging with a widely perceived higher status than before. On the other, these changes made civilians more central to the prosecution of war than ever before. The restructured military needed civilians to do some of the labor that soldiers once did, but even more important was their enhanced value as spectators to or fans of military adventure. For Fayetteville, this has meant the army and the city are both more united and more divided than ever before, as we will see.

New Modes of Warfare

The U.S. Army's current operations manual lists the following forms of what are called *Operations Other Than War:* Evacuation Operations, Arms Control, Support to Domestic Civil Authorities, Humanitarian Assistance and Disaster Relief, Security Assistance, Nation Assistance, Support to Counterdrug Operations, Combating Terrorism, Peacekeeping Operations, Peace Enforcement, Support for Insurgencies and Counterinsurgencies, and Attacks and Raids.[13] With these proliferative functions (many distinguishable from war only in the world of public relations), the pace of "engagements" quickened from about two per year from 1975 through 1991 to four annually in the first seven post–Cold War years.[14] Fort Bragg soldiers went to Somalia, Haiti, Panama, and the former Yugoslavia, and newspaper coverage of soldiers hugging their children goodbye and hello became routine.

On the other hand, some freshly favored forms of war, such as economic sanctions, needed no soldiers at all. By U.N. estimate, the embargo of Iraq through the 1990s killed forty thousand children under five years of age each year.[15] And landmines and unexploded bombs left behind in the world's ex-war zones have gone on killing as well; for example, eleven thousand live cluster bomb elements remained scattered through Kosovo in 1999.[16]

Soldiering became both more onerous and less dangerous work. Onerous because there were more separations from home than ever (with more missions in a smaller army), and less dangerous because some of the new operations minimize the use of weapons or have been fought mainly from the air against thinly defended countries. Of the sixteen million U.S. soldiers in World War II, almost 3 percent died and many more were permanently disabled. In the twenty years from 1980 through 1999, a total of 563 American soldiers died from "enemy" fire. That same number of people die every five days on American highways (this latter fact might be counted as a war casualty in another sense, since the number is much lower in countries that have built smaller armies in the interest of spending more on public transportation).[17] A soldier during this period was much more likely to be murdered or to commit suicide while in the service than to die in combat, although soldiers are less likely than civilians to die from either cause or from disease. Black male soldiers, in particular, are twelve times less likely to be murdered than their civilian counterparts and one-fifth as likely to die from disease.[18] Among American workers, people on construction crews and poultry-processing lines have much higher rates of death and disability.[19]

This does not mean that soldiering is safe and easy work, by any means. While peacetime soldiers die at a rate half that of comparable civilians,[20] and while soldiers over the last two decades have been dramatically less likely to die in accidents than their predecessors,[21] some army occupational hazards may be on the increase. Often denied by officials, these hazards include exposure to Agent Orange in Vietnam, to toxic anti–saran gas pills in the Gulf, poorly tested anthrax inoculations, and to the United States' depleted uranium weapons.[22]

These new missions and lessened risk have threatened to make soldiering less masculine. So, of course, has the rise of women in uniform and the necessity of serving for some missions under the "softer" banner of the UN. When political scientist Cynthia Enloe asked, "Are peacekeepers real men?" she meant to suggest that new ideas about masculinity are required by new forms of warfare.[23] Just as in domestic policing, where violence-centered SWAT teams are seen as more masculine than the community policemen on the beat, so disaster relief soldiers are more feminized in popular imagery than those who attack in combat. Humanitarian missions can also be based in a universal definition of human needs and so undermine nationalism, which is itself gendered male. Moreover, the increased foreign military training that soldiers receive makes them teachers as much as warriors. And their hiring by other nations (as when the United State was compensated by other allied nations who sent few troops to the Gulf War) could remake their image less as protectors of the home front than a kind of exotic export.[24]

When I spoke with John Perry, he was an ROTC student who had grown up in Fayetteville and was preparing to enter the military amid this atmosphere. He emphatically wanted to join as a "traditional" combat GI, not a "humanitarian soldier." When he eventually goes overseas with the Army, he said, "I don't really want to do that. . . . You go to some Third World country, you baby-sit poor people. I wouldn't be worried about getting in a fire fight with somebody because we have them outgunned 6 to 1. We got bulletproofing and night vision. You worry about somebody parking a U-Haul truck outside of your barracks and blowing you to smithereens when you are sleeping." His choice of imagery is common: A baby-sitter is female, and she cares for the childish. Prestige inside the army, he knew (partly from the counter-example of a relative who unhappily did office work in uniform), still would come through manly combat arms, not personnel management, water purification detail, or the finance department, all tasks that required less strength or courage.[25] And, like any reasonably attuned person in Fayetteville, he has heard that becoming a man through military service can begin with violence at the hands of other soldiers at Fort Bragg. In initiation rites, soldiers are sometimes shocked with electricity, made to sit on garbage, have their necks hung with dead fish, and—to symbolize the gender they must never be—smeared with lipstick as camouflage paint.[26]

Whatever work is done to remasculinize the army and whatever people think of the new forms of military work, they suggest to many that the United States is demilitarizing in the wake of the Cold War. A bulldog-tattooed Marine holding a small, frightened boy in the wake of Hurricane Andrew on a 1993 *National Geographic* cover might be taken as a sign of the demilitarizing of the soldier, the draining of violence from his labor and character. Or should it rather be seen as the militarizing of humanitarian labor that social workers and disaster relief experts would have otherwise done, or as a recruiting ad? Or is the issue that the military has become so powerful as to erase the distinction between civil and military worlds, to stand in for the social whole, and so claim ever larger budgets and roles?

This is not a new problem. When Roosevelt used the army to implement some of his domestic policies in the 1930s, he claimed he did so because it was "the most convenient, economical, and efficient agency available."[27] But the number of functions that the military claimed to perform better than civilians, by the 1990s, required no crisis mentality and covered broader ground, from diplomacy to teaching in public schools. And the superiority of the army for these duties was attributed not to the funds they had to do them, but to an intrinsic will and skill in military institutions. So when President Clinton called on the Pentagon to train civilian day care workers at its excellent, well-funded centers, such as the one at Fort Bragg, *Newsweek* wondered whether "perhaps the Pentagon can fight a couple of land wars and simultaneously save the nation's children."[28]

The Army is, in fact, trying to do this in Fayetteville. A new mission—not listed in the official handbook—is improving American character and helping at-risk children. Soldiers drive into Fayetteville to teach or mentor thousands of students each year in the public schools. They do this on the principle that the schools have failed them and military values are irreplaceable vehicles of self-improvement. One method of reaching children is the Junior ROTC program, found in all nine of the county's high schools and in about 1 in 10 American high schools. Taught by uniformed, retired military personnel, it puts children as young as fourteen in uniform and gives them classroom instruction and drill. The Department of Defense pays part of the teachers' salaries but a quarter billion dollars of local school funds nationwide are paid out each year just in personnel costs for the program.[29] The Department of Defense pays less than a third of the program's $800,000 annual cost in the Cumberland County schools (a number which excludes the cost of the rooms used, utilities, maintenance, and some supplies). In keeping with the explicit (but once denied) goal of recruiting, 45 percent of "cadets" who graduate from the program join the military.[30]

Another educational venture started in 1995 partners Fort Bragg military units with each of Cumberland County's eighty-four schools in soldier-student mentoring programs (only one preschool said it had no need of soldier mentors). Hundreds of on-duty soldiers go out to the schools to tutor, read to children, proctor exams, run physical fitness tests, guest lecture about their jobs, or bring students on post to see their work and equipment. The program suggests to schools that they can reciprocate by making partnership banners to hang at the post or in the school, or they can visit the unit with songs or homemade cards. An Army spokesman said that the soldiers "don't recruit, but by being there they get some recruiting value."[31] He also described several Army programs meant "to help at-risk kids by putting them in a military environment." Approximately 460 high school dropouts and troubled teens come to the installation each year for weeklong youth camps. Their rationale is that the military both models upward mobility through many of its individual soldiers and gives poor children the experience with discipline and teamwork that they do not get elsewhere. An underlying premise is that, ultimately, it also fights domestic crime.

The drug wars, too, have allowed the expansion of the military's domestic role. The Army has patrolled the U.S.–Mexico border with automatic weapons, trained local police forces, and spent millions to facilitate surveillance and interdiction at home.[32] Security intellectuals model the problem of drug use and war in indistinguishable terms. Said one prominent theorist:

> Within its own borders the United States faces a potential insurgency of awesome proportions. The gang warfare racking the poorer neighborhoods of all major American cities has so far centered on protecting drug turf. Should the gangs cease to fight each other and combine to extend their operations into other illicit activities and their control over wider urban and even suburban areas, the federal government might find itself conducting a counterinsurgency campaign involving community development, intelligence gathering, and special operations.[33]

Internal military interventions in the United States are not new. The objects of attention are, however, reflecting the new forms of social crisis. Slaves and Indians were the primary targets in the nineteenth century (federal troops fought 943 battles, large and small, against Native Americans from 1865 to 1898), and then attention shifted to striking industrial workers as the century turned.[34] As jobs were taken en masse to nonunion areas overseas in the later twentieth century, military attention shifted to urban unemployed rioters (and to occasional antiwar and school integration protests). The newest types of military intervention emerge from environmental crisis, as climate change has intensified the number and severity of storms and their flooding or icing. And they are a reflection of the new economy, for which the problem is not to hold down wage demands but to manage the huge population of permanently unemployed in the inner cities (accepted by federal policy as the cost of controlling inflation), who turn to property crime and drug use, in Fayetteville and elsewhere.

The Neoliberal Military

The military reorganized more than its missions. Like contemporary business, it chopped the size of its workforce and engaged more heavily in outsourcing and privatization of some of its functions. Organizing these changes was *neoliberalism*—or the belief that unregulated markets provide the best way out of social problems and that government attempts to solve them are wasteful, bungling, and/or arrogant. This belief justified turning previously public matters, such as the running of prisons, over to private companies and the devolution of government functions to more local levels where they might wither away. In business, it called for downsizing and outsourcing operations, reducing workers categorized as redundant and using more temporary and part-time workers, consolidating functions, and trimming inventories through just-in-time deliveries of products. Corporations increasingly relied on subcontractors to do their work, so as to more easily cast off productive capacity when needed as well as shed responsibility for pay levels and working conditions.

So, too, the army. Although it kept its progressive wages and benefits, it dropped hundreds of thousands of employees and turned to rely more on part-time workers, which, for the military, are Reserves and National Guard. Training foreign forces with renewed enthusiasm, it both cut costs (foreign militaries get no retirement benefits) and outsourced its war function and responsibility. For example, for years Fort Bragg sent Special Forces soldiers to train the Indonesian military, calling it both military foreign aid and military diplomacy. The United States has provided massive amounts of armaments, some used in Indonesia's invasion and slaughter of one-third of the population of East Timor in 1975. The killing and other human rights abuses committed by the Indonesian army and the paramilitaries it supported in rampages through Timor in 1999 were disavowable and disavowed.[35] The United States also privatized by using private companies to do military training on behalf of the United States (placing much of it outside congressional oversight).[36] Heavily staffed by high-ranking ex-military officers and defense officials, including especially Special Operations veterans from Fort Bragg and elsewhere, these companies have been contracted to train the Bosnian, Croatian, Saudi Arabian, Liberian, and Angolan armies (and in some cases police). These companies are often located around domestic military bases and their clients in the 1990s included regimes which went on to commit bloody human rights abuses in Croatia, Uganda, and elsewhere.

The Department of Defense merged and eliminated military bases. The army alone cut 112 in the United States and announced 664 closings overseas; however, the United States still maintains 1,324 major active-duty installations worldwide.[37] With this it turned, as it had been doing through the 1980s, to more "flexible" forms of warfare, offering just-in-time delivery of the army to a site of conflict rather than relying on large permanent overseas inventories of bases and soldiers. This all favored Fort Bragg, where hundreds of millions of dollars of new buildings sprang up, a phenomenal expansion that even many local veterans and politicians readily identify as "pork-barrel spending."[38] Fayetteville's citizens, however, ruefully note the barbecue is mostly cooking up elsewhere. With the bidding for these and other contracts done nationally, and no preference given to local communities, most deals go to larger out-of-town businesses, often the "Beltway Bandits" such as Lockheed-Martin with long experience and valuable contacts for influencing and understanding the Pentagon procurement process.[39]

U.S. arms merchants swallowed each other after the Cold War, their mergers blessed and even paid for by the Department of Defense. Shedding almost two million workers was not bad for business. With the help of hundreds of millions of federal "payoffs for layoffs," as critics dubbed them, the giant new companies' stock prices went up as much as 80 percent.[40] The "peace dividend," as the journalist William Greider noticed, "was distributed to shareholders of the major defense companies."[41]

The military has also been "civilianizing" war making, turning more to civilian communication systems and employees (of military contractors or the military itself), who are less expensive than soldiers.[42] Some become quasi-soldiers. During the Gulf War, for example, civilian technicians sat alongside soldiers to help them identify targets with their company's latest technology; such individuals have been put into the category of "surrogate warriors" or "operators" in military journals and "vision statements."[43] Armed private security guards from Triple P Services, for example, trained to use deadly force, watch over Fort Bragg's ammunition supply point and other areas of the installation. And as they do, the line between "legal" and "illegal" war targets and combatants blurs.

The army was also under orders to put many of its functions out to bid, including utilities infrastructure, housing, and shopping outlets. As one local officer described it, "In privatization across the country, the Department of Defense is seeking an advantage that would accrue to the armed forces by getting them out of a business that is not a core competency of the armed forces, so they can be totally focused on providing for the national defense."[44] This privatization was meant as a cost-cutting measure as well, but, like other such efforts, its savings are often costs simply passed on to the general public via, for example, lower wages for the workers involved. These new contracts, too, have mostly gone out of town. Privatization has also accentuated the us–them feeling for some on post. Setting aside the long-standing post civilian workforce—a "skilled and dedicated workforce . . . that is a part of the Army's culture, sharing the Army's values"—the garrison commander has said that "the prospect of changing all this—and in a time of crisis, being forced to rely on some private contractor who is not one of 'us'—is something that, quite frankly, scares the hell out of most all green suiters."[45]

Privatization has also meant that public information is treated as a private commodity by the subcontractor. When Fort Bragg's office of transition services, which helps soldiers return to civilian life, was recently privatized, the company got access to valuable data on separating personnel with high-tech skills that civilian employers want. The city could have used the information to attract new business to town, but the subcontractor is "working himself out of a job if he gives us that information," a chamber official told me, his booster voice flagging.

In addition, Fayetteville is more easily hurt by deployments with the downsized army. In "any future conflict," one Fayetteville planner said, "and if you think there aren't going to be any future conflicts, well, I've got some land in Florida you may want to invest in. But when the next conflict comes, when we have to deploy large numbers of troops, . . . the deployment will be for longer and more people will be involved. So it'll hurt the economy even more than the last go-round [the Gulf War], because we have so many fewer soldiers to send to hot-spots."

So it was that the Gulf War, a dramatic sign of what might come, convinced Joe Riddle, Jr., one of Fayetteville's leading commercial real estate developers, that he needed to diversify his assets. A charming and hyperkinetic man, he bounded about his conference room as we spoke and occasionally centered his energy by taking a big handful of change out of his pocket and arranging the coins in little piles on his hand. The room, hung with aerial photos and color-coded maps of Cumberland County, pointed to his wide holdings. He had just put a sixty thousand-square-foot addition on one of his shopping centers. "I started it in May," he said, "and I had no idea. I mean, if you read the papers, we were friends with Saddam up to a certain point, and then all of a sudden we weren't. So it was hard to figure that one out.

Joseph P. Riddle, III, developer

We didn't really do anything from August of '90 until about January of '91 except build up over there. So for all that time, we had a lot of people gone from our market, and it was as dead as I've ever seen it."

He and other businesspeople paint the city in those war days of 1991 as dust-bowled and shutter-flapping. His commercial renters felt the sudden contraction of business as the soldiers abandoned the city by the tens of thousands and their families either judiciously cut back on spending or went to stay with parents. Although Joe Riddle's capital, first accumulated by his father over the long boom years, had already gone into some limited out-of-town ventures, he would now begin to build in earnest elsewhere.[46]

The army's privatization initiatives have also made his job tougher. The installation's landscape, once a uniformity of lettering style and public architecture, now sprouted Burger King and Kentucky Fried Chicken signs as the military began renting out post property and became his competitor.[47] While the Burger King franchisee in town lost out, the people who cook and clean up at Burger King on or off post won't know the difference: None make a living wage.

The dilemmas of both American capital and labor pale before the ones civilians face overseas where the "core" functions of the U.S. and other militaries are being privatized.[48] In one sense, whenever the U.S. Army has sent military trainers out from Fort Bragg to train security forces in places like Colombia or Guatemala or Indonesia, they have privatized an American military goal. The United States and these armies themselves often work in unacknowledged conjunction with local paramilitary forces.[49] They fight what Mary Kaldor has characterized as the "New Wars." By this she means the wars now fought by paramilitaries without clear lines of command, who target civilians and use maximum violence including torture, systematic rape, and the bombing of hospitals and markets. They often aim "to sow fear and discord, to instill unbearable memories of what was once home, to desecrate whatever has social meaning."[50] Their intention to prevent dissent or even discussion is signified by their frequent maiming of eyes, ears, and tongues.[51] To render people senseless in this way is another form of privatization, if in the near total sense.

Both of these kinds of restructuring—new modes of warfare and institutional renovation—have had important effects on local communities. One is to intensify and reshape the cultural politics of the military in Fayetteville and across the country. On the one hand, there was intense renegotiation over the moral status of soldiers versus civilians, with the army generally emerging triumphant. On the other, civilians became more central than ever before to the prosecution of war, not only as replacement labor for soldiers, but as spectators of military adventure.

CIVILIAN CAMOUFLAGE:
THE NEW MILITARY POLITICS

On a moist summer morning, the gas fumes leave visual ripples as two men pump gas into their cars at the Amoco on Bragg Boulevard. One has lots of visible scalp under a red beret, starched desert camouflage, and several pounds of black boots. The other has gel-styled hair and

Iron Mike

wears lightly pressed Docksiders and a Tommy Hilfiger shirt. Americans have been taught to view this pair through the freighted distinction between *soldier* and *civilian,* categories that have been changing with the emergence of Hot Peace and military restructuring.

Of long standing are these contrasts: A civilian is protected, a soldier the protector. A civilian enjoys peace and safety, the soldier faces danger and war (nuclear warfare's actual collapse of this fact notwithstanding). No matter his or her gender, a civilian is feminized, a soldier masculinized. The status that a warrior accrues is obvious from the frequent mention of veteran status on jobs résumés and in political campaigns: Valor gives value, virility virtue.[52] In stronger terms, the soldier is emotionally disciplined, self-sacrificing, vigorous, and hardworking. By definition, then, the civilian is weak, cowardly, materialistic and wealthy, and self-centered. The civilian is soft, lacking experience with both the physical discipline that hardens muscles and with the hard facts of death and evil that the soldier faces down. The soldier has a calling, most civilians only a job—the exceptions in religion and medicine reveal the assumption that the work is sacred.[53] One ex-soldier driving through Fort Bragg with me pointed out off-duty soldiers jogging in the suffocating Southern summer heat, one toting a full pack on his back: "It's a monastic order," he said.

The distinction has gotten a sharper edge over the last twenty years. "In times of protracted peace, citizens grow fat and lazy and careless," so goes the stereotype in one recently popular book on the military.[54] Another widely read, celebratory book on Marine Corps boot camp, *Making the Corps* by *Wall Street Journal* Pentagon reporter Thomas Ricks, is called by one reviewer "a powerful indictment of many other institutions in American society—especially public schools and parents. In an age of moral relativism, and a narcissistic American society steeped in victimization, individualism, and materialism, what other institutions are as unequivocal about their own ethos and hierarchy of values? As Ricks notes of his recruits, " 'Parris Island is the first place many of them encounter absolute and impersonal standards of right and wrong, of success and failure.' " And in a recent cyberdiscussion on soldiers' tax breaks in Fayetteville, several veterans struck themes of civilian whiney immaturity and overindulgence: "If you want the privileges [of the] military, join! Just remember, you can't quit like a civilian job when things get tough." Said another: "Very few other careers have a global responsibility for protecting and promulgating the objectives of the greatest and freest society that the world has ever known. Local jurisdictions should not look to service members as another group to fatten the tax coffers."

But the evaluation is also reversible, though done much less often and less publicly. When it is, the soldier is a slacker, playing cards and drinking, while the civilian supports him. In a society in which productive and free labor historically represented a pinnacle republican value, the soldier could easily become a pariah.[55] For he is defined by waiting, not activity, and destroying, not producing. And his freedom to come and go is severely restricted. When post–World War II abundance increasingly defined the American Dream in terms of ever higher levels of leisure and consumption, the soldier's spartan life could be seen as a self-indictment. Although the enhanced army pay after 1973 gave some reprieve from this cultural judgment, the prejudices of class and race could continue to stick to a military identity when soldiers so often came from more impoverished or nonwhite backgrounds.

As the word itself suggests, the *civilian* is assumed more civilized or civil, that is, peace loving, polite, or well bred, while the soldier is a barbarian with a club, witlessly pursuing war.[56] Said one soldier, "I came here in 1947 for two weeks' training. And there were signs on the streets downtown: 'Soldiers and Dogs Not Allowed'. . . . The civilian folks who don't deal with the military don't understand at all. We're human beings. We raise our kids like they raise their kids. . . . [But the people in town saw us as] martinets versus real people. . . . The killers were at Fort Bragg, and the real people were downtown."[57] The soldier's "blood sacrifice" (killing others and risk of being killed), while heroic, even Christlike, in one reading of the dualism, is tainted with deviance or sin in another.[58] Around the world and through time, societies have paid attention to the blood on warriors' hands and have explicitly and often ritually worked at "cleansing" and reintegrating them into the social home they left for war.[59]

The relationship between those who have killed and seen killing in battle and those who have not is always fraught with tension, taboo, and unrecognized effects. Studies of World War II soldiers' attitudes toward civilians showed a contradictory mix of desires: to protect people back home from knowledge of the horrors they sometimes saw and made, the wish to have the people understand their experience, and despair for their ability to do so. Civilians, for their part, often wanted simply to believe there was a simple moral clarity to the war.[60] So, too, might there be fear that the soldier's dehumanizing of the enemy (and of himself, at times) might easily spill over to the civilian at home.[61] Little communication would come of such a stew.

Some of the negative judgment of soldiering comes from three aspects of its cultural context. First is the contradiction between the imperative to be free and autonomous—seen as the birthright of each American, but especially of men—and the hierarchy and compulsion of military life. One woman told me about an argument she watched between her husband, a Fort Bragg soldier, and a Marine. In a classic style of interservice rivalry, the Marine said every other branch of service was "full of faggots." To this standard putdown of homosexuality and claim about which service "real men" choose, the soldier retorted that the Marines are "dummies and machines." When she chimed in with the rejoinder, "You're *all* slaves!" she was body-slammed—a playful response, she thought.

Moreover, military work is called *service* because people see soldiers as giving the country something larger than what they take home in their paychecks. It is a never completely reciprocal exchange because of life's sacredness—both their own and those they take in battle. But for this reason, soldiering can have a weak if noble cultural reputation, as do nurses, day care providers, sanitation workers, and others. Even weaker might be the reputation of those who serve the servers, as Fayetteville's citizens do.

Finally, there is the related issue of how to interpret soldiers' dependency on a government wage. Because they receive cash payments from the government and many services in kind, soldiers live in something that bears a strong family resemblance to a social welfare state. This is a potential problem in a nation that does not generally acknowledge a universal right to work or to health care. One solution to the stigma that might otherwise attach to this is to make a sharp cultural distinction between earned and unearned social benefits. The acrimony that goes with the debate over individual military benefits often centers on the dangerous work soldiers do to earn them or the idea of a promise of such made to the soldier in his or her contract.

People define the kind of society they want when they characterize soldiers and civilians. Over the course of American history, some have defined military values as the antidote to the sickness they see in their era, such as materialism, corruption, or selfishness. In Fayetteville, some people use the soldier to identify how their city should change. When they celebrate the military's cosmopolitan experience and racial integration, they at least implicitly criticize the town's parochialism and segregation. Many—though more soldiers than civilians—believe that civilian society would improve if it adopted more military values and customs.[62] In doing this, though, as Michael Sherry has noticed, Americans have "tried to extract the virtues of war from war itself."[63] They set the killing aside and celebrate instead war participants' values of idealism, discipline, courage, strenuous effort, self-sacrifice, and love of country. And they select the values to

Civil-military relations: the boundary between Fort Bragg (*left*) and Fayetteville (*right*)

emphasize: the democratizing effect of standing among a mass of equally endangered soldiers, for example, rather than the authoritarian and coercive character that an institution based in automatic obedience and violence encourages.[64] This view also obscures how some of the same values celebrated as military also or even better characterize civilian service work, from teaching and nursing to building bridges. And it can entail the confusion of economics and culture, with the wealth of army resources conflated with the character of those who use them to maintain their surroundings.

The identities of soldier and civilian are more complicated than this cultural ideology suggests, however. How they effect the so-called crisis in civil-military relations was brought home to me when I met Michael Trimble at a Cross Creek Mall restaurant. At thirty-five years of age, he has spent most of his life in the city, brought there when his father was stationed at Fort Bragg. He is a construction worker who makes a reasonable wage, but he dislikes Fayetteville so much that he plans to someday move. He has experienced the city's crime rate personally, having twice been mugged. When he said, "Fayetteville is like a little New York now," he meant no compliment.

When I asked if he had friends in the military, he glanced around the room, lowered his voice, and said no. In explanation, he pointed to some buzz-cut men at another table and said, sounding angrily perplexed, "I've had a soldier say to me, 'I protect *your* country.'" The implication, he suggested, was that he was negligent for not doing the work himself and obligated to them for their labors. Michael wondered at the soldier's choice of possessive pronoun, and I shared with him a sense that something was amiss. While it may suggest that the volunteer soldier easily sees himself as somewhat mercenary, it can also be heard as a reversal and a rebuke. The civilian world lacks patriotism, so much so that the soldier removes himself from membership in the "imagined community" of the nation, as historian Benedict Anderson calls it. The exchange between these two men might have been an anxious rendering of the contemporary relationship between soldiers and civilians, a relationship journalists and others have increasingly identified as problematic, even explosive.[65]

This man defies the categories of that punditry, however. He should be army-knowledgeable and sympathetic, having lived in a military family and city and doing a job that depends on military spending. His resentments of the military are not based in a broader politics or in a misunderstanding of what the military is about, but in the army's undercutting of his economic and social interests as he sees them. He resents the economic advantages soldiers have that he does not (despite the fact that some members of the lower ranks with children have incomes that qualify them for food stamps). When he goes to bars to meet women in his hometown, he finds many soldiers standing in his way. And, in a more overtly political vein, he is unhappy with the erosion of a former egalitarianism of citizenship between soldiers and civilians.

Despite the monolithic image outsiders often have of it, the army, too, like the civilian world, contains multitudes. The historian Richard Kohn has called it a "pernicious myth . . . that there was, or is, any such thing as the American soldier—a prototypical American in uniform—or that our military forces, either as institutions or as collec-

An army of one

tions of individuals, reflect our true character as a people and as a nation."[66] Some of those in uniform are about to leave the service,
disgusted; others are enthusiasts of army custom and discipline or
ardent nationalists or true believers in the power of violence to get
things done; yet others, pragmatists doing time to get college tuition
(the number one reason given for enlisting).[67] Some love the idea of
American empire, others hate it with libertarian or democratic fer-
vor. Some are part-timers, others lifers. They get socialized into units
with different "personalities" like the Airborne, Quartermasters, or
Seabees. If many think of the army as monolithic, however, it may be
because military propaganda suggests as much, with its images of soldiers all facing their flag, families, and enhanced future in united
enthusiasm. Such images can also motivate soldiers to present them-

selves as conforming to a single, uniform model of why they join, what they do, and what they value.

A tension exists between the impulse to clearly distinguish between two cultures of the military and civilian worlds (often to either celebrate or criticize one of them) and the desire to see a single set of military and civilian values, and a single America. So it was when the Army chief of staff settled on an official set of "seven Army Values and their definitions": loyalty, duty, respect, selfless service, honor, integrity, and personal courage.[68] A Fort Bragg Web master tried to satisfy both desires by heading the list "Soldier/Civilian Values." There are advantages to the military to having it both ways. Democratic values and local citizens can be harmed, however, either with a sharpened distinction (hostility or subordination can be produced, and civilians' responsibility for, and social and cultural connections to, soldiers' actions lost) *or* a blurred one (the genuine differences of interest between the two groups are mystified).

Just as the soldier's identity is more complicated than popular stereotype, so is the civilian's. Many people walking around Fayetteville in blue jeans or business suits are in what can be called "civilian camouflage." They include all the people we have already met who are getting military pensions or benefits, paying war taxes, selling things to GIs, watching war on TV as the twelfth man on the team, or people who are war refugees or war brides. In each of these ways, individuals become less clearly or simply civilians, even when some of them see themselves as having nothing to do with the military or are unsympathetic to it.

Moreover, *civilian* has been a category rarely discussed explicitly in America. This is because it has the quality linguists have discovered in many antonyms. Not simply two sides of a coin, one is "unmarked"—or the dominant, normalized, or culturally unproblematic term—and the other "marked"—the one that more often comes up for explicit discussion because it is seen as presenting some kind of "problem." So, in ordinary conversation, an "unhealthy" state is more often discussed than a "healthy" one. "How deep is the water?" we ask, not, "How shallow?" Throughout American history, black has been marked as a race, white remaining invisible. Female has been a gender, male a kind of prototype human being, without gender. The identity of a civilian is clearly the unmarked of the soldier-civilian pair. Despite the power of the military physically and economically, civilian is the majority, dominant category, and so is less recognizable as such.

Civilian identity has been sharpened, however, by the All Volunteer Force. The punditry has generally agreed to see this as a problem of growing ignorance and hostility toward the military as fewer civilians have enlisted. Instead we might say the civilian has become more visible as many begin to hypervalue the soldier. A kind of "super-citizenship" is offered by military recruiters whose ads promise elevated character to those who join.[69] Their overheated advertising rhetoric is blown forcefully across the country with each year's recruiting budget, which was over $2 billion in 2001.[70] Beyond these ads' influence, civilians are motivated to value soldiers in this way in exchange for not being required to kill or die. Such a barter was not so urgent when the draft meant more families had already given their own children to the army. Some civilians, of course, reject the very idea of this burden or that it should be so constantly and widely created by the drive for American global dominance. Or they see the professional army as simply one occupation among many, duly compensated and requiring no cultural premium.[71] But all civilians become, through this process, "subcitizens." And as first-class citizenship is militarized, those who are excluded explicitly or implicitly, including gays and lesbians and straight women, can see further erosions in their social status.[72]

The civilian has also become more visible as the volunteer army's politics have become more distinct—and more conservative—than civilians' and than the drafted army's. While American voters now are about equally likely to identify themselves as Republicans or Democrats, a recent survey showed 64 percent of elite officers were Republican and only 8 percent Democrats.[73] Among retirees, reservists, and ROTC students, conservatism also dominates. This has given Fayetteville's Republican Party, once a miniscule and forlorn band, a tremendous boost, particularly when veterans retire, register, and become politically active. On the national level, too, veterans are a potent political force, well-organized to press for benefits, recognition, and a stronger military, through the Association of the United States Army (with one hundred thousand members), the Veterans of Foreign Wars, and others. Such groups lobby Congress, send literature into veterans' homes, and help organize informal networks in local communities. The AUSA's position is that the army is "underpaid, overcommitted and underresourced,"[74] but the source of its enthusiasm for higher budgets comes as much from its corporate partners who it offers "'face to face meetings with Army decision-makers and government officials."[75]

One soldier that AUSA might claim to speak for is Eric Fisher. After spending many unhappy years in the city—a favored phrase being "yogurt has more culture than Fayetteville"—his disgust at local politicians finally brought him out to work on the successful campaign of a Republican elected to the state Senate. He also took a lively interest in a local taxpayer revolt group, which was vigorously attacking city government's spending habits. In the regular and reserve Army for twenty-four years, his attraction to being a soldier came from its code of high principle. It is, he said, a job that can sometimes require falling on "the grenade of honor," if that is good for the organization, or sacrificing oneself for the greater good. "The army is like the church to me," he said, because it is where he talks with others about things of ultimate value, like God and country. And he stayed with the military because he "bonded" with other soldiers over these values and over shared hardships. He contrasted the army with the civilian world by pointing to a recent story he had heard on National Public Radio about a furniture factory closing elsewhere in North Carolina. When it and the rest of corporate America downsized, he said, the owners simply discarded their people. When the army cut personnel in the early 1990s, by contrast, the soldier got "a ticket home, his goods moved, and help with the transition." The civilian world, he was saying, has no heart and no soul in comparison with the Army "family."

Such alienation from civilian society indexes erosion of the principle of civilian control of the military that some commentators see as a sign of a coming "crisis in civil-military relations."[76] If people in the military see themselves as sole custodians of authentic American values, their cultural and political leadership might be required to save the country. But while there are overt attempts to expand the military's authority, globally, nationally, and locally, the more basic and pressing problem is that civilian camouflage and the widespread acceptance of a military definition of the situation leaves few to ask questions when soldiers settle into high schools in Fayetteville and around the country to sell the military.

When the question of civil-military relations is raised, people almost invariably talk about the relationship between the army, the president, and Congress. But Fayetteville's history shows that local relations between post personnel and city governments, soldiers and local women, or soldiers and merchants are where the quotidian struggle occurs to define what a soldier and a civilian are, what cultural and economic capital they ought to have, and what authority each ought to have over the other.

I learned some of this from William Reeves, who worked in the schools for decades. "One of the day to day most obvious relations," he said, "people may think of at the end of the month [is] payroll and merchants and whatnot, but [school] was a day to day relation—sometimes good, sometimes bad." His students' parents who were soldiers often complained about their children's schools because they had just emerged from the relatively lushly funded Department of Defense system before they came to the financially more limited city schools.[77] Soldiers, on the other hand, also

> felt that they had a right, because they were defending the nation . . . to be looked after. Somebody needs to take care of us and make sure that our children are safe and happy and well educated. . . . Friends who live at Fort Bragg and work at Fort Bragg, they would wash my face over and over: "You wouldn't be having these [Federal Impact Aid] dollars if it were not for us. So, attend to our wishes." . . . Never mind the fact that we wouldn't need the money if it were not for your children. But you don't tell them that, you see. You have a little bit more diplomacy than that.

He bristled at the dominating attitude officers sometimes brought when they came to school to complain. He noticed that they often came to parent conferences carrying a briefcase, which he saw as a status symbol meant to put him in his place.

> Sometimes he'd open the attaché case [and I would see] two pencils and a pack of cigarettes or something. But they looked the part. . . . And I guess it's good that the military calls people to feel superior because if you want to go in battle with the enemy, you need to feel superior, but not necessarily when you go to the school. [Well, did you ever feel like they were coming in to battle?] Oh yeah, they'd be prepared and the attaché

> case was just like, just like the mortar. . . . So I can understand that if I had
> lived all of my last twenty some days not having dealt with any civilians,
> and everybody around me, under me . . . shows they respect [me]. It's
> hard for a person to just take off that personality, simply because they
> come into the civilian community.

And he saw the dominating approach in officers' relationships with
their children as well.

> I used to feel sorry for some of the children and I said I will not send for
> this parent again because first sergeant, drill sergeant mentality would
> come in and sit and say . . . "If you do that again, boy, if I hear of you do-
> ing that, I'll knock your head through that cinder block wall" and I
> couldn't do that. . . . [In] the city you'll have signs on the bus that says
> "please do not smoke" [but] people get on the bus on the post and the
> sign on the bus is saying "you *will* not smoke." It's just that different. And
> that kind of attitude and framework on the part of the adults. . . . There
> was just no debating, you don't, you don't, you don't. Well, we had to say
> "please don't."[78]

As military and civilian institutions face each other each day in Fayetteville, their contrasting styles, political differences, and variously
funded interests are usually negotiated peacefully. But the changing
political landscape in America includes a growing number who believe the nation is sick and that the cure is the return of a disciplined
traditional race and gender order. A small but also growing number
believe violence will achieve it. While violent white supremacism is
found both in and outside of the military, the death of two people at
neo-Nazi hands in Fayetteville in 1995 had much to do with the consequences of the American century of war and war preparation, as we
will see.

RACE MURDERS AND THE NEW
CIVIL-MILITARY RELATIONS
Three white supremacist soldiers stationed at Fort Bragg set off on a
December night in 1995, fortified with guns and beer, for one of Fayetteville's poorest neighborhoods. One of them, James Burmeister,
was intent on earning the spiderweb tattoo that signifies having killed
an African American or homosexual person. Shortly after midnight,
and within spitting distance of the downtown's towering, modern

county courthouse, they found Michael James and Jackie Burden walking along the road; they approached them and shot Michael. Jackie ran, and they shot her in the back.

Caught sleeping in their off-post trailer later that day, the soldiers were quickly discharged from the Army. Post officials soon posted a notice about extremist groups on barracks' walls: "Army policy does not prohibit passive activities such as mere membership, receiving literature in the mail, or presence at an event, though [these are] strongly discouraged as incompatible with military service."[79] It began an investigation into racist activity on the installation that, a scant two weeks later, reported the problem small. There were, it said, just seven "racist skinheads" among the 14,700 members of Burmeister's 82nd Airborne Corps.[80] These men and their fascism were already well known, though, to their superiors, who simply asked that they reinstall their dogtags where they had hung Nazi insignia. Other commanders allowed or encouraged SS insignia on team T-shirts and white supremacist statements and sympathies. And they most likely also knew of the fascist journal *Resister,* put out by active-duty and former Special Forces soldiers.[81] And everyone knew that one of the country's largest neo-Nazi organizations found the pickings around Bragg good enough to advertise itself on a nearby billboard.[82]

In the city, the NAACP organized some public meetings to discuss racism and the murders, which expanded to hearings in other North Carolina military towns. Local television and newspapers focused on "racial healing," a term that portrays racism as an illness requiring a spiritual or psychological cure. The national press, on the other hand, played up the case's neo-Nazism, although it seemed to resonate more with fear of civil terror just after the Oklahoma City bombing than of racism. Coverage was easily subsumed into longstanding stereotypes of a backward, violent South rather than focused on the murders' emergence in the shadow of the guns of Fort Bragg and a wider national acceptance of violent solutions to social problems.

The people I spoke to about the crime over the next months often pointed first to the fact that the soldiers were not from the city. Many were able to tell me their three home states, Pennsylvania, Kentucky, and Illinois. Many saw the murders as a case of outsiders versus natives, not soldiers against civilians, or even whites versus blacks. Fayetteville's veterans, of course, might be expected to be somewhat defensive about a military explanation. As one grumbled to me: "If Burmeister had worked at Fat Daddy's instead of Fort Bragg, do you think the newspaper would have prefaced every description of him with 'restaurant worker Burmeister . . . '?" Some people also thought citizens failed to rally more behind the victims because they were unemployed and James had been addicted to drugs.

The gunman, James Burmeister, was tried the next year in Fayetteville's courthouse.[83] While Court TV showed up, there were often more empty than occupied seats in the small courtroom on the days I attended the trial. Some residents compared this crime with events of a few years earlier when a white soldier had gone on a shooting rampage in a local restaurant, killing four white patrons. More often, it seemed, people pointed to a double murder by a black man a few years earlier with white victims. The contest over which crime to compare this one to was a struggle over the crime's explanation—are soldiers prone to crazy bursts of violence? Is racial hatred simply mutual and equally lethal to members of each racial group? Or is this an anomaly, the military otherwise promoting racial harmony?

In all of these discussions in town, gender was left hidden in plain sight, the murderers' maleness causing no remark.[84] Class questions were only slightly more visible. It was surely legal advice, though, that changed Burmeister's appearance: While initial newspaper photos showed him in the T-shirt, crew cut, and black, thick-framed glasses that say "white working-class punk," his court dress of blue blazer, tortoise wire-rimmed glasses, and longer haircut was "college student." But in more ways then his dress could recuperate, the cultural citizenship of both this soldier and his victims was stained by their social class.

Several months after the trial, I went to see the murder site.[85] Nothing I had heard to that point prepared me for its misery. It was in an area of dilapidated, near-bare wood housing, the road unpaved. It had never *been* paved in a full century of modernity—its large ruts filled with the muddy water of the last days' rain. There, beside an uncondemned two-room shack, at the two X-like spots where Michael James and Jackie Burden had been shot and dropped to the ground, people had been tending two small memorials. Bitter pieces of broken brick and asphalt, dumped from elsewhere, held up the shrines'

War memorial: neo-Nazi murder site

two bouquets of red and orange plastic flowers, bright as blood or res-
urrection. A man approached me asking for $5 to take a taxi to work,
and, paying him, I left.

These murders happened just blocks away from the 1941 Turman
killings, also the product of white supremacism. But what happened
in Fayetteville and the United States in the fifty years between is
equally important, and the story can be told in two different ways.
The first is as a narrative of racial progress, where Turman's treatment was the Jim Crow norm, Burmeister the freakish exception in a
multiracial, multigender army and "post–civil rights" America. In
some ways, this is true. Nearly one-third African American (the other
services have lower percentages), the Army promotes blacks to its
higher ranks in greater numbers than in most other American work-
places, and it explicitly trains its soldiers in an ideology of racial brotherhood or rather of the irrelevance or harmfulness of race to the military mission.[86] Military leaders teach new recruits that everyone in
the army is "green" (as in olive uniforms) rather than black, white, or
brown.[87] The complete and immediate deference required to rank
means many white privates salute African American sergeants.

But while Burmeister's violence prompted a more unequivocal

military and civilian condemnation, his behavior was treated as aberrant just as Turman's was, leaving everyday practices of physical and symbolic racial violence still unacknowledged. Official military racial neutrality confronts the racism of many soldiers and the communities from which they come, as well as the racist discourses that have supported military actions since the beginning of the Republic. So one does not have to travel in neo-Nazi circles in the army to have heard what one Fort Bragg soldier back from the mission to Haiti said, shaking his head incredulously: There he had seen "the missing link," that is, the interspecies between humans and apes.[88] Even a book on racial equity by the most widely cited sociologist of the military, Charles Moskos, celebrates the tradition of African American soldiers on the frontier without hesitating over the racial evolutionist arguments that made Native Americans, Hawaiians, Cubans, and Filipinos objects of military action in the nineteenth century. So, he and his coauthor, John Butler, intend irony only for the first half of their statement that "the African-American 9th and 10th Cavalry Regiments, commanded by white officers, had the duty of controlling hostile Indians on the Great Plains."[89]

Another explanation for the changes from 1941 to 1995 would focus on the extensive pressures the military has been under. This includes both the civil rights movement and the internal pressure the military came under in an era of affluence, which is how to recruit enough labor. In this context, it became more open to African Americans. But even with this sociologically and historically more adequate view of army desegregation, another explanation is needed.

The differences and similarities in the crimes and their punishment say much, however, about the changing politics of the military in society and to the wages of the military budget. There has been a massive reorganization of the role of the state in public welfare in the period between the two crimes. Turman entered an army funded by a government with strong legitimacy and a vigorous welfare function that had just emerged with the New Deal. Burmeister joined an army that responded to a crisis of state legitimacy during the Vietnam War and racial upheaval of the 1960s by eliminating the draft, raising pay, and, of necessity without conscription, being more welcoming to women of all races and men of color. A constant retrenchment in the state's welfare role from at least the 1960s also meant that soldiers who came to Fayetteville increasingly found there a dramatic example of America's tale of two cities; inequality grew in the 1980s and 1990s, some of it, sociologist Bristow Hardin has demonstrated, as a direct result of how the military budget was spent.[90] So do they sometimes join the consensus that confuses character and racial difference with social stratification resulting from public policy and corporate actions. One older man who discussed the murders with me alluded to this when he said that they were not so much a sign of who Fayetteville's people were as much as they were

> saying something sad about the nation [more] than Fayetteville. And I know we are a part of the nation but I . . . would assign [it] back to people like Senator Jesse Helms and Senator Newt Gingrich and the mind-set that those type people are perpetrating upon the folk in America. I lay some of the blame for that superior feeling and promoting that mood in America that we are sick and tired of these no-good welfare folk, the food stamp people, all those negative things that flow from our national leadership which in my opinion gives a license or heightens the license of people who are on the verge of saying, "yeah I agree and we have to do something [violent] about it."

Burmeister joined forces with paramilitarism that was bred by the legitimation crisis following the Vietnam War. Many people saw that war not as a should-not-have-been-fought war, but as a should-never-have-been-lost war. Lost it was, though, as they see it, by a government and military leadership taken over by Jews, blacks, and feminists.[91] Unlike the MPs who killed Turman in 1941, Burmeister acted outside the chain of command. He replaced his dog tags with a Nazi symbol in order to join that movement in delegitimizing "duly-constituted authority" and to signal whose fault it was that America had lost control.

The crisis of state legitimacy resulted in the shift to an all-volunteer force that was increasingly black and female. Heightened policing of race and gender lines through such things as combat exclusion, and continued harassment of female, nonwhite, and gay and lesbian soldiers has been one response to what political scientist Francine D'Amico calls the deinstitutionalization but not the elimination of racism and sexism in the military.[92] If military work is to continue to confer a kind of white manhood, D'Amico says, masculinity and white identity must be asserted in a coded language of "readiness" and recruit "quality," sexuality managed in the language of "don't ask, don't tell," and the enemy must be even more emphatically racialized and feminized. Burmeister simply transferred this enemy imagery inside the nation.

This all made the crime of 1995 difficult to see as anything but evil or civilian racism bleeding into a military institution that has solved its own race problems. It is hard to see the white supremacist soldiers as recruited from relatively poor communities without jobs to a public works program that provides public housing in barracks and food at the mess hall. And it is difficult to see their murder victims as people privately struggling with the consequences of Fayetteville's low wages and high unemployment rate, problems exacerbated by the military base economy. And when the soldiers involved were disgorged from the army to stand trial in a civilian court, it was hard to see their case as one like many others less visible. Soldiers become mentally ill, are discharged, and show up for mental health services in civilian clothes. Prostitutes servicing the military are arrested or murdered. All cases that together threaten to overwhelm the city's beleaguered public services and further erode its reputation.

The years of militarization since 1941 have raised the military's public stature. Opinion surveys suggest the military has become the most respected American secular institution—more esteemed than the Congress, the courts, or the schools.[93] As the military's values increasingly become identified as America's, the problem of racism takes a new turn. The army's growing conservatism means that soldiering grants citizenship to blacks in a new way. While Ned Turman's contemporaries hoped that personal sacrifice for the nation or battlefield valor would win them this, Burmeister's black colleagues' disciplined and conservative personal politics are what now theoretically set them apart from civilians. Defined as the weaker among us, civilians are so, not just because they need protection, but because their values are flabby. This also reinvigorates the black soldier's masculinity, questioned by racism. As people identify "the government" as a self-serving, bloated, and civilian-centered welfare function and the military as its rational other, the black soldier also comes to stand in contrast to that other huge American population of "group-quartered" young blacks—the imprisoned.

Fed by money, the military-civilian distinction has grown sharp enough to suggest that the civilian is actually outside the nation, which belongs only to those who fight in war. The characteristics rejected from the body politic are transferred all too easily to the civilian world's still unaccepted racial and gender identities. And while mayhem in Fayetteville marks some people's attempt to redefine citizenship in both 1941 and 1995, the murders stand out less than we might at first imagine from the background violence and economic dislocations of the American century of war and war preparation.

WAR AS SPECTATOR SPORT

When our military bus arrived at Sicily Drop Zone (a paratroop landing field) for the yearly All-American Week celebrations, my fellow travelers and I filed out. We included hundreds of white-haired veterans in shirtsleeves and unit caps, military wives or husbands with their children in arms, young soldiers in civvies on a busman's holiday, and other Fayetteville residents out for a pleasant afternoon. Moving on to some bleachers by the side of the vast and sandy open landing area, we sat down to watch the choreographed seizure of an unnamed, perhaps Third World, airfield. Although a little shade would have made things more comfortable, for most it was to be a perfectly entertaining day in the late spring sun.

Despite a warning over the PA system, some of us jumped as jets screamed close overhead to clear the field with faux, but still chest-pounding, explosions. Huge transport planes moved slowly across the sky in their wake. They dropped waves of parachutes, young men dangling from their lines like dandelion seeds. The wind was too high for the planned drop of heavy equipment, the announcer crackled, but the crowd moved on happily to the static displays of weaponry and took their hot dog stand purchases under a two-story-high sand-colored tent. Young soldiers put camouflage paint on children in strollers, and others patiently or enthusiastically explained their machine guns and mobile Geographic Information Systems (GIS) units to the crowds who scuffled by their tables.

Target Audiences and the Team's Twelfth Man

The renewed importance of civilian consent or support for military enterprises gave purpose to that afternoon's events. Even more so than earlier in the decade, our presence was a vehicle for the pursuit of mil-

Recruiting for an all-volunteer army: All-American Week weapons display

itary missions, even a form of civic activism. For civilians around the country have come to be depicted as the team's twelfth man or a "force multiplier." The demonstration joins a sprawling set of mechanisms that every day transmit the military's message and invite people to that role. These include military band concerts, Hollywood films using Defense Department equipment, glossy recruitment ads, uniformed soldiers teaching in public schools, military museums, dry-docked battleships set up as tourist destinations, and intensive explicit and covert use of the U.S. media. Overt training and recruiting efforts of the military services are packaged as entertainment. The Golden Knights, for example, the Army's crack parachute team, leap together from planes in flower-like clusters or make precision landings inside major league ballparks or race car tracks before an estimated twelve million people each year. Based at Fort Bragg, they have several hundred full-time employees and a $2 million annual budget.[94]

Much public relations is accomplished via a new surge of war-themed entertainment in places like the nation's 330 military museums.[95] While some remain dusty destinations on a few military buffs' itineraries, they increasingly incorporate expensive and state-of-the-art interactive exhibits. The ninety thousand-square-foot Mighty Eighth Air Force Heritage Museum in Pooler, Georgia, for example, aims to recreate the feeling of being in a bomber in combat. Eight screens and deafening flak sounds surround visitors, and a whoosh of air hits them at the appropriate moment to simulate the feel of the bomb bay doors' opening.

A daily wave of tourists visits battleships, aircraft carriers, and subs berthed up and down U.S. coasts. War memorials and statuary are among the tourist calling cards of many cities, not always minor, as with Washington, D.C.'s monuments to Iwo Jima, Vietnam, and Korea. Recreational dollars pour into Civil War and other battle reenactments, paintball parks, and veterans' reunions (which Fayetteville business boosters began to aggressively seek out in the 1980s). Military history is a separate section in most bookstores, on par with cooking, biography, or history itself. And war serves as a form of leisure activity for viewers of the many TV war documentaries or news programs, and in Hollywood fiction films like *Top Gun* and *Saving Private Ryan* and even antiwar movies like *Platoon* and *Three Kings*. And in a related if demilitarizing vein, many military installations closed in the last ten years have become theme parks, golf courses, or film production facilities.[96]

These are the devices of what sociologist Michael Mann calls "spectator-sport militarism," or the celebration of military prowess through enthusiastic witnessing rather than military training and fighting.[97] Because much war spectating emerges during the search for leisure experiences, this might also be called military tourism. War as entertainment has more buyers than ever because the military's emphasis on "civilian mobilization" comes at a time when Americans are spending increasing amounts of their wealth on entertainment, tourism, or leisure activities. The new economy is in fact centered on entertainment, both culturally and materially, with many people spending more on it than on health care and clothing.[98]

Civilian means spectator

When the Gulf War began, Latisha Collins was recruited to this civilian role in her Fayetteville high school. Her history teacher required the class to watch the war on CNN and then led discussions afterward, centered not on how the unfolding tragedy might have been avoided but on military strategies for fighting the war better or ending it more efficiently. In her hours of CNN viewing, she watched reporters who had accepted military control of their stories, as well as an unacknowledged disinformation campaign waged by the White House and a public relations firm hired by the Kuwaiti government. Although the incubator babies and Iraqi troops massing on the Saudi border were later shown to be phantoms, their reporting as fact shaped the conversations in Fayetteville classrooms, making a military solution seem obligatory.[99] Like children around the country, she was also given class time to write letters to soldiers. After her teacher suggested to the students that they write about themselves and their families, she sarcastically described the daily routine of the prostitutes and drug dealers in her poor neighborhood, and the several children she once knew who had died violent deaths. She was told her letters were "inappropriate" and would not be sent out.

Fort Bragg is a key to the new waging of cultural war. It is home to a major Psychological Operations unit whose new $8.6 million facility, a spokesperson explained, will use "a CNN-central concept . . . in which psychological operations soldiers develop first-class, world-quality products and export them to remote locations."[100] The product has occasionally been used at home, as already seen, during the Cold War. In the mid-1980s, the unit worked with a National Security Council office to try to shape media coverage of the contra war in Nicaragua. While it pulled out of this cooperative arrangement after a year, apparently with concern about its legality, it recently sent several interns to NPR and CNN to learn how the news is made there.[101] Recognizing the value of television to their efforts, the military has lobbied for advanced production facilities like those on Fort Bragg and more advanced nose video cameras for its fighter jets, to allow more attractively sharp imagery for transmission to CNN and other news networks.[102]

Fort Bragg has long done concerted public relations or propaganda work in the city, and the legitimacy of using public funds to missionize civilians has been taken for granted. An example of how elaborate these efforts have been comes from the early 1960s, when the Air Force flew the city's mayor and other members of the Fayetteville–Pope Air Force Base Civilian Advisory Council to Florida to watch a missile launch, as well as to golf and fish. According to a booklet produced by the military, the trip's goal was to increase "the atmosphere of mutual understanding and cooperation that grows and flourishes each time we meet and that plays an important part in the success of the Air Force mission." Despite the gesture of reciprocity, the civilian was a junior partner, military goals paramount. The civilians received a certificate at the end that proclaimed: "Bearer has completed the [USAF Tactical Missile] School's Ultra-short Course for Novice Missileers. . . . The bearer of this document is a man to be reckoned with as much by the Warlords of communism as by the

Golfers and Fish of Orlando, Florida." Participants also received a photographic journal of their trip, to which the public relations department had added humorous captions. They portrayed the civilians as "manly friends" of the officers, though sometimes brought low with awe before the technowizardry of the missile men or the celebrity of the generals: "How many books of green stamps did you say this cost?" one civilian asks an officer as they stand near a missile launcher. Just a single joke points to civilian control. With the word "Guest" on his name tag, a suited man says to a soldier, "Now, sergeant, you can't be serious about getting that pay raise by 1 October."[103]

Through the years, military officials have listened to city leaders talk about Fayetteville's problems and accomplishments and have appeared in support of various local initiatives, for example, at parades downtown or at conferences on domestic violence. In such contexts, however, the military sees itself as helping the civilian world only as it is consistent with—that is, it ideally advances and must never impede—the military mission. While public relations efforts may present the work as altruistic, soldiers sent to work in the community can be said to be in training for overseas civic action work. If they contribute to efforts to combat domestic violence in town, where many military families are part of the problem and where services for them will often be provided, this can be seen as central to the military mission of caring for military families in the interest of soldier morale and retention. In this respect as well, the restructuring post–Cold War military sharpens the distinction between soldier and civilian and blurs the boundary of army and home front, further obscuring the costs of war and responsibility for it.

The end of the Cold War brought no peace to Fayetteville. The army and its missions were restructured but the goal was more to rearrange budget categories than priorities. As throughout the century, however, the conditions of life for Fayetteville's people were subtly reshaped. They became drawn, even more than previously, into a collaborative role, though the full extent of their job remained camouflaged. Commentators sounded alarms that civilians had veered dangerously away from the army, or vice versa. But many decades of a national security culture and state have obscured the reality that the

Future site of $23 million war museum, downtown Fayetteville

distinction between the civilian and the military has worn down rather than intensified. For the post–Cold War era has seen the rise of the ideas that the sofa spectator is a linchpin of military success and that soldiers shopping at the mall, teaching Junior ROTC to high school students, and getting educated through Montgomery GI Bill benefits are key to the health and wealth of civil society. And as at century's beginning, war and racism were intertwined; the city's 1995 white supremacist murders are one illustration of the complex process whereby the formation of a military welfare state in lieu of a broader sense of public welfare continues to contribute to the poverty and scapegoating of large segments of the black community.

Despite the massive military buildup of the 1980s and continued heavy military spending in the 1990s, Fayetteville today watches the rest of urban North Carolina pass it by in wealth and status. As it does, Fayetteville's people have struggled to imagine another future beyond the base. The millennium opened with a behemoth military museum honoring the Army's Airborne and Special Operations units being the city's major investment in new development. But one local politician dares to imagine, at least in private, the whole base turned back to the city. Its golf courses and basketball courts and residences would house families now in deteriorated mill housing, and businesses would turn to modern ploughshares and the work of social and environmental repair.

Fayetteville's people have enjoyed a unique and cosmopolitan history, but they have also suffered a history only partly of their own making. Like people across America, choices made in Washington about war and war preparation have deeply shaped their lives. Those choices have wreaked havoc on soldiers' bodies and psyches, cost people their sons and daughters, lowered the wages and raised the taxes of most, intensified social inequalities, and yoked the progress of their democracy and egalitarian hopes to war's secrecies, redefined citizenship, and political and racial hatreds. The sacrifice and suffering war exacts from the home front has often been denied by official narratives, even as the costs abroad have been. But however permanent the present may seem, other histories—both of the past and the future—can still be made from the insights of all the people who have lived under war's shadow and nursed its hidden injuries.

From where I sit trying to catch shade at the edge of the press tent, the very small band of dissenters are hardly visible behind the crowd of red-bereted soldiers and other Fayetteville residents who have come for the grand opening of the Airborne and Special Operations Museum. The signs the demonstrators hold—Magic-Markered words on painted cardboard—are small, amateur things beside the firm, new sod, clean concrete, and freshly minted and soaring five-story monument of the museum's entrance, its crisscrossed girders meant to evoke the form of a parachuting soldier. But in any case all eyes are soon drawn skyward as the PA system announces the arrival of the Golden Knights parachute demonstration team. The men appear as tiny motes at first, and as they drift closer, their gentle stunt loops become visible, outlined by the magenta plumes of smoke that begin streaming from small jets on the boots of one parachutist. A voice behind me snaps angrily at someone who walks in front, blocking his view. Someone else to my side blesses the jumpers, and they land, safely and pinpoint, on a target laid out on the museum lawn.

Ross Perot's familiar short form comes to the microphone. His $1 million donation has put him on the dais with General Hugh Shelton and the retired general who spearheaded the fund-raising. Most of the rest of the $22.5 million cost came from the people of Fayetteville or the state at large through their taxes, excess utility payments, and donated public land. This is not the story told from the stage, however, perhaps because city officials who made the transfer risked no referendum on the matter. Moreover, the museum symbolically belongs to the military and to veterans, and so even the city's mayor sits down in the well of folding chairs with a host of others. City officials promise, though, that the museum will launch the permanent "revitalization" of the downtown, putative heart of the city. It is still mainly moribund this day, though, as it had been for decades.

Whatever its economics, the museum's cultural impact will be powerful as it educates yellow busloads of schoolchildren and cars full of sightseers in the military's official version of history. To make a tourist attraction of war requires some heavy lifting and thick screening, however: The history inside is clean and beautiful and, even, fun. The depicted wars all liberated someone but had no politics—not even antifascism. No civilians died or were raped, and soldiers' bodies are all intact, even when injured. There are none of the women on whom war also turns, from military prostitutes to wives raising children alone to weeping or angry mothers. They are wars of sacrifice without killing, wars allowing humans to be their best, helping each other in times of trouble, serving what is called the greater good, and enduring the ultimate risk.

After the speeches, people begin to stream into the museum and I walk over to greet the band of peace activists. Their signs can now be read by everyone going by:

> World War II, 55 million killed, 60 percent civilian
> Vietnam, 2.3 million killed, 58 percent civilian
> Gulf War, including sanctions, 1.3 million killed and counting, more than 75 percent civilian

While most passersby seem to disappear the people and their message with averted, ambiguous gazes, several gray veterans step up to spit out familiar invective. "Get a job," says one. "Go live in Cuba," another, their words indexing a worldview in which criticism of war can only come from people who contribute nothing to the nation and do not belong. Another soldier comes up with a more interested and friendly greeting. Lenore Yarger, who is from a Catholic Worker house in another city and is holding the Iraq sign, tells him she thinks the memory of war should be cause for mourning and horror. He tells her he decided a while ago that he would not be willing to kill and seems neither proud nor ashamed to say so. He is more disturbed to describe his attempts to talk to his fellow soldiers about the ethics of their work: Most are afraid to discuss it, although a few openly agree or disagree with him. He joined the army for college benefits, he says, and would have left after four years of insulting treatment from superiors, but he had been pulled into debt and seemed to have no other option. The army, though, set him in the right direction in life, he says. Child psychology is what he is now headed toward. His friends wait for him at some distance, and he joins them to head back to post, soon indistinguishable from any other man in the crowd.

I move on and talk with a young city worker, cheerfully winding up speaker wires near the now-empty dais, this job a welcome break from his more usual day. He had a family member who died in the army, and so the museum is a good thing, he said, because it expresses gratitude for that sacrifice. But he believes God wants us to live peacefully with each other.

Inside the museum, I meet some Vietnam veterans in front of a helicopter diorama with faux tall Asian grass and two expressionless mannequins in uniform. It is a good day, they say, feeling the museum is theirs, or is for them, in any case. One, Lorenzo Andrews, is a Puerto Rican man from the Bronx. His beret is festooned with military unit pins, which he sells to make a living. He is there with two men who identify themselves as disabled by post-traumatic stress disorder and one man who says he cannot say what work he used to do. Ho Chi Minh was an admirer of George Washington, Lorenzo tells me, and the war perhaps a mistake. But he does not regret having gone to war: It is where he found his lifelong, beloved friends, both those with him today and back in the Bronx, where he and others take care of the homeless and hurt among them. While they have noticed unhappily that the museum mannequins are nearly all white and while they agree that the displays do not even try to represent war's horrific reality, they keep their eyes steadfastly on the details that the museum designers got right: the webbing on the uniform found only in the early years of the war matched with the correct shirt style, just as they remembered it.

Passing out of the building and across the grounds to leave, I walk through another past of forgotten home front battles, their ghostly sites bulldozed by the museum's engineers and by the political will to forget. The building went up virtually on top of the place where Ned Turman, the black private from South Carolina, was killed in 1941. And on the ruins of the "notorious" Hay Street bars, where Korean, Vietnamese, and North Carolinian women sold their bodies to soldiers during the Vietnam War, and where soldiers came to buy them and to drink away the spectral sight of the Southeast Asian dead who followed them there. And where stood just the year before the consid-

erably less grand shelter of some homeless men, now homeless somewhere else.

To remember all of these, despite the museum, may be less arduous labor than that which keeps them buried, for a costly work of
euphemism, erasure, and financing are needed to hold them underground. And it may be safer, too, because preparing for war has required constructing enemy images, both foreign and domestic, and
has sharpened the social inequalities that a war economy creates.
What the museum forgets and what alternatives there are become visible and audible in the suffering and aspirations of the living: the
homeless men, Lenore and Lorenzo, and all the others who have
passed through Fayetteville and made both its sadness and its vibrancy
and iconoclasm. Even more, they embody the longing for another
kind of home. They speak outside the lines of the museum script, remember more than any book can hope to capture, and, with their insights and will, are headed on a different route to safety and service.

Introduction: Making War at Home

1. The military facilities near Fayetteville include the Army's Fort Bragg and Pope Air Force Base. The air base's relatively small size, its location farther from the city than Fort Bragg, and the distinctiveness of the Air Force workforce and history have led me to focus on Fort Bragg. Technically, the Army is said to have installations or posts, the Air Force, bases, but in referring to Fort Bragg as a kind of military facility, I sometimes use the generic term *military base*. Throughout this book, the term *army* is used as the generic term for any military service, with *Army* referring only to that specific service.

2. Randolph Bourne. 1964. *War and the Intellectuals: Essays by Randolph S. Bourne, 1915–1919*. Edited and with an introduction by Carl Resek. New York: Harper Torchbooks.

3. Many claims have been made for the benefits: freedom from foreign tyranny, aggression between other states deterred, military technologies that spin off to civilian use, and youth disciplined through soldier training. With few exceptions, these are unproven or disproven propositions (see, for example, Sam Marullo. 1993. *Ending the Cold War at Home*. New York: Lexington Books).

4. Elaine Scarry has eloquently described this confusion of war's goals with its bodily effects or reality (*The Body in Pain: The Making and Unmaking of the World*. Oxford: Oxford University Press, 1985).

5. Of all the tens of thousands of books on war, a very small but powerful few have been written by those who have lost the most to the violence. War's ravages have been most intense where the gap between rich and poor is widest, and so, too, the hungry and illiterate survivors tell fewer tales in print. But see Victor Montejo. 1987. *Testimony: Death of a Guatemalan Village*. Trans. Victor Perera. Willimantic, CT: Curbstone Press. See also Joshua M. Greene and Shiva Kumar, eds. 2000. *Witness: Voices from the Holocaust*. New York: Free Press. For ethnographies that include survivors' accounts, see Carolyn Nordstrom. 1997. *A Different Kind of War Story*. Philadelphia: University of Pennsylvania Press; Glen Alcalay. 1984. Maelstrom in the Marshall Islands: The social impact of nuclear weapons testing. In Catherine Lutz, ed. *Micronesia as Strategic Colony: The Impact of U.S. Policy on Micronesian Health and Culture*. Cambridge: Cultural Survival Occasional Papers; Janis H. Jenkins. 1996. Women's experience of trauma and political violence. In Carolyn Sargent and Caroline Brettell, eds. *Gender and Health: An International Perspective*. Upper Saddle River, NJ: Prentice Hall; Liisa H. Malkki. 1995. *Purity and Exile: Violence, Memory, and National Cosmology among Hutu Refugees in Tanzania*. Chicago: University of Chicago Press.

6. There, the Air Force Association succeeded in expunging what histori-

ans know about the atomic bombing of Japan; see Edward T. Linenthal and Tom Engelhardt, eds. 1996. *History Wars: The* Enola Gay *and other Battles for the American Past.* New York: Metropolitan Books/Henry Holt and Co.

7. There are related if muted effects emanating from the sites of National Guard armories, large recruiting centers, and clusters of military retirees.

8. C. Wright Mills. 1956. *The Power Elite.* New York: Oxford University Press; Richard Slotkin. 1992. *Gunfighter Nation: The Myth of the Frontier in Twentieth-Century America.* New York: Harper Perennial.

9. Key sources for me have been Fayetteville journalist Roy Parker's excellent history of Cumberland County as well as archives at Fort Bragg and in the local history room at the county library. I also used Fayetteville city council meeting minutes, the *Fayetteville Observer* morgue, National Archive photographs and records from Fort Bragg earlier in the century, and material from University of North Carolina at Chapel Hill's own historical collections, the premier archive on the South.

10. Such interviews, as historian David Cecelski has eloquently described them, help us "understand their search for faith and their struggles to make sense out of the world—because those are our struggles, too. We want to know how they have found dignity, grace and beauty in lives that have never been easy." David Cecelski. 1999. If you could hear what I hear. Address to 25th Anniversary Celebration of the Southern Oral History Program, Chapel Hill, NC.

1. **Encampment: Boosters, Social Crisis, and a Military Solution (1918–1938)**

1. Fayetteville is being advertised, to great advantage. *The Fayetteville*

Observer [hereafter *Fayetteville Observer*], 10/18/16.

2. Fayetteville gets big military camp. *Fayetteville Observer,* 7/24/18. The men present that day included Fred Hale, president of the chamber of commerce and son of the *Fayetteville Observer* editor.

3. John Mueller. 1991. Changing attitudes towards war: The impact of the First World War. *British Journal of Political Science* 21: 1–28. See also Arthur A. Ekirch, Jr. 1956. *The Civilian and the Military.* New York: Oxford University Press; John Whiteclay Chambers III. 1987. *To Raise an Army: The Draft Comes to Modern America.* New York: The Free Press; David M. Kennedy. 1980. *Over Here: The First World War and American Society.* New York: Oxford University Press.

4. Camp notes. *Fayetteville Observer,* 10/10/17.

5. H. Trawick Ward and R. P. Stephen Davis, Jr. 1999. *Time Before History: The Archaeology of North Carolina.* Chapel Hill: University of North Carolina Press.

6. *Ibid.,* p. 256. Palisaded villages became more common at about the time that chiefdoms rose in the Southeast, chiefdoms whose elites could organize the capture of stored surpluses that agriculture had made possible (and whose investments also made people less likely to flee their homes when violence threatened); George R. Milner. 1999. Warfare in prehistoric and early historic eastern North America. *Journal of Archaeological Research* 7 (2):105–151.

7. While the contact zone might have begun to take shape in the Sandhills area beginning with Spanish expeditions of the sixteenth century, the effect on native societies was minimal until the seventeenth.

8. Brian Ferguson and Neil Whitehead (*War in the Tribal Zone: Expanding States and Indigenous Warfare.* Santa Fe: School of American Research

Press, 1992) have called this "the tribal zone": the areas where European colonists, technologies, and diseases affected native peoples, often with devastating population loss.

9. The relatively poor soils of the aptly named Sandhills area and other evidence suggests that the Siouan-speaking Native Americans who used the area did so mainly on a seasonal basis. Christopher Ohm Clement, Steven D. Smith, Ramona M. Grunden, and Jill S. Quattlebaum. 1997. *Archaeological Survey of 4,000 Acres on the Lower Little River, Cumberland, Hoke and Moore Counties, Fort Bragg, North Carolina.* Columbia, SC: University of South Carolina, South Carolina Institute of Archaeology and Anthropology, Cultural Resources Consulting Division.

10. *Ibid.*, pp. 23–24.

11. James H. Merrell. 1989. *The Indians' New World: Catawbas and Their Neighbors from European Contact through the Era of Removal.* Chapel Hill: Published for the Institute of Early American History and Culture, Williamsburg, Va., by the University of North Carolina Press; Gerald M. Sider. 1993. *Lumbee Indian Histories: Race, Ethnicity, and Indian Identity in the Southern United States.* Cambridge. Cambridge University Press.

12. S. A. Ashe. *History of North Carolina,* cited in John Oates. 1950. *The Story of Fayetteville and the Upper Cape Fear.* Charlotte: The David Press, p. 149. The Scots first arrived in the future Fort Bragg area around 1750; Clement et al., *op. cit.,* p. 38. By 1860, there were approximately two thousand people there; Clement et al., *op. cit.* p. 51.

13. Col. Duncan G. MacRae of the FILI speaking in 1889, cited in Oates, *op. cit.,* p. 243.

14. Russell F. Weigley. 1967. *History of the United States Army.* New York: The Macmillan Company, p. 27.

15. *Ibid.*, p. 163. The Army also spent much time building roads and

forts to facilitate further colonial settlement: In this, "any difference between soldiering and pioneering escaped the naked eye;" Geoffrey Perret. 1989. *A Country Made by War: From the Revolution to Vietnam–the Story of America's Rise to Power.* New York: Random House, p. 137.

16. *Eighth Census of the United States,* 1860. Volume I: Population.

17. But as in most other American communities, history often steers around this sensitive topic. Roy Parker's account of this area is an exemplary exception: Roy Parker, Jr. 1990. *Cumberland County: A Brief History.* Raleigh: Division of Archives and History, North Carolina Department of Cultural Resources. Class has also been made through violence and intertwined with race. See Gerald Sider's (*op. cit.*) eloquent account of how Native American ethnicity emerged through violence and uprooting, rather than just being destroyed by them.

18. While 39 percent of rural households had one or more slaves, only a small number had a dozen or more; Parker, *op. cit.,* p. 40. Far fewer slaves were owned in the west where smallholders dominated, including in the area that was to be the future site of Fort Bragg.

19. *Ibid.*, p. 42.

20. *Ibid.*, pp. 49–51. Other factors contributed to the siting of arsenal in Fayetteville as well; Jonathan Phillips, personal communication.

21. Parker, *op. cit.,* p. 43.

22. Parker, *op. cit.,* pp. 43–44. North Carolina was known in the 1700s as a haven for people running from slavery, and the badges were white authorities' attempt to control the situation; Jeffrey J. Crow. 1980. Slave rebelliousness and social conflict in North Carolina, 1775–1802. *William and Mary Quarterly,* 3rd series, 37:79–102.

23. Cited in John Hope Franklin. 1956. *The Militant South, 1800–1861.*

Cambridge, MA: Harvard University Press, p. 156.

24. Edward Lee Winslow, Esq. *Oration Delivered Before the Fayetteville Independent Light Infantry Company on the Semi-Centenary of the Corps,* August 23, 1843. North Carolina Collection. University of North Carolina at Chapel Hill (UNC-CH).

25. J. E. B. Stuart Chapter of the United Daughters of the Confederacy. 1910. *War Days in Fayetteville.* Fayetteville, NC: Judge Printing Co., pp. 10–11.

26. Katherine Beach, Cape Fear Museum, personal communication.

27. Established in 1817, *The Fayetteville Observer's* circulation was surpassed only by the *New Orleans Picayune.* The textile mills employed 550 workers by 1860, most of them children and young women. Their status was low in the eyes of contemporary farmers and craftspeople, who considered them "factory slaves"; Parker, *op. cit.,* p. 62.

28. Clement et al., *op. cit.,* p. 29.

29. Despite the state's hostility to unions, there were strikes in local mills in 1909, 1915, and 1921. The new factories were sometimes joint ventures of locals with mill barons from elsewhere in the state or the country; several mills were erected in 1898, 1900, and 1906; Parker, *op. cit.,* pp. 79, 103–107. Unions were hostile, however, to the interests of black workers; Jeffrey J. Crow. 1992. *A History of African Americans in North Carolina.* Raleigh, NC: Division of Archives and History, NC Department of Cultural Resources, p. 121.

30. *Thirteenth Census of the United States,* 1910. Volume III: Population.

31. H. Leon Prather. 1984. *We Have Taken a City: Wilmington Racial Massacre and Coup of 1898.* Cranberry, NJ: Associated University Presses; and David Cecelski and Timothy B. Tyson. 1998. *Democracy Betrayed: The Wilmington Race Riot of 1898 and Its Legacy.* Chapel

Hill: University of North Carolina Press. For other sources on the making of race in the South in this period, see C. Vann Woodward. 1974. *The Strange Career of Jim Crow,* 3rd revised ed. New York: Oxford University Press; Joel Williamson. 1986. *A Rage for Order: Black/White Relations in the American South Since Emancipation.* New York: Oxford University Press; and Glenda Elizabeth Gilmore. 1996. *Gender and Jim Crow: Women and the Politics of White Supremacy in North Carolina, 1896–1920.* Chapel Hill: University of North Carolina Press.

32. Scion of one of the town's wealthiest and most respected families, Edwin Robeson MacKethan was elected president of the club and later went on to be elected state legislator and city mayor in the early 1920s. *Edwin Robeson MacKethan Papers,* Southern Historical Collection, UNC-CH.

33. A white man's day. *Fayetteville Observer,* 10/22/1898.

34. Cited in Prather, *op. cit.,* p. 85. John Oates's account of the history of Fayetteville (an exhaustive 868 pages, covered in a Scotch-evocative plaid rayon cloth made in a local mill) gives sharp insight into race ideas of the year (1950) it was written in its pacified and extremely terse account of the Red Shirts' activities: "Their purpose was to restore white supremacy in several counties in the State. They wore red shirts and rode on horse back. They paraded from time to time in the towns of this section. . . . There was an intensive political campaign in every county of the State and as a result the Legislature elected in November 1898 was composed of 134 Democrats; 30 Republicans and six Populists" (*The Story of Fayetteville and the Upper Cape Fear,* p. 423). Likewise, Oates erroneously claims the Ku Klux Klan "first appeared in 1868 and practically ceased

to exist in 1870" (p. 422). Oates also presents an historical account of a white man, William J. Tolar, who, in an organized mob action outside the Market House in 1867, had killed a black man accused of the rape of a white woman. He calls Tolar "one of the most beloved men who ever resided in the Cape Fear section." The account notes that when asked years later whether "he had not killed a man in Fayetteville[,] Tolar replied, 'No, I killed a beast in human form'." *Ibid.,* p. 224.

35. Prather, *op. cit.,* p. 83.

36. White supremacists were more successful in taking the 1900 election in the urban and eastern parts of the state where most blacks lived. Seventy-six percent of the Fayetteville voters who went to the polls voted for it while all other county precincts voted 54 percent for it (the county was then 43 percent black). The substantial rural black migration to cities during the 1890s had been seen as a political threat by many whites, contributing to the character of the urban vote that year; Jerry Wayne Cotton. 1973. Negro Disenfranchisement in North Carolina: The Politics of Race in a Southern State. Ph.D. dissertation, University of North Carolina at Greensboro.

37. Parker, *op. cit.,* pp. 79–80; Cecelski and Tyson, *op. cit.;* Leon F. Litwack. 1998. *Trouble in Mind: Black Southerners in the Age of Jim Crow.* New York: Knopf, p. 305. There was even an attempt to establish South African–style Bantustans—separate rural districts for whites and blacks—in the state, an effort that lost a vote in the North Carolina Senate by a slim margin in 1915. It prompted more active black resistance to the many forms of discrimination they faced; Crow. 1992, *History of African Americans,* pp. 122, 124–25.

38. Franklin, *op. cit.* For reconsiderations and refutations, see Marcus Cunliffe. 1968. *Soldiers and Civilians: The*

Martial Spirit in America, 1775–1865. New York: Little, Brown; and Robert E. May. 1978. Dixie's martial image: A continuing historiographical enigma. *The Historian* 60 (2):213–234.

39. In the late 1880s, "a Georgia black leader described his people as essentially under siege, occupying a steadily deteriorating position. . . . 'Open war, with two contending armies in the field, governed by the usages of Christian nations, would be an improvement.' By 1910, in the estimation of a visitor, race relations in the South had become a 'state of war' "; (Litwack, *op. cit.,* p. 411). Black armed resistance was much more common than many have assumed; Timothy B. Tyson. 1998. Robert F. Williams, "Black Power," and the roots of the African American freedom struggle. *Journal of American History* 85 (2):540–570.

40. Catherine Bishir. 1993. Landmarks of power: Building a Southern past, 1885–1915. *Southern Cultures* 1: 5–44. See also Gaines M. Foster. 1987. *Ghosts of the Confederacy: Defeat, the Lost Cause, and the Emergence of the New South, 1865 to 1913.* New York: Oxford University Press.

41. Jacquelyn Dowd Hall. 1998. "You must remember this": Autobiography as social critique. *Journal of American History* 85 (2):439–465.

42. Bishir, *op. cit.*

43. Elizabeth Ellis, interview with Gary Goodwyn, 1980, Local and State History Room, Cumberland County Public Library (CCPL); *Fayetteville Observer,* 2/27/08.

44. Just the previous year, another police chief and an officer had been killed by a black bootlegger who also received the death penalty. He attempted suicide in jail, anticipating, he said, no justice from the court; *Fayetteville Observer,* 2/7/07 and 2/28/07.

45. *14th Census of the United States,*

1920 Bulletin, Population: North Carolina.

46. *Fayetteville City Council Minutes,* May 6, 1920, to April 13, 1925. Mayor John Underwood and Police Chief Merker resign. *Fayetteville Observer,* Extra, 4/30/20. The assistant police chief and two patrolmen were relieved of their duties a year earlier for reasons that appear unmentionable in both city council minutes and the newspaper. It was a board of aldermen at this time and only later became a city council; *Fayetteville City Council Minutes,* August 7, 1916, to April 30, 1920.

47. Alexander Cook, interview, 1980, CCPL.

48. *Fayetteville Observer,* 7/23/21. Unlike his black bootlegging counterpart, Williams was simply imprisoned for his murder. And he was later pardoned by the governor after inventing rifle improvements that were ultimately incorporated into eight million Army weapons; Oates, *op. cit.*

49. Between 1900 and 1918, there were twenty-nine lynchings in the state, twenty-five of black men, but these numbers do not include other such racially motivated slayings. During the years between 1917 and 1919, Fayetteville became the location for one of the ten NAACP branches in the state. During the 1920 to 1943 period, lynchings continued apace, with thirty-seven in the state; Raymond Gavins. 1991. The NAACP in North Carolina during the age of segregation. In Armstead L. Robinson and Patricia Sullivan, eds. *New Directions in Civil Rights Studies.* Charlottesville: University Press of Virginia, pp. 105–25. The application for a Fayetteville branch charter, made in April 1918, notes that it would involve converting an existing group called "The Ants," who were "an organized body of colored people whose purpose is for the uplife and advancement of colored peo-

ple." The Records of the NAACP Branch Files, Group I, Box G-147, Fayetteville, NC 1918–1939. Library of Congress.

50. Charles W. Chesnutt. 1999 (1902). The free colored people of North Carolina. In Joseph McElrath, Jr., Robert C. Leitz III, and Jesse Crisler, eds. *Charles W. Chesnutt: Essays and Speeches.* Stanford, CA: Stanford University Press, pp. 176–177; Matthew Leary Perry. The Negro in Fayetteville. In Oates, *op. cit.,* pp. 695–715. One of the largest mills, the Ashley-Bailey Silk Company, was unusual in hiring an all-black workforce. The Northern owners believed black workers were more adept at handling the slippery material they wove; Parker, *op. cit.,* p. 106.

51. Parker, *op. cit.* In the 1920s, one-third of the black farmers of Cumberland owned their land, with many living east of the Cape Fear River. This turned out to be where land values were not to rise as quickly as they did near the post. Blacks in the closer western part of the county who owned substantial farmland, though, were able to profit from rising land values. In town, there was a gradual decline of black businesses after the war, with some remembering nonrenewal of their business leases around the Market House and a "no loan to Negro" policy in local banks. At this time as well, whites began to go into once black-dominated professions that had become more respectable as "white work" after World War I, including restaurants and services; hotels; laundries; barber, police, fire, and burial services; C. A. Asbury and D. W. Bishop. n.d. The economic and social development of the Negro in Fayetteville, 1865–1967. Manuscript in Gillespie Street Library Auxiliary Club. Scrapbook of the History of Black Citizens in Fayetteville, vols. I and II. CCPL.

52. Michael S. Sherry. 1995. *In the*

Shadow of War: The United States since the 1930s. New Haven, CT: Yale University Press, p. 2. The Civil War is sometimes called the first industrial war, but by World War I, the moniker was much more throughly apt.

53. Walter Millis. 1956. *Arms and Men: A Study in American Military History.* New Brunswick, NJ: Rutgers University Press, p. 207.

54. In telling this story, American military and social history has sometimes been technophobic and sometimes technophiliac. One reason for the latter attitude has been the hope that superweapons would forestall the need for a large standing army (Sherry, *op. cit.,* p. 2). It is also spurred by the compensatory fantasy that either the weapons' horror or efficacy would make wars end more quickly.

55. Parker, *op. cit.,* p. 115.

56. Parker, *op. cit.,* p. 114.

57. Ann Markusen et al. 1991. *The Rise of the Gunbelt: The Military Remapping of Industrial America.* New York: Oxford University Press; Roger W. Lotchin, ed. 1984. *The Martial Metropolis: U.S. Cities in War and Peace.* New York: Praeger.

58. Richard L. Watson. 1979. The North Carolina congressional delegation, 1917–19. *North Carolina Historical Review* 61: 298–323.

59. *Camp Bragg and Fayetteville, N.C.: Sketches of Camp and City.* Richmond, VA: Central Publishing Company, 1919, pp. 11–12. Climate was viewed differently at the start of the twentieth century. The brochure's readers would know that the outdoor life promised to soldiers would improve their health and character and serve as an antidote to modernity's ills.

60. www.braggarmy.mil/www-cpao/bhis.txt. A later version of this Web site includes the claim that "only" 7 percent of the land was "occupied" by 170 families, the claim seeming to anticipate continuing sensitivity to the land ownership issue. It is unclear how that calculation was made, perhaps including only cleared land in current crop use.

61. Clement et al., *op. cit.,* p. 58; Lorraine V. Aragon. 2000. *Sandhills' Families: Early Reminisces of the Fort Bragg Area: Cumberland, Harnett, Hoke, Moore, Richmond, and Scotland Counties, North Carolina.* Fort Bragg, NC: Cultural Resources Program, Environmental and Natural Resources Division, Public Works Business Center. Some trading occurred in the town of Raeford, further to the west.

62. The Army continues to care for several churches and numerous graveyards scattered throughout the area, as required by agreement reached with landowners during the condemnation. B. A. Boyko and W. H. Kern, eds. 1996. *Cemeteries of Fort Bragg, Camp Mackall, and Pope Air Force Base, North Carolina.* Fort Bragg, NC: U.S. Army, XVIII Airborne Corps and Fort Bragg Directorate of Public Works and Environment. About 550 people—white, black, and Native American—are known to be buried there.

63. Clement *et al., op. cit.,* p. 52; Aragon, *op. cit.,* p. 67.

64. 1920 U.S. Census.

65. Bill Kern, Fort Bragg, personal communication.

66. Roy Parker, Jr. 1998. Birth of a century of service. Manuscript, p. 5.

67. Neil S. Blue had over 20,000 acres; Mary Blue, 3500, and W. M. Blue, 2,990; other closely tied members of the extended family held numerous other plots. Neil was one of the largest landowners not only in this area but in the state by the late 1920s. Clement et al., *op. cit.,* p. 65; John G. Reilly. 1969. Tyson and Jones Buggy Company: The history of a Southern carriage works. *North Carolina Historical Review,* 201–213; Jim Wrinn and Edward Lewis.

1992. *The Road of Personal Service: A Centennial History.* Aberdeen, NC: Aberdeen & Rockfish Railroad Company; Samuel Ashe, ed. 1906. *Biographical History of North Carolina,* vol. 5. Greensboro, NC: Van Noppen. While William Blue had begun to help promote the area for government purchase in October 1917, other family members resisted initial government offers. They held out and received better prices. Neil Blue received $29 an acre through a court settlement, while early payments averaged $18.45 an acre; *Completion Report,* Field Artillery Cantonment, Camp Bragg, Fayetteville, North Carolina, July 1919. Office of the Constructing Quartermaster. CCPL. While it is difficult to know the comparative worth of this area's in-use farmland, we can compare that price with the $36 per acre statewide average value of farm real estate in 1918, which went up to $42 in 1919, and $54 in 1920; *North Carolina Historical Crop Estimates, 1866–1974.* Raleigh: North Carolina Crop and Livestock Reporting Service, 1974.

68. Aragon, *op. cit.,* p. 56. They were one of many Northern industrialist families who purchased North Carolina land around the turn of the century for resort use.

69. In her oral histories, Aragon found Scot descendants of the landowners more often describing their ancestors' land as poor, while black descendants "suggest that their grandparents were just beginning to flourish on the land when speculators or the U.S. government arrived and requested them to leave"; *ibid.,* p. 68. In general, moreover, there had been substantial land concentration around the state in the previous decades; Crow. 1992. *op. cit.,* p. 112.

70. Hugh T. Lefler and Albert R. Newsome. 1954. *North Carolina: The History of a Southern State.* Chapel Hill:

University of North Carolina Press. p. 574.

71. Gina Kolata. 1999. *Flu: The Story of the Great Influenza Pandemic of 1918 and the Search for the Virus That Caused It.* New York: Farrar, Straus and Giroux.

72. Turk McFadyen, interview, 1980, CCPL.

73. Rev. R. A. McLeod. 1923. *Historical Sketch of Long Street Presbyterian Church, 1756 to 1923.* Published jointly by the Session of Long Street Presbyterian Church and The Scottish Society of America. Sanford, N.C.: Cole Printing Co., p. 17. The $5,000 they received for the church deed was used to set up a scholarship fund for a ministerial student.

74. Henry Groves Connor. Letters of March 19, 1920, and March 27, 1920, to Honorable Josephus Daniel, Secretary of the Navy, Washington, D.C. *Henry Groves Connor Papers.* Southern Historical Collection, UNC-CH.

75. Elizabeth Ellis, interview, 1980, CCPL.

76. *Fayetteville Observer,* 7/24/18.

77. The name may have signaled the strong influence of North Carolinians in the Wilson administration.

78. It took several years for the government to get all the eventual acreage for the bases. The War Department did most of its buying between 1918 and 1921. By 1941, a total of 120,580 acres constituted Fort Bragg, and by the end of the century, 161,000. A daily average of three thousand to seven thousand men (and some women) worked on the post, with wages ranging from twenty-five to thirty cents an hour for a common laborer to seventy-five cents for a plumber. When completed, the camp had a capacity of 16,300 soldiers, including 536 officers. *Completion Report, op. cit.*

79. One problem was that wage rates

were low compared with those at Norfolk and other installations with large construction crews, with rates set by the War Labor Policies Board; *Completion Report, op. cit.*

80. Jose Trias Monge. 1999. *Puerto Rico: The Trials of the Oldest Colony in the World.* New Haven, CT: Yale University Press, p. 30.

81. Kelvin A. Santiago-Valles. 1994. *"Subject People" and Colonial Discourses: Economic Transformation and Social Disorder in Puerto Rico, 1898–1947.* Albany: State University of New York Press.

82. *Completion Report, op. cit.,* p. 30.

83. Kolata, *op. cit.*

84. Oates, *op. cit.,* p. 285.

85. 1910 U.S. Census; 1920 U.S. Census. The foreign population of the rest of the state was unchanged by the war.

86. A strong endorsement. *Fayetteville Observer,* 9/11/16.

87. 1920 U.S. Census.

88. Margaret DeRosset, interview, 1980, CCPL.

89. Katherine E. Samons, Fort Bragg story is recounted by an early settler. *Spring Lake Times,* May 6, 1965. Fort Bragg Historian's Office, box labeled "Fort Bragg: General History, General Information, Maps, Historical Sites." Samons's parents, Henry Jackson and Isa Belle Goodman, received $3,650 for their 309 acres in late 1918.

90. Oates, *op. cit.,* pp. 768–770, quoting from a Raleigh *News and Observer* story. One Fayetteville resident recounted that Mrs. Ray had lost five sons in the Civil War, and so Mr. Nichols's appearance might have seemed to her, at least, a godsend of male labor and protection (Spencer Currie, interview, 1980, CCPL).

91. Negroes go North by the thousands to war work. *Fayetteville Observer,* 5/16/17.

92. Alvin Walters, interview, 7/9/97.

93. Fort Bragg: Negro drafted men to be furloughed for work there. *Fayetteville Observer,* 11/13/18.

94. Parker, 1990, *op. cit.,* p. 117.

95. West Pointer battled to save Fort Bragg. *Fayetteville Observer,* 9/12/96.

96. General Bowley won battle for Bragg. *Fayetteville Observer,* 9/26/96. It became a permanent Army post in 1922 and was renamed Fort Bragg.

97. American soldiers did not go to the front in numbers until June 1918, however.

98. John Chambers. 1986. Conscripting for colossus. In Peter Karsten, ed. *The Military in America: From the Colonial Era to the Present,* revised ed. New York: The Free Press; John K. Sweeney. 1996. *A Handbook of American Military History from the Revolutionary War to the Present.* Boulder, CO: Westview Press.

99. Chambers, *op. cit.,* p. 300. This argument's basis in the social contract and in hopes for modernization contrasts with today's arguments for the value of military training (whether in the form of JROTC or military recruitment itself). Contemporary Army promoters focus on the value for individual students (the "at-risk" are particularly thought to benefit). The social benefits discussed are usually restricted to reducing youth disruptions or crime.

100. Perret, *op. cit.,* p. 310.

101. Bruce White. 1986. The American military and the melting pot in World War I. In Peter Karsten, ed. *The Military in America: From the Colonial Era to the Present,* revised ed. New York: The Free Press.

102. Chambers, 1986, *op. cit.,* p. 300.

103. Woodrow Wilson, cited in Millis, *op. cit.,* p. 236.

104. Millis, *op. cit.,* p. 236.

105. To the young men. *Fayetteville Observer,* 5/30/17.

106. John Whiteclay Chambers III.

1987. *To Raise an Army: The Draft Comes to Modern America.* New York: The Free Press, pp. 211, 213; Perret, *op. cit.,* p. 316. Perret also notes that Wilson's antimilitarist secretary of war, Newton Baker, devised the plan of using citizen-run draft boards to make selections, deflecting discontent from the Army itself. This format also allowed some boards "to get rid of the town's misfits and halfwits by getting them into khaki" (p. 316). The political landscape of attitudes toward conscription and war itself was complex. In the years leading up to World War I, the religious right was generally pacifist and isolationist, although this was something the war changed. Southerners as a whole saw that war as a northern project, with little importance for them, although the Progressive-influenced road and school builders of the region supported it (Michael Lienesch, personal communication). In a rural area of Tennessee in which the response to conscription has been closely studied it has been shown that the war's many deserters and evaders came from the poorer classes and that their motives were not based in antiwar principles but in their belief "that no one had the right to force them into service, or because their loyalties to family and place were more important to them than abstract patriotism"; Jeanette Keith. 1995. *Country People in the New South: Tennessee's Upper Cumberland.* Chapel Hill: University of North Carolina Press, p. 166.

107. Lefler and Newsome, *op. cit.,* p. 573.

108. *Fayetteville Observer,* 4/11/17. On nativism and the war, see John Higham. 1963. *Strangers in the Land: Patterns of American Nativism, 1860–1925.* New York: Atheneum.

109. Joan M. Jensen. 1991. *Army Surveillance in America, 1775–1980.* New Haven, CT: Yale University Press, p.

177. For more on the war's erosion of freedom of speech, see also Ronald Schaffer. 1991. *America in the Great War: The Rise of the War Welfare State.* New York: Oxford University Press.

110. Kennedy, *op. cit.,* pp. 57–59.

111. *Ibid.*

112. John Monaghan, interview, 1980, CCPL.

113. Frances McColl, interview, 1980, CCPL.

114. Lefler and Newsome, *op. cit.,* p. 574.

115. Weigley, *op. cit.,* pp. 395–397. Some European nations were spending five to ten times as much on their militaries as the United States at the turn of the century (Sherry, *op. cit.,* p. 6). That situation is now reversed on an even larger scale. The critique of militarism was "mainstream." While North Carolina's governor called all to "Rally to the Flag" in April 1917, he also spoke for many when he said he was opposed to universal military service: "I am against the Imperial German Government because it stands for universal military service"; *Fayetteville Observer,* 4/18/17, although the paper that same day editorialized for the draft.

116. Sherry, *op. cit.,* p. 9.

117. Weigley, *op. cit.,* pp. 400–401.

118. George Orwell. 1950. *Coming Up for Air.* New York: Harcourt Brace, p. 144.

119. Sherry, *op. cit.,* p. 10. Ekirch, *op. cit.*

120. *The Minute Man,* Vol. V. Fourth Corps Area, Fort Bragg, NC. Chicago: MTC Association of the United States, 1927. Box "Yearbooks of the CMTC," Fort Bragg Archives, Fort Bragg, NC.

121. *Camp Bragg and Fayetteville, N.C.: Sketches of Camp and City.* Richmond, VA: Central Publishing Company, 1919. The brochure went on to argue for a racial basis to the section's wealth, specifically, the "sturdy Anglo Celtic character" of the (putatively

only significant) inhabitants, which gives the city a purported homogeneity and rigid regard for law and order.

122. Sherry, *op. cit.,* p. 6. As Sherry points out, this increase (which had occurred as well after the Spanish-American War ended in 1898, when the military tripled from prewar levels to 150,000) runs against the myth that America has "recklessly" demobilized after each war.

123. Wade Thomas Saunders, interview, 1980, CCPL.

124. Edward Coffman. 1986. *The Old Army: A Portrait of the American Army in Peacetime, 1784–1898.* New York: Oxford University Press, pp. 401–402.

125. www.bragg.army.mil/www-cpao/lifestya.txt

126. 'Goulash cannon' a high-tech marvel. *Fayetteville Observer,* 2/5/98.

127. Frances McColl, interview, 1980, CCPL; Walter Campbell, interview, 1980, CCPL.

128. Parker, 1990, *op. cit.,* p. 118.

129. M. Ruth Little, Longleaf Historic Resources. 1996. Fort Bragg Main Post, National Register of Historic Places Registration Form. U.S. Department of the Interior, National Parks Service.

130. D. T. Perry. 1934. Fayetteville looks ahead. *Manufacturer's Record* (July): 20–21; Parker, 1990, *op. cit.,* p. 129.

131. This is a pseudonym, as are most names of living persons in this book. The exceptions are those individuals who are either public figures or who specifically declined the offer of confidentiality when I interviewed them.

132. When the United States Air Force came into being in 1947, this field became the basis for Pope Air Force Base.

133. Betty Hanford, interview, 4/23/97.

134. Bill Fields, interview, 3/14/97.

135. Sherry, *op. cit.,* p. 24.

136. *Fayetteville Observer,* 12/24/34.

137. Ruth Little, personal communication. Fort Bragg was headquarters for the thirty-three CCC camps in North and South Carolina.

138. Weigley, *op. cit.,* p. 402.

144. Sherry, *op. cit.,* p. 19. For example, the National Recovery Administration, which put controls on wages, prices, and production, was modeled on the War Industries Board of World War I and used propaganda methods from the war; William Leuchtenburg. 1964. The New Deal and the analogue of war. In John Braeman, Robert H. Bremner, and Everett Walters, eds. *Change and Continuity in Twentieth-Century America.* Columbus: Ohio University Press.

2. Hostess to the "Good War" (1939–1947)

1. National Archives, Record Group (RG) 111 - SCA, Fort Bragg Albums. Fort Bragg, NC. Aerial Views, 211th FA BN, Book 1, SC126357.

2. Studs Terkel. 1984. *"The Good War": An Oral History of World War Two.* New York: Pantheon Books. For a more summary account that deals eloquently with the censored or ignored aspects of World War II, see Michael C. C. Adams. 1994. *The Best War Ever: America and World War II.* Baltimore: Johns Hopkins University Press. See also George H. Roeder. 1993. *The Censored War: American Visual Experience during World War Two.* New Haven: Yale University Press. Other accounts of how World War II was experienced in specific American communities can be found in Marc Scott Miller. 1988. *The Irony of Victory: World War II and Lowell, Massachusetts.* Urbana: University of Illinois Press; Robert Havighurst and

H. G. Morgan. 1951. *Social History of a War-Boom Community.* New York: Longmans, Green; and Paul Levengood. 1999. For the duration and beyond: World War II and the creation of modern Houston, Texas. Ph.D. dissertation, Rice University. See also Arthur Marwick, ed. 1988. *Total War and Social Change.* New York: St. Martin's Press; and Richard Polenberg. 1972. *War and Society: The United States 1941–1945.* Philadelphia: Lippincott.

3. Geoffrey Perrett. 1973. *Days of Sadness, Years of Triumph: The American People, 1939–1945.* New York: Coward, McCann, & Geoghegan, p. 343.

4. Howard Schuman and Jacqueline Scott. 1989. Generations and collective memories. *American Sociological Review* 54: 359–381.

5. Sherry, *op. cit.,* pp. 20, 31.

6. *Ibid.,* pp. 32–44.

7. Roosevelt cited in Sherry, *op. cit.,* pp. 32, 33. This is despite the fact that, as Sherry (p. 34) notes, British armies easily reached America in 1776. In fact, however, German submarines torpedoed American ships at will off the coast of North Carolina during much of 1942 (John S. Duvall. 1996. *North Carolina during World War II: On Home Front and Battle Front: 1941–1945.* Fayetteville, NC: Airborne and Special Operations Museum Foundation).

8. The Red Scare of the previous world war era, of course, generated similar fears of wrong-thinking others.

9. Sherry, *op. cit.,* p. 40.

10. Robert Abzug. 1999. *America Views the Holocaust, 1933–1945: A Brief Documentary History.* Boston: Bedford/ St. Martin's.

11. Duvall, *op. cit.*

12. David Cecelski. 1995. The home front's dispossessed. *Southern Exposure* (summer): 37–41.

13. *Fort Bragg at War: The Station Complement.* 1945. Atlanta: Foote and Davies, p. 15. Again, a nonlocal firm

(from Charlotte, North Carolina) was given the general contracting job for the post expansion, although all hiring was done through the State Employment Service which opened an office at Bragg; *Raleigh News and Observer,* 3/16/ 41. An additional 1,968 buildings went up at Camp Mackall, a nearly 8,000-acre tract ten miles southwest of Fort Bragg that the Army acquired in 1942 for airborne training. The camp was created out of two federal forests, a Dupont Chemical Company hunting preserve (which the company stocked with Mexican quail and used to entertain clients) and private land. Little, *op. cit.,* p. E10–11.

14. *Fort Bragg at War, op. cit.,* pp. 40, 42, 55, 66, 69. While army pay and contracts brought money to the city, the army also brought new expenses, including a new water treatment plant, water lines, and sewers at a cost of over $900,000. One city's war plant—Its water works. *American City* (June 1944), 59:74–75. And on Army paydays near Fort Benning in Georgia, like Fayetteville, "the rush of retail trade is so great that the littered streets take on the look of circus days." Army camps boom trade, increase city budgets. *American City* 56 (December 1941):11. Fort Bragg did not get a sewage disposal plant until July 1941. Up until that point, it put its waste into the Little River which flowed into the Cape Fear, something that was "the subject of much controversial discussion"; *Fayetteville Observer,* 4/5/40.

15. *Charlotte Observer,* 4/26/39. Reel 17, Fayetteville, NC. Clipping File, North Carolina Collection, UNC-CH.

16. Private V. H. Polachek. Fort Bragg, 1941. *The Field Artillery Journal* 31(9): 682, 685.

17. Parker, 1990, *op. cit.,* p. 122. Parker notes that the New Deal had brought a variety of sanitation, mos-

quito control, and school projects to the county in the mid-1930s. The WPA had brought a new city hall in 1939 and a new armory for the local militia, the FILI, three years earlier, and a free library system was instituted, although for whites only.

18. Henry Charles Adley. 1952. A preliminary land use plan for the city of Fayetteville, North Carolina and environs. M. A. thesis, UNC-CH, p. 30.

19. The actual numbers for Fayetteville's population were much higher for the war years as a whole. The number of workmen was in fact 31,544 employed during the nine months of construction (Fort Bragg Historian's Office Web site http://www.bragg.-army.mil/history/).

20. Interview, 4/1/97.

21. This business's fate followed the vicissitudes of the Fayetteville economy in later years. The business closed down as Sears and then other stores relocated to a suburban mall near the post. In more recent efforts at downtown revitalization, the building shell has been remade into a microbrewery and restaurant.

22. Ruth Sivard. 1996. *World Military and Social Expenditures.* Washington, DC: World Priorities.

23. Harry B. Stein. 1980. *Pathway to a Future.* New York: Carlton Press, p. 168.

24. Interview, 1/27/97.

25. Interview, 5/15/98.

26. *The Hypo,* 41st Evac Hospital MtZ., Fort Bragg, November 11, 1942.

27. *Fayetteville Observer,* 11/9/45.

28. *Fayetteville Observer,* 8/8/41.

29. State health officer report on the health of the Army. *Carolina Times,* 8/30/41, p. 5.

30. Parker, 1990, *op. cit.,* p. 137. It was known that most of the venereal diseases soldiers contracted were not through prostitutes; Levengood, *op. cit.*

31. Cumberland VD rate 8 times

that of U.S. *Fayetteville Observer,* n.d. Because the disease clustered mostly among fifteen- to thirty-year-olds, however, an age-adjusted rate, given the youth of military counties, would show a less dramatic but still significant difference.

32. This view of the war's impact on women's work became common sense along with the emerging doctrine that made war or war preparation the central adjustment mechanism for society and economy.

33. Susan M. Hartmann. 1982. *The Home Front and Beyond: American Women in the 1940s.* Boston: Twayne Publishers. See also Leila Rupp. 1978. *Mobilizing Women for War: German and American Propaganda, 1939–1945.* Princeton, NJ: Princeton University Press. Several outstanding books have been written about the making of gender through war and of war through gender more generally. The most celebrated have been about the American and the German militaries: Cynthia Enloe. 1987. *Does Khaki Become You? The Militarization of Women's Lives.* London: Pandora; Klaus Theweleit. 1987. *Male Fantasies.* Vol. 1, *Women, Floods, Bodies, History.* Minneapolis: University of Minnesota Press; Claudia Koonz. 1987. *Mothers in the Fatherland: Women, the Family and Nazi Politics.* New York: St. Martin's Press. See also Cynthia Enloe. 1993. *The Morning After: Sexual Politics at the End of the Cold War.* Berkeley: University of California Press.

34. The female employment rate was 29 percent by the end of the 1940s; Hartmann, *op. cit.,* pp. 21, 24. These numbers do not reflect the full extent of women's work as they were more likely than men to work temporarily during the year and perhaps not be counted in a labor census; *ibid.,* p. 77 (citing D'Ann Campbell. 1979. Wives, Workers and Womanhood: America

during World War II. Ph.D. dissertation, UNC-CH. Certain categories of women were more likely to work. Fully half of soldiers' wives did so, for example; Hartmann, *op. cit.*, p. 78.

35. In 1940, 26 percent of women did manual labor, and 25 percent, in 1947; David Kennedy. 1999. *Freedom from Fear: The American People in Depression and War, 1929–1945*. New York: Oxford University Press, p. 779.

36. Hartmann, *op. cit.*, p. 77.

37. Women were half of all clerical workers in 1940, and 70 percent in 1945; *ibid.*, p. 88.

38. *Ibid.*, p. 93.

39. *Ibid.*, pp. 31–32 (women in uniform), 212.

40. John Duvall, *op. cit.* Between 1942 and 1944, employment in that field grew from 27,000 to 40,000.

41. Kennedy, *op. cit.*, p. 634.

42. *Ibid.*, p. 496.

43. Guilielma Fell Alsop and Mary F. McBride. 1943. *Arms and the Girl: A Guide to Personal Adjustment in War Work and War Marriage*. New York: Vanguard Press. Selection in Judy Barrett Litoff and David C. Smith, eds. 1997. *American Women in a World at War: Contemporary Accounts from World War II*. Wilmington, DE: Scholarly Resources, pp.168–169.

44. Car pooling from the city to post, a distance of just ten miles, could take an hour each way.

45. Hartmann, *op. cit.*, pp. 59, 84.

46. *Ibid.*, p. 58.

47. John Morton Blum. 1976. *V Was for Victory: Politics and American Culture during World War II*. New York: Harcourt Brace Jovanovich, p. 193.

48. The executive order prohibiting employment discrimination in companies with government contracts was only enforced in a limited way on the local level. Moreover, blacks had left the South in massive numbers during World War II for such places as Detroit and California.

49. P. John Devaney. 1955. *Economic Structure and Forecasted Employment*. M. A. thesis, UNC-CH. The figures rose from $9 million to $56 million.

50. John W. Dower. 1986. *War Without Mercy*. New York: Pantheon Books. The people of Fayetteville were exposed to this in news stories and cartoons. In one 1942 panel, Popeye fought a trenchful of "blastid yaps!" "This place is alive wit' em!" he exclaims. "I wist I had some inseck powders." Anti-Semitic attitudes were also considered acceptable. The post's *Reception News* cartoonist drew a couple whose long noses are their most outstanding feature, with the woman pleading, "Hooiman, dear. I don't think we were ment [sic] for each other." February 5, 1943, 2(32). Box 102, Camp Publications, Diaries, and Other Publications, World War II Papers, 1939–1947, Military Collection, North Carolina State Archives, North Carolina Division of Archives and History, Raleigh.

51. Jean Byers. 1950. *A Study of the Negro in Military Service*. Washington, DC: U.S. Department of Defense, p. 61.

52. Warren L. Young. 1982. *Minorities and the Military: A Cross-National Study in World Perspective*. Westport, CT: Greenwood Press. See also Bernard C. Nalty. 1986. *Strength for the Fight: A History of Black Americans in the Military*. New York: The Free Press. The famous "Triple Nickel" unit of black paratroopers, the 555th, was eventually stationed at the installation. It was sent to the U.S. Northwest to put out fires ignited by Japanese balloon-delivered bombs. A veteran of that unit described this as combat duty that was kept secret so the Japanese would abandon the tactic as a failure. It was the first unit to be integrated into the Army when it was

dissolved into the 82nd Airborne in late 1947; Bradley Biggs. 1986. *The Triple Nickles: America's First All-Black Paratroop Unit.* Hamden, CT: Archon Books.

53. Lee Finkle. 1973. The conservative aims of militant rhetoric: Black protest during World War II. *Journal of American History* 60(3): 692–713.

54. Paul T. Murray. 1971. Blacks and the draft. *Journal of Black Studies* 2(1): 57–76.

55. Richard Dalfiume, editorial advisor. 1989. *Papers of the NAACP. Part 9: Discrimination in the U.S. Armed Forces, 1918–1955, Series B: Armed Forces Legal Files, 1940–1950.* Bethesda, MD: University Publications of America, p. xii.

56. Hartmann, *op. cit.*, p. 80.

57. Harvard Sitkoff. 1971. Racial militancy and interracial violence in the Second World War. *Journal of American History* 63(3): 661–681. See also Timothy Tyson. 1998. Wars for democracy: African American militancy and interracial violence in North Carolina during World War II. In David S. Cecelski and Timothy R. Tyson, eds. *Democracy Betrayed: The Wilmington Race Riot of 1898 and Its Legacy.* Chapel Hill: University of North Carolina Press.

58. Tyson, *op. cit.*

59. Nalty, *op. cit.*, p. 164.

60. Sitkoff, *op. cit.*, p. 671.

61. There were no USO or other recreational facilities provided for blacks downtown. A USO was built on the white side of downtown.

62. National Archives. RG 159. General Correspondence 1939–1947. Memorandum for the Adjutant General, August 25, 1941, from Howard McC. Snyder, Acting the Inspector General. Entry 26 E, Box 869.

63. The official investigating officer pressed Poole's companion to "explain" the beating through the victim's behavior:

Q. Was Mac Poole doing anything; making any kind of noise, or cursing, or talking loud?
A. No sir.
Q. Can you think of any reason why they struck him?
A. I couldn't tell why they hit him.
Q. Have you ever seen the MPs hit any soldier without the soldier doing something himself?
A. No sir.

National Archives. RG 159. Records of the Office of the Inspector General. Testimony of Private Frank Allen. Report of Investigation of Incidents at Fort Bragg, N.C. IG 333.9.]

64. *Pittsburgh Courier,* 8/23/41; *Washington Afro American,* 8/16/41; *The Newspaper PM,* 8/11/41.

65. *The Afro-American,* 8/16/41.

66. Finkle, *op. cit.*, pp. 692–713.

67. Phillip McGuire. 1988. *He, Too, Spoke for Democracy: Judge Hastie, World War II, and the Black Soldier.* New York: Greenwood Press, p. 17. See also Phillip McGuire. 1983. *Taps for a Jim Crow Army: Letters from Black Soldiers in World War II.* Santa Barbara, CA: ABC-CLIO Press.

68. National Archives RG 159, *op. cit.*

69. *Ibid.*

70. *Ibid.*, Testimony of Private Ivory Barker.

71. Tom O'Connor. Color line stands out everywhere at Army shooting scene. *The Newspaper PM,* 8/10/41.

72. This concept is from David R. Goldfield (1990. *Black, White, and Southern: Race Relations and Southern Culture, 1940 to the Present.* Baton Rouge: Louisiana State University Press) and describes the code of behavior expected in interracial interaction and the assumptions about black inferiority it indexed.

73. Review of the initial draft of this letter led to several changes. Editors changed the term *colored* to the more polite *Negro*. They also removed reference to the action's having been taken at the behest of General Benjamin O. Davis, a member of the investigating panel who had just become the first African American promoted to that rank, under heavy pressure from black leaders. General Davis worked in the inspector general's office and often undermined the more progressive efforts of Judge Hastie. For example, he argued against Hastie's proposed regulation that would have prevented use of the word *nigger* by commanders. Davis also, against all other evidence, reported black morale to be high based on a series of surveys on army posts taken between October 1941 and September 1943; McGuire, 1988, *op. cit.,* p. 66.

74. National Archives. RG 159. General Correspondence, 1939–1947. Memo, War Department, IGO, October 2, 1941, to the Adjutant General from Virgil L. Peterson, Major General, the Inspector General. Entry 26E, Box 869.

75. North Carolina Division of Archives and History, Raleigh, NC. Military Collection. Camp Publications Diaries, and Other Publications, World War II Papers, 1939–1947. *The Black Panther,* publication of the 578th black division, 8/22/42.

76. Interview, 7/9/97.

77. *Fayetteville Observer,* 11/28/44.

78. *The Carolina Times,* 10/25/41, p. 3; *Fayetteville Observer,* 8/20/41. And at least one other black soldier had been shot in the back and killed on post earlier that year according to a letter sent from Fayetteville to the NAACP national headquarters; Records of the NAACP Branch Files, Group II, Box B-149, Fayetteville, NC. 1918–1939. Library of Congress.

79. Cited in Goldfield, *op. cit.,* p. 7.

80. Albert Parker. The case of Pvt. Ned Turman. *Militant,* 8/23/41. Reprinted in C. L. R. James, George Breitman, Edgar Keemer, et al. 1980. *Fighting Racism in World War II.* Fred Stanton, ed. New York: Monad Press, p. 132. The situation apparently did not improve at Fort Bragg after this report. A letter to Judge Hastie in 1943 from a Fort Bragg soldier complained of 35 black soldiers being jailed for eight or nine months for small infractions. The soldiers were then tried and given six months additional imprisonment; McGuire, 1983, *op. cit.*

81. *Carolina Times,* 11/22/41.

82. James M. Reid. Three incidents brought on trouble at Fort Bragg— Reid. *Pittsburgh Courier,* 8/23/41. The *Courier* appealed to its readers' common sense by putting men and masculinity at the leading edge of freedom struggles. So it was when a few months later, North Carolina's leading white newspaper editor, Jonathan Daniels, said of the U.S. entry into the war: "Americans stand on a continent as men—men again fighting in the crudest man terms—for ourselves and also for that destination in decency for all men of which our settlement, our spreading, was always a symbol. In an America grown magnificently male again we have a chance to fight for a homeland with the full meaning of homeland as a world that is fit to be the home of man"; cited in Arthur Marwick. 1974. *War and Social Change in the Twentieth Century: A Comparative Study of Britain, France, Germany, Russia, and the United States.* New York: St. Martin's Press.

War has been the crucible for making men both men and citizens, making citizenship a question of loyalty rather than resistance, despite this case, and a question of heroics rather than nurturance; J. Elshtain Bethke. 1987. *Women and War.* New York: BasicBooks; Gwendolyn Mink. 1990. The lady and the tramp: Gender, race, and the origins of the American welfare state. In Linda Gordon, ed. *Women, the State and Welfare.* Madison: University of Wisconsin Press.

83. Timothy Tyson, *op. cit.;* Raymond Gavins. 1991. The NAACP in North Carolina during the age of segregation. In Armstead L. Robinson and Patricia Sullivan, eds. *New Directions in Civil Rights Studies.* Charlottesville: University Press of Virginia, pp. 105–125.

84. Receiving just 23 percent of the white school spending level in 1920, black schools increased to 66 percent by 1940; Parker, 1990, *op. cit.,* p. 124. These numbers should not be taken at face value, however, as white administrators might have been tempted to give a generous estimation of the value of the used books and equipment sent to black schools, for example.

85. This was in fact the reestablishment of a city branch, with the initial one in 1918. By 1945, the eastern Carolina cities of Fayetteville and Wilmington had unusually low membership totals (94 and 100, respectively) compared with other North Carolina cities. Raleigh had 595; Durham, 285; Winston-Salem, 1088; and Charlotte, 677; Gavins, *op. cit.*

86. Fayetteville City Council minutes, 1940, p. 115.

87. Black police came first to the larger, Piedmont cities of the state; Davetta Steed. *North Carolina League of Municipalities Report, February 1946.* Report no. 53, pp. 1–2. Raleigh.

88. Parker's history lists five initial policemen, including Josh Council, Joe Campbell, Calvin Bennett, Fred Lonnie Truitt, and Albert Algie Banks (p. 141).

89. Sherry, *op. cit.,* 76; Kennedy, *op. cit.,* p. 646.

90. Two-thirds had died in combat or of combat wounds, one-third of other causes; Duvall, *op. cit.,* p. 65.

91. Approximately two-tenths of a percent of both the state's and the county's population died while in the service. In Cumberland County, 128 men died, 73 of them in battle; Duvall, *op. cit.,* p. 65. Parker (1990, *op. cit.,* p. 138) says "two dozen" died in the war. He also counts 780 whites and 341 blacks as soldiers or sailors during World War II.

92. Little, *op. cit.,* p. E11.

93. National Archives. RG 337. General Correspondence, 1942–1948. "Military Strength Within Continental United States Exclusive of Army Air Forces, by Station and Organization." Box 323, Records of Headquarters Army Ground Forces.

94. After World War II, there was less interest among blacks than whites in a return to civilian life, which some have seen as "not a reflection on the attractions of the military but of the failures of American society as a whole"; Young, *op. cit.,* p. 216.

95. Sherry, *op. cit.,* p. 119.

96. Paul Boyer. 1985. *By the Bomb's Early Light: American Thought and Culture at the Dawn of the Atomic Age.* Chapel Hill: University of North Carolina Press.

97. Oates, *op. cit.,* p. 543.

98. *Fayetteville Observer,* 10/25/45.

99. Barbara Ehrenreich. 1997. *Blood Rites: Origins and History of the Passions of War.* New York: Henry Holt.

100. Excerpt from Clinard F. Davis. A soldier and his woes. *Carolina Times,* 11/22/41, p. 6. This fear existed even before Pearl Harbor.

101. Wecter quoted in Sherry, *op. cit.,* p. 100.

102. *Fayetteville Observer,* 9/4/45.

103. Sherry, *op. cit.,* pp. 110–111.

104. See Aihwa Ong. 1999. *Flexible Citizenship: The Cultural Logics of Trans-*

nationality. Durham, NC: Duke University Press.

105. H. Lacy Godwin, interview, 1980, CCPL.

106. Roger Lotchin. 1994. California cities and the hurricane of change: World War II in the San Francisco, Los Angeles, and San Diego metropolitan areas. *Pacific Historical Review* 63(3): 393–420.

107. Miller, *op. cit.,* p. 205.

108. Lotchin, *op. cit.,* p. 420.

109. Sitkoff, *op. cit.*

110. Benjamin O. Fordham. 1994. *Building the Cold War Consensus: The Political Economy of U.S. National Security Policy, 1949–51.* Ann Arbor: University of Michigan Press.

111. Sidney Lens. 1987. *Permanent War: The Militarization of America.* New York: Schocken.

112. National Archives. RG 111-SCA. Fort Bragg Albums. Aerial Views, 211th FA BN, Book 2.

113. C. Wright Mills. 1956. *The Power Elite.* New York: Oxford University Press.

3. **Simulating War at Home: Counterinsurgencies, Foreign and Domestic (1948–1963)**

1. *Fayetteville Observer,* 5/5/54.

2. National Archives, RG 111-SCA, Fort Bragg Albums. Records of the Office of the Chief Signal Officer, Printed Signal Corps. Photograph of American Military Activity 1900–1981, Contact Prints 457400 through 458597, Box 277.

3. *Ibid.*

4. Ann Markusen and Joel Yudken. 1992. *Dismantling the Cold War Economy.* New York: BasicBooks.

5. The phrase *protection racket* is from Charles Tilly (1985. War making and state making as organized crime. In Peter Evans, Dietrich Rueschemeyer, and Theda Skocpol, eds. *Bringing the State Back In.* Cambridge, U. K.: Cambridge University Press), an historian of European state making. "Someone who produces both the danger and, at a price, the shield against it is a racketeer. Someone who provides a needed shield but has little control over the danger's appearance qualifies as a legitimate protector, especially if his price is no higher than his competitors" (pp. 170–171). He makes important distinctions between states which formed earlier and later in the modern period of international states: Contemporary client states have a much greater disproportion of power between military and civil forces, favoring the former, as the bargains it strikes are with the foreign patron (who provides military assistance in exchange for commodities, labor pools, and access) more than the people within that state.

6. Eisenhower quoted in Sherry, *op. cit.,* p. 218.

7. H. W. Brands. 1999. Review of destroying the village: Eisenhower and thermonuclear war. *Journal of American History* 86(2): 840.

8. A. J. Bacevich. 1986. *The Pentomic Era: The U.S. Army between Korea and Vietnam.* Washington, DC: National Defense University Press.

9. *Ibid.,* p. 29.

10. Barton J. Bernstein. 1999. Reconsidering "invasion most costly": Popular-history scholarship, publishing standards, and the claim of high U.S. casualty estimates to help legitimize the atomic bombings. *Peace and Change* 24(2): 220–248. They included Generals MacArthur, Eisenhower, and Arnold and Admirals Leahy, King, and Nimitz.

11. Col. Shillelagh, cited in Bacevich, *op. cit.,* p. 40.

12. Cited in Bacevich, *op. cit.,* p. 40.

13. Lt. Col. William D. Wise, 1954, cited in Bacevich, *op. cit.,* p. 23.

14. Bacevich, *op. cit.,* p. 28.

15. *Ibid.*, p. 51.

16. *Ibid.*, p. 119.

17. Fort Bragg secondary "target." *Fayetteville Observer,* 11/16/78. At least in the 1970s, North Carolina had thirteen major potential nuclear targets, including Seymour Johnson. "Category two targets" included other military bases such as Fort Bragg, and "category three targets" were major industrial centers such as Winston-Salem and Charlotte; *ibid.*

18. North Carolina Association of County Commissioners, *1958 County Yearbook,* p. 53.

19. Fayetteville City Council Minutes, December 23, 1959, to July 19, 1963.

20. North Carolina Civil Defense Agency. 1965. *State of North Carolina Civil Defense Agency: Cumberland County Operational Survival Plan.* Fayetteville, NC: Author, p. 150. This document identified thirty-three counties as potential targets from which evacuation might be necessary.

21. *1962 Special Warfare Center Historical Report,* p. 44. USASOC Archives, Fort Bragg.

22. Invasion by Yankees? Nope, it's just "angry" troops fighting N.C. battle as delaying action in war games. "Mock commies move in." *Greenville Piedmont,* n.d.

23. National Archives. RG 337. General Records. Records of Headquarters Army Ground Forces, Exercise "Southern Pine."

24. Invasion by Yankees? op. cit.

25. The latter term includes "peacekeeping," hostage rescue, and hurricane relief. See Thomas Mockaitis. 1998. Unconventional conflicts. In Sam C. Sarkesian and Robert E. Connor, Jr., eds. *America's Armed Forces: A Handbook of Current and Future Capabilities.* Westport, CT: Greenwood Press, pp. 387–416. Mockaitis suggests that Special Forces are not considered "respectable

soldiering . . . [and] that an unhealthy interest in special operations significantly shortens one's career" (p. 412). Whether that is the case or not, the American ambivalence toward war is even stronger in relation to these forms, marked linguistically as only quasilegitimate or paramilitary.

26. Michael McClintock. 1985. *The American Connection.* London: Zed, p. 30.

27. USASOC Directorate of History, Archives, Library and Museums. 1997. *Sine Pari: Without Equal: The Story of Army Special Operations.* U.S. Army Special Operations Command Historical Monograph 1, p. 7.

28. Weigley, *op. cit.,* p. 543. Weigley notes that the autonomy of Special Forces became extreme in the Kennedy period, when they sometimes took CIA rather than Army commands (p. 544).

29. The quote is from USASOC Directorate, *op. cit.,* p. 23. See also Anna Simons. 1997. *The Company They Keep: Life inside the U.S. Army Special Forces.* New York: The Free Press.

30. *Fayetteville Observer,* 7/2/53.

31. It rose from $441 million in 1981 to $3.2 billion in 1989, by which time Fort Bragg had ten thousand of the Army's thirty-five thousand Special Operations soldiers. The public relations battle that is constantly waged to justify units and services is waged for Special Operations through the argument that they are "force multipliers," reducing the need for large numbers of conventional troops; *Fayetteville Observer,* 10/15/89.

32. Robin Neilands. 1998. *In the Combat Zone: Special Forces since 1945.* New York: New York University Press, pp. 210, 112–113, emphasis added.

33. Nearby Camp Mackall has been a central place for Special Forces training. A total of 77,006 troops were trained there, at the Sandhills Wildlife

Refuge, and the "Corridor area" between Mackall and Bragg in 1983; Camp Mackall Master Plan, Phase I, Analysis of Existing Facilities and Environmental Assessment Report. Fort Bragg, June 1984.

34. National Archives. RG 337. General Records. Records of Headquarters Army Ground Forces, Exercise "Southern Pine."

35. Neilands, *op. cit.*, p. 113.

36. *Ibid.*, p. 74.

37. Interview, 4/2/97.

38. For example, the *Fayetteville Observer* (2/12/76) reported mercenary recruitment for the war in Angola, which focused particularly on black soldiers in town.

39. William Blum. 1995. *Killing Hope: U.S. Military and CIA Interventions since World War II*. Monroe, ME: Common Courage Press.

40. *Ibid.* To take just one example, the CIA organized a coup against a democratically elected leader in Guatemala in 1954. On election, Guatemala's President Arbenz had modeled his reforms explicitly on the New Deal and in contrast to Communism. His administration had taken four hundred thousand acres of United Fruit land that the company had left unplanted, paid the company the land's declared tax value, and gave the land to landless Guatemalan citizens on which to plant subsistence crops. The CIA parachuted Russian arms into the country, disseminated propaganda of "Soviet influence," sent pilots to strafe several areas of the country, and paid a force of 150 local soldiers to invade and other soldiers to do nothing to stop them. The new military regime was a ferocious police state that left tens of thousands dead. Stephen Schlesinger and Stephen Kinzer. 1984. *Bitter Fruit: The Untold Story of the American Coup in Guatemala*. New York: Anchor Press/Doubleday.

41. Stan Goff. 2000. *Hideous Dream:*

A Soldier's Memoir of the US Invasion of Haiti. Winnipeg, Canada: Soft Skull Press; Douglas C. Waller. 1994. *Commandos: The Inside Story of America's Secret Soldiers*. New York: Simon & Schuster, p. 71.

42. Barbara Christian. 1999. The crime of innocence. In David Batstone and Eduardo Mendieta, eds. *The Good Citizen*. New York: Routledge, pp. 51–64.

43. A. G. Mojtabai. 1986. *Blessed Assurance: At Home with the Bomb in Amarillo, Texas*. Boston: Houghton Mifflin.

44. 363rd Civil Affairs Brigade. *Country Study: Pineland*. Prepared for commander in chief, EastSoutheastern Command, Tampa, Lenoir, p. 11. USASOC Archives, Fort Bragg.

45. *Ibid.*, p. 17.

46. *Ibid.*, p. 15.

47. *Ibid.*, p. 24.

48. Tom Engelhardt. 1995. *The End of Victory Culture: Cold War America and the Disillusioning of a Generation*. New York: BasicBooks.

49. *Fayetteville Observer*, 5/28/70.

50. Engelhardt, *op. cit.*

51. USASOC Directorate, *op. cit.*, p. 15.

52. Historical Supplement, 1969 and 1978, US Army JFK Center for Military Assistance, Fort Bragg, NC. USASOC Archives, Fort Bragg.

53. Soldiers get training, civilians playgrounds. *Fayetteville Observer*, 3/24/70.

54. Stewart L. Udall. 1994. *The Myths of August: A Personal Exploration of Our Tragic Cold War Affair with the Atom*. New York: Pantheon Books; Michael Uhl and Tod Ensign. 1980. *GI Guinea Pigs: How the Pentagon Exposed Our Troops to Dangers More Deadly than War: Agent Orange and Atomic Radiation*. New York: Playboy Press; Carole Gallagher. 1993. *American Ground Zero:*

The Secret Nuclear War. Cambridge, MA: MIT Press.

55. David Loomis. 1993. *Combat Zoning: Military Land-Use Planning in Nevada.* Reno: University of Nevada Press. Loomis notes that much ink has been spilled in the planning literature examining the question of land use for adult theaters and halfway houses, but little on military ranges, whose impact is much greater. Other large military facilities are Fort Greeley (661,000 acres), Fort Irwin (641,000), and Fort Hood (217,000). New Mexico has given two million acres to the White Sands Missile Range, and Arizona one million to the Yuma Proving Ground.

56. Donald F. McHenry. 1975. *Micronesia: Trust Betrayed.* New York: Carnegie Endowment for International Peace.

57. *Camp Mackall Master Plan, op. cit.,* pp. 4–6.

58. *Fayetteville Observer,* 3/18/53.

59. *Fayetteville Observer,* 3/20/53.

60. Richard Misrach (with Myriam Weisang Misrach). 1990. *Bravo 20: The Bombing of the American West.* Baltimore: Johns Hopkins University Press; Mike Davis. 1993. Dead West: Ecocide in Marlboro country. *New Left Review* 200 (July–August): 49–69; Mike Davis. 1999. Berlin's skeleton in Utah's closet. *Grand Street* 69 18(1): 92–100. See also Seth Shulman. 1992. *The Threat at Home: Confronting the Toxic Legacy of the U.S. Military.* Boston: Beacon Press.

61. Davis, 1993, *op. cit.,* p. 50. See also Donovan Webster. 1996. *Aftermath: The Landscape of War.* New York: Pantheon.

62. U.S. military intelligence also monitored and attempted to influence the islands' elections, most infamously in Belau, whose harbor was wanted to berth US Navy nuclear submarines.

63. The term belongs to a man who was once the Pentagon's top environ-mental figure; Davis, 1993, *op. cit.,* p. 50.

64. Shulman, *op. cit.,* See also Chapter 5.

65. Citizen Soldier. 1991. *Real War Stories.* Forestville, CA: Eclipse Enterprises.

66. Joseph M. Rothberg, Paul T. Bartone, Harry C. Halloway, and David H. Marlowe. 1990. Life and death in the US Army: In *corpore sano. The Journal of the American Medical Association* 264(17): 2241(4). In peacetime, this study shows, soldiers are half as likely to die as demographically similar groups of civilians. This is accounted for by mental and physical screening for mili-tary work as well as extensive preventa-tive and clinical health care provided in the military regardless of income level.

67. Jumping in Flash Burn proves safer than highway driving. *Fayetteville Observer,* 5/6/54.

68. Leon F. Litwack (1998. *Trouble in Mind: Black Southerners in the Age of Jim Crow.* New York: Knopf) describes the brutal violence that enforced not only the Jim Crow color line, but the expec-tation of black economic inferiority as well. That meant a black man with a visible new possession could be killed for the presumption it implied.

69. Timothy B. Tyson. 1998. Rob-ert F. Williams, "Black Power," and the roots of the African American free-dom struggle. *Journal of American His-tory* 85(2): 64–90. See also Litwack, *op. cit.,* pp. 422–428.

70. *Fayetteville Observer,* 7/1/53.

71. The nearest high school for Indian students was thirty-five miles away until the building of the Les Max-well High School on the east side of Fayetteville in 1958. Indians were not permitted to attend either white or black schools and had to raise their own funds to build their first local school in 1925. They did not receive public school transportation until 1948; Cum-

berland County Association for Indian People, General History of Community and Indian Center, manuscript.

72. Robert Beatty, interview, 4/23/97.

73. *Your City Government.* 1959–1960. Annual Reports of City. Fayetteville, NC.

74. William Henry Chafe. 1980. *Civilities and Civil Rights: Greensboro, North Carolina, and the Black Struggle for Freedom.* New York: Oxford University Press, p. 7. In 1940, North Carolina did, however, have the highest black registration rate in the South, with the exception of Tennessee, and the eighty-five lynchings its people perpetrated between 1882 and 1930 was the lowest number in the region; Steve Suitts. 1981. Blacks in the political arithmetic after Mobile: A case study of North Carolina. In *The Right to Vote: A Rockefeller Foundation Conference,* April 22–23, 1981. New York: The Rockefeller Foundation, p. 54.

75. Timothy Tyson. 1998. Wars for democracy: African American militancy and interracial violence in North Carolina during World War II. In David S. Cecelski and Timothy B. Tyson, eds. *Democracy Betrayed: The Wilmington Race Riot of 1898 and Its Legacy.* Chapel Hill: University of North Carolina Press, pp. 254–255.

76. Mary Kaldor. 1991. *The Imaginary War: Understanding the East–West Conflict.* London: Blackwell.

77. Ruth Sivard. 1996. *World Military and Social Expenditures.* Washington, DC: World Priorities.

78. Kaldor, *op. cit.*

79. Sherry, *op. cit.,* p. 177.

80. Richard Dalfiume. 1982. *Papers of NAACP.* Frederick, MD: University Publications of America, Inc., p. xv.

81. Gerald Horne's research has been the most thorough and insightful in showing these links during the Cold War. He also posits that black progress during World War II was due to the suspension of red baiting prompted by the alliance with the Soviet Union. Gerald Horne. 1986. *Black and Red: W. E. B. Du Bois and the Afro-American Response to the Cold War, 1944–1963.* Albany: State University of New York Press.

82. *Fayetteville Observer,* 9/13/49.

83. That year, Cumberland County's 32 schools included 18 for white, 13 for "colored," and 1 for Indian students.

84. End of segregation: Now at last we must face it, calmly. *Fayetteville Observer,* 5/18/54.

85. Christian principles: Will amalgamation mean disunity? *Fayetteville Observer,* 5/26/54.

86. And the FBI and military intelligence units investigated thousands of people for simple assembly and acts of speech. Herbert Hoover encouraged public cooperation in spying on neighbors and found enthusiastic assistance from the Veterans of Foreign Wars and other private groups; Joan Jensen. 1991. *Army Surveillance in America, 1775–1980.* New Haven, CT: Yale University Press, pp. 235–236.

87. See also Timothy B. Tyson. 1999. *Radio Free Dixie: Robert F. Williams and the Roots of Black Power.* Chapel Hill: University of North Carolina Press.

88. J. W. Seabrook, The Supreme Court decision of May 17, 1954, as viewed by a North Carolina Negro. Brief presented to the Pearsall Committee. In Gertha Smith Gibson. 1987. *James Ward Seabrook: An Educational Leader in the Black Community.* Ph.D. dissertation, UNC-CH.

89. The phrase is George Kennan's, cited in Frederick M. Dolan. 1994. *Allegories of America: Narratives, Metaphysics, Politics.* Ithaca, NY: Cornell University Press.

90. *Ibid.,* p. 72.

91. Blacks were first elected to city councils in Winston-Salem in 1947,

Greensboro in 1951, Durham in 1953, and Raleigh in 1960; William H. Towe. 1972. *Barriers to Black Political Participation in North Carolina.* Atlanta: Voter Education Project.

92. *Fayetteville Observer,* 5/4/49. Neither alphabetization nor numbers of votes garnered can account for that singular placement.

93. Principal Poole's actions were said to be the first integration move in a Southern federal facility; Parker, 1990, *Cumberland County, op. cit.,* pp. 140–141; see also Lee Nichols. 1993 [1954]. *Breakthrough on the Color Front,* 2nd edition. Colorado Springs: Three Continents Press, pp. 170–173.

94. Wilma Cecelia Peebles. 1984. *School Desegregation in Raleigh, North Carolina, 1954–1964.* Ph.D. dissertation, UNC-CH; Southern Education Reporting Service. 1961, 1963–1964. *Statistical Summary of School Segregation–Desegregation in the Southern and Border States.* Nashville: Author; see also Don Shoemaker, ed. 1970. *With All Deliberate Speed: Segregation–Desegregation in Southern Schools.* Westport, CT: Negro Universities Press. The numbers were quite small to begin with, with six black children in one white school that first year in Fayetteville. Full integration came to county schools only in the early 1970s.

95. *Fayetteville Observer,* 10/3/63.

96. The threat applied to systems taking students who lived on military posts. Soldiers living off post were, in other words, treated as civilians were; *Fayetteville Observer,* 7/20/62. Several of these families ultimately brought suit against the County Board of Education when their applications were denied; *Fayetteville Observer,* 3/14/63.

97. Capus Waynick, John C. Brooks, and Elsie W. Pitts, eds. 1964. *North Carolina and the Negro.* Raleigh: North Carolina Mayors' Cooperating Committee, p. 222. The number of median

income families in Cumberland and Onslow Counties was higher than in many other eastern Carolina counties, but no higher than other urban counties, in the case of Cumberland, or of many other coastal counties, in the case of Onslow.

98. Charles C. Moskos and John Sibley Butler. 1996. *All That We Can Be: Black Leadership and Racial Integration the Army Way.* New York: Basic-Books. While Moskos and Butler's argument acknowledges manpower and morale needs as contributing to the institutional push for racial equity, they see the military's disciplinary culture, skill training, and the job provision per se as more important in creating both equity and a common culture between the African American and white citizens who join. They also argue that the military has provided opportunities for the middle-classing of large segments of the black community, who then serve as role models for the rest. They celebrate the conservatism of the black military family as the root of black success since it focuses not on victimization, but on the future and family success.

99. Sherry, *op. cit.,* pp. 145–146.

100. Leo Bogart, ed. 1992. *Project Clear: Social Research and the Desegregation of the U.S. Army.* New Brunswick, NJ: Transaction Publishers, p. 274. Fort Bragg appears to be "Base B" in the official report.

101. *Ibid.,* p. 264.

102. Richard J. Stillman, II. 1968. *Integration of the Negro in the U.S. Armed Forces.* New York: Praeger.

103. Of the 11 million, 97 percent were white. These figures reflect the numbers through 1963 of those World War II and Korean War vets who got GI home loans; Bristow Hardin. 1991. *The Militarized Social Democracy and Racism: The Relationship between Militarism, Racism and Social Welfare Policy in the United*

States. Ph.D. dissertation, University of California at Santa Cruz.

104. Sherry (*op. cit.,* p. 145) notes that it was only Korean War manpower needs that forced general implementation of Truman's executive order. Moreover, the black casualty rate was twice that of whites as they were pushed into front-line combat assignments; Richard O. Hope. 1979. *Racial Strife in the U.S. Military: Toward the Elimination of Discrimination.* New York: Praeger, p. 31. The last all-black unit was not disbanded until 1954; Alton Hornsby, Jr. 1991. *A Chronology of African-American History.* Detroit: Gale Research, Inc.

105. Like the army, many churches are also highly hierarchical and centralized and can swiftly and widely implement social changes, if leaders wish. Catholic schools were desegregated in 1953 by order of Raleigh's bishop; Jeffrey Crow, ed. 1992. *History of African Americans in North Carolina.* Raleigh: Division of Archives and History.

106. Only two other counties in the state had a lower white registration rate, due to the high rate of out-of-state residence among soldiers. Neighboring counties' black registration rates show a wide range, reflecting both varying registrar racial bias as well as different voter roll purging practices. Hoke County, also bordering Fort Bragg, had 8 percent; Bladen County, 17 percent; Moore, 37 percent; Lee, 20 percent; and Rockingham, 62 percent. Onslow County, another military county, had 21 percent; Donald R. Matthews. 1959. *Voting Participation in North Carolina: Memorandum to North Carolina Advisory Committee on Civil Rights.* Manuscript. Donald R. Matthews. 1961. *Voting and Voter Registration in North Carolina, 1960.* North Carolina Advisory Committee. Manuscript.

107. Aldon D. Morris. 1984. *The Origins of the Civil Rights Movement: Black Communities Organizing for Change.* New York: The Free Press.

108. *Fayetteville Observer,* 2/12/60.

109. *Fayetteville Observer,* 5/27/63.

110. James C. Cobb. 1993. *The Selling of the South: The Southern Crusade for Industrial Development, 1936–1990.* Urbana: University of Illinois Press.

111. Fayetteville Human Relations Advisory Commission and Department. Annual Report, March 1968–March 1979.

112. *Fayetteville Observer,* 7/11/63.

113. *Fayetteville Observer,* 1/18/87.

114. Morris J. MacGregor and Bernard C. Nalty. 1977. *Blacks in the United States Armed Forces: Basic Documents. Vol. XIII: Equal Treatment and Opportunity: The McNamara Doctrine.* Wilmington, DE: Scholarly Resources, p. 231.

115. *Ibid.,* p. 233.

116. *Fayetteville Observer,* 3/11/69.

117. The post commanders, he said, did not place them off-limits strictly for failing to integrate: "They'd put them off limits if they had fights in them, yes. Or [if] the military complained, but, that was not a part of the integration problems." Monroe Evans, interview, 7/2/97.

118. City Council Minute Docket, City of Fayetteville, North Carolina, April 11, 1966, to May 13, 1968.

119. Fayetteville Human Relations Advisory Commission and Department. Annual Report. March 1970.

120. David Cecelski. 1997. Ordinary sin. *Independent Weekly* (March 19–25): 11–15.

4. **Carnival, Carnage, and Quakers: The Vietnam War on Hay Street (1964–1973)**

1. Christian G. Appy. 1999. The muffling of public memory in post-Vietnam America. *The Chronicle of*

Higher Education 45(February 12):
B 4–6.

2. There is one on Fort Bragg.

3. *Fayetteville Observer,* 9/3/98.

4. Jerry Lembcke. 1998. *The Spitting Image: Myth, Memory, and the Legacy of Vietnam.* New York: New York University Press. Lembcke's research shows that the spitting image was consciously promoted by the Nixon-Agnew administration to split the alliance that had emerged of antiwar soldiers and civilians.

5. Fort Bragg was a training center from 1966 through 1970, and, at a 1968 peak, its population had grown to 57,840. Robert B. Roberts. 1988. *Encyclopedia of Historic Forts: The Military, Pioneer, and Trading Posts of the United States.* New York: The Macmillan Company, p. 609.

6. Interview, 7/21/98.

7. Interview, 7/22/98.

8. This store was one of a chain, Tyrrell's, whose exploitative practices included encouraging homesick soldiers to put their girlfriends' photos in the shop window, using the military as a collection agency, and posting in the store a "Vietnam Honor Roll" of customers who had died. It eventually drew pickets from the GI movement at Fort Bragg and elsewhere around the country; David Cortright. 1975. *Soldiers in Revolt: The American Military Today.* New York: Anchor Press/Doubleday, pp. 84–85.

9. Hugh Gusterson. 1991. Nuclear war, the Gulf War, and the disappearing body. *Journal of Urban and Cultural Studies* 2(1): 45–55; Elaine Scarry. 1985. *The Body in Pain: The Making and Unmaking of the World.* New York: Oxford University Press.

10. Geoffrey Perret, *op. cit.,* p. 331.

11. *Fayetteville Observer,* 5/21/70.

12. This was also the acronym for the recruitment jingle, "Fun, Travel, and Adventure."

13. *Annual Historical Supplement for Fort Bragg, North Carolina, 1968.* XVIII Airborne Corps and Fort Bragg History Office Archives. In 1971, the desertion rate in the Army as a whole reached 7 percent of strength and AWOL incidents about one for every five enlisted soldiers; Cortright, *op. cit.,* pp. 12–13.

14. Fort Bragg soldiers spoke of such things in a *Fayetteville Observer* (9/17/71) reprint of a *Washington Post—Los Angeles Times* article. See also Richard A. Gabriel and Paul L. Savage. 1978. *Crisis in Command: Mismanagement in the Army.* New York: Hill and Wang; and Howard Zinn. 1980. *A People's History of the United States.* New York: Harper & Row.

15. David R. Roediger. 1994. *Towards the Abolition of Whiteness.* New York: Verso. In the early 1900s, the term was also used for camp-following prostitutes, in the connected sense of a low person.

16. Blacks were far less likely to get deferments, including physical ones. From 1950 through 1966, 22 percent of whites failed the physical exam, but only 15 percent of blacks did; Paul T. Murray. 1971. Blacks and the draft: A history of institutional racism. *Journal of Black Studies* 2(1): 57–76, 70–71. Protest of this fact led to changes in military policy which yielded racially more proportionate casualties by war's end; Sherry, *op. cit.,* p. 255.

17. Clyde Taylor, ed. 1973. *Vietnam and Black America: An Anthology of Protest and Resistance.* New York: Anchor Books; Cortright, *op. cit.*

18. Installation officials responded with, among other things, a 1972 Harmony Concert that drew thousands of soldiers and civilians. A rainbow coalition of musical styles—Loretta Lynn, Los Travivadies Del Brave, and Jerry Butler—were invited to sing in service to "better race relations." The "racially balanced" crowd included the concert's

instigator, an ex-enlisted man with long hair, an earring, and his own band, Trigger (no doubt the gun part, not the horse). The newspaper celebrated the festival's categorical mixing: "It was hard to distinguish the officer from the enlisted man—the civilian from the military at the concert." Commanding General Emerson himself was wearing an African dashiki, blue jeans, and cowboy boots and gave a green beret ("much to the delight and pleasure of the audience") to black musician Jimmy Witherspoon.

19. They held the prison for over two days; Cortright, *op. cit.*, pp. 70–71.

20. A movement survey of 25 members of GIs United found 17 were volunteers and 16 came from lower middle class families; *ibid.*, p. 222. More generally, a 1972 report by HUMMRO (a contract research firm that has done extensive work for the Army) found higher AWOL rates among volunteers than draftees; *ibid.*, p. 14.

21. David Cortright and Max Watts. 1991. *Left Face: Soldier Unions and Resistance Movements in Modern Armies.* Contributions in Military Studies, Number 107. New York: Greenwood Press, pp. 19–21. A survey two years earlier by a journalist found 44 percent of black and 14 percent of white enlisted men and 27 percent of black and 11 percent of white officers were for immediate withdrawal from the war; Wallace Terry II. 1970. Bringing the war home. *The Black Scholar* 2(3): 6–18, 17.

22. GI Civil Liberties Defense Committee, New York, NY, press release April 19, 1969; Fred Halstead. 1978. *Out Now!: A Participant's Account of the American Movement Against the Vietnam War.* New York: Monad Press; Cortright, *op. cit.*, p. 59. Another antiwar, antiracist GI group, the Black Brigade, was started shortly after.

23. Of the draftees, 51 percent did not pass, two-thirds of them for physi-

cal reasons; James W. Clay, Douglas M. Orr, Jr., and Alfred W. Stuart, eds. 1975. *North Carolina Atlas: Portrait of a Changing Southern State.* Chapel Hill: University of North Carolina Press, p. 287. This rate is worse than World War II's. Rejection rates of those examined at induction over three months in 1942 were between 34 and 43 percent, with most rejections for physical reasons, and with rates significantly higher for blacks than whites; Spencer Bidwell King, Jr. 1949. *Selective Service in North Carolina in World War II.* Chapel Hill: University of North Carolina Press, pp. 227, 256.

24. *Bragg Briefs,* 1:2.

25. In an article discussing a private's recent drug-induced jump from the roof of Womack Hospital, one writer attributed the escapism of drugs to the "olive drab atmosphere of Fort Bragg," a world of "inspections, guard duty, KP, police call and all for no real purpose. Nothing really gets done. The country really isn't being defended. It is just a silly world where the alcoholic lifers and brass play their silly games before another night of drinking at the club" *Bragg Briefs* 2(2)(September 1969): 2.

26. This was in 1972. Cited in Miles D. Wolpin. 1994. *Alternative Security and Military Dissent.* San Francisco: Austin and Winfield. Another estimate is 7,000; Cortright, *op. cit.*, p. 86.

27. Other GI publications on Fort Bragg were *The Fort Bragg Free Press, Sick Slip,* and *Strikeback; Bragg Briefs* 2(1)(August 1969): 3. The authorities' harassment extended to businesses that agreed to distribute the newspapers; *Bragg Briefs* 2(2)(September 1969): 2.

28. Dean Holland, a Bragg soldier from Nebraska who had applied for conscientious objector status and was having a great deal of trouble getting it, went to the Quaker meetings in the summer of 1969 asking for help. Quakers from around the state came and

rented the Ray Street house and supported the people who ran it over the
next three decades. The soldiers who
met at Quaker House included some
who had worked on *Bragg Briefs.*

29. Phil Esmonde, interview,
12/17/98.

30. *Fayetteville Observer,* 1/7/70. On
the response to the GI movements, see
also Tom Wells. 1994. *The War Within:
America's Battle over Vietnam.* Berkeley:
University of California Press, pp. 281–
283, 297, 492–496. See also David
Cortright, *op. cit.*

31. *Bragg Briefs* 2(4)(November
1969): 6.

32. Wells, *op. cit.,* p. 492–496.

33. *Fayetteville Observer,* 5/27/70.

34. Tim Spofford. 1988. *Lynch Street:
The May 1970 Slayings at Jackson State
College.* Kent, OH: Kent State University Press. The van, termed "Thompson's Tank" after the mayor by city
blacks, had been purchased by the city
police along with other armaments in
preparation for the civil rights movement's nonviolent Freedom Summer
of 1964.

35. The M-16 Civilian Coalition
was also behind the rally, a group that
Rennie Davis called "the true supporters of soldiers"; see *Fayetteville Observer,*
5/15/70 and 5/16/70. If people
remember nothing else about the Vietnam War protests, they remember,
often with derision or straight-up
anger, that Jane Fonda came to town.
The failure to remember the GI pro-
testor is consistent with the principle
that memory degrades, not randomly,
but in the direction of cultural expectations of what goes with what, of what
should happen; Roy D'Andrade. 1973.
Cultural constructions of reality. In
Laura Nader and Thomas Maretski,
eds. *Cultural Illness and Health.* Washington, DC: American Anthropological Association, Anthropological
Studies 9. But 1,700 Fort Bragg soldiers

would the next year sign a petition asking for the Jane Fonda antiwar show to
be allowed on the installation.

36. Such observances had been canceled at half of the 43 military installations around the country where demonstrations were planned; *Fayetteville
Observer,* 5/16/70.

37. Cortright, *op. cit.,* p. 67. The
local paper estimated 2,000 participants.

38. Bruce Pulliam, interview with
Brenda Moore, 2/16/94.

39. Absent the violence, this was like
the scene outside the 1968 Democratic
Party Convention in Chicago. Chicago's melee was called then and remembered now as a violent antiwar
demonstration, but was actually a
police riot, even by official investigation. Mayor Daley, who claimed the
police were justified in injuring dozens
of civilians, including journalists, was
in fact personally opposed to the war
and had gotten his two sons into the
National Guard; Harold Evans. 1999.
The American Century. New York:
Knopf, pp. 550–551.

40. Rich Giroux, interview, 5/8/00.
Some suspected agent provocateurs of
raising that rejected prospect; Adolph
Reed. 2000. *Class Notes: Posing as Poli-
tics and Other Thoughts on the American
Scene.* New York: The New Press.

41. *Fayetteville Observer,* 5/21/70.

42. *Fayetteville Observer,* 1/1/70.

43. *Fayetteville Observer,* 5/31/70.

44. Wells, *op. cit.,* p. 495.

45. Joe McGinniss. 1983. *Fatal
Vision.* New York: Penguin.

46. *Fayetteville Observer,* 2/17/70,
2/19/70.

47. *Fayetteville Observer,* 2/17/00.

48. Quaker House fire investigated.
Fayetteville Observer, 5/20/70; *Fayetteville Observer,* 2/16/70. There had been
political violence in many other venues
as well in the preceding year: eighty-
four bombings or attempts and arson on
college campuses, perpetrated particu-

larly by segments of the antiwar movement that advocated destruction of property involved in the war effort, such as ROTC buildings and research facilities doing military work. Watts, *op. cit.*, p. 297.

49. William Carothers, interview, 3/30/97.

50. Bruce Pulliam, interview with Brenda Moore, 2/16/94.

51. *Fayetteville Observer,* 5/28/70.

52. He made a $3,000 down payment and passed the remaining mortgage payments on to the Society of Friends.

53. A 1972 study cited in Cortright, *op. cit.*, p. 85.

54. *Ibid.*, p. 91.

55. *Ibid.*, p. 49.

56. Not all who opposed the war felt this way. Many experienced the loneliness of being different and the weight of their neighbors' condemnation.

57. Samuel Adams had written: "It is a very improbable supposition that any people can long remain free, with a strong military power in the very heart of their country. . . . Even where there is a necessity of the military power . . . a wise and prudent people will always have a watchful and a jealous eye over it; for the maxims and rules of the army, [*sic*] are essentially different from the genius of a free people, and the laws of a free government." Cited in Arthur A. Ekirch, Jr. 1956. *The Civilian and the Military.* New York: Oxford University Press, p. 9. In spite of enthusiasm for independence and armed revolt, these widely shared sentiments made discipline and recruitment problems for the Revolution's militias and Continental army. See also Marcus Cunliffe. 1969. *Soldiers and Civilians: The Martial Spirit in America, 1775–1865.* Boston: Little, Brown; and Richard H. Kohn, ed. 1979. *Anglo-American Antimilitary Tracts, 1697–1830.* New York: Arno Press.

58. Anna Simons, *op. cit.*

59. *Fayetteville Observer,* 9/3/98. The war anguish of cities with military bases grew over the second half of the twentieth century as they increasingly became home to military lineages. Where soldiers once came and went on to make families elsewhere, they became more likely to stay for location-based benefits, such as the exchange and military hospitals, and their children to emulate them. So while only accounting for 2 percent of North Carolina's deaths in World War II, Cumberland County had three times that proportion of the state's Vietnam War dead. While some would argue that these higher numbers have to do with Fort Bragg's cultural influence on the young men of the county, making them more eager to volunteer in general, the cultural influence of the post (as opposed to one's parents) could clearly cut both ways, as we have just seen.

60. Micaela di Leonardo. 1987. The female world of cards and holidays: Women, families and the work of kinship. *Signs* 12(3): 440–453.

61. The same term is often used by university students to refer to natives of the college towns they transiently live in. It has the odd effect of suggesting that the native is an exotic, even alien, species in that environment they share, and the visitor is the norm.

62. Some people in town believe the army both provides customers and has facilitated the immigration of prostituted women.

63. For many examples, see Neil Sheehan. 1988. *A Bright, Shining Lie: John Paul Vann and America in Vietnam.* New York: Vintage Books.

64. *Fayetteville Observer,* 1/7/70, 3/2/71.

65. Daniel C. Hallin. 1986. *The "Uncensored War": The Media and Vietnam.* New York: Oxford University Press, p. 9; see also Sheehan, *op. cit.*

66. Wells, *op. cit.,* pp. 473–474, 491.

67. The situation changed when a second daily newspaper, the *Fayetteville Times,* was started in the city in 1973. Competition for military subscribers pushed the *Observer* to more army coverage.

68. *National Geographic* magazine, for example, which covered the war-devastated countries of Vietnam, Laos, and Cambodia fourteen times from 1960 through 1968, suddenly dropped those areas from view, publishing just one article on them in the next thirteen years; Catherine Lutz and Jane Collins. 1993. *Reading National Geographic.* Chicago: University of Chicago Press, pp. 127–129.

69. *Fayetteville Observer,* 5/16/70.

70. Interview with *Fayetteville Observer* reporter.

71. Joan M. Jensen. 1991. *Army Surveillance in America, 1775–1980.* New Haven, CT: Yale University Press, pp. 240–241.

72. 111th Military Intelligence Group report. Department of the Army, United States Intelligence and Security Command. FOIA Request of Greg Sommers, Quaker House, 7/14/89.

73. FBI memo, 10/29/70. FOIA request to Greg Sommers, Quaker House, 11/6/89.

74. U.S. Government memorandum to SAC (100–10924), 5/21/70, in FOIA request by Greg Sommers, director of Quaker House, to FBI, dated 4/12/89. The FBI withheld fifty-five documents in their entirety, while the CIA requested $323.80 to conduct a search of its records. Nonetheless, it said it would be unlikely to release any documents found because they would be classified.

75. Stewart L. Udall. 1998. *The Myths of August: A Personal Exploration of Our Tragic Cold War Affair with the Atom.* New Brunswick, NJ: Rutgers University Press. See also Carole Gallagher. 1993. *American Ground Zero: The Secret Nuclear War.* Cambridge, MA: MIT Press.

76. Harold Evans. 1999. *The American Century.* New York: Knopf, p. 420.

77. James William Gibson. 1989. Paramilitary culture. *Critical Studies in Mass Communication* 6(1): 90–93. The black budget is a publicly undisclosed segment of the military budget. In the early 1990s, that was estimated at 10 percent of each year's total (Sam Marullo, *op. cit.,* p. 182).

78. Gibson, *op. cit.,* p. 90. See also Elizabeth Traube. 1992. *Dreaming Identities: Class, Gender, and Generation in 1980s Hollywood Movies.* Boulder, CO: Westview Press. The social ramifications of this war were also to have ironic reverberations with other issues of race and ethnic identity in Fayetteville. Defeat in Vietnam was interpreted in a special way by those white southerners whose understanding of the Civil War centered around a sense of loss and injury which, while acknowledging military defeat, emphasized the "chivalry of the losers and the romance of a lost cause"; R. Celeste Ray. 1996. *Scottish-American Heritage: Community and Celebration in North Carolina.* Ph. D. dissertation, UNC-CH, p. 319. For some of the Highland Scots among them—especially those who established the Scottish-American Military Society in 1981—this resonates still further back in time with their defeat at the Battle of Culloden and their perceived exile to America. The Scots who participate in the heritage movement centered around the Highland Games present Scottish history as a sequence of battles and often refer to themselves as a "warrior culture" or a "warrior race," who have "a love of a fray." That this is truly a racial way of thinking is indexed by how the men, many of whom are soldiers or veterans,

say they were "naturally drawn to military careers to begin with and find out why later on"; Ray, *op. cit.*, p. 249.

79. In a survey of registered voters in nearby Chatham County, 65 percent say the effect of the militia and survivalist movement on the country has been bad, 23 percent are not sure, and 3 percent see it as good; Dorothy Holland, Catherine Lutz, Donald Nonini, Lesley Bartlett, Marla Frederick, Thaddeus Guldbrandsen, and Enrique Murillo. n.d. *Restructuring Democracy.* Manuscript.

80. Life in a military town poll. *Fayetteville Observer,* 8/23/98. Thirty years after the war, only half the respondents to a survey had positive things to say about Fayetteville as a place to live, the rest were neutral or negative. And this apparently represented a significant improvement over feelings in the past.

81. Cortright, *op. cit.*, p. 187; David R. Segal, Jerald G. Bachman, Peter Freedman-Doan, and Patrick M. O'Malley. 1999. Propensity to serve in the U.S. Military: Temporal trends and subgroup differences. *Armed Forces and Society* 25(3): 407–427.

82. Geoffrey Perrett. 1990. *A Country Made by War.* New York: Vintage, pp. 537–538. Cortright (*op. cit.*, p. 76) notes that when reveille was eliminated, many soldiers had already refused to get up.

83. Some were incentives-based, keyed to better chances at promotion or advanced training. Others were control-based, as when race relations councils were instituted that channeled political activity and discontent into administrative arenas.

84. Segal et al., *op. cit.*

85. Lembcke, *op. cit.* This is not to say that no soldier was spit on or that some people were not angry with soldiers for prosecuting the war, but that the dominant reality was one where Vietnam veterans' homecoming experience was closer to that in World War II (where most soldiers experienced no parades and plenty of suspicion) and that it included indifference, fear, and the solidarity with civilians described here.

5. Many Reserve Armies: The Faces of Military Dependency (1974–2000)

1. In 1997, the national sales average was $261 per square foot, while Cross Creek Mall stores averaged $400; Bunni Oslund-Fisk, Marketing Director, Cross Creek Mall, interview, 7/1/99.

2. This is in 2000 dollars; Center for Defense Information. 1999. *1999 CDI Military Almanac.* Washington, DC: Center for Defense Information, p. 26. The bases included 890 in the U.S. and its possessions and 375 in 21 foreign countries; Charles Reginald Schrader, ed. 1995. *Reference Guide to United States Military History, 1945 to the Present.* New York: Sachem Publishing Assoc.

3. Marullo, *op. cit.*, p. 156–158. There is tremendous variability in how this percentage is figured—minimized by proponents of a large military (who come out as low as 20 percent) and maximized by opponents (occasionally put at 50 percent). The 44 percent figure includes the Pentagon budget as well as the often-excluded: foreign military aid, veteran's benefits and additional retirement pay, interest on borrowing to pay for past wars, and NASA's military activities.

4. *Ibid.*, p. 150.

5. Lawrence Korb. 1986–1987. The defense budget. In Joseph Kruzel, ed. *American Defense Annual.* Lexington, MA: Lexington Books, p. 41.

6. Sherry, *op. cit.*, p. 6.

7. Center for Defense Information. *op. cit.*, p. 16. In addition, there were 1.4 million reservists in 1998.

8. Marion Anderson. 1982. *The Price*

of the Pentagon. Lansing, MI: Employment Research Associates. While these numbers represent estimates based on assumptions not all of them share, the economists' consensus is that civilian spending creates more jobs. See also Roger Bezdek. 1975. The 1980 economic impact—Regional and occupational—Of compensated shifts in defense spending. *Journal of Regional Science* 15(2): 183–198. While increased military spending generally raises unemployment, the impact of this is unevenly distributed: white men suffer the employment effects least, and black men most; similarly, nonmilitary government expenditures reduce unemployment for all groups, but white men are most benefited and black men, least. Women of both races fall in between; John D. Abell. 1992. Defense spending and unemployment rates: An empirical analysis disaggregated by race and gender. *American Journal of Economics and Sociology* 51(1): 27–42.

9. Markusen and Yudken, *op. cit.,* pp. 58–64.

10. *Ibid.,* pp. 160–161.

11. Bristow Hardin. 1991. *The Militarized Social Democracy and Racism: The Relationship between Militarism, Racism and Social Welfare Policy in the United States.* Ph.D. dissertation, University of California at Santa Cruz.

12. Markusen and Yudken, *op. cit.,* pp. 163–165.

13. They nonetheless often have remained disadvantaged in some welfare programs, such as old-age assistance, that are biased toward male patterns of work and unemployment; Gwendolyn Mink. 1990. The lady and the tramp: Gender, race, and the origins of the American welfare state. In Linda Gordon, ed. *Women, the State and Welfare.* Madison: University of Wisconsin Press. Early American welfare policies focused on women rather than disadvantaged race or class groupings, the latter of which are preferred criteria for assistance in other industrialized countries. According to Mink, this strengthened many Americans' ambivalence about the idea of universal citizenship. See also Theda Skocpol. 1993. *Protecting Soldiers and Mothers: The Political Origins of Social Policy in the United States.* Cambridge, U. K.: Cambridge University Press.

14. Hardin, *op. cit.,* p. 84.

15. Mary Kaldor. 1981. *The Baroque Arsenal.* New York: Hill and Wang; Sherry, *op. cit.,* p. 402 on the B-1.

16. Markusen and Yudken, *op. cit.* As Marullo (*op. cit.,* p. 155) also notes, the acceptance of cost-overruns and guaranteed profits "spill[s] over into the private sector" through a variety of processes, including the need of private businesses to compete with the Department of Defense for resources and personnel.

17. Markusen and Yudken, *op. cit.,* p. 89.

18. Ann Markusen, Peter Hall, Scott Campbell, and Sabina Deitrick. 1991. *The Rise of the Gunbelt: The Military Remapping of Industrial America.* New York: Oxford University Press.

19. Seth Shulman, *op. cit.* On the shaping of science by military priorities, see Stuart W. Leslie. 1993. *The Cold War and American Science: The Military-Industrial-Academic Complex at MIT and Stanford.* New York: Columbia University Press.

20. Mary B. Johnson. 1993. *Challenges of Faith and Family in the Lives of Defense Workers.* Ph.D. dissertation, University of Massachusetts. See also Hugh Gusterson. 1996. *Nuclear Rites: A Weapons Laboratory at the End of the Cold War.* Berkeley: University of California Press; and A. G. Mojtabai. 1986. *Blessed Assurance: At Home with the Bomb in Amarillo, Texas.* Albuquerque: University of New Mexico Press.

21. Marullo, *op. cit.*

22. Marullo, *op. cit.*, p. 148. A GAO report in 1992 estimated that from 10 to 30 percent of military contract dollars fell into the conservatively figured category of "fraud and waste" (cited in Marullo, *op. cit.*, p. 149).

23. A prominent recent example is Togo West, who moved from the Carter Pentagon to lobbying for Northrup Grumman, which makes the $2 billion B-2 bomber, and back to become secretary of the Army under Clinton; Ken Silverstein. 2000. *Private Warriors*. New York: Verso Books, p. 192.

24. Tim Weiner. 1990. *Blank Check: The Pentagon's Black Budget*. New York: Warner Books, p. 16

25. *Fayetteville Observer,* 1/22/00, 1/23/00, 1/24/00.

26. Chris Hables Gray. 1997. *Postmodern War: The New Politics of Conflict*. New York: The Guilford Press; Sherry, *op. cit.*

27. Center for Defense Information, *op. cit.,* pp. 39–42. For the unacknowledged involvement, see Blum, 1995, *op. cit.*

28. Sherry, *op. cit.*, p. 340.

29. David Harvey. 1989. *The Condition of Postmodernity: An Enquiry into the Origins of Cultural Change*. New York: Blackwell.

30. Cynthia Enloe. 1995. The globetrotting sneaker. *Ms.* 5(5): 10–15.

31. The companies that came moved during a rush of recruiting that occurred across the South. States and localities offered subsidies, tax incentives, and industrial bond-funded buildings to companies that would relocate to their communities; Charles Cobb. 1993. *The Selling of the South: The Southern Crusade for Industrial Development, 1936–1990*, 2nd ed. Urbana: University of Illinois Press.

32. By one estimate, 40 percent of the county's employment (excluding soldiers themselves) is directly or indirectly attributable to the military; Governor's Advisory Commission on Military Affairs. 1995. *Study of Military Economic Impact on North Carolina.* Greenville, NC: ECU Regional Development Institute, Appendix, p. 3.

33. These include 40,000 Fort Bragg soldiers and 4,000 Department of Defense civilian employees on average through the 1980s.

34. State Data Center, North Carolina Office of State Planning. 1994 Employment by Sector. www.ospl.state.nc.us.

35. State Data Center, North Carolina Office of State Planning. www.ospl.state.nc.us.

36. Brett Williams. 1994. Babies and banks: The "reproductive underclass" and the raced, gendered masking of debt. In Steven Gregory and Roger Sanjek, eds. *Race*. New Brunswick, NJ: Rutgers University Press.

37. Mary Fisher, Fayetteville Job Service Center, labor market specialist, interview, 10/18/96. The army has not always fully reimbursed soldiers for their off-base housing costs, however; Chester Hartman and Robin Drayer. 1990. Military-family housing: The other public-housing program. *Housing and Society* 17(3): 67–78.

38. Army unfurls its plans for a modern base. *Fayetteville Observer Times,* 10/20/91. The expectation was quite different in the past, when, as at the turn of the century, military men thought "the moral superiority of the military life rested on its freedom 'from the sordidness and misery of the money-getting trade' "; Samuel Huntington. 1957. *The Soldier and the State: The Theory and Politics of Civil-Military Relations.* Cambridge, MA: Harvard University Press, p. 268.

39. Jack Cox, interview, 6/28/99.

40. President's Economic Adjustment Committee. n.d. *The Economic Impacts of Desert Shield/Desert Storm Deployments on Fort Bragg, North Caro-*

lina, Local Communities. Washington, DC: Office of Economic Adjustment, Department of Defense, pp. 1–3. This report estimated military families account for 22 percent of retail sales off post, that PX and commissary sales are 11 percent of all metro area retail sales, and that 30 percent of all purchases made by military families are on post. The overall impact on retail sales of the Gulf War was estimated at just 5 percent.

41. Bunni Oslund-Fisk, marketing director, Cross Creek Mall, interview, 7/1/99.

42. Cynthia Enloe. 2000. *Maneuvers: The International Politics of Militarizing Women's Lives.* Berkeley: University of California Press, p. 46.

43. Cortright and Watts, *op cit.*

44. While cities with bases cannot control federal policies related to the base, they can regulate the conditions under which soldiers come to town. Where there has been little local opposition, towns have not much restricted prostitution, alcohol, drugs, or gambling, or they have even tried to profit from them. Near a Nebraska military base around the turn of the twentieth century, town leaders got their school taxes from taverns and paid their police officers with a $5 a month tax on each prostitute. Residents, however, put pressure on for the development of a red light district to segregate the activity from the sight of respectable families. A rise in VD led the post commander to threaten a boycott of town if control over local women was not taken. The town proceeded to give prostitutes physical exams, which ultimately raised their numbers as business boomed. Fluctuations in the town's attitudes toward this trade were apparently race-dependent: When black troops came in, vice was allowed and a clampdown happened when they moved out; Frank N. Schubert. 1987.

Troopers, taverns, and taxes: Fort Robinson, Nebraska, and its municipal parasite, 1886–1911. In Garry D. Ryan and Timothy K. Nenninger, eds. *Soldiers and Civilians: The U.S. Army and the American People.* Washington, DC: National Archives and Records Administration, pp. 91–103.

45. Lack of industry is Cumberland's missing piece of tax puzzle. *Fayetteville Observer,* 5/28/00.

46. *Fayetteville Observer,* 5/15/97, 9/6/98. The figure for school spending excludes federal and state contributions. Some of the lower spending emerges from the fact that the district's teachers are relatively young and new to the system, something true of many growing schools systems but also true of those, like Fayetteville's, with teacher retention problems. A formula—not always fully funded—determines how much communities are paid in federal impact funds. For 1998–1999, that was $960 per high school student living on post and a smaller amount for off-post children; Susan Jackson, Public Affairs Office, Fort Bragg Schools, interview, 7/1/99.

47. They are admitted in equal percentages but apply in smaller numbers (6 percent of Cumberland's versus 8 to 13 percent of other urban counties').

48. www.ospl.state.nc.us/sdn.

49. Post exchanges approved to sell higher-priced items. *Fayetteville Observer,* 5/9/97. In the late 1940s, Congress tried to reel in the proliferating and expensive number of military stores by legislating that commissaries could be maintained "only where other stores either were not available within a reasonable distance or did not sell food at a reasonable price"; Michael E. Hucles. 1990. *From Haversack to Checkout Counter: A Brief History of the Army Commissary System.* Fort Lee, VA: U.S. Army Troop Support Agency, pp. 89–90. But the bottom line argument that

could always be made—even though retirees were fully one-third of commissary shoppers by the 1980s—was soldier morale and retention. And long gone is the fear that providing for soldier entertainment and consumer goods "fostered indulgence rather than the proper military characteristics of 'self-sacrifice and denial' "; Edward M. Coffman. 1986. *The Old Army: A Portrait of the American Army in Peacetime, 1784–1898.* New York: Oxford University Press, p. 361. Later reforms made the stores self-supporting, with surcharges permitted and turned back to the base.

50. Defense Finance and Accounting Service. Military pay and housing and subsistence allowances as of 1/1/2000. www.dfas.mil/money/milpay/pay/. CEO total compensation averaged $10.6 million in 1998, worker pay $29,000; Sarah Anderson, John Cavanagh, Ralph Estes, Chuck Collins, and Chris Hartman. 1999. *A Decade of Executive Excess: The 1990s.* Sixth Annual Executive Compensation Survey; www.ufenet.org.

51. GE is a significant military contractor that had 150 staff members in its Washington office in the mid-1980s (weapons makers far exceed other corporations in their assault on the capital; the larger Exxon corporation, for example, had just thirteen people in its D. C. office). Infact. 1988. *Bringing GE to Light: How General Electric Shapes Nuclear Weapons Policies for Profits.* Philadelphia: New Society Publishers, p. 81.

52. In 1998, rounded to the nearest $1,000; Army Times Publishing Co., cited in *Military Market Magazine's 1998 Almanac.*

53. www.defenselink.mil/-pubs/almanac/almanac/people/minorities.html. The general population figure is 32 percent for 18- to 34-year-olds; "Resident Population, by Race, Hispanic Origin, and Single Years of Age: 1998," No. 22, p. 22. In *Statistical Abstract of the United States,* 1999. Available from *Statistical Universe* (Online Service). Bethesda, MD: Congressional Information Service.

54. Reynolds Farley and William H. Frey. 1994. Changes in the segregation of whites from blacks during the 1980s: Small steps toward a more integrated society. *American Sociological Review* 59:23–45. They find segregation is also generally low in growing cities, found mostly in the South and West, where many military facilities are located. Growth, then, also likely accounts for Fayetteville's level of integration.

55. It rose by nearly 50 percent in the twenty years after the Korean War; Nancy L. Goldman. 1976. Trends in family patterns of U.S. military personnel during the 20th century. In Nancy L. Goldman and David R. Segal, eds. *The Social Psychology of Military Service.* Beverly Hills, CA: Sage Publications, pp. 119–134. The AVF gave an even stronger boost to marriage rates.

56. Allan Berube. 1990. *Coming Out under Fire: The History of Gay Men and Women in World War Two.* New York: The Free Press.

57. Army investigates homosexual Web site. *Fayetteville Observer,* 5/19/00.

58. Doug Ireland. 2000. Search and destroy: Gay-baiting in the military under "don't ask, don't tell." *The Nation* 271(2): 11–16.

59. Survey of troops finds antigay bias common in service. *New York Times,* 3/25/00. See also Cynthia Enloe, 2000, *op. cit.*

60. Enloe, 2000, *op. cit.,* pp. 194–195. The shift in language may have connoted more equality but it continued to suggest that the spouse had moral obligations to the military.

61. Many soldiers call their control by the army the "cost" of freedom, their disciplining the route to saving lives on the battlefield. Disobedience

kills, according to this view of work conditions in the military. While the superior knowledge of the officer, when absorbed automatically, can help a soldier survive, obedience also kills when the order is to fire on others or when the order, tacitly, is to "die in place."

62. Military Attrition: Better Data, Coupled with Policy Changes, Could Help the Services Reduce Early Separations. GAO/NSIAD-98–213 Research Alert, January 15, 1999.

63. Starting salary for city police officers, for example, was $24,700 in 2000. www.cityoffayetteville.org.

64. 1986–1987, *American Defense Annual, op. cit.*

65. Only 4 of 100 counties approached Cumberland's 11 percent female unemployment rate (one has another large military base), and only 2 were near its 9 percent overall unemployment rate in 1990. The female unemployment rate on Fort Bragg itself was 17 percent; United States Bureau of the Census. 1990. *1990 Census of Population.* Washington; DC: U.S. Department of Commerce, Economics and Statistics Administration, Bureau of the Census. See also J. Brad Schwartz, Lisa L. Wood, and Janet D. Griffith. 1991. The Impact of military life on spouse labor force outcomes. *Armed Forces and Society* 17(3): 385–407.

66. F. John Devaney. 1955. *The Present Economic Structure and Forecasted Employment for Fayetteville and Cumberland County, N.C.* Ph.D. dissertation, UNC-CH, p. 4, table 3. Population changes moderated in the 1990s.

67. Clay et al., *op. cit.,* p. 50.

68. The U.S. military was 14 percent female at both the enlisted and officer level in 1998, ranging from 6 percent female in the Marines to 18 percent in the Air Force; Center for Defense Information. *op. cit.,* p. 17. These women have been considered a social

problem by many, whether in terms of their impact on "readiness" or their sexuality, which is more heavily monitored than their male colleagues'; Cynthia Enloe. 1987. *Does Khaki Become You?* London: Pandora.

69. Defense Manpower Data Center, cited in April 1999 Tidbits. http://-trol.redstone.army.military/mwr/marketing. A soldier can retire at age thirty-eight with a full pension.

70. Jack Cox, interview, 6/28/99.

71. www.bragg.army.mil/pao/99.htm.

72. *Fayetteville Observer,* 6/7/70.

73. Denny Shaffer, interview, 7/28/00.

74. Shulman, *op. cit.,* p. 72.

75. David Armstrong. The nation's dirty, big secret. *Boston Globe,* 11/14/99. Judging by Superfund cleanup costs alone, the federal government's damage has been five times that of all privately owned companies (including all chemical and oil companies, rubber manufacturers, etc.).

76. Suzanne Lynch. 1998. Conservation policy case study: The red-cockaded woodpecker. Manuscript.

77. David Armstrong. A toxic legacy abroad. *Boston Globe,* 11/15/99. See also Dr. Huda A. Ammash. 2000. Toxic pollution, the Gulf War, and Iraq. In Anthony Arnove, ed. *Iraq under Siege.* Boston: South End Press.

78. Don F. Reitz, Edward J. Kaiser, Raymond J. Burby, and Gerard McMahon. 1990. *Fort Bragg–Pope Air Force Base Impact Assessment: Population, Housing, Fiscal, Land Use.* Chapel Hill: The Department of City and Regional Planning, University of North Carolina at Chapel Hill; Gerard McMahon and Edward J. Kaiser, eds. 1992. *Fort Bragg/Pope Air Force Base Military-Civilian Joint Compatible Land Use Study: A Case Study Prepared for North Carolina Department of Economic and Community Development, Division of Community*

Assistance. Chapel Hill: Center for Urban and Regional Studies, University of North Carolina at Chapel Hill.

79. There are relatively few crashes, considering the amount of air traffic. From 1948 to 1985, there were twelve fatal on-post crashes and four off post. In all, sixty-three soldiers died; *Fayetteville Observer,* 3/14/85.

80. Analytical/Environmental Assessment Report, Master Plan, Future Development Plans. Fort Bragg, NC, January 1979, p. 12.

81. Building ambition. *Fayetteville Observer,* 5/23/94.

82. When investing in politics, the rate of return is confidential. *Fayetteville Observer,* 5/23/94.

83. Jack Cox, interview, 6/28/99. Cox now contributes his expertise on a local planning commission.

84. Every American city has similar stories of the intervention of elites in the location of government resources, zoning decisions, and other workings to enhance their property values through state action. As the urban theorists John Logan and Harvey Molotch (1987. *Urban Fortunes: The Political Economy of Place.* Berkeley: University of California Press) note, "place entrepreneurs" are everywhere a potent force. They often unite with others into "growth machines [that] unite behind a doctrine of value-free development—the notion that free markets alone should determine land use" (p. 32) and that this benefits the citizenry in general. A corollary of that doctrine is that property values and attributes emerge from "the qualities inherent in a piece of land, and that places are defined . . . through nature, autonomous markets, or spatial geometry" (p. 45). Place entrepreneurs have been key to how Fort Bragg relates to Fayetteville's economies.

85. The Department of Defense has been the country's largest landlord, for example, housing 1.4 million people in 400,000 units of family housing on and off base in the late 1980s; Hartman and Drayer, *op. cit.*

86. In 1990, Cumberland County ranked 66th (and Onslow County, with Camp LeJeune, 87th) among the state's one hundred counties and was by far the lowest among urban counties; State Data Center, North Carolina Office of State Planning, www.ospl.state.nc.us.

87. The poverty rate decreased during the 1980s, although white poverty declined more precipitously and black poverty hardly at all. The white poverty rate in Fayetteville (and other North Carolina military communities) is very similar to other urban areas, but the overall rate in 1990 was 19 percent. For children under five years of age, the poverty rate was 31 percent. But as with the crime rate, Camp LeJeune's home community of Jacksonville (which has a proportionately much smaller civilian population) looks more like the rest of the state than does Fayetteville; 1990 U.S. Census. Fayetteville's infant mortality rate declined to 9.0 per 1,000 in 1999. For whites, it was 6.8, and for "non-whites," 14.8 (North Carolina Child Advocacy Institute, 2000), www.ncchild.org/ci2000pdflist.htm).

88. In 1995; State Data Center, North Carolina Office of State Planning, www.ospl.state.nc.us.

89. As these problems emerged, so did proannexation sentiment among people with bad septic system problems. It was when the state made tougher septic tank regulations, however, that Billy Clark, the city attorney in the 1970s, said, "The money switched. Now it was cheaper to be on city water and sewer [and] the developers tuned in," and he began to lobby for annexation rights, which the city got in 1983; *Fayetteville Observer,* 2/21/84.

90. The 19 percent rate in Fayetteville compares with 9 percent on Fort

Bragg and 5 percent on Pope Air Force Base; 1990 U.S. Census.

91. Without powers of annexation, Fayetteville went into the postwar era of extensive road building with a much smaller official population, making it ineligible for significant federal funds for roads and other resources often allocated by cities' populations. Nonetheless, the county's lax regulation boosted development at the city periphery, accentuating urban sprawl. The annexation issue created political bad blood between the city and the county, since the city sees the county as using services without paying for them. Speaking without a single voice, the divided area legislative delegation comes home with less than its share of state money.

92. Interview, 3/31/97.

93. State Data Center, North Carolina Office of State Planning, www.ospl.state.nc.us.

94. Fayetteville's image tough to clean. *Fayetteville Observer,* 9/13/98.

95. State Bureau of Investigation. North Carolina Crime Statistics, sbi2.jus.state.nc.us.

96. Drug use is much lower among soldiers than comparable civilians (3 percent versus 10 percent from 1991 to 1992), but has occurred despite a regular drug-testing program. Heavy alcohol use is more prevalent among soldiers (15 percent versus 10 percent for comparable groups of civilians); Jacques Normand, Richard O. Lempert, and Charles P. O'Brien, eds. 1994. *Under the Influence?: Drugs and the American Work Force. Committee on Drug Use in the Workplace.* Washington, D.C.: National Academy Press, p. 70.

97. Higher rates of reporting may also result. In the mid-1990s, 60 percent of Fort Bragg's reported cases of spouse abuse occurred on post, while only 40 percent of married military couples live there; Henry Berry, Family Advocacy Program coordinator, Fort

Bragg, public presentation, 10/1/94. Berry estimates only 1 in 10 such assaults were reported in 1993, the true total being 7,720 per year, out of a population of 45,000 soldiers, or 1 in 6. Data on other crime rates presented in Madeline Morris. 1996. By force of arms: Rape, war, and military culture. *Duke Law Journal* 1996, 45(4): 651–781.

98. Richard R. Gessner and Desmond K. Runyan. 1995. The shaken infant: A military connection? *Archives of Pediatrics and Adolescent Medicine* 149 (April):467–469.

99. Morris, *op. cit.*

100. U.S. Inspector General's Report, 1979, cited in Enloe, *Maneuvers,* p. 189.

101. Media Report to Women. 1997. TV network murder coverage up 700% since 1993. *Media Report to Women* 25(3): 1–3. Coverage of foreign violence increased as well at the same time.

102. Fayetteville Online Commons, 9/8/98, www.fayettevillenc.com.

6. **Military Restructuring, Civilian Camouflage, and Hot Peace (1989–2000)**

1. Center for Defense Information. 1999. *1999 CDI Military Almanac.* Washington, DC: Author, pp. 20–21. Ann Markusen, Peter Hall, Scott Campbell, and Sabina Deitrick. 1991. *The Rise of the Gunbelt: The Military Remapping of Industrial America.* New York: Oxford University Press, p. 147.

2. Military means money. Military worth over $2.1 billion to Cumberland County. *Fayetteville Observer,* 10/11/92.

3. While many factors influence the variable outcomes, communities whose bases have closed have not been devastated. Some have prospered, replacing the jobs lost, gaining a wider tax base, and gaining redirected retiree retail and

medical spending. This includes areas that lost large bases such as South Carolina's Charleston Naval Base, which had 30,000 military and 7,000 civilian employees; Louis Jacobson. 2000. There is life after a military base closes. *National Journal* (April 22): 1292–1294. Charleston's mayor concluded, "I still would not have called for the closing, because we still experienced the trauma and tragedy of people losing their jobs. . . . We did take lemons and made lemonade out of them. But all things being equal, I wouldn't have asked for a bag of lemons to begin with"; *ibid.,* p. 1294. On California base closings, see The East Bay Conversion and Reinvestment Commission's Web site, www.cedar.ca.gov; and Michael Dardia et al. 1996. *The Effects of Military Base Closures on Local Communities: A Short-term Perspective.* Santa Monica, CA: Rand.

4. The decline began in 1987, when the army was 2.2 billion strong. It was 1.4 billion in 1998. Budget calculations are in inflation-adjusted dollars. Center for Defense Information, *op. cit.*

5. It went from $334 billion in 1991 to $274 billion in 1998. It will be $331 billion in 2005. All numbers are given in 2000 dollars; Center for Defense Information, *op. cit.,* p. 26.

6. Samuel P. Huntington. 1996. *The Clash of Civilizations and the Remaking of World Order.* New York: Simon and Schuster; Robert D. Kaplan. 1994. The coming anarchy. *Atlantic Monthly* 273(2):44–76; Ralph Peters. 1997. Constant conflict. *Parameters* 27(2):4–14. Peters's pugnacious analysis claims America's military will know "more about the enemy than he knows about himself" (p. 9) and notes with satisfaction that "everybody is afraid of us. . . . We are magic" (p. 13).

7. The Rwandan genocide, for example, was commonly treated as a timeless conflict between the Hutu and Tutsi ethnic groups. Those racial designations were in fact the product of the Belgian colonial period, and the killing had political, economic, and regional prompts more than ethnic dislike as its cause; Alison Des Forges. 1999. *"Leave None to Tell the Story": Genocide in Rwanda.* New York: Human Rights Watch.

8. Hugh Gusterson. 1999. Nuclear weapons and the other in the Western imagination. *Cultural Anthropology* 14(1):111–143.

9. Richard J. Herrnstein and Charles Murray. 1994. *The Bell Curve: Intelligence and Class Structure in American Life.* New York: The Free Press; Randy Thornhill and Craig T. Palmer. 2000. *A Natural History of Rape: Biological Bases of Sexual Coercion.* Cambridge, MA: MIT Press.

10. Matthew Evangelista. 1999. *Unarmed Forces: The Transnational Movement to End the Cold War.* Ithaca, NY: Cornell University Press. Evangelista's research shows that the Reagan buildup and threat of Star Wars missile defense—said to have caused the Soviets either to bankrupt themselves through compensatory military budget increases or "fold their cards" in submission—were instead treated as business as usual. Gorbachev made peace moves in response to the international movement against war and his own sense of the priority of spending on social development. See also John Tirman. 1999. How we ended the Cold War. *The Nation* (Nov. 1): 13–21.

11. Tirman, *ibid.,* p. 15; National Conference of Catholic Bishops. 1983. *The Challenge of Peace: God's Promise and Our Response.* Washington, DC: United States Catholic Conference.

12. On UN resolutions as well, the United States often voted alone against any limits on its military's prerogatives; votes, for example, were 109–1, 95–1, 98–1, and 84–1 on 1980s resolutions to

ban the proliferation of chemical and biological weapons, and 116–1 and 125–1 on resolutions prohibiting the testing and development of new weapons of mass destruction; William Blum. The U.S. versus the world at the United Nations, cited in David McGowan. 2000. *Derailing Democracy: The America the Media Don't Want You to See.* Monroe, ME: Common Courage Press.

13. Sam C. Sarkesian and Robert E. Connor, Jr., eds. 1996. *America's Armed Forces: A Handbook of Current and Future Capabilities.* Westport, CT.: Greenwood Press, p. 387. The distinction has been made between operations when the goal is to fight and win (war), to deter war and resolve hostilities (conflict), and to promote tranquility (peace); Volker C. Franke. 1997. Warriors for peace: The next generation of U.S. military leaders. *Armed Forces and Society* 24(1): 33–58. Military pundits have spilled much ink worrying about what these new forms do to the "warrior's identity."

14. Thirty-six occurred in the seventeen years from 1975 through 1991, and thirty in the next seven; Center for Defense Information, op. cit., pp. 39–42.

15. Anthony Arnove, ed. 2000. *Iraq under Siege: The Deadly Impact of Sanctions and War.* Boston: South End Press; John Mueller and Karl Mueller. 1999. Sanctions of mass destruction. *Foreign Affairs* 78(3): 43–53; Mueller and Mueller estimate that sanctions, including those placed on Haiti in 1991 and Serbia in 1992, have killed more people during the post–Cold War era than all weapons of mass destruction throughout history. One factor is the absence of the Soviet Union that once provided countervailing support when sanctions were applied. They also note the amount of fear generated by issues of biological and chemical weapons (and terrorism) far exceeds their threat.

16. Center for Defense Information. 1999. Landmines: Hidden deadly killers: Where we are today. *The Defense Monitor* 28(5): 5. Land mines remove limbs and kill on a daily basis; there are more planted land mines in Cambodia, for example, than there are people.

17. U.S. Department of Transportation, National Highway Traffic Safety Administration. 1998. *Traffic Safety Facts 1998.* www.nhtsa.dot.gov/people/ncsa/pdf/Overview98.pdf.

18. They are three times more likely to be suicides and eight times more likely to be homicides than to die in combat; Department of Defense, Directorate for Information Operations and Reports. Worldwide U.S. Active Duty Military Deaths, table 1, (web1.-whs.osd.mil/mmid/casualty/wwt.-pdf). Of the two-thirds of a million Americans deployed in the Gulf War, the official total of military deaths was 383 soldiers (a significant number of whom were friendly fire deaths); Center for Defense Information, *op. cit.,* p. 40. The civilian-military murder rate comparison is from 1986 data examined by Joseph M. Rothberg, Paul T. Bartone, Harry C. Halloway, and David H. Marlowe. 1990. Life and death in the US Army: In *corpore sano. JAMA: The Journal of the American Medical Association* 264(17): 2241–2244.

19. Rothberg et al., *op. cit.*

20. Rothberg, et al., *Ibid.*

21. Department of Defense, Directorate for Information Operations and Reports. Detail Comparison of Strength, Manners of Death, and Manners of Death Per 100,000 Strength—by Military Service and Sex: Totals by Service. web1.whs.osd.mil/mmid/casualty/castop.htm.

22. Uhl and Ensign, 1980, *G. I. Guinea Pigs;* Bill Mesler. 1997. Pentagon poison: The great radioactive ammo cover-up. *The Nation* (May 26): 17–22. The Army's own researchers

found both that low doses of depleted uranium can cause cancer in laboratory animals and that the Army recommended "public relations efforts" to deal with the issue. A VA report suggested the PB pills (pyridostigmine bromide) given to protect against possible nerve gas attack contributed to Gulf War illnesses.

23. Cynthia Enloe. 1993. *The Morning After: Sexual Politics at the End of the Cold War.* Berkeley: University of California Press. See also Stephanie Gutmann (2000. *The Kinder, Gentler Military: Can America's Gender-Neutral Fighting Force Still Win Wars?* New York: Scribner), who asks the question without irony.

24. A conservative, DoD assessment of military exports over the period from 1990 through 1998 totaled $133 billion, making the United States by far the world's largest arms dealer. The dollar figure includes U.S. government and direct industry negotiated sales, transfer of "excess defense articles," and military education and training; U.S. World-Wide Arms Exports, Fiscal Year 1990–98, www.fas.org/asmp/profiles/dscadata.html.

25. Other soldiers I spoke with in Fayetteville liked such undertakings, proud to be doing work they construed as "taking care of" others rather than as a special kind of combat. This care is sometimes supported by racial ideologies of an American or European "civilizing mission" to peoples and nations who are not fully modern, and there is little discussion of how American actions sometimes created or contributed to the problem in the first place. The local Libertarians say, on the other hand, that these expanded missions are a boon to their cause. With their personal and political impulses being to stay home, many soldiers develop sympathy for that party's anti-interventionist platform.

26. Prop Blast rite has bred controversy, camaraderie. *Fayetteville Observer,* 5/20/00. Many soldiers associate combat work, however, with their own childhood play at war games, which for some in Fayetteville could draw on knowledge their older relatives and friends had. Said one, whose older neighbor showed him the ropes, "My friend is a sniper with the Special Forces, and so he has extensive [experience]. And I'd just ask a million questions. . . . I just identified with him and I hung out with him. . . . He was fun. . . . He had cool toys, and he'd come out and play army with us. . . . and show us how to make little shelters out of sticks and stuff. It was really ridiculous, but . . . [I was learning things like] the concept of resourcefulness. That's probably the main thing that I picked up is, just because you don't have something doesn't mean you can't make it."

27. Ekirch, 1956, *The Civilian and the Military,* p. 239.

28. *Newsweek,* 4/28/97.

29. American Friends Service Committee. 1999. *Trading Books for Soldiers: The True Cost of JROTC.* Philadelphia: Author.

30. Catherine Lutz and Lesley Bartlett. 1995. *Making Soldiers in the Public Schools.* Philadelphia: American Friends Service Committee; Harold Jordan. 2000. The new-old face of JROTC. *Youth and Militarism Online* (July), www.afsc.org/youthmil/html/-news/july00/newjrotc.

31. Gene Sexton, Assistant Chief of Staff, Fort Bragg Community Relations, interview, 7/12/2000. The recruiting done through these programs amplifies the other recruiting effects of living next to a base. One man who worked in the schools saw the influence of soldiers' in-town lifestyles on his students. When some students would tire of school routines and tell him they

wanted to drop out and join the army, he'd say:

> "Join the army? Do you realize that you're going to one of the most disciplined places in the world?" . . . They could see the glamour part of the military life. That's coming off the post, coming into town, [owning] automobiles, able to go to the restaurant, go to the Doll House [a somewhat upscale strip bar], and what not. So, I'm gonna join the Army. But again, something happened when they get in there and they get to see, that it wasn't what it looked like from the outside. . . . They see these people come into what looks like a ready-made world of happiness and whatnot, not knowing what really goes on.

32. Peter B. Kraska and Victor E. Kappeler. 1997. Militarizing American police: The rise and normalization of paramilitary units. *Social Problems* 44(1): 1–18. This study of over five hundred police departments shows a striking rise in police paramilitary units, their integration into mainstream policing, and the military's direct involvement with these units. At the time of the study, 30 percent of the departments had received training from police with Special Operations backgrounds, and 46 percent trained with active-duty Special Operations soldiers (p. 11).

33. Sam C. Sarkesian and Robert E. Connor, Jr., eds. 1996. *America's Armed Forces: A Handbook of Current and Future Capabilities.* Westport, CT: Greenwood Press, p. 412.

34. The National Guard was established as essentially an industrial police force, and the term *class warfare* and the army's role in fighting it was discussed in the highest circles; David Adams. 1995. Internal military interventions in the United States. *Journal of Peace Research* 32(2): 197–211. The rate of interventions (about eighteen per year)

has changed little over the years Adams examines, from 1886 to 1990, except after wars, which exacerbate use of the army against the people; the rates of intervention have been markedly higher during and after overseas wars. See also Weigley, *op. cit.*

35. William Pfaff. Beware of a military penchant for a parallel foreign policy. *International Herald Tribune,* 9/22/99. As Pfaff and innumerable human rights reports note, there is little evidence to support the military's contention that its collaboration with some of the world's worst killers of their own people—in Indonesia, Guatemala, Colombia, Paraguay, and Chile—"professionalizes" their army and mitigates human rights abuses.

36. Silverstein, *op. cit.* Central players include Vinnell and Military Professional Resources, Inc., which conduct military and police training overseas. Most contracts fall below the $50 million mark requiring congressional notification.

37. United States Department of the Army. The Army Budget FY 00/01. Washington, DC: Comptroller of the Army, pp. 56–61. The 1,324 major installations include 646 in the continental United States and 678 overseas. Including guard, reserve, and minor installations, there were 3,660 U.S. military sites worldwide in 1999. United States Department of Defense, Office of the Deputy Under Secretary of Defense (Installations). 2000. *Department of Defense Base Structure Report, Fiscal Year 1999.* Washington, DC: Government Printing Office. www.defenselink.mil/pubs/basestructure-1999.pdf.

38. This was also due to a renewed drive to improve soldier retention through quality of life spending and the political consensus on growing the military budget.

39. Businesses with Fayetteville

addresses have won several of the smaller contracts for providing sports officials for Fort Bragg intramural and youth sports, school bus services, and mess hall pest control (although these are small only in comparison: Two companies divide the $680,000 spent on sports refereeing). The multi-million-dollar contracts for operation of battle simulation centers, hospital aseptic services, and housing repair and remodeling have gone elsewhere. As the Fort Bragg business office points out, however, outside corporations get many of their employees and some supplies locally.

40. William Greider. 1999. *Fortress America: The American Military and the Consequences of Peace.* New York: Public Affairs, pp. 76, 78. The most striking examples were General Dynamics' takeover of several other large shipbuilding companies, Boeing's acquisition of McDonnell Douglas, and Lockheed's merging with Martin-Marietta to acquire $12 billion worth of contracts.

41. *Ibid.*, p. 71.

42. Colonel Charles J. Dunlap, Jr. 1997. Technology and the twenty-first century battlefield: Recomplicating moral life for the statesman and the soldier. Paper presented to the Ethics and the Future of Conflict Working Group, Carnegie Council on Ethics and International Affairs. The number of American civilians participating in uniform in the NATO Bosnia operation was 2,200, one-tenth of the number of regular troops; Katherine M. Peters. 1996. Civilians at war. *Government Executive* 28(7): 23.

43. Bryan Bender. 1997. Defense contractors quickly becoming surrogate warriors. *Defense Daily* (March 28): 490 cited in Dunlap, *op. cit.,* p. 12.

44. Geoffrey G. Prosch. Another view of privatization of Fort Bragg utilities. *Fayetteville Observer,* 3/29/00.

45. Letter by Col. William C. David, Garrison Commander, 2/18/98, www.bragg.army.mil.

46. Joseph P. Riddle III, interview, 8/6/99.

47. He had built one fast-food restaurant close to post for a franchisee who, he said, "had no knowledge that there would ever be any on base and he peppered the border of Bragg with Burger Kings. Well, about a year after we opened, the military decided that they were going to allow independent, private businesses to go build things on base. . . . And the franchisee's store that I built for him, the sales went down over a quarter million dollars, because it sucked it dry. And the one on Bragg, and the one that was on Lejeune, were the top two in the country. . . . They were doing an *astronomical* amount of sales." The Burger King franchisees sued the parent company and lost.

48. Unprecedented levels of global mercenary activity have arisen as military work is privatized outside the United States as well. Some of it is freelance as always and some emerges from elaborate commercial enterprises such as Executive Outcomes, a British-based firm that, in the late 1990s, was providing military equipment and training to the Papua New Guinea Defence Force; Simon Sheppard. 1998. Foot soldiers of the new world order: The rise of the corporate military. *New Left Review* 228: 128–138.

49. Human Rights Watch. 1998. *War without Quarter: Colombia and International Humanitarian Law.* New York: Author. On the role of the School of the Americas at Fort Benning in training Latin American militaries, see Jack Nelson-Pallmeyer. 1997. *School of Assassins.* Maryknoll, NY: Orbis Books. See also Jennifer Schirmer. 1998. *The Guatemalan Military Project: A Violence Called Democracy.* Philadelphia: University of Pennsylvania Press.

50. Mary Kaldor and Basker Vashee, eds. 1997. *Restructuring the Global Military Sector: Vol. 1. New Wars.* London: Pinter, p. 16. See also Jeffrey A. Sluka (editor. 2000. *Death Squad: The Anthropology of State Terror.* Philadelphia: University of Pennsylvania Press) on the unparalleled levels of torture and terror now being practiced by states and others.

51. Carolyn Nordstrom. 1997. *A Different Kind of War Story.* Philadelphia: University of Pennsylvania Press.

52. Bruce Lincoln. 1991. *Death, War, and Sacrifice: Studies in Ideology and Practice.* Chicago: University of Chicago Press, p. 40.

53. One of the classic statements of this cultural belief system is Samuel Huntington's *The Soldier and the State* (Cambridge: Harvard University Press, 1957). Contrasting West Point with the nearby town of Highland Falls, he waxes rhapsodic. In town:

> The buildings form no part of a whole: they are simply a motley, disconnected collection of frames coincidentally adjoining each other, lacking common unity or purpose. On the military reservation . . . there is ordered serenity. The parts do not exist on their own, but accept their subordination to the whole. Beauty and utility are merged in gray stone. . . . In order is found peace; in discipline, fulfillment; in community, security. . . . West Point is a gray island in a many colored sea, a bit of Sparta in the midst of Babylon. Yet is it possible to deny . . . that the disciplined order of West Point has more to offer [America] than the garish individualism of Main Street? (p. 465).

54. Gutmann, *op. cit.,* pp. 24–25.

55. Eric Foner. 1995. *Free Soil, Free Labor, Free Men: The Ideology of the Republican Party before the Civil War.* New York: Oxford University Press.

56. Both *civilized* and *civilian* derive from the Latin *civilis,* which means "of or pertaining to the citizen"; *Oxford English Dictionary.* A Beetle Bailey comic strip in the late 1990s, however, showed soldiers "on a tear" on town leave, with a chaplain commenting "Strange. . . . They put on their civvies to act *uncivilized!"* The suggestion here may be that army discipline is a civilizing force, not its antithesis.

57. Jack Cox, interview, 6/28/99. Such signs mainly appeared on bars frequented by local men, not shops, restaurants, or movie houses that welcomed the soldiers; Sgt. Enrique Vila, interview, 7/25/99.

58. Calling for remembrance of soldiers' sacrifices on Memorial Day 1999, the Fort Bragg newspaper, *Paraglide,* promoted the "Moment of Remembrance" movement, begun in 1996. Shopping malls, sports arenas, airports, and bus lines mark that moment at 3 P.M.—the hour of Christ's death on the cross in Christian belief. See also Barbara Ehrenreich. 1997. *Blood Rites: Origins and History of the Passions of War.* New York: Metropolitan Books, 1997; Carolyn Marvin. 1999. *Blood Sacrifice and the Nation: Totem Rituals and the American Flag.* Cambridge, U. K.: Cambridge University Press.

59. Ehrenreich, *op. cit.,* p. 12.

60. Samuel Lynn Hynes. 1997. *The Soldiers' Tale: Bearing Witness to Modern War.* New York: Allen Lane/Penguin Press; Gerald F. Linderman. 1997. *The World Within War: America's Combat Experience in World War II.* New York: Free Press.

61. Lincoln, *op. cit.*

62. In a 1999 survey, 77 percent of officers agreed with this proposition, while 43 percent of civilian elites with military experience and 25 percent of nonveterans did so; Sharp divergence found in views of military and civilians. *New York Times,* 9/9/99. Peter D.

Feaver and Richard H. Kohn. 2000. Project on the gap between the military and civilian society: Digest of findings and studies. Triangle Institute for Security Studies, manuscript.

63. Sherry, *op. cit.*, p. 3.

64. When President Clinton came to North Carolina in 1997 to announce some education initiatives, he declared, "We can make our public schools just like our military, the best on Earth, if, like our military, we are willing to adhere to high, rigorous standards for all people, regardless of their background." Text of President Clinton's Remarks to the N.C. General Assembly. March 13, 1997. The White House, Office of the Press Secretary.

65. Thomas E. Ricks. 1997. *Making the Corps.* New York: Scribner.

66. Richard Kohn. 1987. The American soldier: Myths in need of history. In Garry D. Ryan and Timothy K. Nenninger, eds. *Soldiers and Civilians: The U.S. Army and the American People.* Washington, DC: National Archives and Records Administration, p. 53.

67. Maryann Jones Thompson. Looking for a few good clicks. *The Industry Standard,* 5/3/99, p. 76. Recruiters (the Marines are an exception) consistently deemphasize war and focus on job opportunities.

68. These were promulgated in 1998 and include these definitions: "Loyalty: Bear true faith and allegiance to the U.S. Constitution, the Army, your unit, and other soldiers. Duty: Fulfill your obligations. Respect: Treat people as they should be treated. Selfless-Service: Put the welfare of the nation, the Army, and your subordinates before your own. Honor: Live up to all the Army values. Integrity: Do what's right, legally and morally. Personal Courage: Face fear, danger, or adversity (Physical or Moral)"; Soldier/Civilian Values, www.bragg.army.mil.

69. I am grateful to Donald Nonini for this concept.

70. This was the projected cost for enlisted recruiting and advertising alone. Alphonso Maldon, Jr. Asst. Secretary of Defense [Force Management Policy]. Testimony, Feb 24, 2000, before Senate Armed Service Sub-Committee on Personnel.

71. When the citizen's army became the professional army, according to Michele Kendrick (1994. The never again narratives: Political promise and the videos of Operation Desert Storm. *Cultural Critique* 28:129–147), it was "whitened"—seen as effective because it no longer drew so heavily on "ghetto" residents and was more educated.

72. Enloe, 2000, *op. cit.*

73. Near the beginning of the AVF, the numbers were 33 percent Republican and 12 percent Democrat. Sharp divergence found in views of military and civilians. *New York Times,* 9/9/99.

74. J. Frank Moore III. 1999. The CEO's Report. *Army* (November): 43–48. While such institutions have their own distinctive financial and other incentives, individual members' politics are sometimes filtered through the process that one Marine commandant described as follows: "Many veterans seem to romanticize and exaggerate their own military experience and loyalties . . . [and become more] pugnacious" (Shoup, cited in Wolpin, *op. cit.*, p. 173). An irony is that, World War II aside, "they have generally been shabbily treated by the state once battlefield combat was over. . . . Official studies . . . minimize both the physical and especially the psychological effects of combat."

75. Silverstein, *op. cit.*, pp. 201–202.

76. Richard Kohn. 1994. Out of control: The crisis in civil-military relations. *The National Interest* (spring, no. 35): 3. Col. Charles J. Dunlap, Jr.

1992–1993. The origins of the American military coup of 2012. *Parameters* 22 (winter, no. 4): 2–20. This article, which predicted a military coup by officers who tired of their nonwarrior missions, was taken very seriously and widely discussed in military and civilian circles. Its ultimate fate was to become a made-for-TV movie.

77. Per-pupil spending was $5,360 in civilian schools and $7,100 in Fort Bragg schools for the 1999–2000 school year. Source: Cumberland County and Fort Bragg schools.

78. He also noticed, however, that military families on average were more aware of education's value than civilians. He attributed this to the fact that:

they find themselves in this highly structured, very disciplined, very competitive society, where mobility for rank, which means money, is so built in that they are extrinsically motivated to the highest degree that nobody in public school, preacher, mama, technical institute had been able to [instill in them before]. They get to know that if I am going to progress in this military society, I'm going to have to study my manuals. I'm going to have to be disciplined to expectations, that is the only way I will have upward mobility and that is the only way I can get additional moneys from the Private to the Sergeant to the Lieutenant to the General. All of it becomes very clear to them. . . . And once they had children, to speak in terms of the boys in the street, they would bring smoke on anybody as it related to the educational opportunities of their children.

79. Daniel Voll. 1996. A Few Good Nazis. *Esquire* (April): 108.

80. *Raleigh News and Observer,* 12/23/95. The paper also reported that the local police referred all calls about the case to the Army spokesperson.

81. Haiti protested Special Forces soldiers who violated orders by helping Haitian soldiers and militia hide their weapons from confiscation; Haiti says U.S. troops may have helped foes. *Fayetteville Observer,* 12/8/95. See also former Special Forces Master Sergeant Stan Goff's account of rampant racism in the ranks: *Hideous Dreams: A Soldier's Memoirs of the U.S. Invasion of Haiti.* Winnipeg, Canada: Soft Skull Press, 2000.

82. Race tension a Fayetteville undercurrent. *The News and Observer* (Raleigh, NC), 12/17/95.

83. The second soldier, Malcolm Wright, had his trial moved to Wilmington, and the third cooperated with the prosecution and was not tried.

84. White supremacy itself was treated as a male phenomenon. Though women were involved in the families and networks of supremacists around Fort Bragg (Voll, *op. cit.*), women have often but erroneously been portrayed as peripheral or resistant to such racism; Karen Blee. 1991. *Women of the Klan: Racism and Gender in the 1920s.* Berkeley: University of California Press; Koonz, *op. cit.*

85. When juror-screening procedures should eliminate anyone opposed on principle to the death penalty, the trial's outcome—a life sentence—was surprising, even with a mainly white jury. One juror had apparently refused to vote death on the grounds that she was not convinced that Burmeister had really killed the couple. Although the other jurors believed in his guilt, some of them also believed that he was not downtown that night on a Nazi quest but on a search for drugs. With the deal gone sour, they assumed, guns emerged.

86. The illusion that testing produces a meritocracy is held in the military as in college admissions. The tests that regulate entry into the military eliminate many more blacks who desire

jobs in the military than whites (U.S. Congress, Office of Technology Assessment. 1992. *After the Cold War: Living with Lowered Defense Spending.* OTA-ITE-524. Washington, DC: U.S. Government Printing Office). Blacks also disproportionately remain in lower ranks and less-desirable occupational categories; Janice H. Laurence. 1992. Crew cuts: Effects of the defense drawdown on minorities. In Stacey Nevzer, ed. *Military Cutbacks and the Expanding Role of Education.* Washington, DC: U.S. Department of Education, Office of Educational Research and Improvement.

87. Gender, too, is irrelevant. In 1993, a male Fort Bragg soldier killed a visiting female ROTC soldier when she, according to news accounts, "spurned" his advances. But official accounts prominently featured the explanation of "fraternization," a misdeed in which the officer and enlisted class mix socially and thereby erode military discipline.

88. This comment was described to me by a man I knew who heard it while drinking with the soldier.

89. Charles C. Moskos and John Sibley Butler, *op. cit.,* p. 24.

90. Hardin, *op. cit.* See also Williams, *op. cit.*

91. James Gibson. 1994. *Warrior Dreams: Paramilitary Culture in Post-Vietnam America.* New York: Hill and Wang. On the other hand, states' rights stances made this view of federal authorities one likely shared by the 1941 MPs' commanding officer as well.

92. Francine D'Amico. 1997. Policing the U.S. military's race and gender lines. In Laurie Weinstein and Christie C. White, eds. *Wives and Warriors: Women and the Military in the United States and Canada.* Westport, CT: Bergin and Garvey.

93. Polls show more people expressed much confidence in the military (67 percent in 1993) than in any other institution, including organized religion (53 percent), the Supreme Court (43 percent), the medical system (34 percent), or Congress (19 percent). Religion once led the list but was surpassed in 1989. Princeton Religion Research Center. 1993. *Emerging Trends* 15(6): 3. On its Web site, the DoD reports these findings on a page titled "Polls Rate Us No. 1," though it does not mention the institutions it has bested.

94. The budget figure is for 1990; www.usarec.army.mil/hq/golden-knights/; *Fayetteville Observer,* 11/25/90.

95. American Association of Museums. 1999. *The Official Museum Directory.* New Providence, NJ: National Register Publishing.

96. The rise of entertainment culture and economy has produced similar tendencies in the military itself. Concern for retention and morale is expressed in the many golf courses, pools, intramural sports programs, and fairs at military installations. (There are 183 recreational facilities on Fort Bragg alone.) It is also in the many military competitions sponsored on post for both military and athletic skills.

97. Michael Mann. 1988. *States, War and Capitalism: Studies in Political Sociology.* Oxford, U. K.: Basil Blackwell.

98. Michael J. Wolf. 1999. *The Entertainment Economy.* New York: Times Books, p. 4. In 1995, $400 billion was spent in the United States on entertainment, and 2.5 million people worked in the entertainment industry; Howard Gleckman. 1995. Welcome to the entertainment economy. *Business Week* (August 14): 35. Tourism garnered $344 billion in the United States in 1991.

99. Douglas Kellner. 1992. *The Persian Gulf TV War.* Boulder, CO: Westview Press; John MacArthur. 1992. *Second Front: Censorship and Propaganda in the Gulf War.* New York: Hill & Wang.

100. Jon Elliston. 2000. Target audience: Fort Bragg's propaganda troops at work on the home front. *The Independent* (July 5–11): 19.

101. *Ibid.*, p. 19.

102. The Navy spent $600,000 to upgrade the A-6 bomber cameras shortly after the Gulf War, during which Air Force video was consistently used for press briefings and selected for transmission by television networks;

Cori E. Dauber. n.d. How the Air Force sank the Navy, or, Who won the real battle of Desert Storm. Communications Studies Department, UNC-CH, Manuscript.

103. The civilians reciprocated with their version of a war game, inviting the officers to football at Duke and the University of North Carolina at Chapel Hill.

ACKNOWLEDGMENTS

My gratitude goes first to the many people in Fayetteville who helped me over the years to understand their city and their past, as they have lived it, and to think in new ways. Their insights and generosity are at the core of this book. I regret that it could not be long enough to include more of their thoughts and experiences and that I cannot thank each by name.

There are many other gifts to acknowledge, including the astute questions and research assistance of many students at the University of North Carolina, where I am fortunate to work. My appreciation goes especially to Victor Braitberg and Thomas Chivens, as well as to George Baca, Lesley Bartlett, Geritakor Choe, Jeongmin Eom, Carla Jones, Elizabeth Jones, Suzanne Lynch, Marsha Michie, Maya Parson, Miranda Smith, and Patricia Sanford. Thanks also to Elizabeth Fox for her expert help. I was also generously aided by the staff at the Cumberland County Public Library, Fayetteville State University Library archive, Fort Bragg's archives, and the North Carolina Collection and the Southern Historical Collection at the University of North Carolina at Chapel Hill.

This project would not have come to a timely conclusion without a National Endowment for the Humanities fellowship and the Blackwell Fellowship at the Institute for the Arts and Humanities. I thank Ruel Tyson and my lively cohort at the institute for their interest and support. The research was also facilitated by grants from UNC's Odum Institute for Research in Social Science, with the support of John Reed, the University Research Council, The Center for the Study of the American South, and the Dean's Office.

Several loyal and hardworking friends and colleagues read early drafts and steered me in the right direction: I thank especially my treasured friends Lila Abu-Lughod and Orin Starn, as well as the humane and extraordinarily helpful David Cecelski. I am also very grateful to Carolyn Nordstrom, who knows war's other fronts all too well, and to Kim Allen, Micaela di Leonardo, Dorothy Holland, Jonathan Phillips, Nikhil Singh, and France Winddance Twine for their insights into various pieces of the manuscript; to James Hevia, Richard Kohn, and John McGowan for their many good suggestions; to Deb Chasman at Beacon Press for her great editorial work, and Christina Palaia for her expert help with the manuscript. My smart coworkers Judy Farquhar, Donald Nonini, and Marisol de la Cadena have provided me standards and aspirations, and elin O'Hara slavick's deep commitments and stunning visual insights into the city have been an inspiration. I thank my admired, amusing, and lifelong friend, Nora Huvelle, for sharing her interest and her own fine stories. Other friends in Chapel Hill are entwined in this book because they listened to me first speak its words before writing them, including Beverly Abel, Pierre Barker, Ken Bolin, Barbara Entwistle, Robin Kirk, Emy Scoville, and Richard Scoville.

Writing is not just ideas, but the will to speak. For me, that comes from having chanced into a family prosperous with love, and especially with four kind and good-humored sisters, Mary, Betsy, Karina, and Anne. Each holds up a corner of my sky. Above all, I thank my cherished parents, George Joseph Lutz and Carol Lombard Lutz, whose constancy and worldviews helped guide this quest as, in some sense, any of the others on which I have embarked. My father died as this book was in copyediting, to my devastation: for his experience— as a soldier, as the maker of a family, as a devoutly religious man, and as a relentless seeker of truth and of a better world—introduced me to the questions, frameworks, and dilemmas of its subject. Although I deeply regret he cannot read it, he already knew its contents because he taught me, in the largest sense, how to speak and how to ask more of the world.

Finally, Michael Schechter's faith in me has filled my sails and helped carry me forward through the many years of work and worry that went into this project. And my children, Jonathan and Lianna Schechter, contributed both the means for it—they helped and waited through the thousands of hours I spent away from home or facing the computer screen in research and writing—and the motive—for the future of America and its military is their own.

ML.

12/0